# COPYRIGHT HANDBOOK

# COPYRIGHT HANDBOOK

## Second Edition

## Donald F. Johnston

**R. R. BOWKER COMPANY**
New York & London, 1982

Published by R. R. Bowker Company
1180 Avenue of the Americas, New York, NY 10036
Copyright © 1982 by Donald F. Johnston
All rights reserved
Published and bound in the United States of America

Copyright is not claimed by the author in Appendixes 1–5

**Library of Congress Cataloging in Publication Data**

Johnston, Donald F.
   Copyright handbook.

   Bibliography: p.
   Includes index.
   1. Copyright—United States. I. Title.
KF2994.J63  1982      346.7304'82      82-4218
ISBN 0-8352-1488-5    347.306482      AACR2

# SHORT CONTENTS

# CONTENTS

# PREFACE

This book is about United States copyright law. The U.S. Constitution—in effect since 1789—includes the area of copyright as appropriate for federal action. Congress was given the power to enact laws

To promote the Progress of Science and useful Arts, by securing for limited times to Authors . . . the exclusive Right to their . . . Writings. . . .[1]

By the next year (1790), we had federal copyright legislation. Major revisions occurred in 1831, 1870, 1909, and, after much time and effort, in 1976.[2]

The purpose of the *Copyright Handbook*, second edition, is to explain the 1976 Copyright Act and to report on legal developments that have taken place since it took effect at the beginning of 1978.

Copyright law protects a wide variety of works. Chapter 2 contains a long list of the kinds that can qualify, but if you are not now familiar with the breadth of coverage, you can get some idea of the scope by scanning this listing of copyrighted works: a computer program, a sonnet, a stuffed toy, a blueprint, a motion picture, a fabric design, a greeting card, a photograph, a sound recording, a sculpture, and a catalog.

Given the breadth and diversity of copyrightable items, and the many industries that copyright law affects, complexity in the extreme would be the result if we had a special set of legal rules for each type of work. Admittedly, we do have more than a few special rules, but, by and large, each type of work is governed by the same general copyright principles, and the law is considerably more coherent than it might be under the circumstances.

In order to discuss the general principles without having to name the long list to which they apply, copyright parlance uses the phrase "work of authorship" as the general term. And, in copyright law language, the creator of a work often is referred to as the "author," even though he or she may, in ordinary conversation, be called, say, an artist or a composer. (Actually, "author" in copyright usage has two meanings. Frequently, it means the creator of the work, but, in the statute itself, the word means the *initial owner of copyright* in the work. This is usually but not always the same person as the creator of the work.)

This book is intended for authors and publishers (in the broad sense of those terms) and for those, such as librarians and teachers, who regularly or from time to time need direct access to information about copyright law. It is also intended as a convenient source for attorneys when their particular information needs do not require exhaustive or more focused works, such as treatises, law review articles, or court decisions.

Few people who need to know about copyright law have to or want to know about every aspect of it. This has been taken into account in the organizational structure of the book and by providing a detailed table of contents for locating specific information expeditiously.

The first chapter of this book is an introduction to copyright and to the main features of the law. Chapters 2–6 elaborate on some of the basics of copyright law: What kinds of works are protected? What legal rights does the author have in such works? How are such rights transferred? How long do the rights last? These chapters are relevant not only for those who create or acquire copyrights, but also for those who wish to understand the limitations inherent in the rights of copyright owners.

The next group, chapters 7–10, are principally of interest to copyright owners. Coverage includes topics such as: When should a copyright notice be used on a work? What should it consist of? When must copies of published works be deposited with the Copyright Office? What are the advantages of registering a claim of copyright in a work? How is a registration obtained?

Chapter 11 reports on some aspects of U.S. copyright law that relate to activities outside the United States; for example: To what extent does the United States recognize copyright protection here for works by foreign authors and for works published abroad? What copyright law standards govern importations of works? What are the potential copyright law disadvantages of not using U.S. or Canadian printers? The chapter also includes a brief report on the international copyright treaties to which the United States is a party.

Chapter 12 covers remedies that the copyright law provides when someone has infringed another's right of copyright. It is a transition to the remaining chapters, 13–17, which concern activities that are *not* infringements of copyright even though they fall within the copyright owner's rights as generally phrased. In these chapters, we consider the right of fair use, the library reproduction rights of section 108, and various other special provisions, including the compulsory licensing sections of the law that affect the music recording, jukebox, cable television, and educational television industries.

Following the main text are chapter notes and references, then a number of appendixes that provide primary source materials for reference purposes; for example, the text of the copyright statute and reproductions of the Copyright Office forms used to apply for copyright registrations.

This second edition of *Copyright Handbook*, the first edition having been published in 1978 shortly after the current law took effect, takes into account developments since then, such as congressional, regulatory, and judicial actions implementing, explaining, and modifying the law. There have been many developments during these early years of the statute. "Many of the many" are relatively minor taken alone, but together they assume considerable importance. There also have been some events of enough consequence in themselves to demand a more current edition—a legislative amendment concerning computer programs and data bases; a federal appeals court decision on home videorecording; the issuance of guidelines on videorecording for classroom use; a Federal Communications Commission decision allowing cable systems to carry more television station signals; and the Copyright Royalty Tribunal's royalty-allocation and rate-making decisions affecting copyright owners in the recording, jukebox, and cable television industries.

In the area of copyright law, one important issue or another (usually several) will be pending at any given time. However, many of these issues will take a long time to be resolved by congressional and judicial decisions. Meanwhile, this second edition of *Copyright Handbook* provides current materials reflecting developments that have taken place, and it reports on the more important ones for which action is pending. In addition to providing updated information, this second edition expands first edition coverage in areas of particular interest to authors and publishers, that is, the fair-use doctrine and procedures for registration of copyright claims.

I presently serve as counsel to R. R. Bowker Company, the publisher of this book and a company within the publishing group of the Xerox Corporation. I was helped in the preparation of this edition by the following people whose contributions were generously given and gratefully received: Gerry McColgan Brown, Liz Ellingham, Anita McCray, and Bob Shafter. They are not responsible for any shortcomings in the text, but they deserve much credit for many that were avoided.

Donald F. Johnston

February 8, 1982

# COPYRIGHT HANDBOOK

# GUIDE TO USE

The detailed table of contents provides a reference to each area of the new copyright law. An alternate reference source is the index at the back of the book.

In the text itself, sentences are frequently followed by numbers, letters, and/or words in brackets. For example:

The federal copyright statute provides legal protection for works which have been set down in a suitably tangible form by or under the authority of the author [102(a); 101 "copies," "fixed," "phonorecords"].

The numbers in brackets refer to the relevant section of the 1976 Copyright Act. The letters in parentheses—such as "102(a)"—refer to the relevant subsection of the Act. The words in quotes—such as "fixed"—refer to specific terms defined in section 101 of the statute, a section that is a long compilation of statutory definitions.

At times, the number in brackets is preceded by the phrase "Transitional and Supplementary Provisions." This refers to provisions set forth at the end of the 1976 Act that were included in order to account for the problems in changing over from the 1909 Act to the 1976. Because these provisions sometimes bear the same number as sections in the main body of the 1976 Act, they are distinguished within brackets not only by the phrase just quoted but also by the abbreviation "Sec." For example:

[Transitional and Supplementary Provisions, Sec. 102]

The text of the sections or subsections themselves may be found in Appendix 1.

The use of bracketed citations is intended to provide the reader with an immediate primary reference to the current copyright statute and to reduce the need for footnotes. The latter are, however, used in citations of other materials, such as court decisions and legislative history. The related chapter notes and references are found in the section following Chapter 17.

The appendixes, which follow the chapter notes, contain the texts of the 1976 and 1909 copyright laws; the legislative history's copying guidelines for educators and librarians; and Copyright Office forms and selected regulations.

# 1

# INTRODUCTION

In 1879, Gilbert and Sullivan's *Pirates of Penzance* had its world premiere in New York City. The operetta met with great acclaim. Before long, someone took notes at a performance and prepared a piano adaptation, which was published as *Memories of Pirates of Penzance*. That admirable forthrightness was not matched by any permission to copy. Thus, we had a pirate of *Pirates*, and an unsuccessful one, as it turned out: The authors sued for infringement and won.[1]

As the *Pirates* case illustrates, once an author's work is available, others can find a way to copy or adapt it. Ingenuity and the applied laws of physics so allow. That was true for *Pirates*, even though a printed version of the original work was not available to copy, and tape recorders did not exist. Today's technologies make the task much easier.

Nearly a century before *Pirates*, we decided that we needed a law of society, which we now call a copyright law, as a counterbalance to what the physical laws permit. This book is about the U.S. statute currently in effect, the 1976 Copyright Act.

Copyright law came about in part out of a sense of fairness to authors. But it also has developed under a rationale, the one principally relied on in the United States today, that society benefits from authors' efforts, that it is in our interest to provide a system that encourages them, and that an appropriate system is one that gives them property rights in the works they create. Thus, the legal protection, while it directly benefits authors, serves as an indirect means for expanding our ability to understand and appreciate the world around us and within us. The U.S. Supreme Court put it this way, in a 1975 decision:

> The immediate effect of our copyright law is to secure a fair return for an "author's" creative labor. But the ultimate aim is, by this incentive, to stimulate artistic creativity for the general public good. "The sole interest of the United States and the primary objective in conferring the monopoly," this court has said, "lie in the general benefits derived by the public from the labors of authors."[2] [Citations and footnotes omitted]

No one, incidentally, contends that the system is so finely tuned that it gives us only that which is beneficial or that, without the legal arrangement, nothing worthwhile would be created. If the rights of copyright were too comprehensive, however, side effects would develop that we would find intolerable. For example, suppose that the author of a work were to have complete control over the right to copy any part of it. A book reviewer then would need permission to quote even a brief excerpt for purposes of illustrating a point.

Because of concerns such as this—and there are many others—the statute has been designed expressly to recognize not only the rights of a copyright owner but some limitations as well. These limitations in effect function as users' rights, with authors themselves of course frequently being users of others' works and the beneficiaries of the limitations on many occasions.

## WORKING WITH THE COPYRIGHT LAW

As is the case for many laws, the copyright statute uses the concept of subtraction. That is, the legislation initially sets down some general and generous statements as to the scope of copyright owners' rights. Then it sets down other statements, analogous to subtractors in mathematics, that one takes away from the general statements to arrive at the total scope of protection.

> Example: In section 106 of the law, reference is made to an author's "exclusive rights . . . to reproduce the work." That right is made subject to section 107, which provides that the "fair use" of a work is not an infringement of the author's rights.

There are many such subtractors. But a substantial number of them are narrow in scope, and the rights of copyright are substantial.

For those who dread mathematics, I am pleased to report that the statute does not often adopt the concept of subtraction to the point of assigning number values to the standards it uses. That happy state of affairs has its moments of dissappointment, however, for the imprecision of the statute's words can be frustrating.

Given the form and content of the statute, the process of finding an answer to a particular copyright question can involve many steps. You could, in an orderly manner, determine which general rules to apply and then interpret each of them in the context of the particular facts. Then you could look at each subtractor and, for those relevant, interpret how each applies. In practice, you can be less plodding. Once you have gained some familiarity with the law's provisions, and some experience with their application, it frequently is possible to select rapidly those issues that have the most promise for resolving a particular copyright problem with the least effort. For example, in the case again of the book review, you may have properly wondered whether the book was protected by copyright at all but needed more information to make a good judgment about that. Would you spend time acquiring the information? No, not if your concern was only whether you could use the excerpt without infringing copyright. The fair-use rule would provide a quicker answer.

There are times, of course, when the facts or the law are not kind enough to permit any quick, favorable answer. Other times there will not be a favorable answer even after an exhaustive search. And there are occasions—undoubtedly the ones you will confront—when no one knows the answer with a comfortable degree of certainty until a court is compelled to select one. An old umpire, Bill Klem, while purporting to talk about baseball, summed up some copyright issues this way: "Some things are balls, some things are strikes, and some things ain't nothin' till I call 'em."

In the material that follows, we will briefly review the 1976 law's provisions relating to copyright owners' and users' rights. We also will note the parts of the law concerned with ownership and transfers of copyrights and with some of the formalities of the law. All of these topics are considered in more detail in subsequent chapters.

## WHAT IS COPYRIGHTABLE

Federal copyright protection applies, subject to various subtractors that we will mention later, to original works of authorship that have been set down in a suitably tangible form with the author's consent. The "setting-down" part is easy—handwriting on paper will do. And it is not difficult to meet the remainder of the test either. In Chapter 2, we will provide a list of works that typically, but not always, do. Many have already been mentioned in the preface. If a work qualifies except for the tangible-form requirement, copyright protection under state laws applies.

Even if a work meets the basic criteria for federal protection, there can be some special circumstance that makes it ineligible. We will leave the details about that to Chapter 3, but, just to give one example, U.S. copyright protection does not apply to a work prepared by an employee of the U.S. government as part of that person's official duties. Also, not everything about an otherwise qualified work is protected by copyright. For example, copyright protection does not extend to an "idea" or to a "discovery" or to a "fact." Rather, copyright protects the "expression" of ideas. The idea/expression distinction and other standards affecting the scope of copyright protection are also considered in Chapter 3.

## COPYRIGHT DURATION

Federal copyright protection begins when a copyrightable work is set down in tangible form by the author or with the author's consent. The rules for how long a copyright lasts vary with the circumstances, but the period almost always is quite long. For a new work, the copyright typically lasts until 50 years after the author's death. For copyrighted works published before 1978, or federally registered before then, the initial copyright protection period covers a 28-year period (from the time of first publication or of registration, whichever applies in the particular circumstances). An additional 47-year term is available if timely sought. Copyright duration rules are considered in Chapter 4.

## RIGHTS OF COPYRIGHT

The rights of copyright are, generally, the rights to do, and to authorize others to do, any of the following:

1. reproduce the work;
2. prepare derivative works based upon it;
3. distribute the work to the public;
4. perform the work publicly; and
5. display the work publicly.

Each of these rights is considered in Chapter 5. There are a number of limitations on them. We will come back to them a little later on in this introductory chapter.

## RELATIONSHIP OF COPYRIGHT STATUTE TO OTHER U.S. LAWS

In passing the 1976 Copyright Act, Congress by and large sought to have the statute be the exclusive law governing copyright issues in the United States, and it enacted a preemption provision to accomplish that goal. The scope of the preemption provision is discussed in Chapter 5.

## COPYRIGHT OWNERSHIP AND TRANSFERS

All the topics discussed under this heading are considered in Chapter 6.

Except when a work falls into the statutory category of a "work made for hire," the initial owner of copyright in a work is the person who created it. When a work is in the work-for-hire category, the party for whom the work was prepared—that is, the employer or the one who commissioned the work—ordinarily is the initial owner of copyright.

Each of the rights of copyright and, indeed, subdivisions of them, can be transferred and owned separately, with the transferee being a copyright owner to the extent of the rights transferred. General rules of law, such as contract law, govern transfers of ownership, subject to some special rules grafted onto the copyright statute.

Instead of transferring ownership of a right of copyright, the owner may grant permission to use the work on a nonexclusive basis. The user, having consent, is free of copyright infringement liability to that extent. However, not having acquired any exclusive right, the user is not called a copyright owner but, rather, a nonexclusive licensee. Having obtained only a non-exclusive right, the user may well not be in a position to complain if others also obtain the same rights from the copyright owner.

There are provisions for recording transfers of copyright ownership and nonexclusive licenses in the Copyright Office, a part of the Library of Congress. Recording is not mandated by the statute, but it is sometimes necessary as a practical matter. Even when recording is not necessary for any known immediate purpose, there are some practical and legal advantages to doing so.

The copyright law distinguishes between works of authorship, which it treats as intangibles, and the physical objects in which the works are, as the statute says, embodied. A person can own the object without owning any rights of copyright in it. Similarly, a person may own the rights of copyright but not own a related physical object. In the case of letters, for example, it is common for the recipient to be the owner of the document but not to have the right to publish it. Various provisions in the statute set forth what rights the object-owner-only has vis-à-vis the copyright owner.

## COPYRIGHT FORMALITIES

When a work is published under the authority of the copyright owner, a copyright notice, in conformity with statutory standards, is supposed to be used. The notice standards, and the potential consequences of not meeting them, are considered in Chapter 7.

When a copyrighted work is published in the U.S. with notice of copyright, the statute calls for depositing a copy or copies in the Library of Congress. The circumstances in which the rules apply, and the exceptions, are considered in Chapter 8.

The statute provides a registration system for copyrights. Registration, although not mandatory, is necessary in some situations as a practical matter. Even when that is not the case, registration is often elected because of the legal advantages it brings. All of this is considered in Chapter 9.

The procedure for applying for registration includes the submission of a completed application form together with a fee and, typically, the deposit of two copies of the work to be registered. Registration forms and procedures are considered in Chapter 10.

## TRANSNATIONAL CONSIDERATIONS AFFECTING U.S. COPYRIGHT LAW

Chapter 11 discusses how the U.S. copyright status of a work can sometimes be affected when some of the events relating to it have taken place outside the United States. For example, if the United States has no copyright relations with a particular country, U.S. copyright protection may not be applicable to a work first published in that country and written by one of its citizens living there. Chapter 11 also considers the copyright statute's provisions that affect importations of copyrighted work into the United States.

A table of U.S. international copyright relations is included in Chapter 11, together with a brief description of the principal copyright treaties to which the United States is a party. The copyright laws of other countries often contain many similarities to the U.S. law, and many countries grant to U.S. citizens, and to works first published here, the same rights under their copyright laws as they apply to domestic productions. This book does not, however, attempt to describe the copyright laws of other nations or to describe international agreements in detail. The statements in this book concern only the U.S. copyright law, unless otherwise noted.

## INFRINGEMENT REMEDIES

When a right of copyright is infringed, the potential legal remedies available to the copyright owner include, among others, a court injunction against further infringements; an award of money for damages caused by the infringement; a payment to the copyright owner of the profits made by the infringement; and an award of reasonable attorney's fees to the prevailing party in the litigation.

Copyright infringement also may result in a criminal prosecution when a person infringes a copyright willfully and for purposes of commercial advantage or private financial gain, as in the case of counterfeit records, audiotapes, and videotapes offered for sale. Copyright infringement remedies are considered in Chapter 12.

## LIMITATIONS ON COPYRIGHT

### Fair Use

The "fair use" of a copyrighted work is not an infringement of copyright. The fair-use doctrine is left deliberately imprecise so as to have a versatile and flexible rule for reaching equitable results in a great variety of situations. The general aspects of the fair-use doctrine are considered in Chapter 13.

### Classroom Teaching Activities

To a degree in the statute itself, but mostly in the underlying legislative history, Congress amplified upon the general fair-use standards in the context of teaching activities. These comments, and related guidelines from the legislative history, are reviewed in Chapter 14. Also considered are some specific statutory sections that, in connection with certain teaching activities, place some limitations on copyright owners' rights as to performance and displays of copyrighted works in class.

## Library Reproduction Rights

Section 108 of the law sets forth specific circumstances under which librarians may reproduce and distribute a copy of a copyrighted work without the permission of the copyright owner and without violating any rights of copyright. These provisions, and the relationship between section 108 and the fair-use doctrine, are considered in Chapter 15.

## Miscellaneous Limits on Performance and Display Rights

There are a variety of limitations on the copyright owner's public performance and display rights, some of which have already been noted. In Chapter 16 we will consider others, such as charitable fund-raising performances and performances during religious services.

## Compulsory Licenses

Thus far we have considered copyright limitations, which, when applicable, allow someone to proceed with particular uses without having to obtain permission or make any payment to the copyright owner. Other sets of standards, called compulsory license provisions, allow someone to proceed without permission but only if statutorily required payments and procedures are followed. Four sections of the statute are concerned with compulsory licenses. They relate to cable television systems, the recording industry, jukebox performances, and noncommercial broadcasting. The compulsory licensing provisions are considered in Chapter 17.

# 2

# COPYRIGHTABLE SUBJECT MATTER
# PART I: BASIC STANDARDS

In this chapter, we will consider the general standards for copyrightability and the various types of copyrighted material. In Chapter 3 we consider the limitations on these general concepts; for example, copyright protection does not extend to an "idea."

## AUTHORSHIP; TANGIBLE FORM

### Original Works of Authorship

A threshold test for copyright protection is that there be an original work of authorship [102(a)]. It is an easy test to meet, happening millions of times a day with snapshots, notes, drawings, etc. Although all these works are ordinarily eligible for copyright protection, most of their creators may not know that copyright applies or care if they do know. In most cases that is a sensible way to live. One of the nice things about many areas of law is that we do not need to know them. Only the occasional surprises keep that from being an unmixed blessing.

Copyright law usually is of practical concern only for works with actual or potential appeal to some significant segment of the public (though copyright sometimes serves to protect privacy interests). You, apparently, are both fortunate and unfortunate enough to have some copyright law interest, and so it makes sense to understand something more about "original works of authorship."

Protectible works of authorship take a variety of forms. Here is a list—lengthy but not exhaustive—of materials that typically, but not always, incorporate at least one work of authorship:

articles, biographies, condensations, histories, letters, novels, poems, translations;

forewords, afterwords, indexes, editorial notes, annotations, tests, answer material for tests;

anthologies, magazines, newspapers, pamphlets, catalogs;

music, plays, pantomimes, ballets;

paintings, drawings, prints, maps, charts, atlases, advertisements, art reproductions, fabric designs, posters, cartoons, comic strips, puzzles, games, greeting cards, technical drawings;

sculptures, jewelry, dolls, stuffed toy animals, toys, globes, models;

photographs, motion pictures, filmstrips, radio and television programs, videotapes and disks, sound recordings; and

computer programs and computer data bases.

No lengthy statutory list of material that can qualify as works of authorship exists,[1] but the statute does name seven general categories [102(a)]:

literary works;

musical works, including any accompanying words;

dramatic works, including any accompanying music;

pantomimes and choreographic works;

pictorial, graphic, and sculptural works;

motion pictures and other audiovisual works; and

sound recordings.

The seven categories are not intended to be mutually exclusive and do not necessarily cover everything that can qualify as an original work of authorship.[2] However, as a practical matter they come very close. Each of the seven will be discussed later in this chapter.

The statute does not give a formal definition of the term "work of authorship." Generally, the term connotes intellectual expressive efforts. The legislative history notes that the phrase "implies neither that the subject matter is unlimited nor that the new forms of expression within that general area of subject matter would necessarily be unprotected."[3]

In order to qualify as an original work of authorship, the work need not meet a standard of quality or novelty. Ordinarily, it is enough that the work is original to the author in the sense that he or she did not copy it. The old copyright law did not include requirements of novelty, ingenuity, or aesthetic merit, and there was no intent, in the 1976 law, to impose such standards.[4]

The standards for copyrightability result in, among other things, the possibility that two people may independently create similar works of authorship; in this case each work will be entitled to copyright because each is original to its author. Theoretically, to use an example from one of the cases, someone could independently create anew a poem identical to Keats's *Ode on a Grecian Urn* and be entitled to copyright (although others could copy

Keats).[5] Of course, when similar works do come along, the suspicion of copying, because of the absence of originality, often is present. In the case of the Keats poem, the circumstances would be most incriminating. But the possibilities for honorable and close similarities sometimes are realistic. This is true for many simpler works, each originator perhaps having prepared his or her own work from threads of the same ideas. Even among complex works, the possibilities exist for some similarities in the absence of copying. For example, two textbooks on the same subject may have similarities in their copyrightable content without one having been copied from the other.[6]

A work need not have a significant amount of creativity to qualify as an original work of authorship. Only a modicum is called for; a most banal effort is likely to yield enough. There are limits, however. As one judge put it, "Apply hook to wall" would not make the grade.[7] In another case, a tinkered version of a standard sales form failed to qualify.[8] There also is a general principle that limits copyrightability in situations where there are only a limited number of practical ways to express something, as in the case of some very simple contest rules.[9]

As you can see, the original work of authorship test is not arduous to meet. This is not a foolish arrangement, for it enables the courts to avoid taking a major role in deciding what is "worth" protecting, a probable benefit to us all, judges included. Besides, the author does not obtain exlusive rights to the ideas that he or she expresses, only the right to stop others from copying the author's expression. And even that right has some limitations imposed upon it, such as the fair-use doctrine.

### Tangible Form

The federal copyright statute provides legal protection for works that have been set down in a suitably tangible form by or under the authority of the author [102(a); 101 "copies," "fixed," "phonorecords"]. Before a work so meets the tangible-form stage, state copyright law governs. Thus, if you create a song but do not take it beyond the shower walls, you could not look to federal copyright law for protection if your tasteful, but morally corrupt, neighbor steals it. But you could look for protection under state law.

Original works of authorship frequently reach a suitably tangible form at a fairly early stage. This is especially the case for the kinds of works that people get concerned about from a copyright standpoint. Even when a tangible form is not arrived at expeditiously in the normal course of events, an author often can arrange it. For example, a videotape could be made of a ballet, or an audiotape of a speech, in cases where those works were not to be recorded in written form. This is not to say that state law does not provide adequate protection when it applies. But the federal government has been assigned the principal copyright role for so long that some advantage exists in having its extensive national body of law apply directly.

The formal statutory test for suitable tangibility is that the work be "fixed" in a tangible medium of expression. That happens when the work's

> embodiment in a copy or phonorecord, by or under the authority of the author, is sufficiently permanent or stable to permit it to be perceived, reproduced, or otherwise communicated for a period of more than transitory duration. [101]

Under that standard, there is great tolerance for different media. Microfilm, keypunch cards, magnetic tape, and optical disks—all will do as well as paper, canvas, film, and marble. Would a live television show suffice? Ordinarily, it would not meet the requirement to be of "more than transitory duration." But the statute includes a provision that makes federal copyright law coverage possible immediately: "A work consisting of sounds, images, or both is 'fixed' if a fixation of the work is being made simultaneously with its transmission" [101 "fixed," "transmit"]. This can readily be accomplished by taping the show at the time of transmission.

The statute, through its definitions section, is structured so that a work that is "fixed" is fixed in either a "copy" or a "phonorecord." Even an original painting is, for copyright statute purposes, a "copy" [101]. At first blush, this seems like a congressional exercise of its humpty-dumpty powers: "When I use a word . . . it means what I choose it to mean." However, such a stance is at least partially defensible, as it would be cumbersome for the statute to refer expressly to the original and any copy every time that coverage was needed in the statute.

Generally, a phonorecord is a tangible medium that embodies copyrighted sounds—other than sounds accompanying a motion picture or other audiovisual work—and a copy is a tangible medium that embodies anything else that is copyrighted. More about copies and phonorecords is given later on in this chapter.

## CATEGORIES OF WORKS OF AUTHORSHIP

Broadly speaking, all works are governed by a common set of copyright law standards. Thus, an illustrator, a writer, a film producer, and a computer programmer all are affected by the statute's general rules applying to original works of authorship. However, the statute also mentions more specific categories. Sometimes these are added in order to make it clear that copyright applies, as in the specific statutory reference to pantomimes. At other times, a specific type is mentioned because some different or additional supplementary rules apply. In the material that follows, we will go over the seven general categories of works listed in the statute. Following that, we will explain the terms "compilations" and "derivative works" and then proceed to the special case of computer programs and automated data bases, subject areas that were affected by a December 1980 amendment to the copyright statute.

### Literary Works

Literary works is the first category mentioned in the statutory list [102(a)]. It is broader than the words suggest, functioning as a catchall for works not covered by the other six categories. Literary works are defined as:

> works, other than audiovisual works, expressed in words, numbers, or numerical symbols or indicia, regardless of the nature of the material objects . . . in which they are embodied. [101]

A novel, even one that is not literate, is a literary work. A poem is a literary work. A catalog, a directory, a compilation of data, a computer data base, a computer program—each is ordinarily classified as a literary work for purposes of the statute.[10]

### Pictorial, Graphic, and Sculptural Works

Just as the statutory phrase "literary works" does not connote a legal requirement that some standard of merit or quality be reached, the "pictorial, etc." definition is not intended to require that some standard of artistic taste be met.[11] Some special copyright law standards apply to utilitarian aspects of pictorial, etc. works. We will consider them later in this chapter.

### Pantomimes; Choreographic Works

Pantomimes and choreographic works probably get special statutory mention so as to make clear that copyright protection can apply. The element of fixation (discussed earlier in this chapter) often will be missing for these types of works. However, film, tape, and written notations can supply it. The legislative history states that social dance steps and simple routines are not included in the term "choreographic works."[12]

### Dramatic Works

Dramatic works are included in the statutory list because of the importance of the category and because there are some special provisions for variant terms such as nondramatic musical works.

### Motion Pictures; Audiovisual Works

Motion pictures are defined in the statute as:

> audiovisual works consisting of a series of related images, which, when shown in succession, impart an impression of motion, together with accompanying sounds, if any. [101]

Motion pictures fall within the broader term of "audiovisual works," defined as those

> that consist of a series of related images which are intrinsically intended to be shown by the use of machines or devices such as projectors, viewers or electronic equipment, together with accompanying sounds, if any, regardless of the nature of the material objects, such as films or tapes, in which the works are embodied. [101]

Examples of audiovisual works that are not motion pictures are ordinary filmstrips and slide sets. Note that an audiovisual work does not necessarily have any audio portion.

As noted later in this chapter, under the topic of computer programs, electronic video games have been found to qualify as federally protectible audiovisual works.

## Musical Works

The inclusion of the musical works category in the statutory list is accounted for not only because of the importance of these types of works but also because several special copyright law provisions deal with such works. Musical works have been expressly recognized in U.S. copyright statutes for about 150 years. However, sound recordings had only limited federal recognition until 1971; this is considered in the next section of this chapter.

## Sound Recordings; Phonorecords

The separate mentions of sound recordings and phonorecords in the statute came about for historical and practical reasons. In the first decade of the twentieth century, the Supreme Court interpreted the then existing copyright statute to exclude piano rolls because the statute seemed to cover only humanly readable works.[13] This caused later problems for musical recordings in disk and tape form, and the problems became acute when the unauthorized commercial duplication of musical recordings became widespread. Protection by the federal law against such activity was unclear, as was the scope of available state law protection.[14]

To clear the air, at least prospectively, Congress, in 1971, amended the 1909 Copyright Act to cover sound recordings first fixed after February 14, 1972.[15] Sound recordings first fixed before then are protectible under state copyright law, and this applies to copies of such recordings made after that date [301(c); 101 "fixed"].

Sound recordings are defined as:

> works that result from the fixation of a series of musical, spoken, or other sounds, but not including the sounds accompanying a motion picture or other audiovisual work, regardless of the nature of the material objects, such as disks, tapes, or other phonorecords, in which they are embodied [101].

Of course, a sound recording, like other works, must meet the general criteria of orginal work of authorship to be eligible for copyright. And, as in the case of other types of works, the test ordinarily will be fairly easy to meet.

The legislative history notes that "the copyrightable element in a sound recording will usually, though not always, involve 'authorship' both on the part of the performers and the record producer responsible for setting up the record session, capturing and electronically processing the sounds, and compiling and editing them to make the final sound recording." The report goes on to note that sometimes the record producer's contribution will be too minimal to qualify.[16]

When the typical copyrighted work, such as a novel, is set down in tangible form, the physical object is called a "copy." But sound recording copyrights are set down in "phonorecords":

> "Phonorecords" are material objects in which sounds, other than those accompanying a motion picture or other audiovisual work, are fixed . . . and from which the sounds can be perceived, reproduced, or otherwise communicated, either directly or with the aid of a machine or device. The term "phonorecords" includes the material object in which the sounds are first fixed.

In order to relate sound recordings and phonorecords to older forms of copyright, it is helpful to start out with a musical composition. When the composition is set down on sheet music, the piece of paper is a copy. When an audiotape is made of a performance of the musical composition, an additional work of authorship—a sound recording—comes into being. The audiotape (or a disk, for that matter) is, for the *sound recording* copyright, the counterpart of the sheet music for the musical composition copyright. But, for purposes of the statute, the sheet music is a copy and the tape of the sound recording is a phonorecord.

For most copyright law purposes, the same rules apply to both phonorecords and copies. However, the copyright notice rules for the two are somewhat different (see Chapter 7), and a special provision allows people, without specific permission from the copyright owner of a musical composition, to make recordings of the composition under defined circumstances. That provision is described in Chapter 17.

For most types of works, one of the rights of copyright is the right to perform the copyrighted work publicly. This is true for musical compositions, for example, but it is not presently true for sound recordings [114(a)].

> Example: When a disk jockey broadcasts a song on the radio. The broadcast constitutes a public performance of both the sound recording and of the underlying musical composition. However, copyright permission is presently needed only for the performance of the musical composition copyright.

When the 1976 Copyright Law was enacted, Congress was not willing to establish public performance rights for sound recordings, but it was willing to think about the issue. It directed the Register of Copyrights to study the matter and make a report [114(d)]. In 1978, the Register recommended that it would be appropriate to establish some public performance rights in sound recording copyrights.[17] At this writing, however, no such law has been enacted. The issue is a controversial one, in part because the addition of a new performance right would tend to raise the royalty costs that broadcasters pay.

## Compilations; Derivative Works

A work of authorship often involves the use of preexisting material. When that occurs, as in the case of any of the seven types of works already mentioned, the work will ordinarily fit into the statutory category of a compilation (e.g., an encyclopedia) or of a derivative work (e.g., a film based on a play). A work, of course, may be both a compilation and a derivative work (e.g., a revised edition of an encyclopedia). The term "compilation" and the related term "collective work" are defined as follows [101]:

A "compilation" is a work formed by the collection and assembling of preexisting materials or of data that are selected, coordinated, or arranged in such a way that the resulting work as a whole constitutes an original work of authorship. The term "compilation" includes collective works.

A "collective work" is a work, such as a periodical issue, in which a number of contributions, constituting separate and independent works in themselves, are assembled into a collective whole.

And here is the definition of a derivative work [101]:

A "derivative work" is a work based upon one or more preexisting works, such as a translation or any other form in which a work may be recast or adapted. A work consisting of editorial revisions, annotations, elaborations, or other modifications which, as a whole, represent an original work of authorship, is a "derivative work."

In addition to a "translation," the definition gives these examples: musical arrangement, dramatization, fictionalization, motion picture version, sound recording, art reproduction, abridgment, and condensation.

Compilations and derivative works are copyrightable to the extent that they represent original works of authorship; but the copyright in the derivative work or compilation as such, covers only the later author's contribution. It does not affect the copyright or public domain status of the preexisting material [103(a),(b)].

Chapter 3 covers the limits of copyrightability, but here is a good place to note that when an author uses another's copyrighted material unlawfully,

the author's copyright will not extend to any part of his or her work where
that happened [103(a)]. By way of illustration, the legislative history states:

> Thus, an unauthorized translation of a novel could not be copyrighted at all,
> but the owner of copyright in an anthology of poetry could sue someone who
> infringed the whole anthology, even though the infringer proves that publi-
> cation of one of the poems was unauthorized.[18]

The report adds that lawful use sometimes may take place other than by
obtaining permission, as when the fair-use doctrine is applicable.

## Computer Programs; Automated Data Bases

In December 1980, Congress amended the 1976 Copyright Act so as to
explicitly place copyright owners of computer programs in the same general
copyright law position as owners of other literary works. The 1980 amendment defines a computer program as:

> a set of statements or instructions to be used directly or indirectly in a computer
> to bring about a certain result. [101]

Before the 1980 amendment, the copyrightability of computer programs
was recognized in the legislative history to the 1976 law,[19] but the formal
statutory recognition nonetheless helped to eliminate doubts. The statutory
definition follows the one used in a 1978 report to Congress by the National
Commission on New Technological Uses of Copyrighted Works, commonly
known as CONTU.[20] In its report, CONTU also provided the following
descriptions of some forms a computer program takes:

> A flow chart is a graphic representation for the definition, analysis, or
> solution of a problem in which symbols are used to represent operations,
> data flow, or equipment.

> A source code is a computer program written in any of the several pro-
> gramming languages employed by computer programmers.

> An object code is the version of a program in which the source code
> language is converted or translated into the machine language of the
> computer in which it is to be used.

In a 1981 case, a federal district court in California decided that a computer program embodied in a silicon chip was eligible for federal copyright
protection.[21]

In the field of electronic videogames, a copyright owner sometimes fo-
cuses on claimed infringement of the game display rather than on a claim
that the computer program itself was copied. One reason is that a principal
concern of the owner is that the game not be copied, even if it is possible
to reproduce it with programming that differs in some respects from the
original. Second, it often will be quicker to establish that the videogame

rather than the underlying program has been copied. In a 1982 case involving the spaceship game "Scramble," the defendant contended that the plaintiff's audiovisual display was not an original work of authorship because its features were determined by the underlying computer program.[22] The federal appeals court in New York disagreed:

> The . . . features of the audiovisual display are plainly original variations sufficient to render the display copyrightable even though the underlying written program has an independent existence and is itself eligible for copyright.

The court also dealt with the issue of whether the variable nature of the audiovisual display meant that the game was not "fixed" in a tangible medium of expression. The court rejected this argument, stating in part:

> No doubt the entire sequence of all the sights and sounds of the game are different each time the game is played. . . . Nevertheless, many aspects of the sights and the sequences of their appearances remain constant during each play of the game. . . . It is true . . . that some of these sights and sounds will not be seen and heard during each play of the game in the event the player's spaceship is destroyed before the entire course is traversed. But the images remain fixed, capable of being seen and heard each time a player succeeds in keeping his spaceship aloft long enough to permit the appearances of all the images and sounds of a complete play of the game. The repetitive sequence of a substantial portion of the sights and sounds of the game qualify for copyright protection as an audiovisual work.

*Automated Data Bases.* The 1976 Copyright Law's standards for copyrightability are, by and large, indifferent to the medium in which a work of authorship is embodied. Because compilations of data on paper have often been recognized as capable of qualifying as works of authorship, there would seem to be no special problem in carrying over the context to compilations when in the form of machine-readable materials such as magnetic tapes and disks.

The 1976 Congress was willing to acknowledge that copyright would apply, but it was unsure as to precisely how it should apply in connection with computer uses of computer data bases or, indeed, of other copyrighted works. Consequently, Congress retained the status quo ante while it waited for CONTU to complete its studies and report. The way in which Congress preserved the status quo was to include in the 1976 Copyright Law a provision stating that the law:

> does not afford to the owners of copyright in a work any greater or lesser rights with respect to the use of the work in conjunction with [computers] . . . than those afforded to works under the law in effect on December 31, 1977, as held applicable and construed by a court in an action brought under . . . [the 1976 Copyright Law].[23]

The notion of preserving the pre-1978 law was not a satisfactory long-term solution, as few, if any, people were confident that they knew what the applicable legal standards were. This area of law was quite undeveloped.

CONTU, after studying the issue of computer data bases in the context of the general provisions of the 1976 statute, concluded that the ordinary statutory standards were, by and large, suitable for coping with the issues that arise when works are used in conjunction with computers. And, in order to make the general copyright law provisions applicable to such matters, CONTU recommended that the clause quoted above be deleted from the law.[24] Congress followed that recommendation in its 1980 amendment to the statute.

## STATE COPYRIGHT LAWS

Before the 1976 Copyright Act, the states had the principal copyright role for protecting most types of unpublished works, whether or not set down in tangible form.[25] The 1976 Act expanded federal jurisdiction by covering all copyrightable works that are set down in suitable tangible form [102(a)]. State law continues to govern copyright protection for original works of authorship that have not yet reached the point of being so set down.

In light of the broad federal jurisdiction that has always existed in the copyright area, the state courts have not had the occasion to build up a large body of law on copyright matters. The existing decisions generally support the proposition that the author of a work, or his or her designee, has the right of first publication of it. The right of course may be granted to others.

Federal and state copyright laws are in harmony when, for works not yet set down in tangible form, the state provides copyright protection comparable to that which the federal law would have provided had the work been in tangible form. Conflicts can arise when a state provides protection that the federal copyright law would have denied had the work been in tangible form. As a standard for determining whether a state law improperly conflicts with federal copyright law, the 1976 Copyright Act contains a section dealing with preemption issues, which are considered in Chapter 5.

# 3

# COPYRIGHTABLE SUBJECT MATTER
# PART II: COPYRIGHTABILITY LIMITS

Broadly speaking, two categories of copyright law restraints limit the coverage of federal copyright protection in tangibly fixed original works of authorship. One category limits the scope of the rights in particular situations. For example, the copyright owner's rights with respect to the public performance of works is reduced in certain classroom performances. We will note these sorts of limitations in Chapter 5, after reviewing what each of the rights of copyright is. The other category, which we will consider now, is concerned with works, or aspects of works, that are not entitled to any federal copyright law protection.

## IDEAS, PLANS, ETC.

Copyright protection does not extend to any of the following [102(b)]:[1]

| | |
|---|---|
| ideas | procedures |
| concepts | processes |
| principles | systems |
| discoveries | methods of operation |

The form of expression may be protected by copyright when it contains original work of authorship, but the underlying idea, concept, etc., may not.

The list of exclusions makes considerable sense in terms of public policy. The life of a copyright is a long one, and it would be unwise for the protection to cover anything as fundamental as an idea, etc. But these statutory exclusions from copyright coverage are not founded solely on such practical considerations. Tradition and precedent combine to confine copyright protection to what an author does as author. Whatever that is, and however much it has been expanded to include some "uncreative" works, Congress still thinks of "authorship" when it thinks of copyright. Concepts, systems, principles, processes—and ideas in that context—are more closely associated with other legal areas such as patents and trade secrets (see Chapter 5).

## The Idea/Expression Distinction

Although the exclusions noted in the previous section make sense, they also make for some confusion in practice. Judge Learned Hand put it this way decades ago with respect to ideas and their expression, in ruling on an infringement suit in which a movie, *The Cohens and the Kellys*, was challenged as an infringement of a play, *Abie's Irish Rose*:

> Upon any work, and especially upon a play, a great number of patterns of increasing generality will fit equally well, as more and more of the incident is left out. The last may perhaps be no more than the most general statement of what the play is about, and at times may consist only of its title; but there is a point in the series of abstractions where they are no longer protected, since otherwise the playwright could prevent the use of his "ideas," to which, apart from their expression, his property never extended. . . . Nobody has ever been able to fix the boundary, and nobody ever can.[2]

Judge Hand went on to say that "the line, wherever it is drawn, will seem arbitrary, [but] that is no excuse for not drawing it." Indeed, the courts often are called upon to do the pencil work.

In much of the litigation that arises, the two works in the lawsuit contain a number of similarities, and often the defendant had a clear possibility of copying the plaintiff's work because it was widely distributed. In deciding the infringement issue, the courts frequently apply the test of whether the two works are "substantially similar" and, in determining that, the courts take into account that some similarities are perfectly permissible because copyright does not protect ideas. The following are excerpts from three recent cases:[3]

> *Two turkey decoys.* The *idea* of a turkey decoy is not new. Further, both decoys must resemble a turkey, or they would be useless. The margin for difference is admittedly small; however, the differences in the neck, tail and body fullness between Turkey Decoy No. 1 and Turkey Decoy No. 2 are readily recognizable upon a view of the exhibits.
>
> Plaintiff's copyright does not give him the exclusive right to manufacture turkey decoys. His copyright merely protects his expression of the idea. The only distinguishing feature of plaintiff's decoy incorporated in defendant's decoy is the interbody cavity and the detachable head and legs. These features, however, were in the public domain long before plaintiff received his copyright.
>
> *Two brass duck's heads.* [No. 2's] sculpture has a longer neck and beak, eyes that protrude slightly when the figure is viewed from the back and the [No. 2] sculpture weighs more than plaintiff's. Nevertheless, a "side by side comparison" . . . of the two shows them to be virtually indistinguishable.

*Eggs talking*. Here, the only similarities between [plaintiff's] lecture and the [defendant's] skit are (1) the use of the literary device of personifying an egg . . . (2) the egg's undergoing certain experiences, such as lying under a chicken or in a box with other eggs in a refrigerator where it is cold and a light goes on and off, and (3) the egg reacting to the possibility of being scrambled or fried.

[Plaintiff] argues that the similarities do not necessarily follow from the common idea of an egg personified, since an author has a wide choice of events. . . . For example, [plaintiff] suggests that instead of lying under a chicken, an egg might be hatched in an incubator, . . . boiled (soft or hard), . . . or used raw, such as in an eggnog. However, the occurrences that are common to both works . . . are fairly predictable and usual in the life of an egg, while the alternatives [plaintiff] offers do not "necessarily follow" from the "common theme."

Of course, idea/expression cases involve other areas as well. Recent cases have included the movie *Star Wars* versus the television series "Battlestar Galactica," the Pink Panther character against some commercials for an automobile that included an animated cougar, and various Superman copyrights versus some episodes of the television series "The Great American Hero."[4] In each of these cases, the defendant happened to prevail, but the decision is always an ad hoc one, and defendants, such as the one in the duck's head case, are often enough found to have copied the plaintiff's expression so as to constitute infringement. The legislative history notes: "Wide departures or variations from the copyrighted works would still be an infringement as long as the author's 'expression' rather than merely the author's ideas are taken."[5]

## Recent Copyright Office Developments

During 1979–1981, the Copyright Office gave some special attention to some copyrightability standards and their interaction concerning ideas, concepts, and methods of operation. One proceeding concerned copyrights and the graphic elements involved in the design of books and other printed material. The other was about copyrights and blank forms. Here is a brief report on the two proceedings:[6]

Concerning "blank forms," the Copyright Office considered regulatory modifications to clarify standards concerning the registerability of such works. It elected not to do so, finding the existing regulations valid. Its basic position is that a form that merely serves as a means of recording information is not copyrightable subject matter if it does not itself convey information or contain original pictorial expression. The Office also noted that the mere fact that a form may be accepted for registration does not mean that everything about it is protected by copyright. Cited as example were bank checks with pictorial illustrations.

As for book design, the Copyright Office considered formulating a regulation on the subject. Ultimately, the Copyright Office decided not to do so, concluding that appropriate protection could be procured under established general standards for original works of authorship. It also concluded that some aspects of design are not subject to U.S. copyright protection, stating, "We believe that the arrangement, spacing, or juxtaposition of text matter which is involved in book designs falls within the realm of uncopyrightable ideas and concepts."

### Computer Programs

There is no large body of copyright law concerning copyright of computer programs. The cases thus far typically seem to have involved extensive and exact copying. Thus, we still await the development of examples of how the line is drawn in this area, although, of course, the general copyright standards are applicable.

The 1978 report of the National Commission on New Technological Uses of Copyrighted Works included a comment on the subject of computer programs and "ideas" or "processes."[7]

## FACTS; NEWS; HISTORY

A fact is a fact, although a *New Yorker* cartoon once depicted a wall of file drawers whose labels made a distinction between unconfirmed facts, hard facts, etc. Considerable creative skill and effort may be needed to ascertain a fact; nevertheless, a fact is not an original work of authorship. However, just as the expression of ideas can be entitled to copyright protection, so can the expression of facts, as in the form of news, history, directories, and compilations. Here are some cases from the past few years:[8]

World War II Stories: A book containing a World War II espionage story contained some details that were later included in a work of fiction based on the same time period. The author of the first book, published many years before, claimed that a number of the details were his "inventions." However, in the infringement lawsuit, the court concluded that he had represented the work as factual and that the author of the fictional work reasonably relied on the impression created. Thus, that author was, for purposes of the case, permissibly using the "information."

In the context of a motion for a preliminary injunction, the court found there was insufficient evidence of substantial similarity with plaintiff's copyrighted material and denied injunctive relief.

A Zeppelin: The last voyage and destruction of the *Hindenburg* in 1937 led to an extensively researched book on the subject in 1962, followed by another book in 1972, followed by a movie contract for the latter, followed by the release of the film itself. The author of the 1962 book claimed that the film infringed his work. Although there were many similarities among their works, a federal appeals court in New York found no copyright infringement, concluding that the similarities were of noncopyrightable elements. In the court's view: "To avoid a chilling effect on authors who contemplate tackling an historical issue or event, broad latitude must be granted to subsequent authors who make use of historical subject matter, including theories or plots." The court also noted that the author of the 1972 book had not used only the 1962 work but others as well and also did archival research and interviewing. And the court further noted that the authors of each of the works—the two books and the film—"relate the story of the *Hindenburg* differently."

Kidnapping: A made-for-television movie dramatized a sensational kidnapping and relied significantly on a book about the case. The jury decided that there had been copyright infringement. The judge's instructions to the jury included a statement that "research is copyrightable." The federal appeals court found that instruction incorrect and returned the case to the trial court for further proceedings.

John Wayne: For a 1979 four-page article on John Wayne, a newsweekly was charged with having used too much from a 1978 book on great American war movies. The portions taken principally were six quotations, not by the author of the book but included in the book. The court found no infringement. The court relied significantly on the fair-use doctrine. But it also offered these comments on whether research efforts, as contrasted with the author's expression, are protected by copyright. "The principal reason research . . . should not be given copyright protection is that it does not meet the standard of originality required. . . . Although the court sympathizes with plaintiff's point that the commercial value of the work of an oral historian depends upon the enforceability of the copyright, . . . the . . . statute does not permit the extension of protection which plaintiff seeks."

Gardening Data: The authors of a gardening book were found to have infringed copyright in that, on 27 of the book's 63 pages, virtually all the names and addresses had been copied from another gardening book. (This case probably was not difficult to decide, but it frequently can be difficult to judge how much of a compilation may be used, and in what manner, without running afoul of copyright. Often, and almost always for significant undertakings, it is advisable to consult an attorney.)

Law Student's Article: A newspaper for lawyers published a copy, verbatim and almost in toto, of an article from a law school newspaper. The article was based on many interviews with students and included extensive quotations. The article's author sued for infringement. The defendant contended that he did not own copyrights in the quotations. But the court ruled that the writer owned copyright in the compilation—that is, in the selection, arrangement, and ordering of them. The court found infringement. (The defendant, incidentally, also raised a defense that it had obtained appropriate copying permission. The court found that the various communications did not amount to an effective permission.)

# SCÈNES À FAIRE

In the *Hindenburg* case mentioned above, the court noted that there were a number of claimed common scenes among the two books and the film involved. For example, all three works contain a scene in a German beer hall, in which the airship's crew engages in revelry prior to the voyage. Other claimed similarities concern common German greetings of the period, such as "Heil Hitler," or songs, such as the German national anthem.

Incidents such as those are known as *scènes à faire*, that is, "incidents, characters or settings which are as a practical matter indispensable, or at least standard, in the treatment of a given topic."[9] The federal appeals court in the case went on to explain:

> Because it is virtually impossible to write about a particular historical era or fictional theme without employing certain "stock" or standard literary devices, we have held that *scènes à faire* are not copyrightable.

Of course, it is possible to infringe copyright by tracking another's expression of a *scène à faire* too closely under circumstances where other expressive choices are reasonably available.

## SHORT PHRASES; TITLES; TRADEMARKS

Short phrases, titles, and trademarks often represent creative expression. Nonetheless, they have not been recognized as covered by copyright law.[10] However, there sometimes is a possibility for protection under laws other than copyright. See Chapter 5.

## DERIVATIVE WORKS; COMPILATIONS

As reported in Chapter 2, copyright for a work employing preexisting material "does not extend to any part of the work in which such material has been used unlawfully" [103(a)].

## WORKS IN THE PUBLIC DOMAIN

When people speak of a work being in the public domain, they mean that the work is not subject to protection by copyright law. In other parts of this chapter, and in some of the chapters that follow, we will mention various ways a work may achieve public domain status, e.g., through certain copyright notice omissions (Chapter 7) or through expiration of copyright (Chapter 4).

## CERTAIN WORKS BY U.S. GOVERNMENT EMPLOYEES

U.S. copyright protection is not available for a work prepared by an officer or employee of the U.S. government as part of that person's official duties" [101 "work of the United States Government"; 105]. The prohibition does not preclude copyright protection for all works by such employees; they may copyright works not prepared as part of their official duties.

The statutory prohibition also does not prevent the U.S. government from owning copyrights. For example, the government may accept bequests of copyrights and, at least ordinarily, may obtain copyrights in works prepared by nonemployees under federal funding if the funding contract so provides.[11]

## STATE AND LOCAL GOVERNMENT WORKS

The copyright statute does not contain a section ruling out copyright protection for works by state or local government employees prepared as part of their official duties. However, several decisions under the old copyright law, and one under the current statute, exclude federal copyright protection for the official text of state legislative or state court decisions.[12] It should be kept in mind that some publications that consist largely of such materials will nevertheless have supplementary materials in the form of abstracts, headnotes, and historical notes, which were not prepared by the government.

In 1980, the question arose of whether a state regulation (a building code) was subject to copyright protection where it was substantially the same as the model building code developed by an organization named Building Officials and Code Administrators International, Inc. The organization, BOCA, claimed copyright in its building code. It had granted permission to Massachusetts. But it brought suit against a private publisher who reprinted the Massachusetts regulations. The case came before a federal appeals court in Boston, which stated: ". . . we cannot say with any confidence that the same policies applicable to statutes and judicial opinions may not apply equally to regulations of this nature." However, the court sent the case back to the trial-level court so that the issues could be explored more fully. Before any final decision was rendered, the parties settled the case.

## UTILITARIAN ASPECTS OF USEFUL ARTICLES

Copyright law draws a distinction between works of "applied art," which copyright protects, and "industrial designs," which it does not.[13] The statute provides some clarification of the distinction by its definition of "pictorial, graphic, and sculptural works" [101]. One part of that definition provides that such works:

> include two-dimensional and three-dimensional works of . . . applied art. . . .
> Such works shall include works of artistic craftsmanship insofar as their form
> but not their mechanical or utilitarian aspects are concerned.

The definition goes on to state the extent to which the design of a useful article shall be considered within the pictorial, etc. standard. (A "useful article" is defined as an article having an intrinsic utilitarian function that is not merely to portray the appearance of the article or to convey information. An article that is normally a part of a useful article is considered a useful article.)

> The design of a useful article . . . shall be considered a pictorial, graphic or sculptural work only if, and only to the extent that, such design incorporates pictorial, graphic or sculptural features that can be identified separately from, and are capable of existing independently of, the utilitarian aspects of the article.

Thus, a lamp base in the form of a Balinese dancer is a sculptured design eligible for copyright protection, as found in the 1954 Supreme Court case of *Mazer* v. *Stein*,[14] the leading case in this area. Here are excerpts from the legislative history describing some of the practical applications of the statutory standards.[15] For easier reading, I have split one paragraph of the official text into its four components:

> A two-dimensional . . . drawing . . . is still capable of being identified as such when it is printed on or applied to utilitarian articles such as textile fabrics, wallpaper, containers, and the like. The same is true when a statue or carving is used to embellish an industrial product or, as in the *Mazer* case, is incorporated into a product without losing its ability to exist independently as a work of art.
>
> On the other hand, although the shape of an industrial product may be aesthetically satisfying and valuable, the Committee's intention is not to offer it copyright protection under the bill. Unless the shape of an automobile, airplane, ladies' dress, food processor, television set, or any other industrial product contains some element that, physically or conceptually, can be identified as separable from the utilitarian aspects of that article, the design would not be copyrighted under the bill.
>
> The test of separability and independence from "the utilitarian aspects of the article" does not depend upon the nature of the design—that is, even if the appearance of an article is determined by aesthetic (as opposed to functional) considerations, only elements, if any, which can be identified separately from the useful article as such are copyrightable.
>
> And, even if the three-dimensional design contains some such element (for example, a carving on the back of a chair or a floral relief design on silver flatware), copyright protection would extend only to that element, and would not cover the over-all configuration of the utilitarian aspect as such.

Making the separability distinction is sometimes quite perplexing—a condition also known elsewhere in copyright law, as in the foggy borders of the idea/expression distinction or in the fair-use doctrine. Rules such as these more than justify the description given to copyright as one of the "metaphysical areas of the law."[16] The distinction of separability is easiest to make when, as in the case of the lamp, the feature in question is not abstract. In one recent case, the judges were not blessed with such a situation. Instead, they confronted sculpturally designed belt buckles, in which the designs were somewhat abstract. The federal district court found that the copyrights were invalid because the artistic features were not, in that judge's view, separable and independent. The federal appeals court, splitting two to one, ruled otherwise. The majority opinion, while observing that the case "is on the razor's edge of copyright law," saw in the belt buckles ornamental aspects "conceptually separable from their subsidiary utilitarian function."[17]

The legislative history commented specifically on the design of typeface and concluded that it was not within the statute's definition of pictorial, graphic, or sculptural works. A federal appellate court in New York recently took the same position.[18]

In addition to setting standards as to what "useful articles" are copyrightable, Congress addressed the issue of the rights that the owner of copyright has in a work portraying a useful article. The legislative solution was to enact a clause that preserved the old law without saying what it was [113(b)]. The legislative history explains:

> The 1961 Report of the Register of Copyrights stated, on the basis of judicial precedent, that "copyright in a pictorial, graphic, or sculptural work, portraying a useful article as such, does not extend to the manufacture of the useful article itself," and recommended specifically that "the distinctions drawn in this area by existing court decisions" not be altered by the statute. The Register's Supplementary Report . . . cited a number of these decisions, and explained the insuperable difficulty of finding "any statutory formulation that would express the distinction satisfactorily."[19]

The legislative history commented specifically about architectural plans and drawings, stating that:

> they would, of course, be protected by copyright but the extent to which that protection would extend to the structure would depend upon the circumstances. Purely nonfunctional or monumental structures would be subject to full copyright protection under the bill, and the same would be true of artistic sculpture or decorative ornamentation or embellishment added to the sculpture. On the other hand, where the only elements of shape in an architectural design are conceptually inseparable from the utilitarian aspects of the structure, copyright protection for the design would not be available.[20]

## NATIONALITY CONSIDERATIONS

U.S. copyright protection applies, while a work is unpublished, regardless of the nationality of the author [104(a)]. For published works, it is possible, in certain circumstances, that U.S. copyright protection will not apply. Details concerning this are considered in Chapter 11. Suffice it to say here that nationality considerations do not prevent most works from having U.S. copyright protection. In large part this is because the United States has copyright treaty relations with many countries and the statute accommodates those relations.

# 4

## COPYRIGHT DURATION

How many years does U.S. copyright in a work last? It depends on the circumstances. In the current copyright law, Congress has established some new duration rules, but it has also preserved some old ones. Consequently, the answers to the question can sound like the signals given by a prison quarterback—"28 . . . 47 . . . 75 . . . 100 . . . life plus 50"—and we could even add three more to that list—"2002, 2027, and indefinite." In this chapter we will consider the various rules that resulted in that sentence.

At the outset, you should know that the normal U.S. copyright life of works created in 1978 or later will not expire before the end of 2028. But copyrights in some pre-1978 works expire each year between now and then.

### WORKS CREATED IN 1978 OR LATER

#### Individual Authors

The general rule for works created by individual authors in 1978 or later is that federal copyright protection (1) begins at the time the work is created and then (2) lasts throughout the life of the author and (3) for 50 years after the author's death and (4) through the end of that last calendar year [302(a); 305]. As discussed in more detail in Chapter 2, a work is "created" when it is set down in a suitably tangible form for the first time [101 "created," "fixed"; 102(a)].

> *Example:* You create a novel in 1983 at the age of 22. You die in 2038, at the age of 81. The copyright commences in 1983 and will expire at the end of 2088. (Registration, a topic considered in Chapters 9 and 10, is not a prerequisite for the beginning of the copyright protection.)

In using the life-plus-50 rule here, we are assuming that the work is not a work for hire, a category we will consider shortly.

Before the work is set down in a suitably tangible form by authority of the author, protection under state copyright laws applies (see Chapter 2).

It is generally thought of as having the potential to last indefinitely, that is, until such time as the work is set down in a tangible form, at which time federal copyright jurisdiction applies [301].[1]

Copyright protection for 50 years after the author's death is new to U.S. copyright law. It is a fairly standard duration period under the laws of many other countries, which is what influenced Congress to choose it for the current U.S. law.[2]

Copyright duration based on an author's lifespan results in different works having different copyright durations. Thus, from one perspective it affects authors unequally. However, from another it affects authors equitably because it gives each author the opportunity to benefit from the copyright throughout his or her life and to provide some benefits for successors as well.

To illustrate how disparate the duration of copyrights can be under the life-plus-50 rule, Table 1 shows some hypothetical, and approximate, duration results for some famous authors and their works, had the rule been applicable in the past.[3] It was estimated in the legislative history that 70 to 76 years would be the average copyright duration under the life-plus-50 rule.[4]

## Joint Works

A "joint work," as defined in the current copyright statute, is a work:

prepared by two or more authors with the intention that their contribution be merged into inseparable or interdependent parts of a unitary whole. [101]

Further discussion of the term is included in Chapter 6.

Federal copyright protection for a joint work created in 1978 or later begins when the work is created and ordinarily lasts for the life of the last surviving author plus 50 years and to the end of that last calendar year

### TABLE 1 HYPOTHETICAL COPYRIGHT DURATION OF FAMOUS WORKS

| Author | Work | Hypothetical Copyright Duration (Years) |
|--------|------|-----------------------------------------|
| Poe | The Raven | 54 |
| Browning | Sonnets from the Portuguese | 61 |
| Da Vinci | The Last Supper | 71 |
| Melville | Moby Dick | 89 |
| Stowe | Uncle Tom's Cabin | 94 |
| Verdi | La Traviata | 98 |
| Michelangelo | Sistine Chapel ceiling | 102 |

[302(a),(b); 305; 101 "created"]—"ordinarily" because that is the express rule only for joint works created by two or more authors who did not work for hire [302(b)]. The statute does not expressly say what the duration rule is when only one of the authors did not work for hire. It may be that the longest possible duration rule for the particular case will be the controlling one for purposes of calculating the duration.[5]

### Works Made for Hire

As defined in the current copyright law, a work made for hire includes a work prepared by an employee within the scope of his or her employment. It also includes enumerated types of works, such as an instructional text, if specially ordered or commissioned and if the parties expressly agree in a signed writing that the work shall be considered a work made for hire [101 "work made for hire"]. See the discussion of works made for hire in Chapter 6.

Federal copyright protection for a work made for hire created in 1978 or later begins when the work is created and lasts for either (1) 100 years after that time, or (2) for 75 years after first publication, whichever period expires first [302(c)]. In either case, the copyright extends to the end of the last calendar year involved [305].

### Anonymous and Pseudonymous Works

As defined in the current copyright law [101]:

An "anonymous work" is a work on the copies or phonorecords of which no natural person is identified as author.

A "pseudonymous work" is a work on the copies or phonorecords of which the author is identified under a fictitious name.

The 75 or 100 years' rule, described in the preceding section, applies to anonymous and pseudonymous works created in 1978 or later. But if, before the expiration of the applicable time, the identity of the author is revealed in appropriate Copyright Office records, the copyright duration period shifts to the life-plus-50 standard previously discussed [302(c)].[6]

## PRE-1978 WORKS NOT FEDERALLY COPYRIGHTED BEFORE 1978

Under the 1909 Copyright Act, a work that potentially was eligible for eventual federal copyright protection may not have obtained that status for a number of reasons. Among them were:

1. the work was not published;
2. the work was not eligible to be federally copyrighted as an unpublished work;

3. the work, although unpublished, was eligible, but federal copyright was not sought.

In such situations the author retained state law copyright protection as long as the work remained unpublished and not federally registered.

The 1976 Copyright Law changed the rules. When the current law took effect, at the beginning of 1978, federal copyright jurisdiction was made applicable to all unpublished works of authorship set down in a suitably tangible form with the author's consent. Federal copyright can protect such works provided they did not go into the public domain before then and that they are eligible under general copyright criteria.

The duration rules discussed for works created in 1978 or later—the 75 or 100 and life-plus-50 standards—were made generally applicable to these unpublished works [303].[7] However, one modification was included in order to give the newly covered unpublished works some federal copyright life beyond what the general rules allow. Otherwise, many unpublished works, protected indefinitely by state law copyright on December 31, 1977, would have come within the federal scheme on January 1, 1978, and would have immediately gone into the public domain.

To avoid such consequences, Congress included a provision that copyright in such works would not expire before the end of 2002 and, if published by then, not before the end of 2027 [303].

*Example:* Composer A created a symphony in 1928. It has never been published and it was not registered in the Copyright Office before 1978. The composer died in 1929. If the life-plus-50 rule applied without any modification, the copyright would have expired at the end of 1979. However, the special rule extended the copyright duration period through 2002 and, if the symphony is published by then, through 2027.

## COPYRIGHT OFFICE RECORDS CONCERNING AUTHOR'S LIFE SPAN

Where copyright protection is calculated from the time of the author's death, it sometimes will be difficult to know when the copyright has expired. The copyright law provides three forms of assistance:

Registration Data: The copyright registration forms provide space for the year of the author's birth (optional) and for the year of the author's death (required if known at the time of the registration application). Registration records are available for public inspection.

Recordation of Data in Copyright Office: Any person "having an interest" in a copyright may, by following Copyright Office procedures, have the Office record a statement as to the author's death or a statement that he or she is still living [302(d)].[8] The Copyright Office also may use other reference sources for information concerning an author's death [302(d)].

Reliance on a Presumption of Author's Death: If, at any time, a work is either 100 years old, or was published at least 75 years earlier, the author may, for copyright purposes, be presumed to have died more than 50 years before if a certificate is obtained from the Copyright Office stating, in effect, that the records provided by section 302(d) indicate nothing to the contrary. One must rely on the presumption in good faith for it to have legal value [302(e)].

## WORKS FEDERALLY COPYRIGHTED BEFORE 1978

When the 1909 Copyright Act was in effect, federal copyright generally was obtained in one of two ways: (1) by publication of the work in the United States, under authority of the author, with an appropriate notice of copyright; or (2) in the case of certain designated kinds of unpublished works (such as dramatic works), by registering the work.[9] The term "publication" is considered in Chapter 7. Also considered there are the law's copyright notice standards. Pre-1978 publication without a copyright notice could result in immediate loss of copyright.

Pre-1978 federally copyrighted works were governed by a dual term of copyright under the 1909 Act. The current law retains that structure for them. Following a discussion of the general current rule, we will address two special situations: (1) sound recordings, and (2) English-language works first published outside the United States.

### Initial Term of Copyright

A federal copyright's initial term under the 1909 Act began on the date of first publication (or date of registration, depending on which of the above two categories was involved), lasting 28 years.[10] The 28-year initial term continues to apply to such works [304(a)]. However, the initial copyright term now continues to the end of the last calendar year in which the twenty-eighth year occurs [305]. This makes it possible, for 1978-and-on works, to consider copyright expiration in convenient calendar year terms.

### Renewal Term of Copyright

Under the 1909 Copyright Act, the initial term of copyright could be extended if renewal was properly applied for before the expiration of the initial term.[11] Works so affected by the 1909 Act are still so affected by the current law [304(a)].

For most of the time under the 1909 law, the renewal term was 28 years. Beginning in the early 1960s, Congress recognized (prematurely, as it turned out) that it probably would soon provide for a longer renewal term. To give some of the older extant federally copyrighted works the opportunity to benefit from any lengthened term, Congress from time to time extended the renewal term of such works by two-year periods beyond the original 28 years.[12] Works federally copyrighted as far back as the end of 1906 were kept within the protection period if renewal terms were obtained. Eventually, with the passage of the current law, the renewal term was set at 47 years, resulting in a total potential copyright of 75 years [304]. But to obtain the second term, a renewal registration must be applied for (or have been applied for in the last year of the initial term if that period has already ended). Renewal registrations are considered in Chapter 10.

Here are some examples of how the initial term/renewal term system works out:

*Example:* You, being a different person than the youthful novelist you were in the example at the beginning of this chapter, published a play in late 1906, with correct copyright notice, and obtained a renewal term in 1934. As that renewal term was approaching its end, its life was extended by Congress. Nonetheless, even with that extension, your copyright expired at the end of 1981.

*Example:* You published another play, with copyright notice, in 1920 and did not later apply for a renewal copyright. Your copyright expired some time in 1948.

*Example:* You published another play in 1920, with copyright notice and, for this one, you did obtain a renewal term in 1948. The copyright expiration date is the end of 1995.

*Example:* You published still another play, with copyright notice, in 1956. Your copyright will expire at the end of 1984 unless a renewal registration is filed in that last year. If a renewal term is obtained, the copyright will go on until the end of 2031.

Table 2 indicates copyright renewal and expiration dates for works federally copyrighted through publication before 1978. The table would also apply to the federal copyright in unpublished works that were registered before 1978.

## CONSIDERATIONS BEFORE CONCLUDING THAT A WORK IS IN THE PUBLIC DOMAIN

When calculating whether a work has lived out its copyright life and entered the public domain, several issues should be remembered.

Keep a lookout for all the relevant works. For instance, in a 1980 federal appeals court case, a motion picture was found to have gone into the public domain because the renewal was not obtained for its copyright. However, the film was a derivative work of a published play, George Bernard Shaw's *Pygmalion.* Copyright in the play had been renewed and the court ruled that that copyright was not destroyed by failure to renew the copyright in the motion picture. The net result was that permission from the owner of rights in the play would be necessary in order to have a noninfringing public performance of the film without infringing the play.[13] Translations, revised editions, and books that include supplementary materials (such as forewords

TABLE 2   COPYRIGHT DURATION FOR WORKS
PUBLISHED BEFORE 1978

| Date of First Publication with Copyright Notice* | Year by the End of Which the Initial Term of Copyright Expires(ed)† | Year by the End of Which the Renewal Term of Copyright, if Acquired, Expires |
|---|---|---|
| 1907 | 1935 | 1982 |
| 1908 | 1936 | 1983 |
| 1909 | 1937 | 1984 |
| 1910 | 1938 | 1985 |
| 1911 | 1939 | 1986 |
| 1912 | 1940 | 1987 |
| — | — | — |
| 1953 | 1981 | 2028 |
| 1954 | 1982 | 2029 |
| 1955 | 1983 | 2030 |
| 1956 | 1984 | 2031 |
| 1957 | 1985 | 2032 |
| 1958 | 1986 | 2033 |
| 1959 | 1987 | 2034 |
| — | — | — |
| 1977 | 2005 | 2052 |

\* For sound recordings and ad interim copyrights, see the discussion later on in this chapter.

† 1. If federal copyright protection for a work began in the 1907–1949 period, the year for securing a renewal term of copyright was the twenty-eighth year of the initial copyright term, with the time calculated on the basis of the day, month, and year when the initial federal copyright commenced.

2. For federal copyright protection that began in the 1951–1977 period, a simple calendar year is used for the renewal term. For a federal copyright that began on any month and day in 1951, the time to secure a renewal term of copyright would be the period beginning December 31, 1978, and ending December 31, 1979.

3. For federal copyright protection that began in 1950, the renewal term could be secured during that part of 1977 which was in the twenty-eighth year of the initial term and also at any time in 1978.

or annotations) are other examples in which more than one copyrighted work may enter into duration considerations.

Even if U.S. copyright has expired in the relevant work(s), copyright protection may still be applicable in some other countries where the duration will be different. If your contemplated use would involve such other countries, their copyright laws would have to be considered. In the case of the *Pygmalion* play, for instance, the appeals court noted that the U.S. copyright would last through 1988. But, since Shaw died in 1950, the copyright in many other countries may last more than a decade beyond that. (Many countries have used the life-plus-50 standard for many years, whereas the United States introduced it only in 1976.)

Even within the United States the expiration of copyright in a published work does not always allow any activity you might be contemplating. For example, illustrations that began as copyrighted works may have been adopted to serve as someone's trademark. Any use that would infringe on the trademark could be legally actionable even if the illustration alone has gone into the public domain.[14]

## SOUND RECORDINGS

See Chapter 2 for a description of sound recording copyrights.

Federal copyright law did not provide protection for a sound recording, as such, until February 15, 1972. That remains a key date under the current law. A sound recording copyright that was first recorded before then is protectible under state law up to February 15, 2047 [301(c); 101 "sound recording," "fixed"]. A copyright in a sound recording first recorded on February 15, 1972, or later is directly protected by federal copyright law. The regular duration rules apply. These rules, of course, turn on the usual factors, such as whether or not the work was published before 1978.

## AD INTERIM COPYRIGHTS

The copyright law preceding the present one contained a rule, applicable under defined circumstances to certain English-language works first published outside the United States, that provided for only a short initial term of U.S. copyright protection. At the end of that period, U.S. copyright protection might be lost forever if, by then, the work had not been manufactured in the United States.[15] This short term copyright is called an ad interim copyright. If manufacture in the United States was timely made and appropriate procedures followed, normal U.S. duration rules could then apply.

The legal standards relating to ad interim copyrights changed somewhat from time to time in the 1909–1977 period. During the later years they had a fairly narrow coverage area. Further information about the relevant criteria is included under the manufacturing clause discussion in Chapter 11.

The current law does not use this ad interim system for works first published after June 1977, nor is U.S. manufacturing a critical element to prevent a copyright from expiring in the case of ad interim copyrights obtained after June 1973 [Transitional and Supplementary Provisions, Sec. 107].

## TABLE 3   U.S. COPYRIGHT DURATION STANDARDS

| Category of Work | Period of Copyright Duration |
| --- | --- |
| 1. Works created in 1978 or later | |
| a. Individual author | a. Author's life plus 50 years [302(a)]. |
| b. Joint work | b. Last surviving author's life plus 50 years [302(b)]. (See chapter text if some are work-for-hire authors.) |
| c. Work made for hire | c. Shorter of: 75 years from first publication or 100 years from creation [302(c)]. |
| d. Anonymous, pseudonymous work | d. 75 or 100 years as in (c) but shifts to author's life plus 50 years if author's name is timely revealed in Copyright Office records [302(a)]. |
| e. All works | e. Copyright lasts to end of the last calendar year involved [305]. |
| 2. Works created before 1978 | |
| a. Works not federally copyrighted before 1978 | a. Same rules as in 1(a)–(e) except copyright duration lasts through at least 2002 and, if published by then, through at least 2027 [303]. |
| b. Works federally copyrighted before 1978 | b. Initial term of 28 years from year copyright was secured. Renewal term of 47 years if renewal term is (or was) obtained in last year of initial term [304(a)]. For both initial term and renewal term, copyright now lasts to end of the last calendar year involved [305]. |
| c. Certain English-language works first published abroad before July 1, 1977 | c. The rules in (b) above apply if certain procedures were followed; otherwise the U.S. copyright could have expired shortly after the publication. See Chapter 11. |
| 3. Sound recordings | |
| a. Sound recordings first fixed before February 15, 1972 | a. State law applies and may provide protection through 2047 [301(a)]. |
| b. Sound recordings created after February 14, 1972 | b. Applicable rules in 2 above apply [303, 304(a)]. |
| c. Sound recordings created after 1977 | c. Applicable rules in 1 above apply [302]. |
| 4. Original works of authorship not fixed in tangible medium | State law applies. See Chapter 2. |
| 5. Ways in which copyright protection period may be shortened | Abandonment; forfeiture through copyright notice deficiencies, or ad interim copyright problems, or manufacturing clause problems. |

The old ad interim rules will continue to be significant in judging the present copyright status of English-language works first published outside the United States before July 1977. Where the rules resulted in a loss of U.S. copyright protection, the current law has no rescuscitory powers [Transitional and Supplementary Provisions, Sec. 103].

See Table 3 for an overall listing of standards for U.S. copyright durations.

# 5

# EXCLUSIVE RIGHTS OF COPYRIGHT

In the first part of this chapter we will consider the five rights that the copyright law gives a copyright owner in his or her original work of authorship. These rights form the basis for determining when copyright has been infringed. (The remedies for infringements are considered in Chapter 12.) The rights also are a reference point for transfers and licenses under copyright. (The statute's standards governing such transactions are considered in Chapter 6.) Following the discussion of the five rights is a table listing the various statutory limitations on them. These limitations are discussed in other chapters, as cited in the table.

The second part of this chapter mentions several legal areas, other than copyright, that often are of interest in connection with works of authorship. These other legal rights are beyond the scope of this book, but some brief comments are provided. Also considered is the extent to which copyright law prevails over other laws that deal with the same or similar subjects.

## FIVE EXCLUSIVE RIGHTS

The owner of copyright generally has the exclusive right to do and authorize the following with respect to the copyrighted work [106]:

1. reproduce the work in copies;
2. prepare derivative works based upon it;
3. distribute copies of it to the public;
4. perform the work publicly;
5. display the work publicly.

The ownership of these exclusive rights may be transferred in whole or in part.

### Reproduction

The reproduction rights of copyright refer to making copies or phonorecords of a work. There is no copy or phonorecord unless the physical object holds the work for more than a transitory duration [101 "copy," "phonorecord," "fixed"]. For example, the duplication of a videotape would be the reproduction of a copy, but a continuous playback of the tape ordinarily would not result in a "copy" being made on the screen. In the copyright sense, the playback typically would constitute a "performance" or a "display" of the work [101].

The reproduction right does not, of course, prevent someone else from creating a work, even a similar work, on the same subject. Rather, it is intended to prevent copying. A recent case makes the point quite well. It concerned an artist, an illustrator of birds, who was charged with infringement of his own work. He had transferred some copyrights in one of his bird illustrations— two cardinals among apple blossoms—to the plaintiff, who marketed the work as part of a collection series. Thereafter the artist painted two cardinals among apple blossoms for a different party and a different collection series. The court found that his second painting was an original work of authorship and not a copy of the first. The second work was not classified as a derivative work either. The artist prevailed in the suit. The court did not find that he had violated any agreement not to provide the work for the second collection series.[1] (In other circumstances, however, there could have been an implied agreement.)

It is possible to infringe a copyright without being aware of it at all. George Harrison's song "My Sweet Lord" was found to have infringed an earlier song, even though the court recognized that the copying had been subconscious.[2]

Two of the principal statutory limitations on the exclusive right of reproduction are the fair-use doctrine and the library reproduction rights provisions. For further discussion of these two sections of the law, see Chapters 11 through 13.

## Preparation of Derivative Works

The copyright owner has the exclusive right to prepare derivative works based upon a copyrighted work [106(a)(2)]. A derivative work is a work based upon one or more preexisting works. The statutory definition includes translations, condensations, abridgments, dramatizations, motion picture versions, reproductions, and musical sound recordings [101].

## Public Distribution

The third exclusive right of copyright in the statute is the right to distribute copies (or phonorecords) of the copyrighted work to the public by sale or other transfer of ownership or by rental, lease, or lending [101 "publication"; 106(a)(3)]. The appearance of a work on television or on the stage ordinarily would not, by itself, be a public distribution; such an appearance would be too transitory to qualify as a copy. Of course, public display or performance rights might be involved, depending upon the circumstances. According to the legislative history, distribution to the public means, generally, distribution to persons under no explicit or implicit restrictions with respect to disclosure of the contents of the work.[3]

Once a person obtains ownership of a copy, he or she has certain rights in that physical object notwithstanding the copyright (see Chapter 6).

## Public Performance

The owner of copyright has the exclusive right to perform the copyrighted work publicly, except in the case of pictorial, graphic, or sculptural works [106(4)]. This right does not apply to sound recordings, but keep in mind that copyright in the underlying work is separate from copyright in the sound recording as such [114(a)]. Thus, if someone publicly plays your hit recording of someone else's copyrighted song, you have no copyright case, but the copyright owner of the song may have one. (As noted in Chapter 2, there is some support for amending the law to provide a public performance right in a sound recording copyright.)

The term "performance" covers a variety of activities, such as singing, dancing, acting, reciting, or broadcasting. When you turn on your television set, you are viewing a performance of the work [101 "perform"]. However, the copyright owner's exclusive right covers no more than public performances.

The definitions of "public performances" and "public displays" are combined in the statute. To perform or display a work publicly includes any of the following:

1. performance or display at a place open to the public;
2. performance or display at any place where are gathered a substantial number of persons outside a normal circle of family and its social acquaintances;
3. transmitting or otherwise communicating a performance or display of the work to the public or to one of the places described in (1) or (2) above.

One of the purposes of clause (2) is to make clear that performances in "semipublic" places, such as lodges, factories, summer camps, and schools, are public performances.[4] The term "a family" in clause (2) includes an individual living alone and a gathering of the individual's social acquaintances, which would normally be regarded as private.[5] The legislative history states that routine meetings of business personnel ordinarily would be excluded from the scope of the second clause because a "substantial number" of persons would not be present.[6] Under clause (3), there can be a public performance or display even if the viewers or hearers are not present in the same place or seeing or hearing the material at the same time [101 "publicly"].

Under the 1909 Copyright Act, many of the copyright owner's exclusive performance rights were limited to public performances for profit. Although the new law does away with that broad for-profit distinction, it replaces it with a number of other limitations on the owner's public performance rights. These limitations are considered in Chapters 14, 16, and 17.

## Public Display

The fifth exclusive right of copyright is the right to display the copyrighted work publicly [106(5)]. Like the public performance right, it is not applicable to sound recordings [114(a)].

To display a work means to show the original, or a copy of it, either directly or with mechanical aids, such as a projector. In the case of a motion picture or other audiovisual work, one *displays* a work by showing individual images nonsequentially [101 "display"]. One *performs* a work by showing it in sequence or by making the accompanying sounds audible [101 "perform"].

The public display right was not expressly recognized in the 1909 copyright statute, and its status under the old law was uncertain.[7]

Infringement of a public display right is infrequently claimed. One case concerned some wicker mirrors. The defendant allegedly displayed infringing mirrors at a housewares exhibition in Chicago. Because the alleged infringement occurred in Illinois, it was possible to sue in that state, even though the defendant was from another state and was served with the summons in another state.[8]

The owner of an original work, or of a lawfully made copy of it, is entitled (without the authorization of the copyright owner) to display that copy publicly to viewers present at the place where the copy is located. This may be done directly or by the projection of no more than one image at a time [109(b)].

Table 4 lists various sections of the law that, in defined circumstances, limit what is copyrightable under federal copyright or that limit, again under defined circumstances, the scope of the rights of copyright. The brief descriptions in the table necessarily do not fully describe the provisions referred to which are complex. The statute and the text chapters should be consulted for further information.

The numbers in the fourth column of the table list particular rights potentially affected by the section or topic referred to in the second and third columns. The numbers in the fourth column correspond to the numbers used in section 106 to designate the rights of copyright: (1) reproduction, (2) preparation of derivative works, (3) public distribution, (4) public performance, and (5) public display.

## TABLE 4    STATUTORY LIMITS ON COPYRIGHTABILITY AND RIGHTS OF COPYRIGHT

| Item | Section | Activity or Topic | Exclusive Rights Potentially Affected | Chapter Reference |
|------|---------|-------------------|---------------------------------------|-------------------|
| 1. | 101 | Definition of pictorial, etc., works | 1, 2, 3, 4, 5 | 2 |
| 2. | 102(b) | Uses of ideas, etc. | 1, 2, 3, 4, 5 | 3 |
| 3. | 103 | Use of preexisting material | 1, 2, 3, 4, 5 | 2 |
| 4. | 104 | National origin considerations, post-1977 standards | 1, 2, 3, 4, 5 | 11 |
| 5. | | National origin considerations, pre-1978 standards | 1, 2, 3, 4, 5 | 11 |
| 6. | 105 | Certain works by U.S. employees | 1, 2, 3, 4, 5 | 3 |
| 7. | 106 | Public distribution, public performance, public display | 3, 4, 5 | 5, 6 |
| 8. | | Short phrases, titles, trademarks | 1, 2, 3, 4, 5 | 3 |
| 9. | | Derivative works; compilations | 1, 2, 3, 4, 5 | 3 |
| 10. | | Facts, news, history | 1, 2, 3, 4, 5 | 3 |
| 11. | | *Scènes à faire* | 1, 2, 3, 4, 5 | 3 |
| 12. | 107 | Fair use | 1, 2, 3, 4, 5 | 13, 14 |
| 13. | 108 | Library reproduction, distribution rights | 1,    3 | 15 |
| 14. | 109(a) | Transfer of lawful copy | 3 | 6 |
| 15. | 109(b) | Display of lawful copy | 5 | 6 |
| 16. | 110(1) | Teaching activities | 4, 5 | 14 |
| 17. | 110(2) | Teaching activities | 4, 5 | 14 |
| 18. | 110(3) | Religious services | 4, 5 | 16 |
| 19. | 110(4) | Certain noncommercial performances | 4 | 16 |
| 20. | 110(5) | Use of broadcast receivers in public | 4, 5 | 16 |
| 21. | 110(6) | Agricultural and horticultural fairs | 4 | 16 |
| 22. | 110(7) | Record and tape vendors | 4 | 16 |
| 23. | 110(8) | Aid for disabled | 4 | 16 |
| 24. | 110(9) | Aid for disabled | 4 | 16 |
| 25. | 111(a)(1) | Secondary transmissions, hotels, etc. | 4, 5 | 16 |
| 26. | 111(a)(2) | Secondary transmissions, teaching activities | 4, 5 | 14 |
| 27. | 111(b) | Secondary transmissions, broadcast signals | 4, 5 | 17 |
| 28. | 111(c)(d) | Cable systems, broadcast signals | 4, 5 | 17 |
| 29. | 111(e)(f) | Cable systems, nonsimultaneous broadcast signals | 1,    4, 5 | 17 |
| 30. | 112(a) | Transmission programs | 1 | 17 |

| Item | Section | Activity or Topic | Exclusive Rights Potentially Affected | Chapter Reference |
|------|---------|-------------------|----------------------------------------|-------------------|
| 31. | 112(b) | Transmission programs, teaching activities | 1 | 14 |
| 32. | 112(c) | Transmission programs, certain noncommercial uses | 1 | |
| 33. | 112(d) | Transmission programs, aid for disabled | 1 | |
| 34. | 112(e) | Transmission programs under section 112; derivative works | 1, 2, 3, 4, 5 | |
| 35. | 113(b) | Useful articles | 1,    3,    5 | 3 |
| 36. | 113(c) | Useful articles, pictures of |     3,    5 | 3 |
| 37. | 114 | Sound recordings | 1, 2, 3, 4 | 2 |
| 38. | 115 | Recorded nondramatic musical works | 1, 2, 3 | 15 |
| 39. | 115(a)(2) | Musical works, adaptations of | 1, 2, 3, 4, 5 | 15 |
| 40. | 116 | Jukebox performances | 4 | 15 |
| 41. | 117 | Lawful owner of copy of computer program | 1, 2 | 6 |
| 42. | 118(d) | Noncommercial broadcasting | 1,    3, 4, 5 | 15 |
| 43. | 118(d)(3) | Television programs, teaching activities | 1,    3 | 15 |
| 44. | 201(e) | Copyright obtained by certain involuntary transfers | 1, 2, 3, 4, 5 | |
| 45. | 204(a) | Transfer of ownership not in writing; effect on transferee | 1, 2, 3, 4, 5 | 6 |
| 46. | 205(e) | Conflicting transfer of ownership; effect on transferee | 1, 2, 3, 4, 5 | 6 |
| 47. | 205(f) | Conflicting transfer and license; effect on each | 1, 2, 3, 4, 5 | 6 |
| 48. | 301(c) | Sound recordings fixed prior to 2/15/72 | 1, 2, 3, 4, 5 | 2 |
| 49. | 302–305 | Copyright duration | 1, 2, 3, 4, 5 | 4 |
| 50. | | Abandonment of copyright | 1, 2, 3, 4, 5 | |
| 51. | 405, 406 | Effect of notice errors, omissions | 1, 2, 3, 4, 5 | 4 |
| 52. | 407(e) | Unpublished transmission programs | 3 | 8 |
| 53. | 507 | Statute of limitations | 1, 2, 3, 4, 5 | 12 |
| 54. | | Laches (delay in claiming rights) | 1, 2, 3, 4, 5 | |
| 55. | | Pre-1978 manufacturing clause | 1, 2, 3, 4, 5 | 11 |
| 56. | 601 | Post-1977 manufacturing clause | 3 | 11 |
| 57. | 602 | Importations | 3 | 11 |

TABLE 4   STATUTORY LIMITS ON COPYRIGHTABILITY
AND RIGHTS OF COPYRIGHT (*Cont.*)

| Item | Section | Activity or Topic | Exclusive Rights Potentially Affected | Chapter Reference |
|------|---------|-------------------|---------------------------------------|-------------------|
| 58. | 704(b) | Copies deposited with Copyright Office | 1, 3 | 8 |
| 59. | 704(c) | Copies deposited with Copyright Office | 3 | 8 |
| 60. | | Works in public domain pre-1978 (T&S 103)* | 1, 2, 3, 4, 5 | 4 |
| 61. | | Pre-1910 nondramatic musical works (T&S 103)* | 1, 3 | |
| 62. | | Pre-1978 compulsory licenses in nondramatic musical works (T&S 106)* | 1, 3 | |
| 63. | | Television and radio news programs (T&S 113)* | 1, 2, 3 | 15 |

* "T&S" refers to the transitional and supplementary provisions to the 1976 Copyright Act.


The existence of so many limitations does not mean that copyrights are narrow in scope. Many of the limitations apply only in special circumstances and do not have broad effect.

## EXCLUSIVE RIGHTS OF COPYRIGHT VS. RIGHTS UNDER OTHER LAWS

### Federal Laws

The copyright law does not limit any rights or remedies under any other federal statutes [301(d)]. Eight areas of federal law that sometimes become relevant to copyrighted works are utility patents, design patents, trademarks, unfair competition, antitrust law, federal communications law, the Freedom of Information Act, and the Tariff Act of 1930. Although none is within the scope of this book, some brief remarks are pertinent here.

*Patents.*[9]   The federal patent law concerns new and nonobvious useful inventions. Patent protection covers a period of 17 years. An owner of a valid patent obtains the exclusive right to make, use, or sell the patented invention. This right may apply even when someone else has independently developed the same invention. The patent law, like the copyright law, is going through a period of sorting out as to how it relates to computer programs.[10]

*Design Patents.*[11]    Federal design patent law concerns new, original, and ornamental designs for articles of manufacture. Design patent protection can extend for as long as 14 years. Design patents are issued only after a search is made to determine that the design is novel.

*Trademarks.*[12]    The federal trademark law, the Lanham Act, provides a registration and protection system for those words, names, symbols, and devices that identify the trademark owner's goods and services and distinguish them from others. (Technically, a trademark refers to sources of goods and a service mark to sources of services but, for convenience, both of these are called trademarks here.) Trademark protection can last as long as the mark retains its identifying and distinguishing function. Generally speaking, a valid trademark operates to preclude other businesses from using the same or a similar mark under circumstances where confusion might arise as to the origin of goods.

The federal registration of a trademark—with the United States Patent and Trademark Office—is possible, but not required, once a word, symbol, or other device is used in interstate commerce as a trademark. One of the principal practical advantages of registration is that the mark becomes part of a public record. This record is frequently searched by those selecting trademarks. If a mark is registered, someone who is considering a similar mark may reconsider in order to avoid confusion.

It should be noted that trademarks also can be protectible under state laws.

*Unfair Competition.*    The Lanham Act contains a provision that prohibits false designations of origin and false descriptions of goods and services even when federally registered trademarks are not involved. This section of the law is in a stage of flux and will not be covered in any depth here. However, two recent cases demonstrate some possible effects of the section. In one case, a celebrated author (Ken Follett) had served as editor of someone else's book; when the book was marketed, Follett was named as an author. The Lanham Act played a role in bringing the practice to a stop.[13] In another case, the section protected a publisher of guidebooks that used the term "Instant Guide" against another publisher's use of the phrase "Insti-Guide" on its books, which were otherwise similar in appearance.[14]

State laws also provide protection against "unfair competition." Because this term can embrace a wide variety of claims, it is necessary to evaluate any particular claim in the context of the copyright statute's preemption standards affecting state laws.

One area where state unfair competition laws play a role in copyright-related matters is with respect to titles of works. The mere fact that two works have the same title does not mean that anything is legally wrong. But relief is sometimes provided in cases where customers are likely to be confused and particularly where the second person to choose the title seemed to have done so for the purpose of benefiting from such confusion.

*Antitrust Laws.*[15] The federal antitrust laws prohibit, under defined circumstances, such things as contracts in unreasonable restraint of trade, unfair trade practices, certain kinds of price discrimination, and monopolization and attempts to monopolize.

Although copyright law provides the copyright owner with certain statutory rights, those rights do not provide immunity from the antitrust laws; rather they are taken into account in determining what practices are lawful. Antitrust law has played a particularly important role in the music industry. The practices of leading music performing rights organizations are governed in part by antitrust consent decrees, issued many years ago, which require, among other things, that performance licenses be available on reasonable terms.

*Federal Communications Law.*[16] The Federal Communications Act of 1934 governs broadcast and certain cablecast activities. As considered in Chapter 17, the communications law plays a part in the copyright law's compulsory licensing provisions relating to cable system carriage of broadcast signals. Section 605 of the act prohibits certain unauthorized uses of signals, and it has played a role in preventing some companies from appropriating signals of pay television services.[17]

*Freedom of Information Act.*[18] The Freedom of Information Act allows people access to government records under defined conditions and circumstances. These records can include materials created by people and organizations other than the federal government itself. In most cases, the government presumably may provide a copy of such materials, pursuant to the act, without running afoul of copyright law. In one recent case, however, a publisher's photographs, of commercial value, were involved. A federal appeals court decided that the federal district court should give the publisher-copyright owner an opportunity to participate in the resolution of the Freedom of Information Act request for copies.[19] The matter was resolved, with the request being fulfilled, without the need for a judicial decision to resolve the legal issue.

*Tariff Act of 1930.*[20] Under this act, as amended, the U.S. International Trade Commission can make determinations that the importation of infringing goods should be barred. Recently, the commission issued such a decision with respect to copyrighted material and the importation of competing electronic arcade games.[21] (The proceedings involved both copyright and other legal issues.)

## State and Local Laws

The 1976 Copyright Act aims generally for a uniform national policy on copyright matters. It seeks to accomplish this through what are called the statute's "preemption" provisions [301]. Under the previous law, there was no express statutory provision for issues that arise when a state law deals with the same subject as the federal law. Instead, the courts had to reason out what made sense in particular cases, and, sometimes, there were considerable uncertainties.[22] In the 1976 Copyright Act, Congress included some statutory standards to help resolve such problems. One of the legislative goals was certainty:

> The intention of section 301 is to preempt and abolish any rights under the common law or statutes of a State that are equivalent to copyright and that extend to works coming within the scope of the Federal copyright law. The declaration of this principle in section 301 is intended to be stated in the clearest and most unequivocal language possible, so as to foreclose any conceivable misinterpretation of its unqualified intention that Congress shall act preemptively, and to avoid the development of any vague, borderline areas between State and Federal protection.[23]

But state laws take such a variety of forms and purposes that a body of court decisions crafted from experience is needed before we can conclude that vague borderlines are a thing of the past.

Before considering some borderline areas, let us note briefly two of the preemption provisions that are either less ambiguous than the others or seem likely to raise relatively infrequent problems.

> Sound recordings first fixed before February 15, 1972, may be protected by state law into the middle of the next century. [301(c)]

> Rights and remedies under the state law are not limited by the 1976 Act insofar as the rights and remedies relate to any cause of action arising from undertakings commenced before January 1, 1978. [301(b)(2)][24]

Another area is the provision that nothing in the 1976 Act limits any rights or remedies under state law with respect to works of authorship not fixed in any tangible medium of expression [301(b)]. As examples, the 1976 House report refers to "choreography that has never been filmed or notated, an extemporaneous speech, 'original works of authorship' communicated solely through conversations or live broadcasts, and a dramatic sketch or musical composition improvised or developed from memory and without being recorded or written down."[25] Such unfixed works of authorship generally will be protectible under state law, even if the rights and remedies are equivalent to those of the 1976 Act.[26]

Let us now proceed to three standards that will have to go through a maturation process in the "casks" of litigation before the preemption provisions become clear [301]. One is stated in positive language, the two others negatively.

> (a) . . . all legal or equitable rights that are equivalent to any of the exclusive rights of copyright as specified in section 106 in works of authorship that are fixed in a tangible medium of expression and come within the subject matter of copyright as specified by sections 102 and 103 . . . are governed exclusively by [the 1976 Act] . . . [301(a)].
> (b) Nothing in [the 1976 Act] . . . annuls or limits any rights or remedies under the common law or statutes of any State with respect to—
>> (1) subject matter that does not come within the subject matter of copyright as specified by sections 102 and 103; . . . or . . .
>> (3) activities violating legal or equitable rights that are not equivalent to any of the exclusive rights within the general scope of copyright as specified by section 106.

The last criterion will often be a key one in preemption decisions. When the bill that eventually became the 1976 Copyright Act was near its final form, it contained some direct guidance by providing examples of activities violating rights that are not equivalent to any of the exclusive rights of copyright:

> including rights against misappropriation not equivalent to any such exclusive rights [of section 106], breaches of contract, breaches of trust, trespass, conversion, invasion of privacy, defamation, and deceptive trade practices such as passing off and false representations.[27]

However, in the final days of the lawmaking process, the House deleted the quoted language. Concern was expressed that the reference to "misappropriation" might be construed as authorizing states to pass misappropriation laws, and that such misappropriation laws could be so broad as to render the general preemption approach of the new law meaningless.[28] At the same time, however, the proposer of the clause concurred with another congressman's view that striking the reference was not intended to change the existing state of the law relating to misappropriation. The language of the remarks, as reported in the *Congressional Record*, suggests that the two congressmen may not have had a complete meeting of minds, but only thought they did. Thus, it is difficult to determine with any certainty what Congress intended by the deletion. Although this may affect only the nuances of interpretation of the statute's not-equivalent phrase (even the deleted language did not authorize any and all state laws dealing with misappropriations), the nuances may have significant practical consequences.

If the deletion amendment is viewed as only affecting the misappropriation example, the legislative history for other areas cited—breaches of contract, breaches of trust, trespass, conversion, invasion of privacy, defamation, and deceptive trade practices such as passing off and false representation— remains relevant:

The evolving common law rights of "privacy," "publicity," and trade secrets, and the general laws of defamation and fraud, would remain unaffected as long as the causes of action contain elements, such as an invasion of personal rights or a breach of trust or confidentiality, that are different in kind from copyright infringement. Nothing in the bill derogates from the rights of parties to contract with each other; . . . however, to the extent that the unfair competition concept known as "interference with contractual relations" is merely the equivalent of copyright protection, it would be preempted. . . .

Section 301 is not intended to preempt common law protection in cases involving activities such as false labelling, fraudulent misrepresentation, and passing off even where the subject matter involved comes within the scope of the copyright statute.[29]

A number of preemption cases have been decided under the 1976 Act, but many were preliminary decisions or are decisions now on appeal. Although we cannot do justice to any of the cases in a brief amount of space, for further reference here are some of the topics involved, with citations to the cases given in the chapter notes.[30] The subject matter of the cases and the results thus far are given below; however, as the results often are more complex than the capsule conclusions, the cases themselves should be consulted.

1. New York's "truth-in-testing" statute, involving tests given for use in medical school admissions decisions (preemption issue raised but not decided).
2. One state statute directed against "blind-bidding" practices in the motion picture industry was upheld against a preemption charge, but another state's was found sufficiently different that a court declared that copyright law preemption could apply.
3. A California statute providing, under defined circumstances, for an artist to obtain a portion of the proceeds of a work of art when resold (no preemption under 1909 Act; as for the 1976 Act, issue was by-passed).
4. A Massachusetts statute against theft of intellectual property, in this case, literary property on videotape (preemption).
5. A claim of tortious interference with contractual relations and another claim of conversion (preemption).
6. A "right of publicity" case involving an Elvis Presley poster (no preemption).

It should also be noted that appeals are pending in cases involving the interrelationship of trade secrecy law and copyright law.[31] In one, the federal district court found preemption under the particular circumstances. In another, where a statutory copyright notice had been used on the material, the district court found that that would not automatically negate state trade secrecy protection where the work had only received a "limited publication."

# 6

## COPYRIGHT OWNERSHIP, TRANSFERS, AND LICENSES

In this chapter, we shall consider the 1976 Copyright Act's standards governing the initial ownership of copyright, the transfer of ownership of rights of copyright, and the licensing of rights of copyright on a nonexclusive basis.

## INITIAL OWNERSHIP

### Individual Works

The author of an original work of authorship is the initial owner of the copyright in the work and thus starts out as the owner of the exclusive rights of copyright: reproduction, preparation of derivative works, public distribution, public performance, and public display [106; 201(a)]. In the case of a work made for hire, the employer or whoever commissioned the work is considered to be the "author" in the technical statutory sense of the term [201(b)]. (Works made for hire are discussed later in this chapter.)

### Joint Works

A joint work is a work prepared by two or more authors with the intention that their contributions be merged into inseparable or interdependent parts of a unitary whole [101 "joint works"]. The House report underlying the statute adds:

> The touchstone . . . is the intention, at the time the writing is done, that the parts be absorbed or combined into an integrated unit, although the parts themselves may be either "inseparable" (as in the case of a novel or painting) or "interdependent" (as in the case of a motion picture, opera, or the words and music of a song). The definition . . . is to be contrasted with the definition of a "collective work," . . . in which the elements of merger and unity are lacking. . . .[1]

The report goes on to comment about motion pictures in the context of joint works and derivative works:

. . . although a novelist . . . may write a work with the expectation that it will be used in a motion picture, this is clearly a case of separate or independent authorship rather than one where the basic intention behind the writing of the film was for motion picture use. In this case, the motion picture is a derivative work . . . and . . . the copyright . . . is independent of, and does not enlarge the scope of rights in, any pre-existing material incorporated in it.

The authors of a joint work are co-owners of copyright in the work [201(a)]. As such, each potentially has an independent right to license the use of the work, with a duty to account for the profits received.[2]

Those who collaborate in the preparation of copyrighted works should reach a clear understanding as to whether they intend to create a joint work and as to their respective rights in the work. No agreement, or an ambiguous agreement, may cause future uncertainties and conflicts.

## Collective Works

A collective work is one in which a number of contributions, constituting separate and independent works in themselves, are assembled into a collective whole. Anthologies, periodicals, and encyclopedias are examples [101 "collective works"]. Copyright law makes a distinction between the collective work as a whole and each individual contribution. The work as a whole is one work, and each separate contribution within it ordinarily is a separate work.

The owner of copyright in the work as a whole is not automatically the owner of copyright in each contribution [201(c)]. Under the 1909 Copyright Act, there was some support for the position that, in the absence of sufficient evidence to the contrary, the owner of the collective work acquired copyright ownership in the individual contributions submitted for the collective work.[3] That position still has relevance today in considering the ownership status of pre-1978 contributions.

For transfers in 1978 or later, however, the rule is that, in the absence of an express transfer of the copyright or of any rights under it, the owner of copyright in the collective work is presumed to have acquired only the privilege of reproducing and distributing the contribution as part of (1) that particular collective work; (2) any revision of that collective work; or (3) any later collective work in that same series [201(c)].

Thus, when those standards apply, the publisher of a magazine may, if there is no agreement to the contrary, publish an article (the separate contribution) in a later issue of the same magazine in which it first appeared, but not in a different magazine or a book. Similarly, the copyright owner of an encyclopedia may publish the contribution in a revised edition but not in a different work unless that was expressly agreed to. In this discussion, we have assumed that the contribution was not a work made for hire, a category to be considered later in this chapter.

## Derivative Works

A derivative work is a work based upon one or more preexisting works [101 "derivative work"]. The owner of copyright in a derivative work does not, by creating the derivative work, acquire ownership of copyright in the underlying work. Consequently, when acquiring rights from the author of a derivative work, you must consider whether it is also necessary to acquire related rights in the underlying work. The author of the derivative work, of course, had the same problem. That author may, however, have acquired only rights covering the objective then in mind. He or she may not have acquired the right to pass on the particular right in the underlying work in which you are interested.

In a few situations, the copyright law allows the preparation of a derivative work without the consent of the owner of rights in the underlying work [112(e); 115]. In these situations, the derivative work is not separately copyrightable except with the express consent of the copyright owner of the underlying work [112(e); 115(a)(2)].

## Works Made for Hire

In the case of works made for hire, the employer or whoever commissioned the work is considered to be the initial owner of copyright and is treated as the "author" for purposes of the copyright statute [201(b)]. A work-made-for-hire category has been part of U.S. copyright law for a long time. Congress wanted to retain the concept in the new law, but decided to limit the instances in which the category applies. The current law provides for two categories:

*Certain Works by Employees.* A work prepared by an employee within the scope of his or her employment is a work made for hire [101 "work made for hire"]. The employer is the initial owner of all the rights of copyright in the work unless the employer and employee have agreed otherwise in a written instrument signed by them [201(b)]. This category of work made for hire is substantially the same as existed under the 1909 Act.

Often, the employer-employee relationship is clear, as is the "scope of employment" issue. Sometimes, however, there is at least room for argument. In those situations in particular, the employer should consider preserving a record of the facts establishing the employment and its scope. The employer and employee also should consider, in some cases, drawing up a written agreement that reflects the work-for-hire status of the work or works to be produced.[4]

Theoretically, an employer's work made for hire can be any type of work, as the employer-employee relationship can cover just about any activity. Three of the most frequent types of "employer" works made for hire are motion pictures, periodicals (as collective works), and periodical contributions prepared by employees of the publication. Of course, these are not necessarily works made for hire, but they very often are.

*Specially Ordered or Commissioned Works.* Under the 1909 Act, a work that was specially ordered or commissioned also could qualify as a work made for hire, with the person who ordered or commissioned the work becoming the owner of copyright. The 1976 law narrowed this category; work made for hire must now meet two standards [101 "work made for hire"]. First, the parties must expressly agree in a written instrument signed by them that the work shall be considered a work made for hire. Second, the work must be specially ordered or commissioned for use as one or more of the following:

1. translation;
2. atlas;
3. contribution to a collective work;
4. compilation;
5. part of a motion picture or other audiovisual work;
6. test;
7. answer material for a test;
8. supplementary work;
9. instructional text.

A "supplementary work"—item (8) above—is a work prepared for publication as a secondary adjunct to a work by another author for the purpose of introducing, concluding, illustrating, explaining, revising, commenting on, or assisting in the use of the other work. Examples include forewords, afterwords, illustrations, maps, tables, editorial notes, bibliographies, appendixes, and indexes [101 "work made for hire"].

An "instructional text"—item (9) above—is a literary, pictorial, or graphic work prepared for publication for use in teaching [101 "work made for hire"]. The legislative history reports: "The basic characteristic of 'instructional texts' is the purpose of their preparation for 'use in systematic instructional activities,' and they are to be distinguished from works prepared for use by a general audience."

*Practical Significance of Works Made for Hire.* Why does it matter whether a work is or is not a work made for hire? The work-for-hire status gives the employer or the person who specially commissioned the work the maximum possible rights under copyright. The status of the work sometimes can be legally determinative on five points:

1. initial ownership;
2. rights after 28 years;
3. rights after 35 years;
4. rights after 56 years; and
5. copyright duration.

The initial ownership of copyright is determined by whether the work was made for hire. If, for example, a specially commissioned work is work made for hire, the one who commissioned it has the initial ownership. If it is not, the scope of rights of the one who commissioned the work will depend upon what rights can be shown to have been transferred [201(a),(b); 204(a)]. Initial ownership of the work is important not only to the first parties involved in a transfer of rights but also to any later transferees. They will want to be confident that the rights indeed trace back to the true "initial" owner.

Of the other four points noted above, copyright duration has already been considered in Chapter 4, and the rules concerning the three "number" rules will be considered later in this chapter. They are of practical consequence only for works that still have value 28 or more years after their creation, such as motion pictures. Other works also are vigorous at a late age.

## TRANSFERS OF OWNERSHIP

### General

The initial owner of a copyright may transfer all of the rights, or some of them, or parts of some of them to others [201(a),(d)]. (There is a provision that can defeat certain involuntary transfers of copyright, but it is of narrow scope and will not be considered further here [201(e)]. [5] )

If an exclusive right is transferred, the transferee is a copyright owner to the extent of the right transferred [101 "copyright owner"; 201(d)(2)]. For instance, the transferee is entitled to sue for an infringement committed during the period when the transferee owns the right that was infringed [501(b)].

The idea that the exclusive rights of a copyright can be split up and owned separately is a feature of the current law that was not explicit under the 1909 Act. Under the old law, ownership was sometimes considered to be indivisible, and those who held exclusive licenses were not, by that fact alone, always in the position of owners. [6]

When a right under copyright is licensed on a nonexclusive basis, the licensee is not an owner of copyright, and the statute does not place the licensee in a position to bring an action for infringement [101 "transfer of ownership," "copyright owner"; 201(d)(2); 501(b)].

### Copyright Provisions Concerning Transfers

*Signed, Written Agreements.* A transfer of copyright ownership ordinarily is not valid unless a memorandum or other written record of the transfer is signed by the owner of the rights conveyed or by that person's duly authorized representative [204(a)]. (Incidentally, the certificate of copyright registration is evidence of the copyright but not the copyright itself, a point that should be kept in mind in phrasing transfer agreements.)

*Protection against Inconsistent Other Transfers.* The prompt recording of a transfer of ownership in the Copyright Office can protect the transferee against the possibility of conflicting transfers of ownership, if the work also is registered [205(c),(e)]. Example:

| | |
|---|---|
| January 1 | A, owner of copyright in a work for which registration has been obtained, transfers ownership to B. |
| January 15 | Unbeknown to B, and in violation of the agreement with B, A transfers the same rights to C, who acquires them in good faith and for good money. |
| January 20 | B records the transfer from A in the Copyright Office and does it in such a way that it will be revealed to others through a reasonable search under the title to the work or the registration number. |

In this situation B's title is better than C's, where B has recorded before C.

What can C, or any transferee of ownership, do to protect against a prior inconsistent transfer such as the one between A and B? One of the best answers is to deal with honest and competent people. In addition, C could have obtained some statutory protection by not permanently parting with the money until the following had taken place: (1) C's transfer was recorded (this should be done within one month after execution of the transfer); (2) two months have passed after C's transfer agreement with A was executed; and (3) the Copyright Office records are then checked to see if any inconsistent transfer had been recorded [205(c),(e)]. By following those procedures, with respect to a registered work, C fits within the rule protecting the transferee against either a prior or subsequent inconsistent transfer by A. If those arrangements are not practical, then other forms of protection could be designed into a contract, which would provide C with some financial protection (assuming A has sufficient assets) should C not obtain good title to the copyright.

People frequently do not follow formalities such as those just mentioned. Usually, no problem arises, as not many people make a practice of making inconsistent transfers. However, for very important transactions, consideration should be given to the effect of the recordation rules and the way to use them, together with contractual provisions, so as to maximize the chance of obtaining a good title and, should that fail, of keeping, or getting back, any money paid.

Recording a transfer of ownership is most beneficial if the work is also registered. However, recording of the transfer alone may serve legally to protect the transferee against later inconsistent nonexclusive licenses [205(f)(2)].

*Recordation before Infringement Action.* A person who owns one or more exclusive rights of copyright as a result of a transfer of ownership from another is not entitled to sue for infringement of the exclusive right(s) owned until "the instrument of transfer under which such person claims has been recorded in the Copyright Office" [205(d)].

*Recordation Rules.*  In order to record a transfer of ownership in the Copyright Office, the document submitted must meet certain standards:

> It should either bear the actual signatures of the persons who executed it or should be a legible photocopy or other full-size facsimile reproduction of the signed document, accompanied by a sworn certification or an official certification that the reproduction is a true copy of the signed document.

> It should be legible and capable of being reproduced in legible microform copies.

> In addition, it should be complete by its own terms; for example, if the document states that a schedule or exhibit is attached, the attachment ordinarily should be part of the submission. (However, if the document merely identifies or incorporates by reference another document, the Copyright Office will raise no questions of completeness and will not require recordation of the other document.)

These standards are based on Copyright Office regulations (Title 37 of the Code of Federal Regulations, section 201.4), which should be consulted for further details. They include definitions of the terms "sworn certification" and "official certification," and they describe the circumstances under which an incomplete document may be recorded.

For a document of six pages or less (one title), the fee for recordation is $10. The fee increases thereafter by 50 cents per additional page and by 50 cents per additional title [708(a)(4)]. These fees were set by the copyright legislation passed in 1976 and, of course, may eventually change.

After recordation, the document is returned to the sender with a certificate of record.

## NONEXCLUSIVE LICENSES

When a right under copyright is granted on a nonexclusive basis, no transfer of ownership of the copyright is involved; the licensee, not being a copyright owner, does not, for example, have the statutory right to sue for copyright infringement [501(b)].

Whereas a transfer of copyright ownership should be in writing, no similar copyright law requirement exists for a nonexclusive license [204(a)]. A signed agreement, of course, has advantages, whether or not required by copyright law. Even under the copyright law, it has advantages. If the license is in writing and signed by the owner of the rights licensed, the license will remain valid under its terms despite a later inconsistent transfer of ownership by the copyright owner. It will even remain valid against an inconsistent prior transfer of the license taken in good faith before the ownership transfer was recorded and without notice of the transfer [205(f)].

## PERMISSIONS LICENSES

A common type of nonexclusive license is the so-called permission. The term "permission" generally is used in instances where an author, for his or her work, obtains the exclusive right to include excerpts, or the complete text, or an adaptation of another's work. Permissions are also used by educators, for example, to obtain the right to copy and distribute a work.

Permissions are sought as a matter of courtesy, or when the copying would be beyond fair use, or when the seeker wants to avoid the risk of legal infringement without knowing whether consent is required.

Permissions requests are not as easy to administer as might at first appear. For example, a permissions request to a publisher potentially raises these questions for the publisher:

1. Would the granting of permission be consistent with the language of the publisher's agreement with the author?
2. Is the material to be copied something that the author prepared for the publisher, or was that author using the material by permission? If the latter, was the permission the author received broad enough to allow the granting of this permission request?
3. Exactly what portion of the work does the requesting person want to use, and in what manner?
4. Will a quantity limitation be acceptable? Are copies to be sold? Will a time limitation be acceptable? Will a geographic limitation be acceptable, or must world rights be considered?

The answers to these questions can determine whether the publisher has the right to grant permission and, if so, whether it should be granted at no charge or for a fee and, if the latter, the amount of the fee.

In requesting permissions the potential complexities and delays of back-and-forth communications can be minimized by specifying precisely what is wanted and from what source and by describing what use is planned for the copies. The more limited the proposed use, the more likely it is that the person receiving the request will say yes, will not need to ask for further information, and will not seek a fee or only a minimum fee.

The subject of permissions is integrally related to the doctrine of fair use, which is considered in Chapters 13 and 14. In deciding whether it is appropriate to seek permission to copy some copyrighted material, it often is appropriate to determine first if the contemplated use would be a fair use. In many situations, fair use is clearly applicable or clearly inapplicable. However, in others, it is not so clear. Unless you use excessive caution, you will not always know whether an honest, carefully considered judgment would definitely prevail in court. Uncertainty is sometimes inevitable, for "fair use" is intentionally vague.

Even if you have a high degree of knowledge, skill, and self-confidence, you may conclude that a certain use is a fair use but that your judgment might be contested. In these situations, you may have to ask these practical questions:

1. Would the prospective contestant have a respectable position on the fair-use issue (even though an incorrect one in your view)?
2. Do you want to risk the possible time and expense that a dispute could involve?
3. Are the consequences of various possible adverse decisions, or settlements, tolerable?
4. Could you obtain permission within a reasonable time under reasonable terms (even though you do not think you need it)?
5. Can the use be avoided or reduced without substantial harm to your work?

## OWNERSHIP OF COPYRIGHT—RELATED OBJECTS

### Copyright Ownership—Object Ownership

The rights of copyright are intangible. Ownership of these rights is distinct from ownership in the related material or physical object. Consequently, when making a copyright transfer, you should consider to what extent rights in the physical object will also be, or should also be, transferred. Similarly, when transferring ownership in a physical object that includes a copyrighted work, you should consider to what extent rights of copyright also will be, or should be, transferred.

The copyright law provides that, unless there is an agreement to the contrary, the transfer of rights of copyright does not convey ownership in the related physical object, and that the transfer of ownership of a physical object does not of itself convey right of copyright in the copyrighted work represented by the object [202]. For example, when you acquire ownership of unpublished letters, you do not automatically also acquire the right to publish them. Similarly, when you buy a painting, you do not automatically acquire reproduction rights. (Under the 1909 Act, there was some authority for a legal presumption that sale of a painting included publication rights unless those rights were specifically reserved. [7] The 1976 law provides for a different result, at least for post-1977 transactions.)

As a result of a 1980 amendment to the statute, there is now a special provision allowing the owner of a copy of a computer program to make or adapt a copy of that copy for archival purposes or as an essential step in the utilization of the program [117].

### Object Ownership—Display Rights

The owner of an object, such as a painting, may sometimes not also be the copyright owner of the work. He or she nonetheless may, in the absence of a contrary agreement, display the object publicly to viewers present at the place where the copy is located. (This specific limitation on a copyright owner's public display rights does not cover for the benefit of someone who leases or rents the physical object rather than owning it [109(b),(c)].)

## Object Ownership—Sales Rights

If someone acquires ownership of a lawfully made copy (or original) of a work, such as a book or manuscript, he or she may, without the copyright owner's permission, sell or otherwise dispose of the original or copy without infringing copyright in the work. [8] (This limitation on the copyright owner's right to distribute copies publicly does not apply to material acquired by loan or lease [109(a),(c)].)

This right of disposition by the owner of the object causes some copyright owners to prefer to lease rather than sell material. It sometimes is possible to place valid restrictions on sold copies, but even so, a buyer from the contracting party may not always be bound by the restriction.

## STATUTORY TERMINATIONS OF TRANSFERS AND LICENSES

Ordinarily, a transfer of ownership or a nonexclusive license is governed by the terms of the license agreement. However, there are three exceptions in which the copyright law can override the agreement. These exceptions are the three "number" rules mentioned earlier in this chapter: the 28-, 35-, and 56-year rules.

## The 28-Year Rule

Works subject to federal copyright protection before 1978 had a dual term of copyright protection; for those works, that dual term continues. The second term must be applied for before the expiration of the first term, which is approximately 28 years.

If the work is a work made for hire, the proprietor has the right to apply for the renewal term.

If the initial ownership in the work rested in an individual author, he or she is entitled to the renewal copyright [304(a)]. If the author is deceased, his or her statutory survivors are entitled to the renewal term, even if the author had contractually agreed that another would have the renewal right.

The current copyright law is structured so that no additional dual-term copyright situations will be established. However, those already established under the 1909 Act will be carried over. Renewal copyrights will be applied for even after the turn of the century.

## The 35-Year Rule

The 35-year rule applies to all copyrights, dual term and otherwise, except with regard to works made for hire [203(a)]. The rule relates only to the termination of those transfers of ownership or nonexclusive licenses—of U.S. copyrights—that were executed by the author in 1978 or later. It relates to each such transfer or license, other than by will and other than in the case of a work made for hire [203(a)]. It applies even if the transfer or license says that it does not [203(a)(5)].

The 35-year rule gives the author (or his or her statutory successors) the right to terminate the transfer or license only insofar as rights arising under U.S. copyrights are concerned [205(b)(5)]. The transfer or license of those U.S. copyrights remains unaffected if the termination right is not exercised [203(b)(6)].

A derivative work prepared under the authority of a grant before the grant's termination may continue to be utilized, under the terms of the grant, after its termination [203(b)(1)].

The rationale for the 35-year rule is that authors, while in the initial stages of negotiations for their works, are generally assumed not to be in a very good position to insist that the prospective value of their works, 35 or more years later, be reflected in the transaction.

*Time and Notice of Termination.* The 35-year rule sets up two timetables for termination of these post-1977 grants [203(c)(3)]:

In the case of a grant that does not cover the right of publication, the termination may occur at any time during a five-year period beginning at the end of 35 years from the date of execution of the grant.

In the case of a grant that does cover the right of publication, the five-year period begins at the earliest of two dates: the end of 40 years from the execution of the grant, or the end of 35 years from the date of publication under the grant.

The notice of termination must be served at least two years before the selected termination date, and it may be served as many as ten years before the stated date [203(a)(4)(A)].

Given all of the foregoing, the 35-year rule's first potential application will be to a grant made on January 1, 1978, and the first notice of termination of the rights of U.S. copyright under that grant will not occur until after the turn of the century. Nonetheless, there are several reasons why the rule can, even now, have interest to some.

If you are an author of material with a potentially long life, you should be aware of the existence of the rule for possible future use. You should be aware, for example, that if you are dead when the statutory termination right arises, the right will belong to people who fall within classifications designated in the statute—spouse, children, etc. These will not always be the persons who you will want to have the benefit of the termination right. You cannot change the statutory classifications. However, you can limit their practical effect, by voluntarily agreeing, from time to time, with your existing transferee or licensee to terminate the existing grant and substitute a new one. [9] This possibility permits you to have a "younger" transfer outstanding, and thus delays the time that the 35-year rule will have a practical effect. It is also consistent with the object of the 35-year rule, which is to let you negotiate anew as to the later value of rights in your work.

Just as an author may be interested in negotiating new licenses well ahead of time, so too may a publisher wish to postpone or avoid the possible complexities of negotiating new arrangements with the statutory successors. Also, the publisher should keep the 35-year rule in mind so as not to sublicense such rights in such a way that the obligations to the sublicensee may seem to apply even if the publisher's underlying right is statutorily terminated by the author or the author's successors.

For the sake of simplicity, we have thus far considered the 35-year rule as if only one author would be making the grant. When authors of a joint work have executed a grant of U.S. copyright, termination of the grant may be carried out by a majority of the authors who executed it. If one of the authors is dead, his or her termination interest may be exercised as a unit by those of that author's statutory successors who own and are entitled to exercise a total of more than half of that author's interests [203(a)(1)].

## The 56-Year Rule

This rule relates only to the termination of those transfers (of ownership or licenses of U.S. copyrights) executed before 1978. Moreover, it relates only to works that, on January 1, 1978, were under the dual term copyright system of an initial term and a renewal term (see Chapter 4). Within that confined scope, the 56-year rule applies to each transfer or license (other than by will and other than in the case of a work made for hire) [304(c)]. It applies even if the transfer or license says that it does not [304(c)(5)].

The general rationale for the 56-year rule derives from the fact that the 1976 Copyright Act extended the potential U.S. life of dual-term copyrights from 56 years (under the 1909 Act) to 75 years. Congress concluded that the author should have the opportunity to obtain the full benefit of those extra 19 years (or the portion remaining, in the case of works that were already beyond the 56-year term at the time the 1976 Act took effect [10] ).

The 56-year rule gives the author (or his or her statutory successors) the right to terminate the pre-1978 transfer or license insofar as rights under U.S. copyright are concerned. The transfer or license remains unaffected if the termination right is not exercised [304(c)(6)(F)].

Here is an example of the 56-year rule in operation in a relatively simple case:

| Date | Event |
| --- | --- |
| 1925 | Author makes a transfer of ownership to Publisher B |
| 1926 | Work published |

| Date | Event |
|------|-------|
| 1953 | Copyright renewed |
| 1983 | Author serves publisher with notice that the 1925 grant will terminate on January 3, 1986, insofar as U.S. copyrights are concerned |
| 1983 | Author records a copy of the notice with the Copyright Office [304(c)(4)(A)] |
| 1986 | The 1925 grant terminates insofar as those rights arising under U.S. copyright are concerned |

Termination pursuant to the 56-year rule does not affect rights arising under other laws—federal, state, or foreign [304(c)(6)(E)]. Furthermore, a derivative work prepared under authority of the grant before its termination may continue to be utilized, under the terms of the grant, after its statutory termination [304(c)(6)(A)].

Termination may be effected at any time during a period of five years, beginning at the end of 56 years from the date copyright was originally secured or beginning January 1, 1978, whichever is later [304(c)(3)]. The notice of termination may be served not less than two, nor more than ten, years before the effective date of termination [304(c)(4)(A)].

The statutory succession rules that apply when the author is deceased are similar to those applicable under the 35-year rule [304(c)(2)]. In addition, the law takes into account the fact that some of the basic grants that ordinarily would have been made by an author may instead have been made by his or her statutory successors under the 28-year rule, that is, those who became the copyright owners of the renewal copyright [304(c)]. When a grant was made by such statutory successors and they are deceased, termination can be effected only by the unanimous action of the survivors of those who executed the grant.

The 56-year rule is quite complex. Although the major points have been covered in this chapter, there are many nuances. While you may wish to make specific plans to implement the rule yourself by using the statute and the underlying regulations as guides, it is advisable to consult an attorney before you actually carry out your plans.

# 7

# COPYRIGHT NOTICES

Copyright notices show up in many places: following the title pages of books, on mastheads of magazines and newspapers, at the end of evening news programs on television, on the back of jewelry, on labels sewn to stuffed toys, and on puzzle boxes. In our daily lives, they often go unnoticed. But for copyright owners, such notices are a key to maintaining copyright protection.

The current notice standards, which apply to copies and phonorecords publicly distributed in 1978 and later, are reviewed in the first part of this chapter. Failure to conform to the required standards can result in loss of copyright, as under the previous law. However, under the new law, the circumstances in which this can happen are fewer, there is more tolerance for error, and when a potentially fatal error or omission does occur, there are provisions that sometimes can save the copyright's life.

The stricter standards that applied before 1978 are considered in the second part of this chapter. They continue to have importance today because, in cases in which they were not adequately followed at the time, the copyright concerned may have gone into the public domain.

# PART 1: THE STANDARDS FOR 1978 AND AFTER

## WHEN NOTICE IS REQUIRED

For U.S. copyright protection purposes, a notice of copyright should be used on all copies or phonorecords of copyrighted works that are publicly distributed, in the United States or elsewhere, by authority of the copyright owner [401, 402].[1] The requirement begins once the work is published by the owner's authority.

The terms "copies" and "phonorecords" have already been considered in Chapter 2. Generally, they embrace all of the material objects in which copyrighted works are embodied, even the original of a work. The term "copies" relates to works that are visually perceivable, directly or indirectly, and to audiovisual works; "phonorecords" relates to sound recordings [101 "copies," "phonorecords"].

Remember that publicly distributed copyrighted works are not only those for which a registration has been obtained. A work ordinarily is "copyrighted" at the moment it is created. See Chapters 2 and 4.

When planning your copyright notice practices, it is important to consider not only the copies or phonorecords you directly authorize—the first generation, so to speak—but also any copies or phonorecords that you authorize to be made by those who obtain the first generation copies. For example, if you provide a copyrighted data base embodied in a magnetically encoded disk and authorize printouts to be made through use of the disk, you should consider not only the notice requirements for the disk itself but also what notices should be provided for the printouts when they fall within the definition of publicly distributed copies.

The statute does not directly define the terms "published" or "publicly distributed," but, rather, the term "publication." The definition has three parts: Two say what publication is; one, what it is not.

Publication is the distribution of copies or phonorecords of a work to the public by sale (or other transfer of ownership) or by rental, lease, or lending [101]. The legislative history says that "to the public" means, generally, to persons under no explicit or implicit restrictions with respect to disclosure of the work's contents.[2]

Publication is also the offering to distribute copies or phonorecords to a group of persons for purposes of further distribution, public performance, or public display [101]. Thus, when books or records are distributed to wholesalers for further distribution, they have been "published."[3]

The third part of the definition is that "the public performance or public display of a work does not, by itself, constitute publication" [101]. The legislative history states:

> No copyright notice would be required in connection with the public display of a copy by any means, including projectors, television, or cathode ray tubes connected with information storage and retrieval systems, or in connection with the public performance of a work by means of copies or phonorecords, whether in the presence of an audience or through television, radio, computer transmission or any other process.
>
> It should be noted that . . . there would no longer be any basis for holding, as a few court decisions have done in the past, that the public display of a work of art under some conditions (e.g., without restriction against its reproduction) would constitute publication of the work. . . .[4]

In analyzing the third part of the statutory definition, keep in mind that it includes the phrase "performance . . . display . . . does not *of itself* constitute publication" (emphasis added). It is necessary to look at the total activity relating to a work, in the context of all three aspects of the definition, before deciding whether or not "publication" has taken place.

## SIGNIFICANCE OF OMISSION OF REQUIRED NOTICE

If a required copyright notice is omitted, the work can fall into the public domain. Although the statute does not expressly say that, it is the logical implication of a section that sets forth three circumstances in which an omission of a required notice, in 1978 or later, does not invalidate the copyright [405(a)]. The legislative history confirms that the implication was intended.[5]

### When Omission of Required Notice Does Not Invalidate Copyright

An omission of notice, when required, is not always fatal. Sometimes preventive medicine will save the situation. Other times, the case will be a mild one. And when a serious case does arise, sometimes a successful cure is possible.

The copyright owner's preventive medicine is to have agreements with licensees that expressly require "in writing that, as a condition of the copyright owner's authorization of the public distribution of copies or phonorecords, they bear the prescribed notice . . ." [405(a)(3)].[6] When a notice is omitted in violation of such an agreement, the omission does not invalidate the copyright. In the absence of an agreement, it is possible for the copyright owner to be adversely affected by a licensee's omission, even though the copyright owner expected that a notice would be used.

Copyright also would not be invalidated when the required notice "has been omitted from no more than a relatively small number of copies or phonorecords distributed to the public . . ." [405(a)(1)].

In a serious case, it may still be possible to cure the mistake by making a reasonable effort "to add the notice to all copies or phonorecords that are distributed to the public in the United States after the omission has been discovered . . ." [405(a)(2)]. In order for this treatment to be successful, the work must have been registered within five years after the publication without the required notice. A registration before the notice problem ever arose, of course, would meet that test. In fact, such an early registration would serve in part as preventive medicine. Sometimes an unrecognized flaw—such as a date much too late—in a notice is tantamount to a notice omission. If the flaw is not recognized for many years, the discovery could come too late to meet the five-year limit. With an "early" registration, that problem does not arise.

Note that "reasonable effort" refers to the copies or phonorecords distributed to the public after the omission has been discovered; thus, it could be called for immediately in the case of an intentionally omitted notice.

The curative opportunity is new with the 1976 Copyright Act and has already been used to save at least one copyright in an infringement suit.[7]

But the cure is not as easily or as certainly accomplished as might at first appear. It may be impractical or inconvenient to add the notice; also, if the copyright owner ever needs to sue for infringement of the copyright, the effectiveness of the efforts may be challenged.[8]

## Infringer's Defense of Reliance on Notice Omission

When a required notice is omitted, and the copyright's life is saved by one of the means mentioned above, the copyright is fairly healthy; however, it is potentially vulnerable in the case of an innocent infringer.

When a person "innocently infringes a copyright, in reliance upon an authorized copy or phonorecord from which the copyright notice has been omitted," the full panoply of legal remedies for infringement is not available if that person proves that he or she was misled by the omission. In such situations, the infringer does not incur liability for damages with respect to any infringing acts committed before receiving actual notice that registration of the work has been made. In addition, a court may disallow recovery of any of the infringer's profits attributable to the infringement. Further, a court also may permit the continuation of the infringing undertaking, either at no charge or at a reasonable license fee set by the court [405(b)].

In Part 2 of this chapter, we will consider each component of a copyright notice. We will also discuss the types of notice errors that do, and do not, equate to a notice omission. Keep in mind that the error and omission rules are applicable to copies and phonorecords of copyrighted materials publicly distributed by authority of the copyright owner. The owner is not responsible for notice omissions or defects on copies that he or she did not authorize in some way.

## ELEMENTS OF COPYRIGHT NOTICE

A required copyright notice ordinarily has three elements:

1. a signal of a copyright claim;
2. the year when the work was first published; and
3. the name of the owner of copyright.

The statute mentions the elements in the order just given but does not state that the same order must be used in the notice.[9] A fourth element, sometimes applicable, may apply to works that incorporate material prepared by U.S. government employees as part of their jobs.

In discussing copyright notices here, we are talking only about the statutory standards. Copyright owners sometimes choose, for reasons other than legal requirements, to include additional statements about copyright or to use a copyright notice in more than one location.

In general, each work should have its own copyright notice. However, that generalization does not always apply to collective works. A collective work is a work, such as an issue of a magazine, in which a number of contributions, constituting separate and independent works in themselves, are assembled into a collective whole [101]. There could be many copyright notices in such works if each separate contribution had to have its own copyright notice. However, that is usually not required by the copyright law, although separate notices sometimes are used.

In general, the appropriate notice for the overall collective work suffices to keep the contribution from being classified as having a notice omission [404(a)]. Quite frequently the person named in that single notice will not be the owner of copyright in some of the contributions. Technically, there is a notice "error." It is not fatal to the copyright in the contribution [404(a); 406(a)]. The potential adverse consequences are discussed later on when we consider the effects of a name error.

There is an exception to the general rule. When the separate contribution to the collective work is an advertisement, a separate notice is supposed to be used for the copyright in the ad unless the ad is on behalf of the owner of copyright in the overall work [404(a)]. The absence of the separate notice, when called for, apparently means that the ad will be treated as if it had been published without a copyright notice.

## Signal of Copyright Claim

*Basic Standards.*   The copyright signal serves to establish that copyright is claimed.

In the case of "copies," the word "Copyright" or the abbreviation "Copr." or the symbol © may be used [401(a); 101 "copies"]. The © symbol is common. Its use can mean that some foreign countries will, by virtue of the Universal Copyright Convention, excuse you from some of the formal requirements they might otherwise impose as a condition of copyright protection in their countries.[10] Because some people may not recognize that the © signifies a copyright claim, copyright owners often use "Copyright" or "Copr." together with the © symbol.

In addition to using a statutorily required signal, you may wish to use "All rights reserved." This may be of benefit in some Latin American countries that are not parties to the Universal Copyright Convention.[11] Usually, when the phrase is used, it is placed at the end of the notice.

In the case of phonorecords, the symbol ℗ is used in the copyright notice to indicate a claim of federal copyright protection in a sound recording [402(b)].[12] (See Chapter 2 for a discussion of sound recording copyrights.) A notice of copyright in the underlying copyrighted work, such as a musical composition, is not required because the phonorecord is not considered a "copy" of the underlying work [101 "copies," "phonorecords"].[13] However, if copyright is claimed in some text or illustrations, such as on the album cover, a notice of the type used on "copies" would be used in addition to the ℗ for the sound recording copyright.

*Significance of Omissions or Errors after 1977.*   If a publicly distributed copy or phonorecord of copyrighted material bears no appropriate signal that copyright is being claimed, the notice error would be sufficiently serious to amount to a notice omission. (The new law does not expressly say so, but that seems to be the logical conclusion.) There could well be some tolerance for mistakes where notice of the copyright claim is nonetheless fairly given. An example of such a situation might be the use of the letter C with parentheses rather than within a circle.[14] This sometimes occurs for works in machine-readable form where the programming, or the printout equipment, has not been designed to generate a ©. Whereas (C)—that is, a C within parentheses—might be upheld if tested, it makes sense at least to consider doubling up with the use of "Copr." or "Copyright."

## Date of First Publication

*General Rule.* The general rule is that a copyright notice should include the year of first publication of the copyrighted work [401(b)(2); 402(b)(2)]. That is all that the current statute seems to require, even when the copyright involved is in a renewal term under the old law or began its copyright life under the old law by means of a registration rather than a publication.[15] However, to avoid the possibility of future argument, it makes sense to use the date of first publication and also include an indication of a renewal copyright, as shown below:

Copyright A. B. Sea 1950, copyright renewed 1978

If, in a year subsequent to first publication, additional copies or phonorecords of the very same work are produced, the original year date would continue to be used in the copyright notice. It would still remain the year of first publication of the work.

*Compilations; Derivative Works.* When a compilation or derivative work incorporates previously published material in copyright, the year date of first publication of the compilation or derivative work is sufficient on copies [401(b)(2); 101 "collective work," "compilation," "derivative work"]. We are assuming here that the compilation or derivative work has enough new original authorship in it to qualify as a separately copyrightable work. If not, the date of first publication of the original work would be used. In cases of doubt as to whether there is enough new material, the date of the prior work should be included, for example, Copyright A. B. Sea 1980, 1982.

The statutory rules expressly allowing for a single-year date in the case of compilation and derivative work "copies" are not paralleled by similar express provisions for "phonorecords" [see 401 and 402]. It may be that a similar result will be arrived at through judicial interpretation.[16] The opportunity for a ruling apparently has not yet come up under the current law.

*Works Not Requiring Year Date.* Works for which the year date is not required include pictorial, graphic, or sculptural work reproduced in or on greeting cards, postcards, stationery, jewelry, dolls, toys, or any useful articles. The right to omit the year date applies even though there is accompanying textual matter [401(b)(2)].

*Certain Works Published before 1978.* In the case of a work published before 1978, compliance with the notice provisions of the 1909 Act (as in effect at the end of 1977) is acceptable in 1978 and later even if that compliance would not meet the newly established standards [Transitional and Supplementary Provisions, Sec. 108]. For example, the old copyright law exempted the year date from a broader class of pictorial, graphic, and sculptural works than are covered by the current law's year-date exemption for greeting cards and other types of works listed above.[17] Although you might want to take advantage of this provision for any old copies still around, it is worthwhile to consider using the general notice standards of the current law when producing new copies. The 1909 Act is fading out of mind, and a notice without a year date will appear to some, however wrongly, as an incorrect notice unless the particular material is within the exemption in the current law.

*Significance of Omissions and Errors as to Date.* When a year date for a work is called for and none is given that could reasonably be considered a part of the copyright notice, the work is considered to have been published without any notice [406(c)].

When a year date is called for and the one given is earlier than the actual year date of first publication, the error is not equal to the omission of a copyright notice. However, where a copyright's duration is calculated on the basis of the date of first publication, the year date used in the notice may be used for the calculation [406(b)]. Copyright duration rules were considered in Chapter 4.

When the year date given is more than one year later than the actual year date of first publication, the error is equal to an omission of copyright notice [406(b)(2)]. The statute seems to call for this result even in cases where the duration of the copyright does not turn on the year date of first publication.

The statute does not expressly discuss the situation when the year date, although later than the actual year date of first publication, is later by no more than one year. Given the resolutions of other types of year-date errors, the implication seems to be that an incorrect year date of this type would not be equal to an omission of copyright notice. The legislative history supports that view, at least in part. The legislative committee stated:

> Notices postdated by one year are quite common for works published near the end of a year, and it would be unnecessarily strict to equate cases of that sort with works published without notice of any sort.[18]

## Name of Owner

*Basic Standard.* A second element in a statutorily required copyright notice is the name of the owner of copyright in the work. An abbreviation by which the name can be recognized is acceptable, as is a generally known alternative designation of the owner [401(b); 402(b)]. (In the case of a sound recording, if its producer is named on the phonorecord labels or containers, the producer's name is considered a part of the notice if no other name appears in conjunction with the notice [402(b)(3)].)

The exclusive rights of a copyright can be split up, and several persons can become copyright owners of a work [101 "copyright owner"; 201(d)]. When that occurs, it will not always be clear what name(s) to use in the copyright notice. Fortunately, an error will not be fatal.

*Significance of Post-1977 Omissions and Errors as to Owner Name.* If a copy or phonorecord does not contain any name that could reasonably be considered a part of the notice, it is considered to have been published without any notice [406(c)]. If a copyright notice contains the name of someone other than the name of the owner of copyright, the error is not equal to an omission of copyright notice [406(a)]. However, a person relying on the wrong name may have a defense to an infringement claim. The statute provides that:

> any person who begins an undertaking that infringes the copyright has a complete defense to any action for such infringement if such person proves that he or she was misled by the notice and began the undertaking in good faith under a purported transfer or license from the person named therein, unless, before the undertaking was begun—
>
> (1) registration for the work has been made in the name of the owner of copyright; or
> (2) a document executed by the person named in the notice and showing the ownership of the copyright has been recorded. [406(a)]

Whether a person was misled or began in good faith is a question that often can be answered only by a full examination of the particular circumstances. An honest belief in having a valid license may not always alone be enough to establish good faith. The reasonableness of the belief may also be relevant.[19]

## Works Incorporating U.S. Government Works

*General Standard.* A work prepared by an officer or employee of the U.S. government as part of that person's official duties is not eligible for U.S. copyright protection [105; 101 "work of the United States Government"] (see Chapter 3). When another eligible work happens to consist preponderantly of one or more of those ineligible materials, the copyright notice should include a statement identifying those portions protected by U.S. copyright. The statement may be by way of inclusion or exclusion [403].

This notice requirement, new to U.S. copyright law, lets the informed reader know that some of the material is not subject to copyright protection.

*Significance of Omissions or Errors after 1977.* The legislative history states that a failure to meet this notice requirement would be treated as an omission of the notice.[20]

## Notices for Group Registration Purposes

One of the effects of the statute's registration rules, which are considered in Chapters 9 and 10, is to impose a heavy burden, in terms of completing application forms and paying registration fees, on an individual who owns copyrights in many published periodical articles and who wants to register the copyright claim in each. The law provides some relief by allowing, under defined circumstances, such an individual to apply for a single registration covering the group of articles [408(c)(2)].

Several criteria must be met in order for the individual to take advantage of the statutory relief provided. The criteria are:

1. each of the contributions, as first published, should bear its own copyright notice;
2. the name of the owner of copyright in each such notice should be the same;
3. the contributions to be registered by means of the single application and fee should be by the same individual author; and
4. the works should all have been first published as contributions to periodicals (including newspapers) within a 12-month period.

For a contribution to "bear its own copyright notice," several placement options are possible. Copyright Office regulations provide many examples, some of which allow the notice to appear on the page bearing the copyright notice for the collective work as a whole. The regulations are included in Appendix 2.

# COPYRIGHT NOTICE PLACEMENTS

## Sound Recordings

In the case of sound recordings subject to federal copyright protection, the copyright notice for the sound recording copyright should be placed on the surface of the phonorecord, or on the phonorecord label or container, in "such a manner and location as to give reasonable notice of the claim of copyright" [402(c)]. If that test is not met, the notice presumably will be considered to be omitted. But it seems a fair prediction that the courts are not likely to interpret "reasonable" too narrowly.

## Works Other Than Sound Recordings

The copyright notice for works other than sound recordings should also be affixed to the copies in "such manner and location as to give reasonable notice of the claim of copyright" [401(c)]. But for these works, unlike sound recordings, Copyright Office regulations provide dozens of examples of compliance. Although the official examples do not cover all the ways to give reasonable notice on copies [401(c)], they do provide a useful selection and your use of them makes it less likely that your notice placement will ever be successfully challenged. The text of the regulations is included in Appendix 2. The examples are grouped under the following headings: (1) works published in book form, (2) single-leaf works, (3) separate contributions to collective works, (4) works published in machine-readable form, (5) motion pictures and other audiovisual works, and (6) pictorial, graphic, and sculptural works. (Whether a notice meets the regulatory examples "depends upon its being permanently legible to an ordinary user of the work under normal conditions of use, and affixed to the copies in such manner and position that, when affixed, it is not concealed from view upon reasonable examination.") Following is a sampling of regulatory examples:

Work published in book form:
  Notice on the title page
  Notice on the page immediately following the title page

Magazine or newspaper:
  Notice on the title page
  Notice on the page immediately following the title page
  Notice as a part of the masthead

Motion pictures and other audiovisual works:
  Notice embodied in the copies by a photomechanical or reformatted electronic process in such a position that it ordinarily would appear whenever the work is performed in its entirety, and that is located (1) with or near the title; or (2) at or immediately preceding the end of the work

Pictorial, graphic, and sculptural works:
  Where a work is reproduced in two-dimensional copies, a notice attached durably, so as to withstand normal use, to the front or back of the copies
  Where a work is reproduced in three-dimensional copies, a notice sewn, so as to withstand normal use, to any visible portion of the work
  If the work is permanently housed in a container, such as a puzzle box, a notice reproduced on the permanent container is acceptable

Work reproduced on magnetic tape:
  A notice that appears at the user's terminal at sign-on
  A notice that is embodied in the copies in machine-readable form such that on visually perceptible printouts it appears either with or near the title, or at the end of the work

## FRAUDULENT NOTICE SANCTIONS

If a person fraudulently places on an article a notice of copyright that the person knows to be false, then a fine of $2,500 or less may be imposed in a criminal proceeding by the U.S. government [506(c)]. The same fine may be imposed in a criminal proceeding against a person who, with fraudulent intent, publicly distributes (or imports for public distribution) any article bearing a notice of copyright that the person knows to be false [506(c)].

A fine of $2,500 or less also may be imposed in a criminal proceeding against a person who, with fraudulent intent, removes or alters a notice of copyright appearing on a copy of a copyrighted work [506(d)].

## INFORMATION DERIVABLE FROM COPYRIGHT NOTICES

When you see a copyright notice on a work that was first published in the United States, what information can you derive from it about the work's copyright status, assuming that the notice is accurate? The answer is surprisingly little for certain, but quite a bit in terms of probabilities.

Let us consider this notice on a book:

© Name of Author 1982

From the copyright notice itself, you know that copyright is claimed by the named author in something related to the book. However, the notice does not tell you in what. The book may contain much material in the public domain or for which the copyright is owned by others (the author, for example, having used the material with permission). Here are some illustrations:

An anthology: The author of the book may be claiming only a copyright in the compilation of the stories included in it. He or she may have authored none of the stories. Others may own those copyrights.

A translation: The author may be claiming only copyright in the translation. Copyright in the work that was translated may belong to someone else. If you want permission to adapt the translation, you would ordinarily need authorization that covers both the translation and the work translated.

A reprint of a very old classic. The author's claim of copyright may relate only to his or her introduction. However, it also is possible that the author edited the classic. If the changes were more than minimal, the author may be claiming copyright in the revision. You might need permission to copy the revision even though you would be free to copy the original version.

Thus, a copyright notice does not tell much for certain. You can, however, become familiar with possibilities such as those above. You can then make reasonably good judgments as to what the copyright is likely to cover. Many books list "credits" that provide further information. Additional information may be obtainable from the author, the publisher, or from existing Copyright Office records about the work. (The Copyright Office has a helpful publication, Circular R22, *How to Investigate the Copyright Status of a Work*. A free copy may be obtained from the Register of Copyrights, Library of Congress, Washington, D.C. 20559.)

Copyright information that can be derived from the date of publication in a notice also is a weak indicator. As we have discussed earlier in this chapter, a single date in a notice does not necessarily mean that all of the material in the publication was first published in the year given. Some of the material may have been published much earlier, either in the same form or in an earlier and different edition.

When the date of first publication is more than 75 years ago, the U.S. copyright has expired, assuming that the publication occurred with the permission of the copyright owner. When the date of first publication was less than 75 but more than 28 years ago, a U.S. copyright in the particular work has expired unless the copyright was renewed. However, the expired work may incorporate some preexisting material that is still in copyright through renewal or for some other reason. Before you can freely use the material that has expired, it may be necessary, as indicated in Chapter 4, to obtain permission from the owner of the material covered by renewal copyright.

## COPYRIGHT NOTICES AND UNPUBLISHED WORKS

The copyright statute does not require copyright owners to place copyright notice on "unpublished" works. Nonetheless, when you release a copy or phonorecord of an unpublished work you may want to include some sort of legend to alert anyone who may come across it of your claim of rights. The language to use will vary with the circumstances and the objective, as no standard language meets all needs at all times. (For a full discussion, matters beyond the scope of this book, such as contracts and protection of ideas, would have to be considered.) The following example will serve as a point of departure for preparing an appropriate copyright notice statement.

> [Title of work], by [Author's name]. This material has not been published and all rights, including copyrights, are reserved.
> [Month, day, and year]

When unpublished material includes trade secrets, the legend you use should take that into account; indeed, it would be appropriate to obtain legal advice as to the standards you should follow to protect trade secrets. (The subject is beyond the scope of this book.)

It is not always legally clear whether a work has been "published" or whether a particular copy has been "publicly distributed." The notice in the above example is based on the assumption that neither term applies.

However, the notice has a potential hedge built into it, as it includes a signal of a copyright claim, a name, and a date (albeit not a date that purports to be a publication date).

# PART 2: NOTICES ON COPIES PUBLISHED BEFORE 1978

The current copyright law does not provide copyright protection for works that were already in the public domain when it took effect [Transitional and Supplementary Provisions, Secs. 102, 103]. One of the ways a work entered the public domain was for it to be published by authority of the copyright owner and for the published copies to have no notice of copyright or a notice with a fatal defect. The law governing these issues before 1978 was the Copyright Act of 1909 as amended from time to time. The text of the Act, as it was in effect just before 1978, is set forth in Appendix 5.

The notice rules could be quite unforgiving. Indeed, a House committee report underlying the current law notes: "One of the strongest arguments for revision of the . . . [1909 Act] has been the need to avoid the arbitrary and unjust forfeitures now resulting from unintentional or relatively unimportant omissions or errors in the copyright notice."[21]

Because of the potential harshness of the 1909 Act, courts are willing to look at a situation two or three times to see if loss of copyright really has to be the legal result in a particular case. When the statutory wording or binding precedents do not compel that result, the courts often will be willing to accept interpretations that avoid it. There is some flexibility, along with some unpredictability, in current court decisions in this area.

## WHEN COPYRIGHT NOTICE IS NEEDED

The 1909 Act generally provided that notice of copyright "shall be affixed to each copy . . . published in the United States by authority of the copyright proprietor . . ." [1909 Act, Sec. 10]. As a result of a 1947 amendment to the law, if the required notice was omitted from only a few copies, the copyright did not necessarily fall into the public domain [1909 Act, Sec. 21]. The copyright might be forfeited, however, if a licensee omitted the notice in violation of an implied agreement.[22] But in general, omission of the notice from works published by authority of the copyright owner were fatal. As a result, the term "published" took on tremendous significance.

One set of concepts that developed was that a "general" publication without notice amounted to a forfeiture of copyright, but a "limited" publication did not.

A general publication has been described as occurring when "by consent of the copyright owner, the original or tangible copies of a work are sold, leased, loaned, given away, or otherwise made available to the general public, or when an authorized offer is made to dispose of the work in such manner even if a sale or other such disposition does not in fact occur."[23]

A limited publication has been described as a publication "to a definitely selected group and for a limited purpose, and without the right of diffusion, reproduction, distribution or sale. . . . [T]he circulation must be restricted both as to persons and purpose, or it can not be called a . . . limited publication."[24]

The distinction is not easy to draw in practice. For example, a federal district court recently saw a general publication in the circulation of a particular motion picture, whereas the federal appeals court in California saw only a limited one.[25] The same thing happened 3,000 miles away with a federal district court and the federal appeals court in Massachusetts.[26] The concept of publication, as the appeals court in California said, is "an arcane and uncertain area of the law." It will continue to come up as an issue in litigation for years to come.

In another recent case, in 1977, a copyright owner of a shopping center directory rented out a mailing list of shopping center addresses. The list was in the form of a computer printout that could be cut into individual labels. Once the process is finished, the renter no longer possesses the list. The list bore no copyright notice. Into the public domain? No, said a federal district court judge in 1979, it was a limited publication. Also in 1977, an architect filed his drawings for a house with a building permit agency, but omitted the copyright notice. A publication? No, said a Florida state court judge in 1980, noting that past decisions on this issue had been in conflict. The court said that the "better view" was that this was a limited publication.[27]

The decision is not always in the copyright owner's favor. For example, in 1972, a photographer authorized use of one of her photographs in a magazine that was available to the general public. The photograph bore no copyright notice. The magazine was not introduced into evidence, and no evidence was introduced that it bore a copyright notice. A federal district court, in a 1981 decision, ruled that the copyright had gone into the public domain.[28]

In most of these cases, the person claiming to be the copyright owner was suing for infringement and, because of the absence of a copyright notice, preferred that there not have been a "publication." But sometimes, under the old law, the plaintiff had a copyright notice and needed "publication" in order to have a federal copyright (under the prevailing standards) in order to be entitled to sue in the federal courts. Conceivably, the "limited publication" rule, which served to prevent forfeitures, could also be used to block the federal claim. When forfeiture of copyright was not involved, the courts were less reluctant to read the term "publication" narrowly. As a result, a standard for "investive" publication developed that was less strict than the one for "divestive" publication.[29] As the California court said, publication under the 1909 law is "an arcane and uncertain area."

But we are not through yet. If 10,000 people saw a play, was that alone a "publication" under the 1909 Act? No, not at all. Mere performance or exhibition of a work was not a publication. (See also the definition of publication in section 101 of the current law.) As the California court said. . . .

## COPYRIGHT NOTICE ELEMENTS UNDER THE 1909 ACT

The three basic elements for a required copyright notice under the 1909 Act were very much the same as for the 1976 law. The 1909 Act called for a signal of copyright claim, a naming of the copyright proprietor, and, for most works, a date of first publication [1909 Act, Secs. 19, 26].

The © came into the law for certain types of works as far back as 1909, and for other types of works several decades later.[30] The ℗ signal became part of the statute in 1971 (see Chapter 2).

The "name of the copyright proprietor" element caused quite a few problems under the old notice rules. Conceptually, a copyright was "indivisible"; it had a single point of "ownership." But because transfers of ownership and major licenses took place all the time, people did not always use the right name in the notice, and loss of copyright could result. On occasion, the courts were able to avoid such consequences. For example, when a magazine included only a copyright notice in the name of the magazine proprietor, a court sometimes would prevent copyright in an outside contribution from going into the public domain by ruling that the magazine acquired "legal" ownership of title to the copyright. This made the notice acceptable. The author's rights in the article itself sometimes were then protected by a ruling that he or she remained the "equitable" owner of the rights and the "legal" owner was obliged to transfer the title back to the author when requested.

The more liberal notice standards of the 1976 Copyright Act sometimes influence how the courts today will interpret the 1909 Act. That was the case in a recent federal appeals court decision, which found no forfeiture where a sound recording copyright notice was in the name of a licensee.[31] The court decided that the error did not destroy the copyright. As the court interpreted the 1909 Act, forfeiture was not required where, as in this case, there was no significant chance that anyone would be misled. Notwithstanding that favorable development, pre-1978 "wrong-name" notices will continue to be challenged as destroying the copyright under the 1909 Act's standards.

When the 1909 Act notice provisions called for a date to be included, courts were willing to rule that a date that was too early was not fatal because it did not purport to lengthen the copyright term (generally calculated from the date of first publication, that is, beginning in the same year as the year date in the notice). However, when the year used was more than one year later than the year date of first publication, copyright could be lost, even though no one had relied on the year date to conclude that copyright had expired.

## COPYRIGHT NOTICE PLACEMENT UNDER THE 1909 ACT

The current law's "reasonableness" standards for copyright notice placements were not applicable under the 1909 Act. Instead, it had a series of specific standards [1909 Act, Sec. 20]. Failure to have the notice in the right location or affixed in an adequate manner could result in loss of copyright.

# 8

# DEPOSITS FOR THE LIBRARY OF CONGRESS: SECTION 407

One of the purposes of the copyright statute is to augment the collections of the Library of Congress by deposit of copyrighted material by copyright owners. Two sections in the law call for deposits: the registration provisions of section 400, considered in Chapter 10, and the deposit provisions of section 407, the subject of this chapter.

Because registration is not mandatory, the section 408 deposit provisions alone would not automatically result in the Library receiving all the desired materials. Section 407 meets that problem by independently requiring deposits. Does that mean that the Library in effect receives a "double deposit" whenever there is a registration? Although this can happen, when both provisions apply, the double deposit may be avoided by using copies deposited under section 407 to satisfy the registration deposit provisions of section 408 [408(d)]. See Table 5 for a comparison of deposit provisions under the two sections.

## GENERAL DEPOSIT RULES; EXCEPTIONS

Section 407 is concerned with deposits of (1) certain published works and (2) certain broadcast and other transmission program materials that have not yet been "published" in the copyright law sense. We will defer discussion of the second item to the end of this chapter, under the heading "Broadcast and Other Transmission Programs."

If a work is published with notice of copyright in the United States, the general rule of section 407 is that two copies of the best edition of the work should be deposited with the Copyright Office within three months after publication [407(a),(b)].[1] (The term "publication," and the standards concerning notice of copyright, were considered in Chapter 7.)

The general rule enables the Library of Congress to acquire a vast amount of copyrighted materials. But the general rule, if left unqualified, could result in unnecessary efforts, expenses, and inconveniences to the Library

## TABLE 5   DEPOSIT PROVISIONS IN SECTIONS 407 AND 408

| Section 407 | Section 408 |
| --- | --- |
| 1. Applies almost exclusively to published works. | 1. Applies in connection with registration of copyright claims, which can relate to both published and unpublished works. |
| 2. Operates as a formal requirement; sanctions apply for failure to deposit after a demand. | 2. Registration is optional (although on occasion it is a practical necessity). |
| 3. Calls for deposit within three months after publication of work in the United States with notice of copyright. | 3. Registration may be made at any time. Exception: One year is allowed for renewal registrations, when applicable. |
| 4. Purpose is to benefit the Library of Congress. | 4. Purpose is to benefit the Library of Congress and also to provide the Copyright Office with information to aid in determining whether a registration should be issued. |
| 5. Many exemptions are applicable. | 5. Some form of deposit always required when registering (other than for certain registrations with respect to works previously registered). |
| 6. Underlying regulations include many variations from the basic deposit standards. | 6. Underlying regulations include many variations from the basic deposit standards, but the particular variations are not always the same as section 407 variations. |

and to depositors. Atrocious two-ton sculptures could be sent and, worse, arrive. Hundreds of thousands of items of little interest to the Library could pour in, such as advertisements and promotional materials. And some materials, such as works published on computer tape, would be received with no suitable indication of what material was recorded. Such problems are taken into account by Copyright Office regulations providing that:

1. for some works, no section 407 deposit is required;
2. for some works, only one copy need be deposited;
3. for some works, a substitute deposit, such as a color slide of the work, is either allowed or required;
4. for some works, supplementary information relating to the work must be included; and
5. for special situations, the prospective depositor may ask for special relief.

The modifications to the general rule cover a variety of works and situations. They can be quite complex. For instance, the section 407 deposit may be omitted for

> Literary works, including computer programs and automated data bases, pub-
> lished in the United States only in the form of machine-readable copies (such
> as magnetic tape or disks, punched cards, or the like) from which the work
> cannot ordinarily be visually perceived except with the aid of a machine or
> device. Works published in a form requiring the use of a machine or device
> for purposes of optical enlargement (such as film, filmstrips, slide films and
> works published in any variety of microform), and works published in visually
> perceivable form but used in connection with optical scanning devices, are
> not in this category and are subject to the applicable deposit requirements.

Another modification of the general rule allows omission of the section
407 deposit for

> Three-dimensional sculptural works, and any works published only as repro-
> duced in or on jewelry, dolls, toys, games, plaques, floor coverings, wallpaper
> and similar commercial wall coverings, textile and other fabrics, packaging
> material, or any useful article. Globes, relief models, and similar cartographic
> representations of area are not within this category and are subject to the
> applicable deposit requirements.

Given such qualifying remarks, it often is not possible to reduce the rules
to brief and accurate phrases. However, because most people are concerned
with only a few categories, the complexity of the rules as a whole becomes
somewhat irrelevant. The application of the right rule usually becomes clear
enough without too much trouble.

Rather than try to paraphrase all the rules, or include them verbatim here,
we have included the regulations in Appendix 2. Here are some examples
of rule applications:

Novels: two complete copies of the best edition.

Greeting cards, picture postcards, stationery: no section 407 deposit.

Advertising matter published in connection with the sale of articles of
merchandise: no section 407 deposit.

Globes: one copy of the best edition instead of two.

The section 407 deposit burdens are not great in most cases, and the
cause is a worthy one. Consequently, in close cases, some people may
decide to deposit rather than spend time trying to figure out whether a
deposit must be made. However, you may feel that the cost of the copy or
copies is substantial or that the Library's acquisition of free copies represents
a potential "lost sale" of consequence. Or these factors may become of
concern when the cumulative impact of all your potential deposits in a
particular category of works is considered. If so, you will want to know the
impact of the deposit requirements in your particular case.

## Criteria for "Best Edition" and "Complete Copy"

The terms "best edition" and "complete copy," discussed below, are
part of the relevant standards.

*Best Edition.* The statute defines the "best edition" of a work as "that edition, published in the United States at any time before the date of deposit, that the Library of Congress determines to be most suitable for its purposes" [101]. When differences exist between two editions of a work and those differences do not represent variations in copyrightable content, the Library of Congress has established some criteria, in a "Best Edition Statement," for determining which edition is the "best" for its purposes. A copy of the statement is included in Appendix 4.

When differences exist between two editions of a work and those differences represent variations in copyrightable content, each "edition" is considered to be a different work for purposes of section 407's deposit rules. Thus, in such a situation, separate deposits could be called for.

*Complete Copy.* It is not at all uncommon for someone's copyrighted work to be published in such a form that it is physically integrated with someone else's copyrighted work or with some material that is not protected by copyright at all. What the Library of Congress wants to receive is the entire work as it was published, not merely excerpts of some copyrighted part of it. For purposes of section 407, a "complete" copy includes:

> all elements comprising the unit of publication of the best edition of the work, including elements that, if considered separately, would not be copyrightable subject matter or would otherwise be exempt from the mandatory deposit requirements.

The regulations provide additional criteria for motion pictures (such as providing for the inclusion of a brief synopsis) and for certain musical compositions.

*Complete Phonorecord.* For section 407 deposit purposes, a "complete" phonorecord:

> includes the phonorecord, together with any printed or other visually perceptible material published with such phonorecords (such as textual or pictorial matter appearing on recorded sleeves or album covers, or embodied in leaflets or booklets included in a sleeve, album, or other container).

See Chapter 2 for a discussion of the difference between "phonorecords" and "copies."

## WHO DEPOSITS

The statutory obligation to make a section 407 deposit falls upon either the owner of copyright or the owner of the exclusive right of publication in a work published with notice of copyright in the United States [407(a)]. The Register of Copyrights may demand the required deposit from any of the persons having the obligation to make it [407(d)]. If, in a particular case, more than one person has the statutory obligation, they may choose to agree among themselves as to who will actually do it. Of course, that agreement would not be binding on the Register.

## SANCTIONS

A required deposit is supposed to be made without a request for it. However, the statute contains no penalty provisions for the simple failure to deposit. It does have sanctions for the failure to deposit after a demand by the Register of Copyrights.

At any time after publication of a work covered by section 407, the Register may make a written demand for the deposit on any of the persons having the deposit obligation [407(d)]. If the deposit is not made within three months after the demand is received, the person upon whom the demand was made is liable to pay a fine of as much as $250 and to pay the retail price of the copies demanded or, in appropriate circumstances, the cost to the Library of Congress of acquiring the copies [407(d)(1),(2)]. If there is willful or repeated failure to comply with a demand, an additional $2,500 fine can be imposed [407(d)(3)].

The subsection of the current law that establishes the deposit obligation provides that its deposit requirements are not a condition of copyright [407(a)].

## DEPOSIT PROCEDURE

There are no specified formalities for making a section 407 deposit. You can just send the material in to the Copyright Office.

If you want a certificate of receipt for the deposit, you should request it in writing at the time of the deposit and should include the applicable fee [407(b)]. The fee was set at $2 in 1976 [708(a)(3)]. A request for a certificate may be made after the date of the section 407 deposit, but the Copyright Office will issue one only if the requesting party is identified in the records of the Copyright Office as having made the deposit.

## DISPOSITION OF DEPOSITED MATERIALS

The physical materials deposited pursuant to section 407 (as contrasted with the underlying copyrights) are the property of the United States [704(a)]. They are available to the Library of Congress for its collections or for exchange or transfer to other libraries [704(b)].

If the Library of Congress does not elect to take particular published materials that were deposited, the Copyright Office retains them for a period both it and the Library consider practicable [704(d)]. Thereafter, the materials ordinarily may be destroyed, or otherwise disposed of, at the discretion of the Library and the Copyright Office [704(d)].

As mentioned earlier, a deposit under section 407 may sometimes also serve as a deposit under section 408 [408(b)]. A depositor under section 408 (or the copyright owner of record) may request retention, under the control of the Copyright Office, of the deposited material for the full term of copyright in the work. Eventually, there will be regulations relating to that provision [704(e)].

The "disposition" rules relating to section 407 deposits also are applicable to copies of published works deposited solely under section 408. But, unlike section 407, section 408 also relates to unpublished materials, about which there are special disposition rules. Section 408 is considered in Chapters 9 and 10, but this is a convenient point to consider also the disposition rules relating to the deposit of unpublished works pursuant to section 408:

1. as in the case of deposited published works, the deposited material becomes the property of the U.S. government [704(a)];
2. the Library of Congress is entitled, under regulations that the Register of Copyrights shall prescribe, to select any deposits of unpublished works for its collections or for transfer to the National Archives of the United States or to a federal records center [704(b)];
3. before transferring the material to the Library, the Copyright Office is authorized to make a facsimile reproduction [704(c)];
4. if the material is not selected by the Library, it shall be retained under the control of the Copyright Office for the period of time it and the Library determine but, in the case of unpublished works, ". . . no deposit shall be knowingly or intentionally destroyed or . . . disposed of during its term of copyright unless a facsimile reproduction of entire deposit has been made a part of the Copyright Office records. . . ." [704(d)]; and
5. as in the case of published works, a depositor under section 408 (or the copyright owner of record) may request retention, under the control of the Copyright Office, of the deposited material for the full term of copyright in the work [704(e)].

## BROADCAST AND OTHER TRANSMISSION PROGRAMS

Congress wanted to make it possible for the Library of Congress to obtain, via section 407, copies of broadcast and other material. Section 407, as discussed thus far, does not always suffice for that purpose. Why? Because the coverage has concerned "published" works. As noted in Chapter 7, a widely disseminated work may not have been "published" in the technical sense in which that term is used in the copyright statute. Congress thus included, at the end of section 407, a provision allowing the Copyright Office to establish regulations for obtaining for the collections of the Library of Congress "transmission programs that have been fixed and transmitted to the public in the United States but have not been published" [407(e)].

The statute includes definitions for the terms "transmission program," "fixed," "transmitted," and "publication" [101]. Generally, section 407, when implemented by regulations, would enable the Library of Congress to acquire unpublished programs that were sent from one place to another (e.g., via broadcasting or cablecasting) and that were taped or otherwise recorded.

In February of 1982, the Copyright Office promulgated proposed regulations to implement the unpublished-transmission-program feature of section 407.[2] Under prescribed circumstances, they would allow the Library of Congress to make a tape of an unpublished transmission program, or permit the Copyright Office to demand a copy of such a program from "the owner of the right of transmission in the United States." In the latter case, the owner would be entitled to be recompensed for the copy supplied.

# 9

# COPYRIGHT REGISTRATIONS
## PART I: REGISTRATION ADVANTAGES

The current U.S. copyright statute, like its predecessors, provides a system for the registration of claims to copyright. In order to seek registration, the applicant files a completed form together with a required fee (usually $10) and, typically, two copies of the work [408; 708(a)(1),(2)]. The Copyright Office, after reviewing the applicant's submission and deciding that a registration is appropriate, issues a certificate of registration.

We will go over the application form in some detail in Chapter 10. Here we will consider the benefits that registration provides.

## BENEFITS OF REGISTERING

The copyright statute does not literally require that copyrighted works be registered. And only for a portion of copyrighted works does registration become a practical necessity. However, registration has many advantages (some of them applicable to only special situations).

Except in the case of renewal registrations and a few others, a copyrighted work can go through its entire life in perfect health without having been registered. And, sometimes, when trouble arises and registration is needed, it can be obtained in time. However, sometimes unforeseen trouble cannot be dealt with on an ideal basis unless a registration is already in effect. Thus, in some ways obtaining a registration is like obtaining an insurance policy.

Let us consider each of the advantages of registration.

### Renewal Registrations

For works published before 1978 (and unpublished works federally registered before 1978), registration is a prerequisite for obtaining a renewal of copyright, that is, one that adds 47 years to the work's initial copyright term of 28 [304(a)]. The procedures for obtaining a renewal registration are

considered in Chapter 10. Renewal registrations are sought in the last calendar year of the initial term [304(a),305].

Historically, renewal registrations have not been requested in a high
percentage of cases. For decades, initial registrations have been at the rate
of 200,000 or more each year, but renewal registrations have been at levels
of around 30,000. Works in the fields of music and motion pictures receive
special renewal attention by copyright owners because so many of them
have a long economic life.

## Placing Information about Work on Public Record

When a work is registered, information about it goes into the records of
the Copyright Office, where it is available for public inspection [705]. The
information is available not only at the Copyright Office in Washington but
in Copyright Office publications of registration information, which may be
found in various libraries around the country. In addition, the Copyright
Office will provide research services, the current charge being $10 an hour
[705, 708(10)].

Sometimes, you will not want to register because of the public information
it provides. For example, to register a private diary, a copy of the work must
be provided. That copy becomes the property of the U.S. government
[704(a)]. Perhaps you could obtain special relief so that the copy is returned
to you, but in any event you would want to proceed with caution. The same
is true with works of authorship that include trade secrets. For such works,
you should consult an attorney before registering.

## Commencement of Infringement Suits

The statute provides, generally, that a lawsuit for copyright infringement
shall not be instituted until registration has been made [411]. There are two
exceptions. One relates to certain live broadcasts and other transmissions.
The second relates to unsuccessful attempts to register. Both will be considered below.

The need to obtain a registration before commencement of suit means,
at first blush, no more than that you will register if you ever need to sue.
But suppose that you have not registered and you come across what you
think is an infringement. You may find that you want to stop the infringement
immediately and that the alleged infringer shows no interest in accommodating you. You may wish to go into court on your copyright claim right
away—but you will be handicapped. In the ordinary course of events, it
may take weeks to obtain a registration. And even if the Copyright Office,
in its discretion, processes your application on an expedited basis, it will
still take time. A matter of days may be important to you. Thus, an advantage
to registering is that you will be ready to sue promptly if necessary. Statis-
tically, it is not often necessary to sue on very short notice. But for some
copyrights, it makes sense to be in a position to do so.

Let us return to the two exceptions to the rule that registration is a prerequisite to suit:

*Registration Refusal.* In a case when the deposit, application, and the required fee for registration have been delivered to the Copyright Office in proper form and registration has been refused, the applicant is entitled to bring a copyright infringement suit despite the absence of a registration. As part of the process, the Register of Copyrights receives notice of the suit and a copy of the complaint. The Register may elect to become a party to the case on the issue of registerability [411(a)].

*Certain Broadcasts.* In the case of some broadcasts, the first time the work becomes eligible for federal copyright protection, and for registration, is at the time of broadcast, when the work is taped and thus put into a suitably tangible form. And yet, the moment of broadcast also may be the most likely moment the work will be infringed. Must the copyright owner wait until the registration process is completed before bringing an infringement suit? No, not always. The law contains a provision that allows the copyright owner to bring the suit before the work is registered. The provision, and its underlying regulations, are quite detailed [411(b)]. A principal requirement is that the copyright owner have served notice on a potential infringer prior to the broadcast.

## Good Evidence

If a work is registered before, or within five years after, first publication of the work, the certificate constitutes prima facie evidence of the validity of the copyright and of the facts stated in the certificate. That means, generally, that the copyright owner can be off to a good and fast start in establishing critical elements of proof in an infringement case. (If a certificate does not qualify as prima facie evidence, the weight to be given it is within the discretion of the court [410(c)].) Thus, the prima facie evidence rule can be especially valuable in infringement suits where quick resolution is being sought. The rule also can be of special value in suits that arise years after a work was first published. The facts of years earlier are sometimes difficult to ascertain and prove to the degree that you would like in the time that you have available. Lawsuits relating to older copyrights are not uncommon. In the past few years, for example, there have been court cases involving copyrights relating to "Superman," "Hopalong Cassidy," "Peter Pan," "Mickey Mouse," *Gone with the Wind*, and "Pygmalion." True, less celebrated older works are more likely to be forgotten than infringed, but they do come up from time to time in late litigation.

## Litigation Remedies

*Statutory Damages.* When a copyright is infringed, it is often difficult for the copyright owner to prove how much economic harm was caused, for example, what sales were lost. The statute recognizes this problem and allows a court to award the copyright owner an amount, within certain ranges, that the court considers just, what we call "statutory" damages [504(b)]. Eligibility to seek this type of award depends on when the infringement commenced in relation to the effective date of registration of the infringed work.

Published Works: No award of statutory damages is authorized for any infringement of copyright commenced after first publication of the infringed work and before the effective date of its registration, unless such registration is made within three months after the first publication of the work. [412(b)]

Unpublished Works: No award of statutory damages is authorized for any infringement of copyright in an unpublished work commenced before the effective date of its registration. [412(a)]

The effective date of a registration is the day when an application, deposit, and fee, which are later determined by the Register of Copyrights or by a court of competent jurisdiction to be acceptable for registration, have all been received in the Copyright Office [410(d)]. Thus, the effective date precedes the issuance of the actual certificate of registration.

For the broadcast situation noted on the previous page, statutory damages may be obtained even though the infringement precedes the effective date of registration [411(b), 412].

*Attorney's Fees.* By law, the court has discretion to award a reasonable attorney's fee to the prevailing party in a copyright infringement suit [505]. However, the eligibility of a copyright owner to seek an award of such fees depends upon whether the effective date of the registration occurred soon enough in relation to the time the infringement commenced [412]. The applicable rules are the same as those set forth above in the case of statutory damages.

In much copyright litigation, particularly where the infringement is caught at an early stage, the principal relief obtained may not be a recovery of substantial actual or statutory damages, but rather an injunction against further infringement. Thus, it is nice also to be eligible to seek recovery of reasonable attorney's fees so that your legal bill will not have to be paid entirely out of your own pocket. Moreover, even when a substantial monetary reward is obtained, the legal costs of obtaining it may be high and, again, it is nice to have the chance to get the other side to pay at least part of the legal bill.

It should be noted that, when you do sue for copyright infringement and have registered early enough, your eligibility to seek to recover reasonable attorney's fees may backfire on you if you lose the case. The statute speaks of the award of fees "to the prevailing party" [505].

## Protection against Copyright Notice Problems

*Curing Copyright Notice Omissions.* Under some circumstances, the absence of a copyright notice on published works may result in loss of copyright (see Chapter 7). However, for post-1978 omissions a curative process is sometimes available, after the omission has been discovered, to prevent such a disastrous consequence [405(a)(2)]. Registration of the work is one of the required elements.

The existence of the curative process is not merely an argument for registering when you find out you have the problem. For example, if the omission of a required copyright notice is discovered very late—more than five years after publication—the process is available only if the work already has been registered earlier [405(b)]. Thus, the registration of a work for copyright before you know that you need it has some insurance value, for curing the omission of copyright notice, should it be necessary. The contingency protected against is remote, but, as discussed in Chapter 7, not as remote as first appears.

*Protection against a Notice Inaccuracy.* As discussed in Chapter 7, when a copyright notice includes the wrong name as the owner of copyright, someone who relies on a permission from that person may have a valid defense in a suit brought by the correct owner [406(a)]. The correct owner may eliminate the availability of that defense by registering the work in his or her name, provided that happens before the infringing undertaking has begun [406(a)(1)].

## Avoiding Double Deposits

As discussed in Chapter 8, a copy or copies of a work may have to be deposited twice with the Copyright Office, once to meet the deposit requirements of section 407 of the law and once to meet the registration requirements of section 408. If you are planning to register a work eventually, an early registration makes it possible to use one deposit to meet the requirements of both statutory provisions. This is especially worth considering if the deposits you would have to make are expensive.

## Ownership Protection

When ownership of a right of copyright is transferred, the party who receives the right may obtain some statutory protection against an earlier or later inconsistent transaction by the one who transferred the rights. In order to obtain this protection, the transfer should be recorded in the Copyright Office at an early stage and registration should be made for the work [205(c),(e)]. See Chapter 6 for a fuller discussion of this issue.

More generally speaking, the recording of a transfer operates, when registration of a work has also been made, as "constructive notice" of the transfer [205(c)]. In effect, this sometimes eliminates the defense (not always applicable) of "Gee, I didn't know." The law, by means of the "constructive" notice rule, says that public records provided the opportunity to find out and it doesn't matter whether or not you knew. (Sometimes, however, actual notice of the transfer is required [405(b)].)

## Mechanical Recording Rights

As will be discussed in Chapter 17, a copyright owner of a musical work is entitled, under defined circumstances, to some government-set royalties when someone produces and markets recordings of the work pursuant to statutory authorization [115]. Registration is one of the means by which the copyright owner's name and address may be put on record so as to receive the royalties and to be notified of another's intent to use the work pursuant to the statutory license [115(b)(1),(c)].

## Access to Information about Possible Unlawful Imports

The owner of copyright in a work may, if the work has been registered, take advantage of a procedure under which the Customs Service will seek to give notice of imports that appear to be copies of the work [602(b)]. Government assistance in preventing unlawful imports also is possible for registered works [603].

## Manufacturing Clause Considerations

As will be discussed in Chapter 11, a copyright owner sometimes will need an import statement in order to import copies of the copyrighted work that were manufactured abroad [601(b)]. Copyright Office regulations provide that it ordinarily will not issue an import statement until after the effective date of registration for the work.[1]

As also discussed in Chapter 11, when an American-authored English-language work is manufactured abroad, a person who infringes the work but manufactures it here sometimes has a defense if the copyright owner made unlawful imports. The possibility of that defense may be reduced by registering the work and manufacturing additional copies in the United States [601(d)].

## Copy Preservation Possibilities

When an unpublished work is registered, the Copyright Office is not supposed to dispose of the work during its term of copyright unless a facsimile copy is made [704(d)]. For a published work, the Copyright Office is not obligated to retain even a facsimile copy of what was deposited [704]. Thus, registration is not, by itself, a guarantee that the Copyright Office will preserve a copy of a published work. However, the statute allows for a procedure, under regulations, for the owner to request that the material deposited for registration be retained. As of this writing, regulations have not been adopted.

For an overall view of the advantages of registration, see Table 6.

## DECIDING WHETHER TO REGISTER

Set forth below are some examples of the kinds of register-or-not decisions that might be made in practice. In each of these examples, we will assume that the work under consideration includes no confidential information.

Here are some reasons that make registration an easy decision:

1. You have contractually agreed to apply for registration of the work.
2. You believe someone has infringed the work and want to sue for infringement.
3. You believe the work has considerable commercial value and may well attract infringers, and you want to be in the maximum position to be able to sue quickly, recover statutory damages and attorney's fees, and have the benefit of the prima facie evidence rule.
4. The work is one for which copyright will expire unless a renewal term of copyright is obtained and you feel that the work is still of enough importance that you do not wish the copyright to lapse.
5. You acquired the copyright from someone else and it is of such

### TABLE 6   SOME REASONS FOR REGISTRATION

| Reason | Section |
|---|---|
| 1. To have information about the work in records available for public inspection | 705 |
| 2. To obtain renewal registration, when applicable | 304(a) |
| 3. To commence suit | 411 |
| 4. To benefit from the prima facie evidence rule | 410(c) |
| 5. To be eligible to seek statutory damages and recovery of reasonable attorney's fees in lawsuits | 412; 505 |
| 6. To be able to compensate for certain notice omissions or inaccuracies | 405; 406 |
| 7. To avoid double-deposit requirements | 407; 408(b) |
| 8. To protect ownership in certain circumstances | 205(a),(c),(e) |
| 9. To be on record for mechanical license statutory royalties | 115(b)(c) |
| 10. To have access to information about possible unlawful imports | 602 |
| 11. To import certain American-authored English-language works first published outside the United States | 601(b)(2) |
| 12. To have a copy of unpublished work retained under Copyright Office control | 704 |

value to you that you want to record the transfer of ownership, and register the work, so as to obtain protection against a prior or subsequent inconsistent transfer by the one who transferred the rights to you, no matter how unlikely such an act might be.

Here are some examples of cases in which you might decide not to

TABLE 7   REGISTRATION STATISTICS, FISCAL YEAR 1980

| Category of Material | Published | Unpublished | Total |
|---|---|---|---|
| Nondramatic Literary Works | | | |
|   Monographs | 97,538 | 21,683 | 119,221 |
|   Serials | 117,898 | | 117,898 |
|   Machine-readable | | | |
|     works | 986 | 866 | 1,852 |
|   Total | 216,422 | 22,549 | 238,971 |
| Works of the Performing Arts | | | |
|   Musical works | 27,771 | 92,427 | 120,198 |
|   Dramatic works, | | | |
|     including any | | | |
|     accompanying music | 921 | 7,121 | 8,042 |
|   Choreography and | | | |
|     pantomimes | 20 | 43 | 63 |
|   Motion pictures and | | | |
|     filmstrips | 7,437 | 1,038 | 8,475 |
|   Total | 36,149 | 100,629 | 136,778 |
| Works of the Visual Arts | | | |
|   Two-dimensional | | | |
|     works of fine and | | | |
|     graphic art, | | | |
|     including prints and | | | |
|     art reproductions | 9,738 | 6,489 | 16,227 |
|   Sculptural works | 2,179 | 774 | 2,973 |
|     Technical drawings | | | |
|     and models | 447 | 387 | 834 |
|   Photographs | 590 | 657 | 1,247 |
|   Cartographic works | 817 | 8 | 825 |
|   Commercial prints and | | | |
|     labels | 4,527 | 197 | 4,722 |
|   Works of applied art | 12,220 | 2,125 | 14,345 |
|   Total | 30,516 | 10,637 | 41,153 |
| Sound Recordings | 8,098 | 4,680 | 12,778 |
| Multimedia Works | 1,958 | 123 | 2,081 |
|   Grand Total | 290,143 | 138,618 | 431,761 |
| Renewals | | | 32,982 |
|   Total, All | | | |
|     Registrations | | | 464,743 |

register, even though you recognize that situations may arise in which you will wish you had decided differently:

1. The work has not yet been published; you have no present plans to disclose the work to others, do not feel that it is important, through registration, to establish when you created the work, do plan to revise the work before publication, and think it unlikely that anyone will have the opportunity to copy the work now.

2. Each year your company creates, and owns copyrights in, thousands of advertisements and brochures. Your experience has been that, as wonderful as these materials are, no one has ever infringed the copyright in any of them and you believe that will continue to be the case. To register any one of these materials would only cost $10, but to register all of them would cost more than $10,000 a year. In such a situation, you might elect to register none of the works until a pressing need arises, or you might elect to register only the most important ones, or the most important categories.

## REGISTRATION STATISTICS

Table 7 presents some registration statistics from the Register of Copyrights Annual Report for the fiscal year 1980. There were over 450,000 registrations that year, up from about 300,000 in 1970 and 200,000 in 1950. Registrations have numbered more than 100,000 a year since 1904.

# 10

## COPYRIGHT REGISTRATIONS
## PART II: HOW TO REGISTER

A copyright registration is sought by filing with the Copyright Office a completed application form together with the appropriate fee and, typically, two copies of the best edition of the work to which the application relates. The Copyright Office reviews the submission to see if the requested registration is appropriate. If necessary, the Office seeks further information or clarification from the applicant. Assuming that matters are in order, a certificate of registration is issued. If for some reason registration is denied, the Office informs the applicant of the reason.

### SELECTING THE REGISTRATION APPLICATION FORM

Table 8 lists the various Copyright Office application forms and the purpose of each. Applications should be submitted in the form most appropriate to the nature of the authorship in which copyright is claimed. When that would be covered by two or more forms, the most appropriate one should be used, except that if registration is sought for a work including a sound recording copyright, the form for sound recordings should be used.

A reduced-format copy of each form is reproduced in Appendix 3. Copies of the forms may be obtained by writing to the Copyright Office, Library of Congress, Washington, D.C. 20559. Also, in 1981 the Copyright Office established a telephone hotline to provide quick service to people who know what application forms they need and who do not need the services of an information specialist. The hotline number is 202-287-9100.

Following Table 8, registration forms, is Table 9, which notes the elements required in each case for a complete submission.

### FORMS TX, SE, PA, VA, AND SR

Before filling out an application for registration on one of these five forms, it is helpful to consider these four questions:

## TABLE 8   COPYRIGHT OFFICE REGISTRATION APPLICATION FORMS

| Form | Purpose |
|---|---|
| RE | When applying for a renewal of copyright, regardless of the type of work involved |
| TX | When the work to be registered consists principally of textual material |
| SE | When registering individual issues of a serial, such as a magazine or newspaper (not to register an individual contribution to a serial) |
| VA | When the work to be registered consists principally of works of the visual arts |
| PA | When the work to be registered consists principally of works of the performing arts |
| SR | When the work to be registered is a sound recording |
| GR/CP | In conjunction with one of the above forms, when making a single registration for a group of contributions to periodicals |
| CA | As a supplementary registration, when registration already has been made and you wish to correct or amplify the facts that are on the record |

## TABLE 9   REQUIREMENTS FOR A COMPLETE APPLICATION

| Item | Type of Registration | | |
|---|---|---|---|
| | Initial—Forms TX, SE, VA, PA, SR | Renewal— Form RE | Supplementary— Form CA |
| Completed application form | Yes | Yes | Yes |
| Accompanying application fee | $10 | $6 | $10 |
| Deposit of copies of the work, or some other deposit relating to the work | Yes | No | No |
| Prior basic initial registration required | No | Yes | Yes |
| Presentation of the requisite items together | Yes | Yes | Yes |

References: Copyright statute, Secs. 304(a), 408(a)–(d), 409, 708; Forms TX, SE, VA, PA, SR, RE, CA; Copyright Office regulations 37 CFR Secs. 202.3, 202.17, 202.20, 202.21.

1. Has there already been a registration for the same work? (The Copyright Office has rules limiting the number of registrations per work.)
2. Who is entitled to submit an application for registration?
3. Who is entitled to be listed as the "copyright claimant" in an application?
4. How many works may be covered with the registration? (The Copyright Office has some grouping standards.)

## Number of Times a Work May Be Registered

The Copyright Office has a general rule that only one basic initial copyright registration may be made for the same version of a particular work.[1] There are three exceptions:

1. When a work has been registered as unpublished, another registration may be made for the first published edition.
2. When someone other than the "author" is identified in a registration as a copyright claimant, the author may make another registration for the same version in his or her own name as copyright claimant.
3. When an applicant for registration alleges that an earlier registration for the same version is unauthorized and legally invalid, a registration may be made by the applicant, assuming eligibility in other respects.

In adopting a general standard of only one registration per work, the Copyright Office concluded that "the allowance of multiple registrations for the same work would thoroughly confuse the public record designed to be made by the registration system."[2]

## Applicant Eligibility; Copyright Claimant Eligibility

As noted in Chapter 6, the rights of a copyright owner may be split up, with the result that more than one person owns an exclusive right of copyright in the work. As such an owner of an exclusive right, he or she (or it for that matter) is entitled to sue another for infringement of that right while he or she owned it.

Because registration generally is a prerequisite for bringing the suit, it is understandable that the owner of any exclusive right is one of the persons who is entitled to apply for registration of the work. But the statute and the registration form call for the naming of a "copyright claimant." Should the owner of just one of the exclusive rights be named the copyright claimant? The Copyright Office decided that should not happen, stating:

We do not believe that the concept of divisibility of copyright was intended to allow the owner of an exclusive right or rights to claim, or appear to claim, on our records, ownership of the entire copyright. . . . [S]uch a result would lead to a misleading and inaccurate public record, and subvert the purpose of the registration system.[3]

The regulations provide that only certain persons are entitled to be listed as a copyright "claimant." Each is eligible to apply for registration, and so are some others. Table 10 compares those eligible to apply for registration and those eligible to be listed as copyright claimant.

## Number of Works per Registration

*Published Works.*[4]  In the case of published works, the general rule is that an application should relate only to a single work. The rules state that for registration purposes the following would be considered a single work:

All copyrightable elements that are otherwise recognizable as self-contained works, that are involved in a single unit of publication, and in which the copyright claimant is the same.

Here are two examples of the general standard of one work per registration:

Publisher P published 52 issues a year of a magazine, of which P is the copyright owner. A separate registration would be required for each issue.

TABLE 10   PERSONS ELIGIBLE TO APPLY FOR REGISTRATION AND PERSONS ELIGIBLE TO BE LISTED AS COPYRIGHT CLAIMANT

| Eligible to Apply for Registration | Eligible to be Listed as Copyright Claimant |
| --- | --- |
| 1. The author* of the work. | 1. The author* of the work. |
| 2. Someone who has acquired ownership of all the rights of copyright in the work. | 2. Someone who has acquired ownership of all the rights of copyright in the work.† |
| 3. Someone who has obtained from either of the above the contractual right to claim legal title to the copyright in an application for registration of the work. | 3. Someone who has obtained from either of the above the contractual right to claim legal title to the copyright in an application for registration of the work. |
| 4. The owner of any exclusive right of copyright in the work. | |
| 5. A duly authorized agent of any of the above. | |

* The regulations provide: "An 'author' includes an employer or other person for whom a work is 'made for hire.' "

† The statute provides that a transfer of copyright ownership, other than by operation of law, is not valid unless the transfer is reflected in writing signed by the owner of the rights conveyed or that person's agent [204(a)].

Author A is the copyright claimant for an anthology and also for some of the individual short stories within it. Author A may use a single application for the anthology as a whole and for each story of which A is the copyright claimant. But neither A nor the authors of the other individual stories should assume that the registration A obtains will cover the other stories.

If, in the latter example, author A's registration was clearly to cover another author's work, then contractual arrangements should be made so that A would qualify as a copyright claimant for that work at the time of registration.

*Unpublished Works.*[5] As for unpublished works, the general rule of one registration per work also applies. However, it is possible to put together a collection of individual works and register the material with a single registration and a single fee. The regulations provide that a single registration may be used for

all copyrightable elements that are otherwise recognizable as self-contained works and are combined in a single unpublished "collection."

In order to constitute a "collection" for these purposes, there are four criteria:

1. the elements should be presented in an orderly form;
2. the combined elements should bear a single title identifying the collection as a whole;
3. the copyright claimant, in all the elements and in the collection as a whole, should be the same; and
4. all the elements should be by the same author, or, if they are by different authors, at least one of the authors should have contributed copyrightable authorship to each element.

## COMPLETING APPLICATION FORMS TX, SE, PA, VA, AND SR

Each of the five forms asks for information under these nine topical headings:

| | |
|---|---|
| Title | Author(s) |
| Creation and publication | Claimant(s) |
| Previous registration | Compilation or derivative works |
| Fee and correspondence | Certification |
| Address for return of certificate | |

Forms TX and SE have these additional headings: (a) Manufacturing, and (b) License for Handicapped.

In the registration forms, each of these elements is grouped within an area referred to as a "space" in the form's instructions. We will use that designation in the material that follows.

After the first four years of operation of the 1976 Copyright Act, the Copyright Office issued new forms TX, PA, VA, and SR. In their significant aspects, they are substantially the same as the forms originally issued. The redesigned forms serve principally to make the information requests clearer and to make it easier to complete the application (such as by making the spacing coincide with typewriter lines). In addition to revising the existing forms, the Copyright Office issued a new form, SE, for use in applying for registrations in works such as magazine and newspaper issues. After June 1982, Form SE should be used for serials, that is, for "works issued or intended to be issued in successive parts bearing numerical or chronological designations and intended to be continued indefinitely."

## Title Information

Information about the title of the work is necessary to identify the work, serving as one of the principal reference points for gaining access to Copyright Office records. To some extent, the forms ask for the identifying information in different ways, as Table 11 indicates.

On forms PA and VA, where "nature of work" is requested, appropriate responses would be "music," "song lyrics," "drama," "oil painting," or "charcoal drawing."

## Author Information

The following (a–g) is what each of the five forms asks for (in space 2) regarding the author(s) of the work. The forms state that, unless the work

TABLE 11    INFORMATION REQUESTS IN SPACE 1
OF APPLICATION FORMS

| Information | Request on Form |
|---|---|
| 1. Title of this work | TX, SE, VA, PA, SR |
| 2. Previous or alternative titles | TX, SE, VA, PA, SR |
| 3. If a periodical or serial give volume, number, and issue date | TX, SE, VA |
| 4. If this work was published as a contribution to a periodical, serial, or collection, give information about the collective work in which the contribution appeared: title of collective work, volume, number, date, pages | TX, VA |
| 5. Nature of this work | VA, PA |
| 6. Catalog number of sound recording, if any | SR |
| 7. Nature of material recorded (check which): musical, dramatic, musical dramatic, literary, other | SR |

is a collective work, information should be given about every author who contributed any appreciable amount of copyrightable matter to the version of the work to be registered. (For the meaning of "author" in the context of a work made for hire, see example b below.)

In the case of registration for a collective work, such as a periodical issue, it is sufficient to give information for the author of the collective work as a whole. (As discussed earlier, the registration for a collective work does not necessarily cover every contribution within it.)

The form provides entry space for three authors. If more authors are to be reported, "continuation sheets" are used.

Much of the following commentary is taken from the instruction portions of the forms.

a. *Name of author.* If an author's contribution is anonymous or pseudonymous, it is not necessary to name the author. In the case of an anonymous work, the line may be left blank or "anonymous" inserted. In the case of a pseudonymous work, the line may be left blank, or the pseudonym may be given and identified as such, or the author's real name may be given, making clear which is the real name and which is the pseudonym.

See item b, below, concerning a work made for hire.

In one recent case involving a song,[6] the author had assigned all his rights to three individuals. They applied for registration and incorrectly named themselves as authors. When they later sued another for infringement of the song, the validity of the registration was attacked. However, the federal district court in Pennsylvania, which decided the case, concluded that the error was immaterial in the context of the particular suit. If you should find, after obtaining a registration for a work, that the information is incorrect or in need of amplification, it may be appropriate to file a supplementary registration (Form CA). Supplementary registrations are discussed later on in this chapter.

b. *Was this author's contribution to the work a "work made for hire"?* This is potentially confusing because of the meaning of "author" in the context of a work made for hire (see chapter 5). The "author" of a work made for hire is the employer. Thus, for the name of the author, the full legal name of the employer would be used, and the answer to this question would be yes. It is permissible to give a credit to the employee. Form TX gives this example: "Elster Publishing Co., employer for hire of John Ferguson."

c. *Year date of author's birth.* This space would be left blank in the case of a work made for hire. It may be left blank in other cases as well, but, as the forms state, it is useful as a form of identification. It may also eventually be useful, in some cases, in determining whether a copyright has expired.

d. *Year date author died.* The forms state that if the author is dead, the year of death must be included in the application unless the work is anonymous or pseudonymous. The date is useful, in some cases, in determining when the copyright expires.

e. *Author's nationality or domicile—citizen of (name of country) or domiciled in (name of country).* This information sometimes is relevant for determining whether the work is eligible for U.S. copyright. See Chapter 11.

f. *Author of (briefly describe nature of this author's contribution).* Form TX provides these examples: "Entire text"; "Co-author of entire text"; "Chapters 11–14"; "Editorial revisions"; "Compilations and English translation"; "Illustrations." The other forms provide additional examples.

g. *Was this author's contribution to the work: anonymous? pseudonymous?* The yes or no answer would be noted for each category.

## Creation and Publication Information

Set forth below is what each of the five forms asks for (in space 3) regarding the creation and publication (if any) of the work.

a. *Year in which creation of this work was completed.* A work is "created" when it is fixed in a copy or phonorecord for the first time. The year that should be given in the form should be the year the author completed the version for which registration is sought. The forms make the point that "creation" should not be confused with "publication."

b. *Date and nation of first publication—date (month, day, and year), nation (name of country).* If the work has been published, the month, day, and year of the publication should be given and the name of the country where publication first occurred. This information is relevant in determining if U.S. copyright applies. See Chapter 11. For a discussion of the term "publication," see Chapter 7.

## Copyright Claimant(s)

Set forth below is what each of the five forms asks for (in space 4) regarding the copyright claimant(s) in the work.

a. *Name(s) and address(es) of copyright claimant(s).* Earlier in this chapter we considered who is eligible to be a copyright claimant with respect to a particular work.

b. *If the copyright claimant(s) named in space 4 are different from the author(s) named in space 2, give a brief statement of how the claimant(s) obtained ownership of the copyright.* As indicated by the earlier discussion in this chapter, it is possible to acquire important ownership interests in a copyrighted work and not be a copyright "claimant" for purposes of the registration form. When that is the case, the interests acquired may be reflected in Copyright Office records by recording the transfer of ownership. See Chapter 6.

## Previous Registration

Set forth below is what each of the five forms asks for (in space 5) regarding any prior registration of the work. In light of the general one-registration-per-work rule, considered earlier in this chapter, the information requested here helps the Copyright Office to determine if the registration should be rejected or if an exception to the general rule applies.

The instruction parts of the forms state that "If the work has been changed, and you are now seeking registration to cover the additions or revisions, check the third box [see item c, below] in space 5, give the earlier registration number and date [room is provided on the form], and complete both parts of space 6."

a. *Has registration for this work, or for an earlier version of this work, already been made in the Copyright Office?*

b. *If the answer is yes, give previous registration number and year of registration.*

c. *Also, if the answer is yes, why is another registration being sought? (Check appropriate box.) (1) This is the first published edition of a work previously registered in unpublished form. (2) This is the first application submitted by this author as a copyright claimant. (3) This is a changed version of this work, as shown by space 6 of this application.*

## Compilation or Derivative Work

The instructions for this part in each of the five forms state: "Complete both parts of space 6 if this work is a compilation, or derivative work, or both, and if it incorporates one or more earlier works that have already been published or registered for copyright, or that have fallen into the public domain." The statutory definitions of "compilation" and "derivative work" are also set forth in relevant parts. Here are the definitions from the statute:

> A "compilation" is a work formed by the collection and assembling of preexisting materials or of data that are selected, coordinated, or arranged in such a way that the resulting work, as a whole, constitutes an original work of authorship. The term "compilation" includes collective works.
>
> A "derivative work" is a work based upon one or more preexisting works, such as a translation, musical arrangement, dramatization, fictionalization, motion picture version, sound recording, art reproduction, abridgment, condensation, or any other form in which a work may be recast, transformed, or adapted. A work consisting of editorial revisions, annotations, elaborations, or other modifications which, as a whole, represent an original work of authorship, is a "derivative work."

Set forth below is what each of the five forms asks for (in space 6) regarding preexisting works.

a. *Identify any preexisting work or works that this work is based on or incorporates.* Each of the forms gives examples of responses. Here are two from Form PA, the first for registration of a compilation, the second for a derivative work: "Compilation of 19th century military songs"; "French version of Hugo's 'Le Roi s'amuse.'"

In one recent case,[7] a registration of a stuffed toy gorilla lost its prima facie evidence status (see Chapter 9) because it failed to reveal that it was based on a prior work (another stuffed toy gorilla) in the public domain.

b. *Give a brief, general statement of the material that has been added to this work and in which copyright is claimed.* Again, each of the forms gives examples of responses. Those from Form TX are "Foreword, selection, arrangement, editing, critical annotations"; "Revisions throughout; chapters 11–17 entirely new."

## Manufacturing

This category is included only on Forms TX and SE (space 7) and refers to the "manufacturing clause" of the law, which will be considered in Chapter 11. The form states:

> If this is a published work consisting preponderantly of nondramatic literary material in English, the law may require that the copies be manufactured in the United States or Canada for full protection. If so, the names of the manufacturers who performed certain processes, and the places where these processes were performed, must be given (see instructions for details).

The manufacturing clause is discussed in Chapter 11. The form's instructions are given in Appendix 3.

## License for Handicapped

This category too is included only on Forms TX and SE (space 8). It refers to a Library of Congress program that provides Braille editions and special recordings of works for the exclusive use of the blind and physically handicapped. To produce such editions, appropriate permission from copyright owners must be obtained. The purpose of this section of the form is to simplify and speed up the permissions process.

The section of the form states:

> Signature of this form at space 10, and a check of one of the boxes here in space 8, constitutes a non-exclusive grant of permission to the Library of Congress to reproduce and distribute solely for the blind and physically handicapped and under the conditions and limitations prescribed by the regulations of the Copyright Office: (1) copies of the work identified in space 1 of this

application in Braille (or similar tactile symbols); or (2) phonorecords embodying a fixation of a reading of the work; or (3) both.

The Library of Congress program already includes a large collection. But for the benefit of blind and other handicapped readers, it would be nice if more works could be added through space 8 on Form TX. However, that is entirely optional. If a license is given, it may be terminated upon 90 days' notice. Further information is provided in Copyright Office Circular R63, which may be obtained from the Copyright Office, Library of Congress, Washington, D.C. 20559.

Before checking a box in space 8, you should first determine whether you have the rights to grant the license it entails.

## Fees and Correspondence

Set forth below is what each of the five forms calls for regarding fees and correspondence (space 9 on Forms TX and SE, space 7 on Forms VA, PA, and SR).

a. *Deposit account (if the registration fee is to be charged to a deposit account established in the Copyright Office, give name and number of account).* For people who have frequent transactions with the Copyright Office, it is possible to establish a deposit account by depositing an amount of money in advance. Copyright Office fees may then be charged against the account, which avoids the inconvenience of making out a check for each application.

The account is not a charge account and must always contain enough to cover the charge involved. For example, if you rely on a depleted deposit account for your registration application fee, the Copyright Office probably would treat your submission as incomplete, thus delaying not only the issuance of a registration but also postponing the effective date of registration.

The criteria for a deposit account are: (1) The initial deposit, and all later deposits, must amount to at least $250; (2) there must be at least 12 transactions a year; and (3) if fees are to be charged against the account, the exact name and number of the account must be given. For further information and an application form, write the Copyright Office and ask for Circular R5, *How to Open and Maintain a Deposit Account in the Copyright Office.*

When a deposit account is not used, a separate payment should accompany the application. For Forms TX, SE, VA, PA, and SR, the registration fee was set by Congress in 1976 at $10. As of this writing, it has not changed.

The Copyright Office has had some problems with bounced checks. In 1981 it announced that when "a check received in payment of the registration fee is returned . . . uncollectible, the Copyright Office will take immediate steps to cancel any registration for which the dishonored check was submitted."

b. *Correspondence (give name and address to which correspondence about this application should be sent).* When the Copyright Office reviews an application for registration, it may need clarification or otherwise wish to correspond about the application. If there is no reply to the Office's correspondence, the file may be closed and the application process may have to be started all over again.

### Certification

Applications for copyright must be signed. The forms (space 10 in Forms TX and SE, space 8 in Forms VA, PA, and SR) provide for the signator to certify that

a. he or she is eligible to submit the application, that is, is (i) the author or (ii) other copyright claimant, or (iii) the owner of an exclusive right, or (iv) an authorized agent of one of those; and
b. that the statements made are correct to the best of the signer's knowledge.

It is a criminal offense knowingly to make a false representation of a material fact in an application for copyright registration, or in any written statement filed in connection with the application [506(e)]. A fine, which can be as high as $2,500, is possible. Also, in some circumstances the knowing falsity could be used, should an infringement suit arise, as a basis for claiming that the registration is valid.

### Address for Return of Certificate

The forms are designed so that the mailing address, as provided by the applicant (space 11 on Forms TX and SE, space 9 on Forms VA, PA, and SR), is ordinarily used in the window envelope in which the certificate of registration is sent. (The application form, when processed and annotated by the Copyright Office, becomes the master sheet for the actual certificate.)

## DEPOSIT OF COPIES OF THE WORK TOGETHER WITH THE APPLICATION

As part of the application process for forms TX, SE, VA, PA, and SR, a copy or copies of the work (or a suitable substitute deposit) is submitted together with the application. The material becomes the property of the government and can serve the collections of the Library of Congress (see Chapter 8). However, the material also is used as part of the registration process in the Copyright Office. For example, if you submitted an application for a work you reported as published in 1970, and the copy of the work showed the date but no copyright notice, you might possibly not be entitled to a copyright (see Chapter 7). There are other situations in which the work can provide relevant information for the Copyright Office in making registration judgments and in evaluating whether the facts given in the application are consistent with those facts ascertainable from the copy submitted; for example, whether the copy submitted contains a "work of authorship" (see Chapter 2). Unless the facts to the contrary are obvious, however, the Copyright Office will have to take your word that it is your work of authorship.

Because of the "inspection" need of the section 408 deposit, there are no total exemptions from the obligation to deposit, as there are in the case of the section 407 deposits considered in Chapter 8. However, that does not mean that the section 408 deposit rules are short and simple. There are four different general rules and many modifications to them, some permissive and some mandatory. Many of the modifications are carved out to fit very particular situations and, as often is true when that is the case, the rules are quite lengthy. A copy of them is included in Appendix 2. Table 12 gives the subject areas of the individual rules and provides references to the rules themselves. Fortunately, most people will deal with only one or two categories and so can avoid most of the complexity.

## GROUP REGISTRATION: FORM GR/CP

Form GR/CP is for use, as an adjunct to forms TX and VA, for a single registration for a group of published works. It allows a person to use a single basic form and a single application fee for a group of works. However, the criteria for eligibility to use this approach are not broad. Here are the tests to be met:

1. each of the works is by the same individual author;
2. all were first published as contributions to periodicals;
3. all were published within a 12-month period;
4. the special copyright notice practices described in Chapter 7 were followed;
5. the application identifies each work separately (including the periodical containing it and the date of first publication); and
6. the deposit for each consists of one copy of the entire issue of the periodical or, in the case of a newspaper, the entire section in which each contribution was published.

Because of the specific copyright notices that are required—item (4) above—it is necessary to plan ahead to use this group registration procedure.

If you wanted to use Form GR/CP and also to maximize eligibility to seek statutory damages and attorney's fees in an infringement suit, you would group the works so as to register each within three months of the date of the first publication of the first in the group (see Chapter 9).

Form GR/CP cannot be used to register a group of unpublished works.

## TABLE 12 REFERENCES TO DEPOSIT RULES FOR REGISTRATION APPLICATIONS*

### I. THE FOUR GENERAL RULES [408(b)]

| Type of Work | Deposit Required |
|---|---|
| 1. Applications with respect to unpublished works | 1. One complete copy or phonorecord |
| 2. Applications with respect to works first published in the U.S. on or after 1/1/78 | 2. Two complete copies or phonorecords of the best edition |
| 3. Applications with respect to works first published in the U.S. before 1/1/78 | 3. Two complete copies or phonorecords of the work as first published |
| 4. Applications with respect to works first published outside the U.S., whenever published. Note: If a work is simultaneously first published within and outside the U.S., the work shall be considered, for registration purposes, to be first published in the U.S. | 4. One complete copy or phonorecord of the work as first published |

### II. MANDATORY AND OPTIONAL DEPARTURES FROM THE FOUR GENERAL RULES

| Topic | Citation to Regulation Subsection |
|---|---|
| A. Definitions: | |
| "Best edition" | 202.20(b)(1); 202.19(b)(1) |
| "Complete" copy or phonorecord | 202.20(b)(2) |
| "Secure test" | 202.20(b)(4) |
| "Unpublished motion pictures" | 202.20(b)(6) |
| B. Published three-dimensional cartographic representations of area, such as globes | 202.20(c)(2)(i)(A) |
| C. Certain published diagrams relating to science, technology, engineering, and architecture | 202.20(b)(2)(i)(B) |
| D. Published greeting cards, postcards, and stationery | 202.20(b)(2)(i)(C) |
| E. Certain lectures, sermons, speeches, and addresses published individually | 202.20(c)(2)(i)(D) |
| F. Published contributions to a collective work | 202.20(c)(2)(i)(E) |
| G. Certain published musical compositions | 202.20(c)(2)(i)(F) |
| H. Certain published multimedia kits | 202.20(c)(2)(i)(G) |
| I. Published or unpublished motion pictures | 202.20(c)(2)(ii); 202.20(b)(6) |
| J. Holograms | 202.20(c)(2)(iii) |
| K. Unpublished pictorial or graphic works | 202.20(c)(2)(iv) |

* The rules are included in Appendix 2.

TABLE 12  REFERENCES TO DEPOSIT RULES FOR REGISTRATION
APPLICATIONS (*Cont.*)

## II. MANDATORY AND OPTIONAL DEPARTURES FROM THE FOUR GENERAL RULES

| Topic | Citation to Regulation Subsection |
|---|---|
| L. Certain published pictorial or graphic works | 202.20(c)(2)(iv) |
| M. Certain commercial prints and labels | 202.20(c)(2)(v) |
| N. Certain published tests; secure tests | 202.20(b)(4); 202.20(c)(2)(vi) |
| O. Certain machine-readable computer programs | 202.20(c)(2)(vii) |
| P. Certain machine-readable data bases | 202.20(c)(2)(vii) |
| Q. Works produced in or on sheetlike material, such as wallpaper, textile fabric, wrapping paper | 202.20(c)(2)(viii) |
| R. Three-dimensional sculptural works | 202.20(c)(2)(ix) |
| S. Certain works reproduced in or on three dimensional objects, such as jewelry, toys, games | 202.20(c)(2)(ix)(A) |
| T. Certain works reproduced by intaglio or relief printing methods on two-dimensional materials such as paper or fabrics | 202.20(c)(2)(ix)(B) |
| U. Three-dimensional cartographic representations of area, such as globes | 202.20(c)(2)(ix)(B) |
| V. Certain works that are part of certain kinds of educational kits | 202.20(c)(2)(ix)(B) |
| W. Certain published works exempt from the deposit requirements of section 407 of the statute | 202.19(c); 202.20(c)(2)(ix)(B) |
| X. Certain published works consisting of multiple parts that are published in a box or similar container of less than a certain size | 202.20(c)(2)(ix)(B) |
| Y. Certain works reproduced on certain three-dimensional containers which can be made adaptable for flat storage and which, when so made, are less than a certain size | 202.20(c)(2)(ix)(B) |
| Z. Certain works fixed or published only as embodied in a soundtrack | 202.20(c)(2)(x) |
| AA. Oversize deposits | 202.20(c)(2)(xi) |
| BB. Provisions for applying for special relief | 202.20(d) |
| CC. Circumstances under which deposits for section 407 may be used to meet section 408 deposit requirements | 202.20(e) |

Earlier in this chapter we reported on a way in which a group of such works sometimes may be registered, with a single application and fee, as part of a collection (see "Number of Works per Registration").

## SUPPLEMENTARY REGISTRATIONS: FORM CA

The purpose of a supplementary registration is to correct or amplify the information on another registration form—TX, PA, VA, SR, GR/CP, or RE. (It is not for use to record the transfer and licensing of copyrights. For that, see Chapter 6.)

A supplementary registration augments, but does not supersede, the earlier registration. It may be made by any of the following persons or their authorized agents: any author of the work, any copyright claimant of the work, or the owner of any exclusive right in the work.

### Corrections

The use of a supplementary registration is appropriate to correct an earlier registration when the information in the earlier registration was incorrect at the time the registration was made and, the regulations add, when "the error is not one that the Copyright Office itself should have recognized." Examples of corrections would be cases in which the work was given the wrong date of publication on the application or where the author's name was incorrectly given.

### Amplifications

A supplementary registration also is appropriate for amplifying an earlier registration (other than an earlier supplementary registration):

1. to clarify information given in the basic registration; or
2. to provide additional information that could appropriately have been given in the basic registration at the time that basic registration was made; or
3. to reflect changes in facts that have occurred since the basic registration was made.

Examples of appropriate amplification statements are (a) providing a coauthor's name, when omitted in the basic registration; (b) clarifying a statement of "additional matter" that was made in the basic registration; and (c) providing a statement noting that the title of the work has been changed.

Although Form CA has separate sections for "corrections" and for "amplifications," the Copyright Office recognizes that the line between the two sometimes may be unclear. Thus, the placement of the information in the wrong category does not make the application form unacceptable.

## Supplementary Registrations and Renewal Registrations

A supplementary registration may not be used as a substitute for a renewal registration, but it may be used to supplement such a registration in the same manner as for other registrations. However, Copyright Office regulations provide that:

1. a supplementary registration is not appropriate to add a renewal claimant; and
2. a supplementary registration to correct a renewal claimant (or the basis of a claim in a basic renewal registration) may be made only if the application for supplementary registration and the applicable fee are received in the Copyright Office within the statutory time limits for the renewal registration.

## RENEWAL REGISTRATIONS: FORM RE

A renewal registration extends an initial 28-year term of U.S. copyright into a renewal term of an additional 47 years. The current copyright law did away with this dual term of copyright for many types of works. However, it was applicable under the 1909 Copyright Act to pre-1978 federally protected works and, for such works, the dual term still applies. See Chapter 5. The second term, for 47 years, is only available if it is (or was) applied for during the right time period.

Renewal registrations are applied for when an eligible work is in its twenty-eighth year of copyright. For works first published (or otherwise federally copyrighted) in the year set forth in the left-hand column of Table 13, a renewal registration, if desired, must be applied for during the period set forth in the right-hand column. The table could continue, ending in the left-hand column with 1977 and in the right-hand column with 12/31/2004–12/31/2005.

The Copyright Office will not extend the time limit for applying for a renewal term. So even just a little late is too late. It is wise to apply long

TABLE 13    APPLICATION DATES FOR COPYRIGHT RENEWAL

| Year Work First Published or Federally Copyrighted | Period within Which to Apply for Renewal Term of Copyright |
|---|---|
| 1954 | 12/31/81–12/31/82 |
| 1955 | 12/31/82–12/31/83 |
| 1956 | 12/31/83–12/31/84 |
| 1957 | 12/31/84–12/31/85 |
| 1958 | 12/31/85–12/31/86 |
| 1959 | 12/31/86–12/31/87 |
| 1960 | 12/31/87–12/31/88 |

before the deadline. Then, if your application has an error that makes it incomplete, you will have time to correct the situation and submit a valid application on time.

Some works are eligible for a renewal registration because the initial term was started through a registration. See Chapter 5. But when the initial copyright term of a work began through publication with copyright notice, an initial registration may not have been obtained. In that case, you must apply for both the initial registration and the renewal registration. Because the double application presents more opportunities for error, and may require more preapplication time to put together the facts and the material to deposit, it is particularly appropriate to begin the process well before the renewal registration period expires.

The renewal application form has eight sections, or "spaces."

The first calls for the name(s) and address(es) of the renewal claimant(s) and for a statement of claim. The instructions accompanying the form explain who is eligible as a renewal claimant, and the "statement" used is expected to be the applicable choice as described in the instructions.

Space 2 of Form RE requests the title of the work in which renewal is claimed. In addition, if the work for which copyright is being renewed was itself a new version of another work, space 2 asks for a general statement of the new matter on which copyright was claimed. If the renewal relates to a contribution to a periodical, information identifying the periodical issue is requested.

Space 3 asks for the name(s) of the author(s) who contributed copyrightable material in which the renewal term is claimed.

Space 4 asks for the original registration number and the name of the original copyright claimant. If the original registration for the work was made for the work in a published form, the date of publication (month, date, and year) is requested. If the original registration was made for the work in an unpublished form, the date of the registration (month, date, and year) is requested.

Space 5 is used for a renewal of a group of works by the same author as contributions to periodicals. Information identifying the contributions and providing data about the periodical issues is requested.

Space 6 and 8 relate to fees, correspondence, and certificate mailing, topics reviewed above in the discussion of forms TX, SE, VA, PA, and SR.

Space 7 is the place where the signator certifies that the statements made are true to the best of his or her knowledge and that he or she is a renewal claimant with respect to the initial copyright or is a duly authorized agent of one.

# 11

# TRANSNATIONAL ASPECTS OF U.S. COPYRIGHT LAW

## U.S. COPYRIGHT PROTECTION FOR NON-U.S. CITIZENS

### Unpublished Works

If an unpublished work is subject to U.S. copyright protection under general copyright criteria, it has that protection while it remains unpublished, regardless of the citizenship or domicile of the author [104(a)].

### Published Works—First Published after 1977

The copyright status of published works depends on U.S. international copyright relations and the status of the author at the time the work is first published. Works first published in 1978 or later are subject to U.S. copyright protection if, at the time the work is published, any of the following are true:

1. the work is first published in the United States;
2. one or more of the authors of the work is a national or domiciliary of the United States;
3. the work is first published in a foreign nation that is a party to the Universal Copyright Convention;
4. one or more of the authors of the work is a national, a domiciliary, or a sovereign authority of a foreign nation that is a party to the Universal Copyright Convention or to another treaty to which the United States is a party;
5. the work comes within the scope of a presidential proclamation extending U.S. copyright protection to nationals, domiciliaries, or the sovereign authority of a foreign nation (or to works first published in that nation);
6. the work is first published by the Organization of American States or by the United Nations or any of its specialized agencies; or
7. one or more of the authors of the work is a stateless person.

By the time all these possibilities have been considered, not a great deal will be excluded from U.S. copyright protection because of nationality considerations. Table 14 lists the status of U.S. copyright relations with various countries. As you will see, it is quite extensive.

### Published Works—Works First Published before 1978

The rules discussed in the preceding section are based on the 1976 Copyright Act, which took effect on January 1, 1978. The 1976 law does not bring into U.S. copyright a work that had gone into the public domain before 1978 [Transitional and Supplementary Provisions, Sec. 103]. Consequently, it is necessary to understand whether a work that was first published before 1978 and outside the United States was protected by U.S. copyright under the law that applied at the time of first publication. This can involve tracing the status of the U.S. law at the time and the application of that law in the context of the U.S. international copyright relations at the time. If often will turn out that U.S. copyright applies. This is because the U.S. copyright law has generally recognized that U.S. copyright protection applies for works authored by a citizen of, or first published within, a country with which the United States had copyright relations at the time of first publication.[1] As Table 14 indicates, the United States has had extensive international copyright relations for a number of years.

Table 14 lists the status of U.S. copyright relations with other countries. Column A indicates that the country named in the first column is a signator to the Universal Copyright Convention (UCC) as enacted at Geneva; column B gives the same information for the Paris revision; column C refers to the Phonogram Convention; and column D refers to the Buenos Aires Convention of 1910. Each column includes the year signed. Column E gives the status of U.S. bilateral relations with particular countries. All of the foregoing information in the table is based on Copyright Circular R38a. Countries marked by an asterisk are members of the Berne Union.

## TABLE 14   U.S. COPYRIGHT RELATIONS

| Country | A | B | C | D | E |
|---|---|---|---|---|---|
| Afghanistan | | | | | None |
| Albania | | | | | None |
| Algeria | UCC-G 73 | UCC-P 74 | | | |
| Andorra | UCC-G 55 | | | | |
| Angola | | | | | Unclear |
| Argentina* | UCC-G 58 | | Ph 73 | BAC 50 | 1934 |
| Australia* | UCC-G 69 | | Ph 74 | | 1918 |
| Austria* | UCC-G 57 | | | | 1907 |
| Bahamas, The* | UCC-G 73 | UCC-P 76 | | | |
| Bahrain | | | | | None |
| Bangladesh | UCC-G 75 | UCC-P 75 | | | |
| Barbados | | | | | Unclear |

## TABLE 14 U.S. COPYRIGHT RELATIONS (Cont.)

| Country | A | B | C | D | E |
|---|---|---|---|---|---|
| Belgium* | UCC-G 60 | | | | 1891 |
| Benin* | | | | | Unclear |
| Bhutan | | | | | None |
| Bolivia | | | | BAC 14 | |
| Botswana | | | | | Unclear |
| Brazil* | UCC-G 60 | UCC-P 75 | Ph 75 | BAC 15 | 1957 |
| Bulgaria* | UCC-G 75 | UCC-P 75 | | | |
| Burma | UCC-G 75 | UCC-P 75 | | | |
| Burundi | | | | | Unclear |
| Cambodia | UCC-G 75 | | | | |
| Cameroon* | UCC-G 73 | UCC-P 74 | | | |
| Canada* | UCC-G 62 | | | | 1924 |
| Cape Verde | | | | | Unclear |
| Central African Republic* | | | | | Unclear |
| Chad* | | | | | Unclear |
| Chile* | UCC-G 55 | | Ph 77 | BAC 55 | 1896 |
| China | | | | | 1904 |
| Colombia | UCC-G 76 | UCC-P 76 | | BAC 36 | |
| Comoros | | | | | Unclear |
| Congo* | | | | | Unclear |
| Costa Rica* | UCC-G 55 | | | BAC 16 | 1899 |
| Cuba | UCC-G 57 | | | | 1903 |
| Cyprus* | | | | | Unclear |
| Czechoslovakia* | | | | | 1927 |
| Denmark* | UCC-G 62 | UCC-P 79 | Ph 77 | | 1893 |
| Djibouti | | | | | Unclear |
| Dominican Republic | | | | BAC 12 | |
| Ecuador | UCC-G 57 | | Ph 74 | BAC 14 | |
| Egypt* | | | | | None |
| El Salvador | | | | | 1908 |
| Equatorial Guinea | | | | | Unclear |
| Ethiopia | | | | | None |
| Fiji* | UCC-G 70 | | Ph 73 | | |
| Finland* | UCC-G 63 | | Ph 73 | | 1929 |
| France* | UCC-G 56 | UCC-P 74 | Ph 73 | | 1891 |
| Gabon* | | | | | Unclear |
| Gambia, The | | | | | Unclear |
| German Democratic Republic* | UCC-G 73 | | | | 1892 |
| Germany, Federal Republic of* | UCC-G 55 | UCC-P 74 | Ph 74 | | 1892 |
| Ghana | UCC-G 62 | | | | |
| Greece* | UCC-G 63 | | | | 1932 |
| Grenada | | | | | Unclear |
| Guatemala | UCC-G 64 | | Ph 77 | BAC 13 | |
| Guinea* | | | | | Unclear |
| Guniea-Bissau | | | | | Unclear |
| Guyana | | | | | Unclear |
| Haiti | UCC-G 55 | | | BAC 19 | |
| Holy See (Vatican)* | UCC-G 55 | | | | |
| Hungary* | UCC-G 71 | UCC-P 74 | Ph 75 | | 1912 |

TABLE 14    U.S. COPYRIGHT RELATIONS (*Cont.*)

| Country | A | B | C | D | E |
|---|---|---|---|---|---|
| Iceland* | UCC-G 56 | | | | |
| India* | UCC-G 58 | | Ph 75 | | 1947 |
| Indonesia | | | | | Unclear |
| Iran | | | | | None |
| Iraq | | | | | None |
| Ireland* | UCC-G 59 | | | | 1929 |
| Israel* | UCC-G 55 | | | | 1948 |
| Italy* | UCC-G 57 | | Ph 77 | | 1892 |
| Ivory Coast* | | | | | Unclear |
| Jamaica | | | | | None |
| Japan* | UCC-G 56 | | | | |
| Jordan | | | | | Unclear |
| Kenya | UCC-G 66 | UCC-P 74 | Ph 76 | | |
| Korea | | | | | Unclear |
| Kuwait | | | | | Unclear |
| Laos | UCC-G 55 | | | | |
| Lebanon* | UCC-G 59 | | | | |
| Lesotho | | | | | Unclear |
| Liberia | UCC-G 56 | | | | |
| Libya* | | | | | Unclear |
| Liechtenstein* | UCC-G 59 | | | | |
| Luxembourg* | UCC-G 55 | | Ph 76 | | 1910 |
| Madagascar* | | | | | Unclear |
| Malawi | UCC-G 65 | | | | |
| Malaysia | | | | | Unclear |
| Maldives | | | | | Unclear |
| Mali* | | | | | Unclear |
| Malta* | UCC-G 68 | | | | |
| Mauritania* | | | | | Unclear |
| Mauritius | UCC-G 68 | | | | |
| Mexico* | UCC-G 57 | UCC-P 75 | Ph 73 | BAC 64 | 1896 |
| Monaco* | UCC-G 75 | UCC-P 74 | Ph 74 | | 1952 |
| Mongolia | | | | | None |
| Morocco* | UCC-G 72 | UCC-P 76 | | | |
| Mozambique | | | | | Unclear |
| Nauru | | | | | Unclear |
| Nepal | | | | | None |
| Netherlands* | UCC-G 67 | | | | 1899 |
| New Zealand* | UCC-G 64 | | Ph 76 | | 1916 |
| Nicaragua | UCC-G 61 | | | BAC 13 | |
| Niger* | | | | | Unclear |
| Nigeria | UCC-G 62 | | | | |
| Norway* | UCC-G 63 | UCC-P 74 | | | 1905 |
| Oman | | | | | None |
| Pakistan* | UCC-G 55 | | | | |
| Panama | UCC-G 62 | | Ph 74 | BAC 13 | |
| Papua New Guinea | | | | | Unclear |
| Paraguay | UCC-G 63 | | | BAC 17 | |
| Peru | UCC-G 63 | | | BAC 20 | |
| Philippines* | | | | | 1948 |
| Poland* | UCC-G 77 | UCC-P 77 | | | 1927 |

TABLE 14   U.S. COPYRIGHT RELATIONS (*Cont.*)

| Country | A | B | C | D | E |
|---|---|---|---|---|---|
| Portugal* | UCC-G 56 | | | | 1893 |
| Qatar | | | | | None |
| Romania* | | | | | 1928 |
| Rwanda | | | | | Unclear |
| San Marino | | | | | None |
| Sao Tome and Principe | | | | | Unclear |
| Saudi Arabia | | | | | None |
| Senegal* | UCC-G 74 | UCC-P 74 | | | |
| Seychelles | | | | | Unclear |
| Sierra Leone | | | | | None |
| Singapore | | | | | Unclear |
| Somalia | | | | | Unclear |
| South Africa* | | | | | 1924 |
| Soviet Union | UCC-G 73 | | | | |
| Spain* | UCC-G 55 | UCC-P 74 | Ph 74 | | 1895 |
| Sri Lanka* | | | | | Unclear |
| Sudan | | | | | Unclear |
| Surinam* | | | | | Unclear |
| Swaziland | | | | | Unclear |
| Sweden* | UCC-G 61 | UCC-P 74 | Ph 73 | | 1911 |
| Switzerland* | UCC-G 56 | | | | 1891 |
| Syria | | | | | Unclear |
| Tanzania | | | | | Unclear |
| Thailand* | | | | | 1921 |
| Togo* | | | | | Unclear |
| Tonga | | | | | None |
| Trinidad and Tobago | | | | | Unclear |
| Tunisia* | UCC-G 69 | UCC-P 75 | | | |
| Turkey* | | | | | None |
| Uganda | | | | | Unclear |
| United Arab Emirates | | m3.6 | | | None |
| United Kingdom* | UCC-G 57 | UCC-P 74 | Ph 73 | | 1891 |
| Upper Volta* | | | | | Unclear |
| Uruguay* | | | | BAC 19 | |
| Venezuela | UCC-G 66 | | | | |
| Vietnam | | | | | Unclear |
| Western Samao | | | | | Unclear |
| Yemen (Aden) | | | | | Unclear |
| Yemen (San'a) | | | | | None |
| Yugoslavia* | UCC-G 66 | UCC-P 74 | | | |
| Zaire* | | | | | Unclear |
| Zambia | UCC-G 66 | | | | |

# MANUFACTURING CLAUSE

For decades, the so-called manufacturing clause has been a feature of U.S. copyright law. Its purpose has been to provide some protection for the U.S. printing industry. The means used have varied over the years: The 1909 act was amended in this respect in 1919, 1949, 1955, and 1976.[2]

## The 1976 Copyright Law

*General.* The copyright law passed in 1976 restricts the importation into the United States of certain works manufactured outside the United States or in Canada [601(a)]. When the clause is applicable, the general rule is that copies of a work that fail to meet the manufacturing requirements may not be imported or publicly distributed in the United States [601(a)]. There are, however, a number of important exceptions to that general rule.

The manufacturing clause only restricts importations before July 1, 1982 [601(a)], but a bill is pending in Congress to keep the clause in effect. Under the 1976 law, the Register of Copyrights was asked to report to Congress in 1981 on whether that time limit should be extended or other provisions made.[3] The Register's report recommended that no change be made and that the manufacturing clause be allowed to expire.

*Works Covered.* To be subject to the manufacturing clause currently in effect, the work must consist at least preponderantly of nondramatic literary material in the English language that is protected by U.S. copyright law [601(a)].

The term "preponderantly" recently became an issue before a federal district court in New York.[4] The case involved a book that combined textual and photographic materials. The U.S. Customs Service had refused to allow the importation of copies on the grounds that the work consisted "preponderantly"—in terms of importance—of "nondramatic literary" material. The federal court overruled the decision, declaring that a subjective test as to the importance of the literary material was inappropriate; instead, a quantitative test should have been applied. Because only a minor portion of the work as whole was taken up with text, the photographs accounting for far more of the space, the limits on importation were removed.

Even when a work does consist preponderantly of "nondramatic, etc.," material, the manufacturing clause is inapplicable if either of the following is true: (1) the work is not a work made for hire and the author of any substantial part of the "nondramatic, etc.," material is not a citizen or domiciliary of the United States, or (2) the author of any substantial part of the "nondramatic, etc.," material is a citizen of the United States, but has been domiciled outside of the United States continuously for a year or more [601(b)(1)]. The author's status is evaluated at the time importation of the work is sought or when public distribution is made in the United States [601(b)(1)].

The work made for hire exception provided for in item 1 above applies only if a substantial part of the work was prepared for an employer (or other person) who is not a national or domiciliary of the United States or a domestic corporation or enterprise [601(b)(1)].[5]

*Manufacturing Criteria.* To meet the manufacturing criteria when the manufacturing clause is applicable, the printing (or other final process of producing copies) and any binding of the copies of the "nondramatic, etc.," material must be done in the United States or in Canada [601(c)(3)].

If the copies of the "nondramatic, etc.," material are printed directly from type that has been set or directly from plates made from such type, the setting of the type and the making of the plates must be performed in the United States or in Canada [601(c)(1)]. Alternatively, if the making of the plates by a lithographic or photoengraving process is a final or intermediate step preceding the printing, the making of the plates must have been performed in the United States or in Canada [601(c)(2)]. By virtue of this latter clause, reproduction proofs may be imported without incurring manufacturing clause problems, as long as the plates from which the copies of the materials are themselves made in the United States or in Canada and the printing or binding takes place in the United States or in Canada.[6]

*Import Restrictions.* Although, in general, copies of a work that fail to meet the manufacturing requirements may not be imported or publicly distributed in the United States [601(a)], the copyright owner may—once a work is registered—obtain an import statement from the Copyright Office that authorizes the import of up to 2,000 copies [601(b)(2)]. Copyright Office Form IS, *Request for Issuance of an Import Statement,* is used. It is a short form, asking for identification of the work (title, name of author, name of copyright claimant[s]); the name and address of the person in whose name the import statement should be issued; and a certification statement. The application fee is $3 [708(a)(7)].

*Effect on Copyright.* Violation of the current law's importation-distribution limitations does not result in a loss of copyright. However, an infringer whose infringing copies are manufactured in the United States or in Canada can, under defined circumstances, have a defense against the infringement suit if the import or distribution limitations have been violated by the copyright owner [601(d)].

### The Pre-1978 Copyright Law

Under the manufacturing clauses that existed in the U.S. copyright law between 1909 and 1977, loss of U.S. copyright arguably could result if a work covered by the clause was not manufactured in the United States [7] If loss occurs, the new law does not revive the copyright [Transitional and Supplementary Provisions, Sec. 103].

## IMPORT RESTRICTIONS UNRELATED TO THE MANUFACTURING CLAUSE

### Certain Reproduced Copies

The statute provides that: "In a case where the making of copies or phonorecords would have constituted an infringement of copyright if this title [i.e., the 1976 Copyright Act] had been applicable, their importation is prohibited" [602(b)].

### Unauthorized Imports

When copies or phonorecords of a work have been acquired outside the United States, their importation into the United States is within the U.S. copyright owner's general right of public distribution even if the copies or phonorecords were lawfully made outside the United States [602(a)]. There are three circumstances in which the importation may be made without the copyright owner's permission and without violating the copyright owner's right of public distribution.

A *personal use* exception applies when the importation is for the private use of the person doing the importing and not for distribution. The exception covers copies or phonorecords forming part of the individual's personal baggage. When the person doing the importing is already in the United States, the exception covers no more than one copy or phonorecord of any one work at any one time [602(a)(2)].

A *governmental* exception covers copies or phonorecords imported under the authority of, or for the use of, a local or state government or the federal government. The exception does not go so far as to include copies or phonorecords for use in schools. Also, copies of audiovisual works are not covered by this exception if they are imported for purposes other than archival use [602(a)(1)].

An exception for *certain scholarly, educational*, or *religious* purposes applies if the copies or phonorecords are imported for one of those purposes and not for private gain. Also, the copies must be imported by or for an organization operated for one or more of the three stated purposes. The exception applies to no more than one copy of audiovisual works, for the organization's archives. With respect to works of another type, the exception applies to no more than five copies (or phonorecords) for the organization's lending library or archives. Even then, the exception does not apply if the importation is part of an activity consisting of a systematic reproduction or distribution engaged in by the organization in violation of the library re-production and distribution provisions of subsection 108(g)(2) of the Copy-right Act [602(a)(3)]. Subsection 108(g)(2) is considered in Chapter 15.

## COPYRIGHT LAWS OF OTHER COUNTRIES

The copyright laws of other countries are not within the scope of this book. Copyright law is a territorial concept, and each nation has its own rules. Nonetheless, the concepts and rights are often similar to or compatible with U.S. standards. (One of the typical differences between U.S. copyright law and the copyright laws of other countries is that most other countries do not have the formal copyright notice and registration provisions of the U.S. law. However, works published in other countries often will bear a copyright notice, in part because of the U.S. law provisions discussed in Chapter 7.)

The Bureau of National Affairs and UNESCO publish an English-language compilation of copyright statutes and treaties—Copyright Laws and Treaties of the World—for reference purposes. An updated supplement is generally published every year.

## INTERNATIONAL TREATIES

The material that follows is taken, substantially verbatim except for deletions, from Copyright Office Circular 38. Material in brackets is not taken from the circular.

### The Universal Copyright Convention

The Universal Copyright Convention (the UCC) is an international treaty to which the United States is a party. The UCC, as drafted at Geneva in 1952, came into force on September 16, 1955. The UCC, as revised at Paris in 1971, came into force on July 10, 1974.

As a general rule, the UCC requires a participating country to give the same protection to foreign works that meet the Convention requirements as it gives to its own domestic works. To qualify for protection under the Convention, a work must have been written by a national of a participating country, or must have been published for the first time in a participating country.

### The Berne Convention

The Berne Convention of 1886 and its five revisions (Paris,1896; Berlin,1908; Rome,1928; Brussels,1948; Paris,1971) have established the International Union for the Protection of Literary and Artistic Works, better known as the Berne Union.[8] Protection under these conventions is extended without formalities to works by nationals of any country on the sole condition that first publication take place in a country that belongs to the Berne Union.

[Note: The United States is not a member of the Berne Union. With the 1976 Copyright Act, it took a major step toward eligibility by making changes in portions of its domestic law (e.g., the copyright duration rules) that were barriers to entry, but some blocks still remain. Many, if not all, of the countries that are members of the Berne Union also are parties to the Universal Copyright Convention, or otherwise have copyright relations with the United States. In part because the overlap is not complete, U.S. works sometimes are published "simultaneously" in the United States and in a Berne Union country so as to obtain some union benefits. This practice is sometimes called the "back door" to Berne.]

## The Buenos Aires Convention of 1910

This convention has been ratified by the United States and 17 Latin American nations. It specifies that authors of any contracting country who have secured copyright in their own country will enjoy in each of the other countries the rights it accords its own works, if the work contains "a statement indicating the reservation of the property right."

## The Phonogram Convention

The Phonogram Convention, or the Convention for the Protection of Producers of Phonograms against Unauthorized Duplication of Their Phonograms, came into force in 1973. Adhering countries provide international protection against the making or importation of unauthorized duplicates of phonograms (sound recordings) for distribution to the public.

# 12

# REMEDIES FOR COPYRIGHT INFRINGEMENT

The principal remedies in a civil action for copyright infringement are:

1. an injunction against the infringing activity;
2. recovery of actual damages;
3. recovery of the infringer's profits arising from the infringement;
4. recovery of statutory damages; and
5. recovery of reasonable attorney's fees in the infringement action.

We will consider each of these in this chapter. Also, in this chapter, two tables list these and other sanctions, civil and criminal, provided for violations of the copyright law. See Tables 15 and 16.

Generally speaking, an infringer is one who "violates any of the exclusive rights of the copyright owner as provided by sections 106 through 118 or who imports unauthorized copies in violation of section 602 [501(a)]."

A person may be liable as an infringer not only by directly infringing but also by being responsible for the acts of employees. Also, there are standards for what is called vicarious infringement and for contributory infringement.

Concerning vicarious infringement, the legislative history states, in the context of performance rights:

> A well-established principle of copyright law is that a person who violates any of the exclusive rights of the copyright owner is an infringer, including persons who can be considered related or vicarious infringers. To be held a related or vicarious infringer in the case of performing rights, a defendant must either actively operate or supervise the operation of the place wherein the performances occur, or control the content of the infringing program, and expect commercial gain from the operation and either direct or indirect benefit from the infringing performance.[1]

A recent case, involving home videorecording equipment, used this standard for contributory infringement:

> [O]ne who, with knowledge of the infringing activity, induces, causes, or

## TABLE 15   CIVIL REMEDIES

| Remedy | References* |
|---|---|
| 1. Injunction | 502; 510(a) |
| 2. Actual damages | 504(a),(b); 510(a) |
| 3. Infringer's profits from the infringement | 504(a),(b); 510(a) |
| 4. Statutory damages | 504(a),(c); 510(a) |
| 5. Costs of suit | 505; 510(a) |
| 6. Attorney's fees | 505; 510(a) |
| 7. Impoundment of infringing material | 503(a); 510(a) |
| 8. Destruction or disposition of infringing material | 503(b); 510(a) |
| 9. Suspension of right to compulsory license (cable system) | 510(b) |
| 10. Importation exclusions | 602(b); 603 |
| 11. Limited remedies against the U.S. Government | 505, 28 U.S.C. 1498 |

* Denotes sections of the 1976 Copyright Act except for the reference in item 11 to Title 28 of the United States Code.

materially contributes to the infringing conduct of another, may be held liable as a "contributory" infringer.[2]

In this case, a federal district court ruled that contributory infringement had not taken place because the equipment was a "staple article of commerce." The court stated:

Selling of a staple article of commerce—e.g., a typewriter, a recorder, a camera, a photocopying machine—technically contributes to any infringing use subsequently made thereof, but this kind of "contribution," if deemed sufficient as a basis for liability, would expand the theory beyond precedent and arguably beyond judicial management.

The federal appeals court that later reviewed the case decided that videotape recorders did not qualify as a staple article of commerce because, in the court's view, they were not suitable for substantial noninfringing use.[3]

## COMMENCEMENT OF A COPYRIGHT INFRINGEMENT SUIT

### Who May Sue

The owner of an exclusive right of copyright is entitled to sue for any infringement of that right committed while he or she is the owner of it [501]. Either the legal owner or the beneficial owner may bring the suit. According to the legislative history, the "beneficial owner" would be, for example, an author who parted with legal title in exchange for royalties based on sales or license fees.[4]

## TABLE 16   CRIMINAL LAW SANCTIONS

| Sanction | References* |
| --- | --- |
| 1. Criminal infringement generally: | |
| Fine | 506(a) |
| Imprisonment | 506(a) |
| Forfeiture | 506(b) |
| Destruction or disposition of infringing material | 506(b); 509; 603 |
| 2. Fraudulent copyright notice—a fine | 506(c) |
| 3. Fraudulent removal of copyright notice—a fine | 506(d) |
| 4. False representation, copyright registration applications—a fine | 506(e) |
| 5. Fraudulent activity, jukebox license—a fine | 116(d) |
| 6. Phonograph records, counterfeit labels | 18 U.S.C. 2318 |

* Denotes sections of the 1976 Copyright Act, except for the reference in item 6 to Title 18 of the United States Code. As of this writing, legislation is proposed to increase the sanctions for record, film, and tape piracy and related counterfeit labeling (S. 691).

In the case of certain infringements by means of secondary transmissions by cable systems, the statute sometimes allows a broadcast station or the primary transmitter to sue even if the station does not own an exclusive right of copyright [501(c),(d)].

### Copyright Law Requirements for Commencement of Suit

For a copyright infringement action to commence, a claim of copyright in the work ordinarily must have first been registered in the Copyright Office [411].

The specific statutory exceptions to the register-before-suit standard have already been considered in Chapter 9. In a recent case where these exceptions were not applicable, a court nevertheless allowed the registration to be made after commencement; however, one could not count on this to occur in all cases.

If the copyright owner claiming the infringement became the owner as the result of a transfer of ownership, the person is not entitled to sue unless "the instrument of transfer under which such person claims" has been recorded in the Copyright Office [205(d)]. Again, one court recently made an exception, but other courts will not necessarily follow that lead. It remains to be seen whether only the transfer to the person suing need be recorded before commencement of the suit, or whether earlier transfer papers in the chain of title also must be recorded.

Another copyright law formality for the commencement of the lawsuit exists when the so-called manufacturing clause requirements apply and the suit is for infringement of reproduction and distribution rights. In such situations, manufacturing data about the work infringed should be included in the complaint [601(a),(e)]. The manufacturing clause provisions, which apply only to a narrow class of works, were considered in Chapter 11.

Copyright infringement suits should be commenced within three years after the claim for infringement accrued [507(b)].

Claims arising under the copyright statute are subject to federal jurisdiction. Contract disputes involving copyrights sometimes will not qualify, for purposes of establishing federal jurisdiction, as claims "arising" under the copyright statute.

In a copyright infringement suit, if another person has a claim or interest in the copyright being sued upon, the court may order the person bringing the suit to serve written notice of it on that other person [501(b)].

A provision in the statute requires the clerks of the courts to provide notifications about copyright infringement cases (and about final orders and judgments) to the Copyright Office for inclusion in the Office's public records [508].

## INJUNCTIONS

The copyright law gives the court the power to grant temporary and final injunctions to prevent or restrain infringement of copyright [502(a)]. Temporary injunctions, when sought, are usually sought early in the case, before it is fully ready for trial. In determining whether to grant temporary injunctions, the court takes into account the strength of the proof that infringement has indeed occurred and, in some cases, the relative harm that will be caused the respective parties should the temporary injunction be granted or denied pending the final outcome of the litigation.

The injunction remedy is not available against the U.S. government or, in some cases, against infringements arising under federal contracts. In these circumstances, the copyright owner's remedy is for the recovery of reasonable compensation.[5]

## ACTUAL DAMAGES

The court may award the copyright owner an amount equal to the actual damages caused the owner as a result of the infringement [504(a)]. It often is difficult to prove what the actual damages are. For example, only part of the plaintiff's work may have been used as only part of the defendant's work; thus, it may be very difficult to select an exact figure for the amount of financial harm caused.

## DEFENDANT'S PROFITS

One of the remedies for copyright infringement is the right to recover any profits of the infringer that are attributable to the infringement and are not taken into account in computing the actual damages. The copyright owner's obligation is merely to establish the infringer's gross revenue. It is the infringer's burden to prove what the deductible expenses were and also to prove the elements of profit, if any, that were attributable to factors other than the infringed work [504(b)].

The legislative history reports as follows on the relationship between a recovery of actual damages and an award of defendant's profits:

> Damages are awarded to compensate . . . for losses from the infringement, and profits are awarded to prevent the infringer from unfairly benefiting from a wrongful act. Where the defendant's profits are nothing more than a measure of the damages suffered by the copyright owner, it would be inappropriate to award damages and profits cumulatively. . . . However, in cases where the copyright owner has suffered damages not reflected in the infringer's profits, or where there have been profits attributable to the copyrighted work but not used as a measure of damages, subsection (b) authorizes the award of both.[6]

## STATUTORY DAMAGES

As noted earlier, it sometimes is difficult to establish what the actual damages in a case are. Also, the infringer's profits attributable to the infringement may be uncertain or nonexistent. Recognizing these possibilities, the statute allows the copyright owner to elect to recover "statutory" damages instead of actual damages and the infringer's profits. The statutory damages provision permits the court to make an award of from $100 to $50,000, a range we will consider later on. The election of the statutory damages remedy may be made at any time before final judgment is rendered [501(c)(1)]. As discussed in Chapter 9, statutory damages sometimes can be unobtainable if the infringement took place before registration of the work infringed.

For all the infringements in the lawsuit with respect to any one work, the general rule is that the statutory damage award, if made, should be not less than $250 and not more than $10,000 [504(c)(1)]. However, some special rules extend this range in certain cases:

1. If the copyright owner proves that the infringement was committed "willfully," the amount of the statutory damage award may be increased to as much as $50,000 [504(c)(2)].
2. If the infringer proves that he or she was not aware, and had no reason to believe, that his or her acts constituted an infringement, the court, in its discretion, may reduce the award of statutory damages to as low as $100 insofar as that infringer is concerned [504(c)(2)].
3. If the infringer was an employee or agent of a nonprofit educational institution, library, or archives, acting within the scope of his or her employment, the court will not order the award of statutory

damages if the work was infringed by reproducing it, and the person believed and had reasonable grounds for believing that his or her use of the copyrighted work was a fair use under section 107 of the law. The standards in this paragraph also apply if the institution itself is being sued, rather than or in addition to the individual [504(c)(2)].

4. The court will not award statutory damages if the infringer is a public broadcasting entity (or a person acting as a regular part of the entity's nonprofit activities) that infringed copyright by performing a published nondramatic literary work or by reproducing a transmission program of such a work, provided that the infringer believed, and had reasonable grounds for believing, that the use was a fair use under section 107 [118(g) "public broadcasting entity"; 504(c)(2)].

When statutory damages are authorized, a court ordinarily may only make one statutory damage award with respect to the infringement of a single work [504(c)(1)]. The legislative history indicates that the general rule is not affected merely because there is (1) more than one infringement, or (2) more than one right of copyright infringed, or (3) more than one copyright owner involved, or (4) more than one infringer involved.[7] On the other hand, separate statutory damage awards may be made in the case of separate infringements by persons who are not jointly liable.[8]

When multiple works are involved, the statutory damage range applies to each. However, for these purposes, the legislative history states that all the parts of a compilation or derivative work are considered to constitute one work [504(c)(1)].[9]

One of the unsettled issues about statutory damages is whether a defendant is entitled to a jury trial if statutory damages are the only relief sought or the only relief in addition to injunctive relief.[10]

## ATTORNEY'S FEES

In an infringement suit, the court may, in its discretion, award a reasonable attorney's fee to the prevailing party [505]. However, as discussed in Chapter 9, not all infringements can be met with an award of attorney's fees. Registration for the infringed work must have occurred at the right time in relation to the infringement.

## IMPOUNDMENT

During a copyright action, the court has the power to order impoundment of materials claimed to have been made or used in violation of the copyright owner's exclusive rights. In its final judgment, the court may order destruction of copies, plates, etc. [503].

# 13

## FAIR USE: SECTION 107

The fair use of a copyrighted work is not an infringement of copyright. Fair use generally allows such activities as:

quotations of excerpts in a review or criticism for purposes of illustration or comment;

quotations of short passages in a scholarly or technical work for illustration or clarification of the author's observations;

summary of an address or article, with brief quotations, in a news report;

incidental and fortuitous reproduction in a broadcast of a work located in the scene of an event being reported; and

reproduction of a work in legislative or judicial proceedings.[1]

Fair use has been part of U.S. copyright law, as a judicial doctrine, for more than a century. George Washington, who signed the first U.S. copyright law, was involved in one of the first fair-use cases, albeit posthumously. A minister had prepared a book, *Life of Washington in the Form of an Autobiography*, with more than one-third of its 866 pages consisting of many of Washington's letters and of other documents that had appeared in an earlier 7,000-page work entitled *Writings of Washington*. An 1841 court decided that the minister's book went beyond a "justifiable use" of the larger work.[2] The general criteria used in that 1841 case were quite similar to those in use today, while the "fair use" label has been used since at least 1869.[3] Fair use prevailed as a judicial doctrine until the enactment of the 1976 Copyright Law, when it was codified into section 107.

In incorporating the doctrine into statutory language, Congress intended to maintain the rule as it had developed over the decades, including the flexible nature of the standard. Here is how the legislative history reports the congressional intent:

The bill endorses the purpose and general scope of the judicial doctrine of fair use, but there is no disposition to freeze the doctrine in the statute, especially during a period of rapid technological change. Beyond a very broad statutory explanation of what fair use is and some of the criteria applicable to it, the courts must be free to adapt the doctrine to particular situations on a case by case basis. Section 107 is intended to restate the present judicial doctrine of fair use, not to change, narrow, or enlarge it in any way.[4]

Each of us undoubtedly has superb notions of fairness, but they are not always the same notions. The job of the courts and the statute is to try to make it possible for us to operate under some common notions of what is fair use. Because the doctrine is deliberately imprecise, the task is not perfectly achievable, or even nearly so, but that does not mean there are no guidelines at all.

## STATUTORY FACTORS AFFECTING FAIR-USE DECISIONS

As an aid in resolving particular fair-use cases, the legislature adopted four criteria, derived from the court cases:

1. the amount and substantiality of the portion used in relation to the copyrighted work as a whole;
2. the effect of the use upon the potential market for or value of the copyrighted work;
3. the purpose and character of the use; and
4. the nature of the copyrighted work.[5]

These factors are not the only ones that can properly be taken into account in deciding whether or not a use is a fair use,[6] but they ordinarily serve as big enough umbrellas to cover everything that is relevant. We will take a closer look at these four factors.

### Extent of Use

The extent of use can be measured in five different ways:

1. the quantity of copyrighted material taken;
2. the quantity of material taken in proportion to the work it was taken from;
3. the quantity of material taken in proportion to the work in which it was used;
4. the significance of the material taken relative to the work it was taken from; and
5. the significance of the material taken relative to the work in which it is reused.

When the extent of the use is significant in all five respects, the above criteria might translate into colloquial terms such as: "You took a lot of my stuff and a good portion of the total, added very little of your own, left out only the most incidental aspects of my work, and used my stuff as the heart of yours." Often, the case is less one-sided.

Except for some "fair use in education" guidelines (to be considered in Chapter 14), no official mathematical rules exist for determining how much may be safely used under fair use. It all depends upon the context and the circumstances. For example, let us suppose that you are taking less than 1 percent of another work. That seems like a small amount; it becomes more significant, however, if, say, the work taken becomes 30 percent of your work. Or, you may be taking only 25 words, but they are 25 words from a short poem.

## Effect of Use on Value of Work Used

The more that reuse of a work is likely to affect adversely the potential market for, or value of, the work, the more likely it is that fair use will not be available. However, this factor is not meant to be applied so as narrowly to restrain criticism.

The legislative history states that this "effect on value" factor

> must almost always be judged in conjunction with the other three criteria. With certain special exceptions (use in parodies or as evidence in court proceedings might be examples) a use that supplants any part of the normal market for a copyrighted work would ordinarily be considered an infringement.[7]

## Purpose and Character of Use

One of the reasons for the fair-use doctrine is that we recognize that there can be some very good reasons to make some reasonable use of another's copyrighted work. For example, people should be able to use brief excerpts from a work for purposes of criticism without having to obtain the copyright owner's consent. Similarly, we recognize that knowledge builds upon what has gone before, and we want scholars to be able to quote from previous works to a reasonable extent without having to have permission. Those two purposes—criticism and scholarship—have been expressly recognized in the statute, as have teaching, research, commentary, and news reporting. Some other purposes, such as parody, also have favorable potential. An officially blessed purpose, however, is not an unlimited credit line—it is more like having an account that may not be large enough for all your needs. The size of your fair-use account depends not just on the purpose, but on other fair-use factors as well.

A commercial purpose can operate as a detriment to a fair-use determination. However, in our society, fair use would be of extremely limited application if the presence of any commercial purpose was always fatal, especially if we equated "commercial purpose" with "purpose of monetary gain."

Fair-use cases turn on a combination of factors and, as a result, it is difficult to make unequivocal statements about any particular factor. However, it seems reasonable to conclude that the courts recognize that the degree of commerciality is relevant in fair-use determinations. Here is a recent case in which a commercial purpose helped to bring about a decision of no fair use. The case involved an article, in a general-interest magazine, on why people fall in love. The article referred to many scholarly materials, including those of a professor of social psychology. His doctoral dissertation included a "love scale" and a "liking scale" that contained questions designed to elicit a person's feeling about another. The magazine article used the scales verbatim within a large box captioned "The Test of Love. How to Tell If It's Really Real." The federal district and appeals courts in Massachusetts each rejected the fair-use defense, the appellate court stating, among other points:

> The defendants' claim that their purpose "was to acquaint the community with research" is belied by the format and the contents of the alleged infringing publication. They irrefutably showed that the copyrighted material was used as a quiz to entertain readers of a magazine of general circulation. Plainly, the district judge correctly concluded that the defendants' use of the plaintiff's copyright was "of a commercial nature."[8]

The statutory standard of fair use calls for a consideration of the "character" of the use as well as the purpose. Here is an example, from a few years back, of how the "character" of a use may become a factor. The case concerned a consumer magazine that had just issued a report commenting adversely on an aspect of a particular company's microwave oven. A few years earlier, the magazine had included a favorable comment on the same aspect. After the later article was published, the manufacturer issued a brochure quoting from the earlier article but not mentioning the more current comment. The court found the use not to be a fair one.[9]

## Nature of the Copyrighted Work

Some types of works, such as reference works and public speeches, "invite" a degree of fair use. Other types of works almost implicitly contain a warning that fair use should proceed with some caution. For example, the application of fair use to unpublished letters would, under ordinary circumstances, be very narrow. Still other works, because of their compactness, suggest narrow limits of fair use, poems and songs, for example. But, again, there are no absolute rules.

## FAIR USE AND THE FIRST AMENDMENT

The First Amendment to the U.S. Constitution provides: "Congress shall make no law . . . abridging the freedom of speech, or of the press. . . ."[10]

Some conflict potentially exists between copyright law—which itself has a constitutional base—and the First Amendment. The tension is reduced by the copyright law's distinction between copyright-unprotected "ideas" and protectible "expression." It also is reduced by the fair-use doctrine.

During the last 15 years or so, it has been quite common, in copyright infringement cases, for a First Amendment defense to be raised under circumstances where, in earlier times, a fair-use defense alone might have been asserted. Thus far, the courts have found either that neither defense was entitled to prevail or that fair use sufficed to resolve the particular case.

## RECENT FAIR-USE CASES

One good approach to fair-use deliberations is to try to place yourself in the other person's position. This provides a useful perspective, though it is one most easily obtained by those, such as publishers and authors, who are sometimes on one side of the fence and sometimes on the other.

Another way to gain perspective for fair use is to obtain some familiarity with what has happened in some court decisions. The following brief reports are truncated, noting aspects of interest rather than providing a comprehensive summary.

### Commercial Use Cases

A company operated stores that sold, among other things, consumer electronics equipment. In one of its humorous television commercials, it copied from a "Superman" television series. Sued for infringement, it raised the defense of fair use through parody. The court ruled against the company, concluding that the commercial represented

> a detailed copying of the plaintiff's . . . [material], the only variations occurring when defendant's name and business purpose is substituted for the Superman character's name and purpose. . . . I find that defendant's commercial is not parody. This is not a case of fair use, but one of unjustifiable appropriation of copyrighted material for personal profit [11]

The commercial purpose in that case was a strong factor in the decision, as it was in another recent case involving a cable television network that videotaped Boston Red Sox baseball games and Boston Bruins hockey games off the air. The cable network used brief segments of the videotapes as part of a program of sports highlights which it distributed to cable systems. The station that telecast the games sued for copyright infringement. The cable network raised the fair-use defense, asserting that it applied because only brief excerpts were used for news purposes. A federal district court in Massachusetts ruled against the defense, noting, among other points, that the excerpts used, "although of relatively short duration, are of the 'high-

lights' of each broadcast and as such their use may be considered substantial."[12]

A commercial purpose is not always fatal to the fair-use defense. For example, the defense prevailed recently for a market research company's use of television commercials. The company videotaped some commercials off the air. It then prepared survey questionnaires that used five or six isolated frames from a given commercial and contained a series of questions about the commercial being tested. The questionnaires were sent to randomly selected households and the results received were tabulated and analyzed. The results of the studies reportedly enabled researchers to evaluate the strengths and weaknesses of various advertising concepts and commercials. The research company provided the raw data to academic researchers and also made the data and survey reports available to advertisers and others.

A federal district court in California found the research company's use of the commercials to be fair use. The court noted, among other things, that "deriving a profit from a subsequent use does not render such use unfair." The court also relied on its judgment that the use was not in competition with the commercials and did not lessen the value of those copyrighted works.[13]

Another case where a commercial purpose proved not to be fatal involved a "comparative advertising" television commercial. A newspaper, in promoting its new Sunday TV supplement, showed a cover of an older issue of *TV Guide*, by way of comparison with the larger-format supplement. A federal appellate court ruled that the use was a fair use.[14]

## Parody

In the electronics store commercial mentioned above, the defense of fair use through parody was unsuccessful. On the other hand, the parody defense recently prevailed in a case involving a skit aired in 1978 on the television program "Saturday Night Live." The state and city of New York had been conducting a promotional ad campaign, using the theme, and the themesong, "I Love New York." As the federal district court judge described the situation:

> The success of the campaign did not go unnoticed in the entertainment world. . . . [T]he popular weekly variety program "Saturday Night Live" ("SNL") performed a comedy sketch over defendant National Broadcasting Company's network. In this sketch the cast of SNL, portraying the mayor and the members of the city Chamber of Commerce of the biblical city of Sodom, are seen discussing Sodom's poor public image with out of towners, and the effect this was having on the tourist trade. In an attempt to recast the City's image in a more positive light, a new advertising campaign emphasizing the less sensational aspects of Sodom's life is unveiled. As the highlight of this campaign the song "I Love Sodom" is sung *a cappella* by a chorus line of

three SNL regulars to the tune of "I Love New York," with the words "I Love Sodom" repeated three times.[15] [footnotes omitted]

The court found the skit to be permissible fair use through parody. The appellate court agreed, stating: "Believing that, in today's world of often unrelieved solemnity, copyright law should be hospitable to the humor of parody, and that the District Court correctly applied the doctrine of fair use, we affirm Judge Goettell's thorough opinion."[16]

In the SNL decision, the parody was upheld both as a parody of the copyrighted song and as a satire of "the way in which New York City has attempted to improve its somewhat tarnished image through the use of a slick advertising campaign." However, another recent case took the position that the defense of parody works only if the parody is of the copyrighted work itself.[17]

In the SNL case, the material taken from the copyrighted work was characterized as "significant" but not "extensive." One of the risks of parody is that the parodist may take too much of the work being parodied. A federal appellate court in New York recently commented:

Suffice it to say that while the [parody] defense might be applicable to those isolated instances in which a nearly identical line from the plaintiff's script or express reference to one of the plaintiff's characters was made, we question whether the defense could be used to shield an entire work that is substantially similar to and in competition with the copyrighted work.[18]

In several recent cases, the parody defense has been rejected because the claimed parody adhered too closely to, and took too much from, the original.[19] Several of the recent cases in which the parody defense has been unsuccessful happened to include sexual references that some would find distasteful. Those references may not have controlled the results in terms of copyright law theory, but they may have had a significant practical effect on the legal outcome in at least some of the cases.[20]

## News Reporting

In the cable system case mentioned earlier, the defense of fair use through news reporting was unsuccessful for the sports highlight segments. Here are three other recent "news reporting" cases, in two of which the defense of fair use prevailed.

A financial newspaper was regularly using copyrighted research reports of brokerage houses; its use included significant excerpts from the reports, to the degree that a federal district court in New York concluded that the newspaper's reports sufficed to substitute for the original reports. The defense of fair use was rejected.[21]

A television crew filmed the annual San Gennaro Festival in Manhattan. The film included a float upon which a band was playing a copyrighted song. Portions of the film, including the song, were aired on the television news that evening. A company claiming copyright ownership in the song sued for infringement. A federal district court in New York ruled that fair use applied.[22]

A 1979 *Newsweek* article, entitled "John Wayne: End as a Man," used six quotations that had been included in a book, *Guts and Glory—Great American War Movies*. The author of the book sued for copyright infringement. He did not claim copyright ownership in the quotes themselves—others had said them—but rather contended that his selection and arrangement of the quotations were entitled to protection and were infringed. The court concluded that there was not sufficient appropriation to constitute infringement, as the material copied amounted to a very small part of plaintiff's book.[23]

## Feature Programs and Articles

In two recent cases, one involving a program making Charlie Chaplin's death and the other involving a feature story about a college wrestler, the fair-use defense was found wanting.[24]

Charlie Chaplin died in 1977. But, as far back as 1973, CBS had begun work on a retrospective program for use at the time of his death. CBS had made various requests of the copyright owner of some Chaplin films to use excerpts from them. These requests were turned down. When Chaplin died, and CBS decided to air a retrospective program, it had the choice of using only film in the public domain or of including some copyrighted film as well. It elected the latter, and about 40 percent of the film used was in copyright. A jury found copyright infringement. A federal district court in New York was asked to overrule the verdict on the ground that the use was fair use as a matter of law. The court declined.

The wrestling case involved a 28-minute film entitled *Champion*, which was prepared in 1970–1971 about an Iowa University wrestler. The Iowa University Research Foundation was the copyright owner in the film. In 1972 the wrestler concerned was headed for an Olympics medal, and ABC was headed for coverage of the events. ABC admitted three uses of the film: (1) seven to twelve seconds on a pre-Olympic telecast; (2) two and one-half minutes as part of a report on the wrestler before his first Olympic match; and (3) eight seconds in connection with a program, a year and a half later, in which the wrestler was a participant.

The copyright owner sued for infringement and won. Disagreement as to whether ABC had obtained consent was resolved against ABC. In addition, the federal appeals court in New York found fair use inapplicable. Among other things, the court noted that ABC's programming material using the *Champion* excerpts was of the same genre as *Champion* and fulfilled the same function. The court also felt that the amount used was not insignificant, the court observing that ABC "broadcast approximately eight percent of *Champion*. . . ."

An interesting aspect of the case was that the evidence indicated that the market value of the copyright owner's film *increased* after ABC's infringement, in the sense that there was an upsurge in demands for rentals. Remarking on that point, the court stated: "Nevertheless, we believe that ABC did foreclose a significant potential market . . .—sale of [the] film for use on television in connection with the Olympics."

## FAIR USE AND TECHNOLOGICAL APPLICATIONS

The general principles of fair use are as applicable to technological uses— for example, use in conjunction with computers, videotape equipment, and photocopying—as to other uses. Nonetheless, there sometimes is a marked lack of consensus as to how fair use operates in such fields. The opinions of the "referees"—courts and other official bodies—are thus particularly helpful. Set forth below are some recent developments.

### Photocopying

*Pre-1976 Cases.* In a 1962 case, a choir director, without copyright authorization, adapted a copyrighted religious song, reproduced 48 copies of the arrangement on a duplicating machine, and had the arrangement performed, once by a school choir and once by a church choir. Fair use was found inapplicable and he was held to have infringed the copyright.[25]

A decade later came the vastly more complex *Williams & Wilkins* case in the U.S. Court of Claims.[26] A publisher of medical journals sought copyright infringement damages with respect to the article-photocopying practices of the National Library of Medicine and of the National Institutes of Health. The initial judge's decision was infringement; the full Court of Claims' decision, no infringement, by a 4–3 vote. The case went to the U.S. Supreme Court, where the appellate decision was anticlimactically affirmed by an equally divided court, 4–4, with no opinions issued. (In such a situation that action is not a binding precedent for other cases. In any event, it is impossible to tell what principles the Supreme Court precedent stood for, because no opinions were issued and various combinations of several different rationales may have supported the 4–4 tally.)

The *Williams & Wilkins* case involved a combination of numerous facts and theories and does not point unequivocally to a particular result, one way or the other, in a future case. The Court of Claims majority intended it that way. It said its fair-use conclusion rested on all of the elements in the case and not upon any combination less than all. Some of the conclusions underlying the majority's decision were:

1. that the publisher did not show it was being "harmed substantially";

2. that the library and the institutes are nonprofit institutions;
3. that the libraries of both institutions enforced what the court termed "reasonably strict" limitations that kept the copying "within appropriate confines"; and
4. that the problem of accommodating to competing interests calls fundamentally for legislative guidance and, in the period before that is forthcoming, risk of harm should not be placed upon medicine.

*The 1976 Copyright Act.*   The *Williams & Wilkins* decision predates the enactment of the 1976 Copyright Law. Although Congress might have had a great deal to say about the case in the context of the new statute, it did not. The Senate committee report noted:

> It is still uncertain how far a library may go under the Copyright Act of 1909 in supplying a photocopy of copyrighted material in its collection. The recent case of . . . [*Williams & Wilkins*] failed to significantly illuminate the application of the fair use doctrine to library photocopying practices. . . .
>
> While the several opinions in the *Wilkins* case have given the Congress little guidance as to the current state of the law on fair use, these opinions provide additional support for the balanced resolution of the photocopying issue . . . preserved in section 108 by this legislation. As the Court of Claims opinion succinctly stated, "there is much to be said on all sides."[27]

Section 108 is considered in Chapter 15.

Congress included in section 108 a provision requiring the Register of Copyrights to report to Congress by the beginning of 1983, setting forth the extent to which section 108 "has achieved the intended statutory balancing of the rights of creators, and the needs of users." The report also is to "describe any problems that may have arisen, and present legislative or other recommendations, if warranted" [108(i)]. This pending report has had an effect, discussed below, on a national commission's report issued in 1978, concerning photocopying issues.

In addition to the library reproduction provisions of section 108, Congress took photocopying (and other reprographic technologies) into account in the text of section 107 in the context of teaching activities:

> the fair use of a copyrighted work, including such use by reproduction in copies or phonorecords . . . for purposes such as . . . teaching (including multiple copies for classroom use) . . . is not an infringement of copyright.

That aspect of section 107 is considered in Chapter 14.

*National Commission's Report.*   In 1974 Congress established the National Commission on New Technological Uses of Copyrighted Works (CONTU) to study and report to Congress and the president on a number of issues, including on the reproduction and use of copyrighted works by various forms of machine reproduction.[28] The commission issued its final report in July 1978, just seven months after the current copyright law went into effect.

Except for one recommendation concerning commercial copy shops,[29] the commission recommended no changes to the 1976 Copyright Law concerning fair use and photocopying. The absence of experience under the new law was one of the cited reasons.[30] The commission also took into account the fact that the Register of Copyrights would be reporting to Congress on photocopying at the beginning of 1983 and recommended that the Register construe the reporting responsibility broadly and not confine the required study to library photocopying. In particular, CONTU recommended that the Register should examine how the educational and music fair-use guidelines (see Chapter 14) have worked out in practice.[31]

*Court and Other Decisions after 1976.* A few copyright decisions involving photocopying (or other forms of document copying) have been issued since the 1976 Copyright Law took effect. For instance, in 1980, a federal district court in Minnesota enjoined a "yellow pages" directory company from photocopying pages from the similar-purpose directory published by Northwestern Bell. The directory company was using the photocopies as part of its order solicitation papers when seeking advertisers. The court rejected a fair-use defense.[32]

In 1981 some music publishers settled a copyright infringement suit with a college concerning alleged infringements by the college's music department of five Christmas songs. The college reportedly agreed to a payment and to refrain from any further such photocopying.[33]

In 1980 and 1981, some book publishers settled infringement suits with two different commercial copyshop chains. The defendants agreed that before making multiple copies of published copyrighted materials, either they would obtain an express consent from the copyright owner or, if the copying was pursuant to the educational and music fair-use guidelines (see Chapter 14), they would obtain an appropriate certificate to that effect.[34]

In a suit by a hymnal publisher against churches in Chicago (technically, against "Catholic Bishop of Chicago, a corporation") for unauthorized copying from hymn books, the publisher was denied relief because its conduct, in the view of a federal district court in Illinois, was improper. The trial court found improper the publisher's practice of offering a blanket license to the publisher's repertoire without being willing to negotiate licenses for individual songs. An appeals court reversed, ruling that it was not, under the circumstances, improper per se and returned the case to the trial court for further proceedings.[35]

## Computers

The National Commission on New Technological Uses of Copyrighted Works, in its 1978 Final Report, made several comments concerning copyrights and computers.[36] On the subject of placing a copyrighted work into a computer memory solely to facilitate an individual's scholarly research, CONTU concluded:

> that such a use, restricted to individual research, should be considered fair. To prevent abuse of fair use principles, any copy created in a machine memory should be erased after completion of the particular research project for which it was made.

The commission also offered as a fair-use example "the creation of a copy in a computer memory to prepare a concordance of a work or to perform a syntactical analysis of a work, which but for the use of a computer would require a prohibitive amount of human time and effort." The commission went on to note that any copies created for such research purposes should be destroyed upon completion of the research project, or permission from the copyright owner should be obtained for any retention for archival purposes or future use.

On the subject of storing a data base in a computer, CONTU stated:

> Making a copy of an entire work would normally, subject to some possible exceptions for fair use, be considered exclusively within the domain of the copyright proprietor. One would have to assume, however, that fair use would apply rarely to the reproduction in their entirety of such compendious works as data bases. That only one copy is being made, or even that the owner of the computer system intends to exact no fee for providing access to the work, would no more insulate the copies from liability for copyright infringement than would similar circumstances insulate a public library which made unauthorized duplications of entire copyrighted works for its basic lending functions. [Footnotes omitted]

As for the use of a computerized data base, the commission's report first set forth its views about the copyright owner's general rights and interests and then added some comments about fair use. CONTU stated:

> Similar also to a telephone directory, copyright in a dynamic data base protects no individual datum, but only the systemized form in which the data are presented. The use of one item retrieved from such a work—be it an address, a chemical formula, or a citation to an article—would not under reasonable circumstances merit the attention of the copyright proprietor. Nor would it conceivably constitute infringement of copyright.

As for retrieval and reduplication of a larger amount:

> The retrieval and reduplication of any substantial portion of a data base,

whether or not the individual data are in the public domain, would likely constitute a duplication of the copyrighted element of a data base and would be an infringement. In any event, the issue of how much is enough to constitute a copyright violation would likely entail analysis on a case-by-case basis with consideration of fair use bearing on whether the unauthorized copying of a limited portion of a data base would be noninfringing. Fair use should have very limited force when an unauthorized copy of a data base is made for primarily commercial use. Only if information of a substantial amount were extracted and duplicated for redistribution would serious problems exist, raising concerns about the enforcement of proprietary rights.

## Videotaping

*Legislative History.* The three principal legislative reports underlying the 1976 Copyright Law had little to say specifically about the fair-use doctrine as it might specifically relate to off-the-air videotaping. A few comments, relating to teaching activities, are considered in Chapter 14.

*CONTU.* The CONTU report did not take up the subject of videotaping, concluding that Congress intended that the commission's study of machine reproduction focus on photocopying. Also, "the Commission believed that the issues involved in off-the-air videotaping were essentially matters requiring public policy decisions not related to technology per se, and that these matters were being tested in a legal action"[37] (footnote omitted). The legal action referred to was the *Sony* case, considered below.

*Cases.* The market research case concerning survey studies of television commercials, mentioned earlier in this chapter, involved some unauthorized videotaping. So did the case involving the film about the college wrestler, in which the broadcasting company was found to have infringed the film by making an unauthorized copy of it.

We will leave to Chapter 14 another recent case involving off-the-air videorecording and subsequent tape reproductions by a nonprofit institution for school use. The institution was a Board of Cooperative Education Services (BOCES) in New York State. Also in that chapter, we will consider some guidelines that were negotiated in 1981 concerning off-the-air videotaping of programs for use in classes.

The major case thus far concerning videotaping is the case of *Universal City Studios, Inc.* v. *Sony Corporation of America.* In that case a federal appeals court in California recently ruled that home videotaping of copyrighted entertainment programming was not fair use.

The case started in 1976. Universal City Studios joined with Walt Disney Productions to sue Sony, the manufacturer of the Betamax videotape recorders, for copyright infringement. Also named in the lawsuit were the distributor of the recorders, certain retailers who sold the recorders, Sony's advertising agency, and an individual who used his Betamax recorder to copy Universal's and Disney's broadcast material for his own home use.

In 1979, the federal district court handling the case ruled that there was no infringement by any of the parties because, among other reasons, the recording of broadcast programs off-the-air by a person in his home for private use constituted a fair use.[38] In 1981 a federal appellate court overruled that decision, concluding that fair use did not apply.[39]

At the heart of the appeals court decision was the view that fair use traditionally has related to the use by one author of another author's work and has not related to the reproduction of a work for the purpose of using it in the same manner as the original work was intended to be used—that is, for what the court called the "intrinsic" use of the work. The court considered the distinction to be an appropriate line of demarcation for fair-use decisions. And the court was critical of the *Williams & Wilkins* photocopying case considered earlier in this chapter.

> We believe that the Court of Claims approach—in treating intrinsic use of such a work as within the bounds of fair use—created doctrinal confusion that raises the spectre of the evisceration of the traditional workings of the copyright scheme. . . .
>
> We hold that, particularly in the context of new technology, there is a danger to including the sort of copying involved in *Williams & Wilkins* within the scope of the fair use doctrine. New technology, which makes possible the mass reproduction of copyrighted material (effectively taking control of access from the author), places a strain upon the fair use doctrine. A court, if it decides that fair use is applicable, is required to weigh—in "balancing the equities"—the "benefit" of an extremely popular increase in access with the "harm" to the plaintiff. The harm to a copyright plaintiff is inherently speculative and . . . a plaintiff is faced with the unenviable task of proving the nonexistence of fair use, which has typically been viewed as a defense.

The court reinforced its general views about fair use by also considering each of the four fair-use factors referred to in the statute.

In considering the "purpose and character of the use," the court felt that copying entertainment works for convenience was not a powerful purpose in the context of section 107. (The district court also had given great emphasis to the idea that we should be sensitive to privacy considerations in interpreting fair use. The appellate court instead concluded that it "seems more appropriate to address the privacy concerns . . . in fashioning the appropriate relief.")

Addressing the second statutory factor—"the nature of the copyrighted work"—the court stated:

> the legislative history and the case law dealing with this factor are rather sparse, but there seems to be some indication that the scope of fair use is greater when informational types of works, as opposed to more creative products, are involved. . . . If a work is more appropriately characterized as entertainment, it is less likely that a claim of fair use will be accepted.

Concerning the "amount and substantiality of the portion used," the court noted that home use recording usually involves copying the entire work. The court also concluded that, in considering this factor, it is not also necessary to find that the plaintiff has been harmed by the copying.

With respect to the fourth fair-use factor—"the effect of the use upon the potential market for or value of the copyrighted work"—the court believed that the district court was too strict in requiring the plaintiffs to establish harm. The appeals court considered that it is too great a burden in a case such as the one before it, to require that plaintiffs prove actual damages from the activities of specific defendants; attention has to be paid to the cumulative effect of mass reproduction of copyrighted works made possible by videorecorders.

The appeals court's decision did not bring the *Sony* case to an end. One reason is that there were some relevant issues remaining for the district court to decide. These issues, not spelled out in detail in the court opinions, involve various defenses to the basic copyright infringement claim, e.g., a claim of prejudicial delay in bringing suit.

The appellate court did not decide what specific relief should be granted to the plaintiffs should the defenses not be established. The federal district court will decide the "relief" issue in the first instance. However, the appellate court did note, as one of the possibilities, the award of a continuing royalty.

Several proposed pieces of legislation are now before Congress that would make home-use videotape recording not an infringement of copyright. Another proposal would provide for fees to be added to the selling price of videorecorders and tapes, with the sums collected to be allocated among copyright owners under the rules of the Copyright Royalty Tribunal, the organization that administers some aspects of various compulsory licenses (Chapter 17). It is not presently clear whether Congress will choose to act on such proposals at any time soon or whether it will first wait for the outcome of further court proceedings in the *Sony* litigation. If Congress does give considerable attention to the possibility of imposing "surcharges" on videorecorders and videotapes, it may also give some consideration to possible similar arrangements with respect to audiotape recorders and tapes and, possibly, to document reproduction equipment such as photocopiers. It is too early to say what, if anything, will develop or at what pace.

# 14

## COPYRIGHTS AND TEACHING ACTIVITIES

Teachers and teaching activities are not set apart in the copyright law by a set of isolated rules. For example, many teachers are authors as well as users of materials authored by others, and are governed by general copyright standards in that capacity. However, teachers, and school administrators as well, do have a special interest in what practices the copyright law permits with respect to copyrighted materials when consent of the copyright owner is not obtained, and the copyright law has a number of specific opinions dealing with each issue. Some of the principal concerns are the reproduction and use of copyrighted print material for use in class, the off-the-air videotaping of material for classroom use, and the performance of copyrighted works as part of teaching activities. In the absence of consent from the copyright owner, these practices sometimes can run afoul of the owner's rights to reproduce, publicly distribute, and publicly perform the copyrighted work (see Chapter 5). Two of the most promising lawful ways to copy material and distribute or perform it in class without the copyright owner's consent lie in the fair-use doctrine of section 107—the subject of Part 1 of this chapter—and the performance and display provisions of section 110, considered in Part 2.

## PART 1: FAIR USE IN EDUCATIONAL ACTIVITIES

In incorporating the fair-use doctrine into the copyright law, much attention was devoted to issues concerning teaching activities in not-for-profit educational institutions. The legislation itself makes reference to fair use in educational contexts. The legislative history presents many comments on the subject. In addition, with the encouragement of Congress, fair-use guidelines for educational activities were developed by representatives of authors, educators, and publishers, and were incorporated into the legislative history.

More recently, some further guidelines were developed with respect to audiovisual materials.

By no means did Congress take a clear stand on all the issues or even on all those considered. However, a considerable amount of guidance has been provided.

## THE STATUTORY LANGUAGE

As shown by the following excerpts, the fair-use provision of the statute makes several specific references to fair use in the context of teaching activities:

> the fair use of a copyrighted work, including such use by reproduction in copies or phonorecords . . ., for purposes such as . . . teaching (including multiple copies for classroom use), scholarship or research is not an infringement of copyright. In determining whether the use made of a work in any particular case is a fair use the factors to be considered shall include—(1) the purpose and character of the use, including whether such use is of a commercial nature or is for nonprofit educational purposes; . . .

The House Judiciary Committee's 1976 report underlying the statute notes that the wording of section 107 " . . . is the result of a process of accretion, resulting from the long controversy over the related problems of fair use and the reproduction (mostly by photocopying) of copyrighted material for educational and scholarly purposes." The report goes on to put several of the section 107 phrases in a fuller perspective.[1]

> the reference to fair use "by reproduction in copies or phonorecords or by any other means" is mainly intended to make clear that the doctrine has as much application to photocopying and taping as to older forms of use; it is not intended to give these kinds of reproduction any special status under the fair use provision or to sanction any reproduction beyond the normal and reasonable limits of fair use. Similarly, the newly-added reference to "multiple copies for classroom use" is a recognition that, under the proper circumstances of fairness, the doctrine can be applied to reproductions of multiple copies for the members of a class.
>
> The Committee has amended the first of the criteria to be considered—"the purpose and character of the use"—to state explicitly that this factor includes a consideration of "whether such use is for . . . nonprofit educational purposes." This amendment is not intended to be any sort of not-for-profit limitation on educational uses of copyrighted works. It is express recognition that, as under present law, the commercial or nonprofit character of an activity should be weighed along with other factors in fair use decisions.

## LEGISLATIVE HISTORY EXAMPLES

The legislative reports underlying the statute include many comments—some general, some highly focused—concerning fair use in the context of teaching activities. Excerpts from the 1975 Senate report are quoted in the material that follows.[2] An earlier House report, in 1967, included many similar comments, which the later 1976 House report acknowledged still had value as an analysis of various aspects of the problem.[3]

## General Commentary

As a general comment about fair use in the context of the classroom, the Senate report stated:

> Fair use is essentially supplementary by nature, and classroom copying that exceeds the legitimate teaching aims, such as filling in missing information or bringing a subject up to date, would go beyond the proper bounds of fair use. Isolated instances of minor infringements, when multiplied many times, become, in the aggregate, a major inroad on copyright that must be prevented.

The last quoted sentence serves to illustrate that fair-use issues in educational contexts are not set apart from the overall fair-use standards. The sentence was a part of the rationale of the federal appeals court ruling in the *Sony* home videotaping case considered in Chapter 13. And, particularly if that court's decision holds up, it, in turn, will play some role in determining the shape of fair use in educational contexts.

The Senate report also addressed fair-use considerations as they relate to the nonprofit factor, individual teacher copying decisions versus school decisions, and single-multiple copying. Here are Senate comments (captions added).

> *The Nonprofit Factor:* Although it is possible to imagine situations in which use by a teacher in an educational organization operated for profit (day camps, language schools, business schools, dance studios, et cetera) would constitute a fair use, the nonprofit character of the school in which the teacher works should be one factor to consider in determining fair use. Another factor would be whether any charge is made for the copies distributed.

> *The Person Making the Copying Decision:* The fair use doctrine in the case of classroom copying would apply primarily to the situation of a teacher who, acting individually and at his own volition, makes one or more copies for temporary use by himself or his pupils in the classroom. A different result is indicated where the copying was done by the educational institution, school system, or larger unit or where copying was required or suggested by the school administration, either in special instances or as part of a general plan.

> *Multiple Copies:* Depending upon the nature of the work and other criteria, the fair use doctrine should differentiate between the amount of work that can be reproduced by a teacher for his own classroom use (for example, for reading or projecting a copy or for playing a tape recording), and the amount that can be reproduced for distribution to pupils. In the case of multiple copies, other factors would be whether the number reproduced was limited to the size of the class, whether circulation beyond the classroom was per-

mitted, and whether the copies were recalled or destroyed after temporary use.

## Commentary on Particular Types of Works or Activities

The 1975 Senate report also commented on a number of types of copyrighted works and teaching activities. Excerpts are set forth below. (Captions are added; excerpts appeared in a different sequence in the legislative report.)

*Textbooks; Consumables; Periodicals:* Textbooks and other material prepared primarily for the school markets would be less susceptible to reproductions for classroom use than material prepared for general public distribution.

Where the copyright work is intended to be "consumable" in the course of classroom activities—workbooks, exercises, standardized tests, and answer sheets are examples—the privilege of fair use by teachers or pupils would have little if any application.

With respect to material in newspapers and periodicals, the doctrine of fair use should be liberally applied to allow copying of items of current interest to supplement and update the students' textbooks, but this would not extend to copying from periodicals published primarily for student use.

*Entire Works, Extracts, Forming Anthologies:* In general terms it could be expected that the doctrine of fair use would be applied strictly to the classroom reproduction of entire works, such as musical compositions, dramas, and audiovisual works including motion pictures, which by their very nature are intended for performance or public exhibition.

In general, and assuming the other necessary factors are present, the copying for classroom purposes of extracts or portions, which are not self-contained and which are relatively "not substantial in length" when compared to the larger, self-contained works from which they are taken, should be considered fair use. Depending on the circumstances, the same would also be true of very short self-contained works such as a brief poem, a map in a newspaper, a "vocabulary builder" from a monthly magazine, and so forth. This should not be construed as permitting a teacher to make multiple copies of the same work on a repetitive basis or for continued use.

Spontaneous copying of an isolated extract by a teacher, which may be fair use under appropriate circumstances, could turn into an infringement if the copies were accumulated over a period of time with other parts of the same work, or were collected with other material from various works so as to constitute an anthology.

*Typing, Practice Lessons, and So On:* There are certain classroom uses which, because of their special nature, would not be considered an infringement in the ordinary case. For example, copying of extracts by pupils as exercises in a shorthand or typing class or for foreign language study, or recordings of performances by music students for purposes of analysis and criticism, would normally be regarded as a fair use unless the copies of phonorecords were retained or duplicated.

A single copy reproduction of excerpts from a copyrighted work by a student calligrapher or teacher in a learning situation would be a fair use of the copyrighted work.

Some legislative commentary relating to fair use and off-the-air video-taping are considered later in this chapter.

## LEGISLATIVE HISTORY GUIDELINES

With the encouragement of Congress, representatives of authors, educators, and publishers developed guidelines about certain educational uses of copyrighted materials that they agreed would ordinarily constitute fair use.[4] Two sets of guidelines were developed in time for incorporation into the House Judiciary Committee's report preceding the enactment of the 1976 Copyright Act. These guidelines cover (a) books and periodicals, excluding musical works, and (b) musical works.

The House committee report concludes that the guidelines "are a reasonable interpretation of the minimum standards of fair use. Teachers will know that copying within the guidelines is fair use. Thus, the guidelines serve the purpose of fulfilling the need for greater certainty and protection for teachers."[5] The Senate-House Conference Committee report, which immediately preceded the passage of the law, stated: "The conferees accept [the guidelines] as part of their understanding of fair use."[6]

The complete text of the guidelines appears in Appendix 4.

### Books and Periodicals Guidelines

*Teacher Copies.*   Under the guidelines, which by their own terms apply only to not-for-profit educational institutions, a teacher may, under defined conditions, make or acquire single copies of any of the following for scholarly research or for preparation for teaching or for use in actual classroom teaching:

1. an article from a periodical;
2. a short story, essay, or poem;
3. an illustration from a periodical or book;
4. a chapter from a book.

The meaning of "teacher" is broad enough to include institutional specialists working in consultation with actual instructors.[7]

To be within the guidelines, the copy must be made either by the teacher or at the teacher's individual request. Other restrictions on the scope of the teacher's copies are included at the end of the following discussion. These caveats also apply to the classroom-use guidelines. The guidelines do not claim to define the maximum that may be done under fair use.

*Classroom Uses.* The number of copies for classroom use in not-for-profit educational institutions should not exceed the number of students in the course. The copies must be made by or for the teacher giving the course, for classroom use or discussion. Each copy must include a notice of copyright.

The copying also must meet the guidelines criteria of spontaneity, brevity, cumulative effect, and some overall standards.

As regards *spontaneity*, the copying must be at the "instance and inspiration" of the teacher. Further, the decision to use the work must be so close in time to the moment of its use for maximum teaching effectiveness that it would be unreasonable to expect a timely reply to a permission request.

In considering *brevity*, the amount copied from any particular material must be sufficiently short, as specified in the guidelines. The standards for various types of works are as follows:

Illustrations: One illustration per book or periodical issue.

Poetry: (a) A complete poem, if less than 250 words and if printed on not more than two pages; (b) 250 words from a longer poem, and to the completion of the line.

Prose (other than a "special work"): (a) 10 percent but not more than 1,000 words; (b) in any event, 500 words; (c) a complete article, story, or essay, if less than 2,500 words.

Special Work: The guidelines describe special works as "certain works in poetry, prose or 'poetic prose' which often combine language with illustrations and which are intended sometimes for children and at other times for a more general audience fall short of 2,500 words in their entirety." The guidelines do not authorize the reproduction of special works in their entirety; up to two of the published pages, or not more than 10 percent of the text, may be reproduced.

The cumulative effect of the copying must meet several criteria:

1. no more than nine instances of multiple copying for one course during one class term;
2. no more than three excerpts from any one collective work or periodical volume may be copied during one class term. This limitation, however, does not apply to newspapers, current news periodicals, or current news sections of periodicals;
3. no more than one complete item (short poem, article, story, essay) or two excerpts by any one author may be copied during one class term.

The guidelines for cumulative effect also provide that the copying of any particular material is authorized "for only one course in the school in which the copies are made."

In regard to *overall standards*, the guidelines do not authorize:

1. copying from works intended to be "consumable," such as workbooks or standardized tests;
2. copying used to substitute for the purchase of books, publishers' reprints, or periodicals;
3. copying to create anthologies or compilations or to replace or substitute for them.

*Reactions to the Guidelines.*   The National Education Association supported the copyright revision bill (which became the 1976 Copyright Law), and took the position that, in the context of the legislative history, the bill represented "a major breakthrough in establishing equitable legal guidelines for the use of copyright materials for instructional and research purposes."[8]

A different position was taken by representatives of the American Association of University Professors and of the Association of American Law Schools. Those representatives wrote to the House Judiciary Committee, strongly criticizing the guidelines in the context of university teaching. The committee's report on the copyright revision bill noted the objection and made these three comments: representatives of higher education helped to develop the guidelines; the purpose of the guidelines was to state the minimum and not the maximum standards of educational fair use; and the guidelines themselves acknowledged that there may be instances not within the guidelines that nonetheless are within fair use.[9]

*Recent Litigation.*   The guidelines have not to our knowledge been discussed in any judicial opinions. However, two copyright infringement suits were brought by some publishers against commercial copy shop companies. In at least one of those cases, it was alleged that considerable unauthorized copying of copyrighted material was taking place in connection with student courses. Neither case went to trial, and none of the defendants admitted any wrongdoing. Both cases were settled under consent judgments. The defendants agreed not to make multiple copies of published copyrighted materials unless there was suitable consent of the copyright owner or a signed certificate by a teacher that the copying was in compliance with the guidelines.[10]

## Music Guidelines

The music guidelines are less complex than the books and periodicals guidelines. And, unlike those guidelines, they cover activity outside as well as in not-for-profit educational institutions.

*Copying Sheet Music.*   Subject to the general caveats to be considered later, the guidelines authorize emergency copying to replace purchased copies when they are not available for an imminent performance, so long as purchased replacement copies are substituted in due course. Apart from this specific instance, the guidelines do not authorize copying sheet music for the purpose of performances.

For academic purposes other than performances, single or multiple copies of excerpts of musical works may be made, not to exceed one copy per pupil, as long as (1) the excerpts do not comprise a part of the whole that would constitute a performable unit, such as a selection, movement, or aria; and (2) the excerpts do not total more than 10 percent of the whole work.

The guidelines do not authorize any other copying of sheet music for a class. However, for purposes of a teacher's scholarly research or class preparation, the guidelines permit a single copy of an entire performable unit, such as a section, movement, or aria, to be made if (a) the copyright proprietor confirms that it is out of print or (b) it is unavailable except in a larger work.

*Copying a Sound Recording.* Subject to the general caveats considered later, the guidelines authorize the making, for evaluation or rehearsal purposes, of a single phonorecord of recordings of performances by students. The phonorecord—which of course ordinarily will be in the form of a tape recording—may be retained by the educational institution or the individual teacher.

The guidelines also provide that a single phonorecord of a sound recording of copyrighted music may be made from sound recordings owned by an educational institution or an individual teacher for the purpose of constructing aural exercises or examinations. (This standard relates only to the underlying copyrighted music. No guidelines have been developed concerning the duplication of the sound recording itself.) The phonorecord may be retained by the educational institution or the individual teacher.

*General Caveats in the Guidelines.* The copying must include the copyright notice that appears on the printed copy.

Copying to create, replace, or substitute for anthologies, compilations, or collective works is not authorized, nor is copying from works intended to be consumables.

The guidelines expressly recognize instances in which copying not within the guidelines may nonetheless be allowed under fair use.

*Recent Attorney General's Opinion.* The attorney general for Kansas recently issued an advisory opinion that referred to the music guidelines.[11] The State Department of Education had asked whether music educators may duplicate musical scores for distribution to judges in music performance competitions, at state music festivals. The attorney general concluded that such a practice would go beyond fair use. His opinion stated, in part:

While these guidelines are not conclusive upon judicial construction of section

107, we believe the courts are constrained to give considerable weight to the House Judiciary Committee's approval of these guidelines as an expression of Congressional intent. Accordingly, we have relied, in part, on these guidelines. . . . Specifically, we believe that such duplication of musical scores contravenes the prohibition in these guidelines as to copying as a substitute for purchasing music. . . . In fact, we note from the correspondence submitted with your request . . . the underlying motive of the music director . . . who questions the necessity of the public school system "adding the cost of multiple-score purchase(s) to the greater burden of inflated musical works."

# VIDEORECORDING

The legislative history and guidelines considered thus far focus principally on the application of fair use to photocopying and other means of reprography of documents. We will now consider off-the-air videotaping of copyrighted programming. We will mention some legislative history, some guidelines that were developed in 1981, and some other official developments.

## Legislative History—Videotaping for General Educational Uses

The 1976 House committee report on the copyright revision legislation states:

The problem of off-the-air taping for nonprofit classroom use of copyrighted audiovisual works incorporated in radio and television broadcasts has proved to be difficult to resolve. The Committee believes that the fair use doctrine has some limited application in this area, but it appears that the development of detailed guidelines will require a more thorough explanation than has thus far been possible. . . . [T]he Committee . . . urges the representatives of the various interests . . . to continue their discussions actively and in a constructive spirit.[12]

## The Negotiated Guidelines of 1981

By the fall of 1981, a set of off-the-air videotaping guidelines had been negotiated by a group of representatives of educational organizations, copyright proprietors, and creative guilds and unions.[13] The group, called the negotiating committee, had been selected by the House subcommittee responsible for copyright matters. The negotiating committee's guidelines were described, in the letter forwarding them to the House subcommittee, as reflecting "the Negotiating Committee's consensus as to the application of 'fair use' to the recording, retention, and use of television broadcast programs for educational purposes."

*General Guideline Coverage.* The guidelines, a copy of which is included in Appendix 4, apply only to off-the-air recording by nonprofit educational institutions of "broadcast programs," described as "television programs transmitted by television stations for reception by the general public without charge." The guidelines cover the making, duplication, and retention of tapes and uses of such tapes for educational and evaluation purposes. Educational institutions are expected to establish appropriate control procedures to maintain the integrity of the guidelines.

*Guideline Standards on Recording Programs; Duplication and Retention.* Under the guideline standards, a broadcast program may be recorded off the air simultaneously with broadcast transmission (including simultaneous cable retransmission). The recordings may be made only at the request of and used by individual teachers. They may not be regularly recorded in anticipation of requests. Also, no broadcast program may be recorded off the air more than once at the request of the same teacher, regardless of the number of times the program may be broadcast.

A limited number of copies may be reproduced, within the guidelines, from each off-the-air recording to meet the needs of teachers. Each copy is subject to all provisions governing the original recording.

The copies made may be retained for a period not to exceed 45 calendar days after the date of recording. All copies should then be erased or destroyed immediately.

All copies should include the copyright notice on the broadcast program as recorded.

The guidelines recognize two types of use of the recorded material—classroom use and teacher evaluation use.

*Classroom Uses.* Under the guidelines, off-the-air recordings may be used "once by individual teachers in the course of relevant teaching activities, and repeated once only when instructional reinforcement is necessary." Use should occur in classrooms and similar places devoted to instruction within a single building, cluster or campus, or in the homes of students receiving formalized home instruction.

Use may be made during the first 10 consecutive school days within the 45-calendar-day retention period. ("School days" are school session days, excluding weekends, holidays, vacations, examination periods, or other scheduled interruptions.)

The off-the-air recordings may not be altered from their original content or combined so as to make up teaching compilations or anthologies.

*Use for Evaluation by Teachers.* The recordings may also be used to determine whether or not the broadcast program should be used in the teaching curriculum. This is the only authorized use in the 45-calendar-day retention period once the 10-school-day teaching use period has expired.

*Reactions to the Guidelines.* Congressman Robert Kastenmeier, who as head of the House subcommittee responsible for copyright matters guided the 1976 Copyright Act through the House, inserted the following remarks into the *Congressional Record* concerning the guidelines:

> I thank, and congratulate, the negotiating committee for their efforts which will, I believe, greatly assist in clarifying the procedures which educators may follow in their use of broadcasted copyrighted materials. These guidelines will help solve an important problem, hopefully without further legislation and litigation. . . . I share the view of the negotiating committee that these guidelines reach an appropriate balance between the proprietary rights of copyright owners and the instructional needs of educational institutions. I recognize that beyond these guidelines specific permissions from copyright proprietors may be required under Copyright Law.

The Motion Picture Association of America has gone on record as taking no position on the guidelines but, in its letter to that effect, it listed several member companies that assented to the guidelines.[14]

The Board of Directors of the Association of Media Producers voted not to endorse the guidelines, stating in part that "we are fearful that they may seriously jeopardize the future well-being of the small but vital educational media industry . . . and the availability of a broad variety of instructional materials essential to maintaining quality education programs." It is reported that the margin of the vote was a narrow one.[15]

Should future litigation arise involving off-the-air videotaping of copyrighted materials for use by nonprofit educational institutions, the guidelines may well be given appreciable weight in any court decision on how the fair-use doctrine applies. Nonetheless, these guidelines do not have quite the same "official" strength as those discussed earlier in this chapter, which were developed before passage of the 1976 Copyright Act and were part of the legislative record underlying the bill on which Congress voted.

The 1981 guidelines were developed during the period when the district court decision in the *Sony* case was on appeal and were released prior to the appellate decision. (See Chapter 13 for a discussion of the *Sony* case.) The videotaping guidelines were not hedged by any stated assumptions about the law, so the *Sony* decision does not render them outdated. Nonetheless, their context in time is relevant.

## The BOCES Case in New York[16]

The Board of Cooperative Educational Services of Erie County (BOCES) is a nonprofit corporation in New York organized to provide educational services to county public schools. It maintained videorecording equipment to tape programs off the air and to duplicate tapes. It distributed to teachers within the county school districts catalogs describing the available programming. In the 1976–1977 school year, it duplicated approximately 10,000 videotapes. Schools requesting a program would provide a blank tape (or a recorded tape to be erased) to BOCES, which would provide a tape of the program. The schools were not required to return the tape, although they often did so as part of another order.

Three copyright owners of educational audiovisual materials sued BOCES for copyright infringement. (But theirs were far from the only materials represented in the 10,000 copies.) The copyright owners requested pre-trial relief in the form of a court order that BOCES activities be stopped. The court granted that relief, but permitted BOCES, if it kept appropriate records, to continue some of the activity pending resolution of the case at trial.

In its pretrial ruling granting a preliminary injunction motion, the court found the pretrial relief appropriate in part because the copyright owners were able to show a sufficient likelihood of success at trial. Concerning fair use, the court considered various factors and concluded that the scope of BOCES activities was "difficult to reconcile with its claim of fair use," but reserved a final decision on that point, stating that the "applicability of the defense of fair use raises numerous questions of fact which cannot be re-solved without a full trial on the merits." The court went on to say: "At this stage in the proceedings, I find that the substantiality of the copying and the possible impact of the market for educational films tip the balance in favor of the plaintiffs, outweighing BOCES' noncommercial, educational purposes in copying the films."

## Legislative History Continued

The 1975 and 1976 legislative reports underlying the statute included some comments on off-the-air videotaping and educational uses for the hearing-impaired and for use in remote geographical areas.

*Aid for the Hearing-Impaired.* The Senate-House Conference Committee on the bill that became the 1976 Copyright Act endorsed the view that, assuming no other factors would make the use "unfair," the doctrine of fair use is broad enough to permit the making of an off-the-air copy of a television program by a nonprofit educational institution for the deaf and hearing-impaired. Permitted activities included the making of a captioned version; the performance of that version, solely for educational purposes, within the institution for its students; and the sharing of the captioned version among other such institutions. Emphasis was placed on the point that the activity would have to be noncommercial in every respect, and that each of the institutions involved would have to assure against unauthorized reproduc-tion or distribution, and against performance or retention for other than educational purposes.[17]

*Videorecording in Remote Areas.* The 1975 Senate committee report on copyright revision legislation focused on ". . . the special problems involved in the reception of instructional television programs in remote areas of the country":[18]

A particular difficulty exists when such transmissions extend over several time zones within the same state, such as Alaska. Unless individual schools in such states may make an off-the-air recording of such transmissions, the programs may not be received by the students during the school's daily schedule. The committee believes that the making, by a school located in such a remote area, of an off-the-air recording of an instructional television transmission for the purpose of a delayed viewing of the program by the students of the same school constitutes a fair use. . . . The committee does not intend to suggest, however, that off-the-air recording for convenience would, under any circumstances, be considered "fair use." [The committee also noted that to] meet the requirement of temporary use the school may retain the recording for only a limited period of time after the broadcast.

# PART 2: PROVISIONS, OTHER THAN FAIR USE, RELATING TO TEACHING ACTIVITIES

## STATUTORY PROVISIONS OTHER THAN FAIR USE

Although fair use is an important aspect of the law as it relates to teaching activities, other provisions are also directly applicable. The principal ones, contained in section 110 of the copyright law, limit a copyright owner's exclusive rights to perform and display the copyrighted work publicly.

### Face-to-Face Teaching

Nonprofit educational institutions generally may perform or display works in the course of face-to-face teaching activities without the need to obtain consent of the copyright owner [110(1)]. In order to qualify under this provision, the activities should be carried out by instructors or pupils in the classroom or similar place devoted to instruction.

The legislative history sets forth interpretations of the legislative language:[19] (1) the exemption does not cover performances given for recreation or entertainment; (2) the exemption does not cover the case of performers brought in to put on a program; however, an "instructor," within the meaning of the statute, can be a guest lecturer whose instructional activities remain confined to classroom situations; (3) the legislative phrase "classroom or similar place devoted to instruction" can include places such as an auditorium or gymnasium, when used in the context of instructing a class, but not where the audience is broader in scope, such as a school assembly or a general athletic event; (4) the reference in the exemption to "pupils" means, in general, the enrolled members of a class.

As part of this exemption language, section 110(1), the provision states that in the case of an audiovisual work, the performance or display of an unlawfully made copy is not authorized if the person responsible for the performance had reason to believe the copy was not lawfully made.

## Instructional Transmissions

Nonprofit institutions may perform or display works, under defined circumstances, by transmissions primarily to students [101 "transmit"; 110(2)].

There are no limits as to the types of copyrighted works that may be *displayed* under this provision. However, it authorizes the *performance* of only nondramatic literary and nondramatic musical works. Thus, the exemption does not cover the performance of such works as motion pictures, operas, musical comedies, or filmstrips.[20] Moreover, because the exemption covers only performances and displays, it does not authorize the development of a derivative work from a copyrighted work.[21]

The section only authorizes those transmissions that are a regular part of the *systematic instructional activities* of a governmental body or of a nonprofit educational institution. The legislative history equates the italicized phrase with *curricula*.[22]

The performance or display must be directly related to and of material assistance to the teaching content of the transmission. Furthermore, the transmission must be made primarily (not solely) for one of these three purposes:

1. reception in classrooms or similar places normally devoted to instruction;
2. reception by persons to whom the transmission is directed because special circumstances, such as their disabilities, prevent their attendance at class;
3. reception by government employees as part of their official duties.

The "primary purpose" test can turn on such facts as subject matter and the time of transmission. "Special circumstances" can include not only disability but also the case of those who cannot attend class for other reasons, such as having to take care of their preschool children.[23]

Under defined circumstances, copies of the transmission program may be made and distributed to other parties eligible under section 110(2), who are permitted to use them for section 110(2) purposes [112(b)].[24] Ordinarily, the transmission program could not be separately copyrighted [114(e)].

## Public Broadcasting

The statute provides for a statutory license for public broadcasting entities to perform nondramatic musical works and to display published art. These provisions are considered in Chapter 17.

At one stage in the development of the current copyright law, there was a draft provision that would have placed nondramatic literary works within the statutory license provision just mentioned. That provision was not included in the final law, as Congress, instead, wanted the parties to work out voluntary arrangements for the licensing of nondramatic literary works for public broadcasting.[25] The parties did work out such arrangements.

# 15

# LIBRARY REPRODUCTIONS: SECTION 108

The right to reproduce copyrighted works is one of the copyright owner's five exclusive rights [106]. For libraries and librarians, two of the most significant limitations on those rights are the fair-use provisions of section 107 and the library reproduction rights of section 108.

Under section 108 an eligible library (and its employees acting within the scope of their employment) may reproduce and distribute a copy or phonorecord of designated types of works without the permission of the copyright owner and without infringing copyright. The types of material that may be reproduced fall into five general categories, and each type is linked to a particular permissible purpose, as indicated by Table 17 (and subject to various qualifications, which we will consider later on).

In discussing section 108, we first consider its relationship with fair use (section 107). Next, we consider the general eligibility criteria a library must meet to exercise section 108 rights. Then we take up each of the particular activities that section 108 authorizes.

Section 108 covers libraries and archives. For convenience, both are referred to as "libraries." Section 108 also covers library employees acting within the scope of their employment [108(a)]. For convenience, we will generally not mention employees separately.

Section 108 applies to both copies in the traditional sense and to phonorecords, such as records and audiotapes. We will use "copies" to refer to all of these and will note distinctions where appropriate. (As you will see, there are significant limitations in the case of published musical, graphic, and audiovisual works.)

## RELATION OF SECTION 108 TO SECTION 107

### Interactive Effects of the Sections

The first point to make on this topic is that the relationship between sections 108 and 107 is not entirely clear. In the statute, Congress declared that nothing in section 108 "in any way affects the right of fair use as

## TABLE 17 CATEGORIES OF COPYING AUTHORIZED
## BY SECTION 108*

| Type of Material | Purpose |
|---|---|
| Unpublished work | Preservation and security; deposit for research use in another library |
| Published work | Replacement of damaged, deteriorated, lost, or stolen copy |
| Periodical article, contribution to copyrighted collection, a small part of any other copyrighted work | To fulfill a user's request |
| Entire work or a substantial part | To fulfill a user's request |
| Audiovisual news programs[+] | For use in research |

* Section 108 does not give a blanket authorization for copying these materials; a number of statutory conditions must be met, which are considered later in this chapter.
[+] These provisions are considered at the end of this chapter.

provided by section 107" [108(f)(4)]. When the law was developing, the Register of Copyrights recommended to the relevant Senate committee that its report on the legislation describe the relationship between sections 107 and 108. The committee responded as follows:

> The doctrine of fair use applies to library photocopying, and nothing contained in section 108 "in any way affects the right of fair use." No provision of section 108 is intended to take away any rights existing under the fair use doctrine. To the contrary, section 108 authorizes certain photocopying practices which may not qualify as fair use.
>    The criteria of fair use are necessarily set forth in general terms. In the application of the criteria of fair use to specific photocopying practices of libraries, it is the intent of this legislation to provide an appropriate balancing of the rights of creators, and the needs of users.[1]

Does the legislative standard—"nothing is section 108 in any way affects the right of fair use"—mean that a library's copying activities under section 107 are to be judged without regard to its activities under section 108? The difficulty with a simple yes answer is that both sections seek to reach a balance of the rights of copyright owners and users, as is evidenced by the following two excerpts from the underlying legislative reports, the first a partial repeat of the material quoted previously:

> In the application of the criteria of fair use to specific photocopying practices of libraries, it is the intent of this legislation to provide an appropriate balancing of the rights of creators, and the needs of users.[2]

> While the several opinions in the *Wilkins* [library photocopying] case have given the Congress little guidance as to the current state of the law on fair

use, these opinions provide additional support for the balanced resolution of the photocopying issue . . . preserved in section 108.[3]

If each section represents, in a general sense, the legislative balancing, then an imbalance would result if, say, a library could use its fair-use and section 108 rights additively and independently, for example, use its section 107 rights without regard to its section 108 rights, and then use its section 108 rights without regard to the activities under section 107.

One way to avoid concluding that such a seeming imbalance actually results from the statute is to recognize the flexibility that the fair-use doctrine potentially has by virtue of its capacity to take all facets of a situation into account. Under that approach, one of the circumstances to be considered in determining the application of a library's "right of fair use as provided by section 107" would be the extent of a library's related copying activities taken through the use of section 108. Such an interpretation would address the "additive imbalance" issue, while at the same time would recognize that section 108 does not operate to make section 107 irrelevant to library copying activities.

Regardless of whether or not the suggested approach is correct, it at least seems clear that section 108 is not to be read as establishing the absolute boundaries of the scope of a library's statutory rights to reproduce copyrighted works without permission. This viewpoint seems to be inherent in the statutory language itself; it also is supported by some comments in the legislative history made in the context of the fact that, generally speaking, musical works and some others are not covered within section 108:

> Although subsection (h) generally removes musical, graphic, and audiovisual works from the specific exemptions of section 108, it is important to recognize that the doctrine of fair use under section 107 remains fully applicable to the photocopying or other reproduction of such works. In the case of music, for example, it would be fair use for a scholar doing musicological research to have a library supply a copy of a portion of a score or to reproduce portions of a phonorecord of a work. Nothing in section 108 impairs the applicability of the fair use doctrine to a wide variety of situations involving photocopying or other reproduction by a library of copyrighted material in its collections, where the user requests the reproduction for legitimate scholarly or research purposes.[4]

Even when a type of work is within section 108, it seems unlikely that Congress concluded that the section should leave no room whatsoever for fair use—that equitable rule of reason—to come into play. If you accept that, the question arises as to how much room, particularly when the issue comes up in a context where section 108 expressly allows the copying within express limits. Put another way, to what extent will the courts treat the specific section 108 standard as a guide for converting the vague fair-use criteria into a concrete yes-or-no decision in a particular fair-use case?

It may well be that the courts will never give a very precise answer to that question. It is a difficult one, and chances are that any particular dispute can be decided without having to answer it. Nonetheless, section 108 has some characteristics that give it the potential to influence scope-of-fair-use decisions. The section is sometimes detailed, complex, occasionally ambiguous, and, in spots, awkwardly phrased. That combination suggests, correctly, that the section is the result of a difficult-to-reach political and legislative compromise. The features of that compromise will not likely be ignored completely by a court seeking to resolve fair-use issues in a context involving facts of the type addressed fairly specifically by section 108. Thus, although nothing in the section literally affects the right of fair use, the practicalities are that the provisions of section 108 are likely to play at least some role—admitted or otherwise—in interpreting the scope of fair use in the context of library reproduction activities.

### Differences between Sections 107 and 108

There is no restriction as to who may utilize section 107; section 108 applies only to libraries. (When a library uses section 108 as authority for the making of, for example, a copy of an article for someone other than another library, the person receiving the copy does not have explicit section 108 rights. He or she ordinarily must rely on fair use or some other justification for the copy.)

Section 108's coverage of copying activities is sometimes narrower and sometimes broader than section 107's. For example, section 108 ordinarily does not cover more than one copy of a piece of material at any one time, whereas section 107 sometimes permits multiple copies on a single occasion [107; 108(a)–(e),(g)]. Section 108, on the other hand, may be broader in the rights it gives to copy from unpublished works for deposit in another library [108(b)]. Fair use might not cover such activities to the degree that section 108 does.

Because the scope of section 107's coverage is often vague, it may be difficult to say whether a particular right of section 108 is broader or narrower than fair use would allow. One of section 108's attractive features is that it allows a library, at least on occasion, the luxury of not worrying about whether section 107's fair use does or does not apply. Although in some cases a library will have to worry about whether section 108 does or does not apply, for many libraries, in many situations, section 108 does resolve legal uncertainties.

## ELIGIBILITY STANDARDS: ACCESSIBILITY OF COLLECTIONS

A library is eligible to exercise section 108 rights if its collections are open to the public. Even when that is not the case, a library is eligible to exercise section 108 rights if its collections are available not only to researchers affiliated with the library or with the institution of which it is a part but also to others doing research in a specialized field [108(a)(2)]. Some libraries, perhaps especially in some for-profit institutions, may choose not to meet either test and thus may be ineligible for section 108 copying rights.

The statute does not attempt any special definition of the terms "library" or "archives."

## GENERAL COPYING STANDARDS
### No Purpose of Commercial Advantage

*General.* The rights under section 108 apply only to copies made or distributed "without any purpose of direct or indirect commercial advantage" [108(a)(1)]. This means that a library cannot use section 108 as a basis for operating a for-profit copying center. The legislative history states that it also means that a library in a nonprofit institution could not rely on section 108 to arrange with a commercial copying service to carry out the copying and distribution functions of the library.[5]

*Profit Organization Libraries.* Does the no-commerical-advantage restriction mean that a library in a for-profit organization may not avail itself of section 108 to provide copies to the organization's employees for their research activities?

The answer is not clear. The language of the statute was interpreted differently in the Senate and House committees. Although the joint Conference Committee report reflected agreement, it is not certain that a court would find the statutory language flexible enough to embrace the committee's interpretation. Moreover, even if the general answer is that the library's copying for such a purpose is authorized by section 108, the practical utility of that right may be limited both for libraries in for-profit organizations and for the organizations themselves. All of these issues are considered in this chapter, but it is advisable for libraries in for-profit institutions to obtain legal advice from their attorneys as to the interpretation of the law that should be followed.

Let us look at some legislative history. The November 1975 Senate Judiciary Committee report states that the no-commercial-advantage clause was

> intended to preclude a library or archives in a profit-making organization from . . . [using section 108 to provide] . . . photocopies of copyrighted materials to employees engaged in furtherance of the organization's commercial enterprise unless such copying qualifies as a fair use, or the organization has obtained the necessary copyright licenses. A commercial organization should purchase the number of copies of a work that it requires, or obtain the consent of the copyright owner to the making of the photocopies.[6]

This is clear enough. However, the later House Judiciary Committee report (September 3, 1976) concluded otherwise. The committee recognized that section 108 covers only a copy that is made and distributed "without any purpose of direct or indirect commercial advantage." But, said the committee's report:

the "advantage" referred to in this clause must attach to the immediate commercial motivation behind the reproduction or distribution itself, rather than to the ultimate profit-making motivation behind the enterprise in which the library is located.

The House committee concluded that a library in a for-profit institution can have section 108 rights.[7]

The Senate-House Conference Committee report (September 29, 1976) generally went along with the House interpretation:

As long as the library or archives meets the criteria in section 108(a) and the other requirements of the section, . . . the conferees consider that the isolated, spontaneous making of single photocopies by a library or archives in a for-profit organization without any commercial motivation, or participation by such a library or archives in interlibrary arrangements, would come within the scope of section 108.[8]

It may be that the conference report will be considered to represent the legal outcome of the interpretive conflict between the House and Senate reports and that a court would follow the conference report as long as that court concluded that the statutory phrase "commercial advantage" could reasonably be given the House report's narrow interpretation. Right now, the outcome is unknown. Should the issue eventually be decided in court, the outcome will be affected not only by the factors that have already been considered but also by precedents at the time concerning the degree of emphasis that should attach to the statute's legislative history.

Assuming that the no-commercial-advantage clause does not bar a library in a for-profit organization from using section 108 for providing copies to employees does not exhaust the interpretive issues present in the statute. For example, in the case of article copying, section 108 also calls for a library to have had no notice that the copy would be used for any purpose other than "private study, scholarship, or research" [108(d)(1); see also 108(e)(1)]. If the library has notice that the use is for the organization's research activities, is such a purpose one of "private study, scholarship, or research"? If it is not, then section 108 would not apply to the copy made.

None of the three principal congressional reports discussed above directly interprets the phrase "private study, scholarship, or research." However, the House report, interpreting the no-commercial-advantage clause, reflects a clear intent on the committee's part to make section 108 capable of covering an article copy made by a library in a for-profit organization for research activities, on behalf of the organization, by one of its employees:

Isolated, spontaneous making of single photocopies by a library in a for-profit organization, without any systematic effort to substitute photocopying for subscriptions or purchases, would be covered by section 108, even though the copies are furnished to the employees of the organization for use in their work.[9]

Consequently, it is possible, but certainly not certain, that the word "private" in "private study, scholarship, or research" will be construed not to modify "research," or that the employee's research will be considered "private research" within the meaning of the section. (Either interpretation also could affect even a library in a not-for-profit institution. Such a library— assuming compliance with section 108 in other respects—could rely on section 108 to fulfill an article copy request for a for-profit organization even when the library happens to have had notice that the article would be used for the for-profit organization's research purposes.)

Even assuming that the "no commercial advantage" and "private study, scholarship, or research" clauses are construed favorably to the library in a for-profit organization, the remainder of the organization, and thus the organization itself, nonetheless may need a legal justification for the copy in addition to section 108. Nothing in section 108 "excuses a person who requests a copy under subsection (d) [which covers article copies] from liability for copyright infringement for any such act . . . if it exceeds fair use as provided by section 107" [108(f)(2)].

## Multiple Copy Restrictions

Section 108 ordinarily authorizes only the making of a single copy of a piece of material on any one occasion [108(a)–(e),(g)]. (A second or subsequent copy may be made on one or more "separate occasions," as discussed below. This restriction should be kept in mind as one of the significant limitations of section 108.)

The rights of reproduction and distribution under section 108 extend to the "isolated and unrelated" reproduction or distribution of a single copy of the same material on separate occasions. However, they do not extend to cases when a library, or its employee, has substantial reason to believe that it is engaging in the "related or concerted" reproduction of multiple copies of the same material (1) whether made on one occasion or over a period of time, and (2) whether intended for aggregate use by one or more individuals or for separate use by the individual members of a group [108(g),(g)(1)].

The Senate report underlying section 108 gives the following as an example of the above provisions: "if a college professor instructs his class to read an article from a copyrighted journal, the school library would not be permitted, under subsection (g), to reproduce copies of the article for the members of the class."[10]

All the complex language—"isolated and unrelated," "related or concerted"—may well cause baffling problems in many situations. However, 90 percent of the point may be covered in this manner: Section 108 authorizes only one copy of something at any particular time. You can sometimes use section 108 properly to make a later copy of that material. However, this is not a carte blanche. You may not make one copy, walk around the copying machine, and then make another.

## Notice of Copyright

Copies made under section 108 must carry notice of copyright [108(a)(3)]. A notice repeating the original one will ordinarily suffice, although section 108 does not state that such a complete notice is required.

An unresolved issue is whether section 108's call for a "notice of copyright" here calls for the notice elements in sections 401–405 of the law (see Chapter 7) or whether it suffices to give a general statement such as "This material may be protected by copyright."[11] (Whatever the correct answer for purposes of section 108, a library's failure to use the notice elements called for in sections 401–405 will ordinarily not jeopardize the owner's copyright because section 108 copies are not publicly distributed by authority of the copyright owner [405(a); 406].)

TABLE 18   GENERAL CRITERIA FOR SECTION 108 LIBRARY COPYING

| Criteria | Copyright Law Section |
|---|---|
| Collections Accessibility. Are the library's collections sufficiently accessible to outsiders? | 108(a)(2) |
| No Commercial Advantage. Will the copy be reproduced and distributed "without any purpose of direct or indirect commercial advantage"? | 108(a)(1) |
| Single Copy. Will only one copy of the work be made or distributed at this time? | 108(a) |
| Isolated-Unrelated Copy. If this is a second or subsequent reproduction of the same material, is it a reproduction that is "isolated" from and "unrelated" to earlier ones? | 108(g) |
| No Related-Concerted Copying. Is it true that the library does not have any "substantial reason to believe that it is engaged in the related or concerted reproduction of the same material. . ."? | 108(g)(1) |
| Copyright Notice. Will the copy bear a "notice of copyright"? | 108(a)(3) |
| No Conflicting Agreement. Is it true that the reproduction or distribution will not violate any contractual obligation of the library? | 108(f)(4) |

### Conflicting Agreements

The fact that section 108 may generally authorize a copy of a work to be made does not "in any way" affect any contractual obligations assumed at any time by the library when it obtained a copy of the work in its collections [108(f)(4)]. In the case of unpublished works and works only leased, contractual restrictions against copying may have a broad and legally valid scope. Contractual restrictions as to copying from published works purchased by the library might also be held valid in particular circumstances, but perhaps not in as many cases as for unpublished or leased material.

The legislative history notes that this provision is "intended to encompass the situation where an individual makes papers, manuscripts or other works available to a library with the understanding that they will not be reproduced."[12]

The general standards for library copying under section 108, listed in Table 18, apply for each of the four copying purposes covered in section 108. However, further conditions must be met for each of the four, and they are considered in the following material.

## UNPUBLISHED WORKS: COPYING FOR PRESERVATION AND SECURITY

A library that is eligible to exercise section 108 rights may make a copy of an unpublished work for purposes of preservation and security or for deposit for research use in another library that has section 108 eligibility. The work must be duplicated in facsimile form, for example, a manuscript cannot be converted into computer data.[13] The "general copying standards" mentioned in the previous section of this chapter also apply. In addition, the library making the copy must have the unpublished work in its current collections [108(b)].

Unlike some other parts of section 108, this one extends to any type of work so long as it is unpublished, for example, to unpublished photographs, motion pictures, and sound recordings.[14] In some cases, however, the library will have contractually agreed not to make reproductions of such works. And in some situations, it could be inappropriate, for invasion-of-privacy considerations, to reproduce particular material for deposit in another library.

## PUBLISHED WORKS: REPLACEMENT COPYING

Section 108 allows an eligible library to make a copy, in facsimile form, of a published work where the copy is made solely for the purpose of replacement of a copy that is damaged, deteriorating, lost, or stolen. However, the library must first have determined, after a reasonable effort, that an unused copy cannot be obtained at a fair price [108(c)]. The reasonable effort may vary with the circumstances but, according to the legislative history, it will

> always require recourse to commonly known trade sources in the United States in the normal situation also to the publisher or other copyright owner (if such owner can be located at the address given in the copyright registration), or to an authorized reproducing service. . . .[15]

The general copying standards considered earlier in this chapter also apply.

## USER REQUESTS: COPYING ENTIRE WORKS

An eligible library under section 108 may, under defined circumstances, make and distribute a copy of an entire work (or a substantial part of it) pursuant to a user's request made at the same or another library [108(e)]. This particular right under section 108 does not apply to:

1. a musical or sculptural work;
2. an audiovisual work (including motion pictures) other than an audiovisual work dealing with news; or
3. pictures or graphic arts except where they are published as illustrations to material that is eligible to be copied and is copied. [108(h)]

For the application of fair use in the case of these excluded materials, see the excerpt from the legislative history quoted earlier in this chapter, under the discussion of the relationship of sections 107 and 108.

Before making a copy pursuant to section 108(e), the library must first have determined, on the basis of a reasonable investigation, that a copy cannot be obtained at a fair price [108(e)]. The previously quoted reasonable effort standard is also applicable here to the reasonable investigation standard.[16]

A further requirement of section 108(e) is that the copy must become the property of the user [108(e)(1)]. The rationale for this provision may be that the legislature thought it would be inappropriate for the copies to be added to the collections of the library.

Still another requirement of this section is that the library must have had no notice that the copy would be used for any purpose other than "private study, scholarship, or research" [108(e)(1)]. And the library must include a "warning of copyright" on its order forms and prominently display a warning of copyright at the place where orders are accepted [108(e)(2)]. The language for this warning, provided by Copyright Office regulations, is as follows:

NOTICE WARNING CONCERNING
COPYRIGHT RESTRICTIONS
The copyright law of the United States (Title 17, United States Code) governs
the making of photocopies or other reproductions of copyrighted material.

Under certain conditions specified in the law, libraries and archives are authorized to furnish a photocopy or other reproduction. One of these specific conditions is that the photocopy or reproduction is not to be "used for any purpose other than private study, scholarship, or research." If a user makes a request for, or later uses, a photocopy or reproduction for purposes in excess of "fair use," that user may be liable for copyright infringement.

This institution reserves the right to refuse to accept a copying order if, in its judgment, fulfillment of the order would involve violation of copyright law.

The regulations also include standards for type size and other matters.[17]

The material that follows in this chapter concerns the rights that relate to, among other things, journal articles. In one copyright sense at least, a typical journal article could be considered an "entire work" because an article, although within a "collective work" comprising the journal issue, may itself be a separate and independent work [101 "collective work"; 201(c)]. In such a situation, does a library follow section 108(e) or 108(d), or may it choose which one it prefers?

Because section 108(d) is specifically designed to relate to article copying, it may be followed. It also seems likely that section 108(e) could be followed in the alternative, particularly as it requires a reasonable effort to obtain an authorized copy.

## USER REQUESTS: COPYING ARTICLES AND EXCERPTS

### General Coverage

An eligible library under section 108 may, under defined circumstances, make and distribute a copy of an article (or other contribution to a copyrighted collection or periodical issue) pursuant to a user's request. The same is true for a copy or phonorecord of a small part of any other copyrighted work [108(d)]. Some of the rules applicable to user requests for a copy of an entire work, considered in the previous section, also apply here:

1. the warning of copyright notices must be used;
2. the library must have had no notice that the material would be used for any purpose other than "private study, scholarship, and research"; and
3. the section does not apply to musical, sculptural, and other works as already enumerated earlier when considering copying entire works. [108(d)(1),(2); 108(h)]

### Isolated and Unrelated Copies

Right of reproduction and distribution under section 108(d) does not extend to cases when the library "engages in the systematic reproduction or distribution of single or multiple copies . . . of material described in subsection (d)" [108(g)]. This clause does not seem intended to preclude a library from using section 108 merely because the library receives enough requests from its own patrons to warrant having a system for handling them efficiently. Rather, it was apparently intended primarily to preclude the substituting of photocopying arrangements for subscriptions or purchases. At the time of the Senate Judiciary Committee report underlying the law, the focus was on interlibrary transactions:

> Systematic reproduction or distribution occurs when a library makes copies of such materials available to other libraries or to groups of users under formal or informal arrangements whose purpose or effect is to have the reproducing library serve as their source of such material. Such systematic reproduction and distribution, as distinguished from isolated and unrelated reproduction and distribution, may substitute the copies reproduced by the source library for subscriptions or reprints or other copies which the receiving libraries or users might otherwise have purchased for themselves, from publishers or the licensed reproducing agencies.[18]

As we shall see, this problem received special attention in a proviso subsequently added to section 108(g)(2). The point at the moment is that concern about subscription or purchase substitution seems to be the primary relevance of the basic clause, even in a situation not involving interlibrary arrangements. However, because "systematic" is not formally defined, it may be argued that the term has a broader scope.

## Interlibrary Arrangements

*The Statute.* The anti-"systematic" clause raised a storm of controversy concerning the extent to which restrictions would prevent the continuation and development of interlibrary networks and other arrangements involving the exchange of photocopies. To resolve this, a proviso was added to the statute, stating that the exclusion of systematic copying or distribution did not prevent a library, under section 108(d), from

> participating in interlibrary arrangements that do not have, as their purpose or effect, that the library . . . receiving such copies or phonorecords for distribution does so in *such aggregate quantities as to substitute for a subscription to or purchase of such work* [108(g)(2)]. [Italics added]

*The CONTU Guidelines.* The National Commission on New Technological Uses of Copyrighted Works, with the concurrence of representatives of authors, librarians, and publishers, developed guidelines interpreting the italicized words above from section 108(d). The legislative history states that the guidelines are not intended, and cannot be considered, as explicit directions covering all cases, but nonetheless are a reasonable interpretation of the aggregate-quantities standard in the most common situations to which the standard applies today.[19] These section 108(g)(2) guidelines are set forth in Appendix 4.

Concerning article copies, the guidelines consider only what might be called "recent" articles and issues, that is, articles published in issues within five years before the date of a library's request for a copy from another library. The guidelines leave "to future interpretation" the application of the aggregate-quantities standard to copies of articles from older issues.

A calendar year is the base period for applying the guidelines. If, during such a period, the requesting library receives a total of no more than five copies of articles from recent issues of the same publication, it is within the guidelines. The sixth copy is beyond the guidelines. The five copies may be of the same article or a combination of different articles from that publication. (As previously mentioned, section 108 does not authorize obtaining multiple copies of the same article on the same occasion.)

Sometimes an interlibrary request will be made even though the requesting library has a subscription in force or on order. When that is the case, the copy requested will not count as one of the five copies if the material to be copied was not reasonably available for use by the requesting library itself. (This part of the guidelines theoretically allows abuses but, as noted, the guidelines are not intended as explicit directions covering all cases.)

In addition to the quantitative "rule of five" (five copies, five years of issues), the guidelines have some procedural rules.

1. The copy request is not supposed to be made unless the requesting library could have made and supplied the copy under section 108 had the article been in the library's own collections.
2. The supplying library is supposed to fulfill another library's recent-article request only if the requesting library represents that the request conforms with the guidelines.
3. The requesting library is supposed to maintain a record of its interlibrary requests for section 108(d) materials and fulfillments of such requests.
4. The records just referred to are supposed to be kept during the calendar year of the recorded event and for three calendar years thereafter.

It should be noted that, although the guidelines speak in mandatory terms—for example, "no request shall be fulfilled," "the requesting entity shall maintain"—they are only guidelines, not a statute. It is beneficial to comply with the guidelines, even though they are not explicitly mandated.

Interlibrary guidelines also exist for other section 108(d) materials, such as for a copy or phonorecord of a small part of any other copyrighted work covered by section 108(d). A library may fulfill requests for such materials from other libraries. The guidelines state that during any calendar year the copies to be provided should not total more than five interlibrary copies from any given work. The requested copy does not count as one of the five copies if the requesting library has the material or has it on order, but it is not reasonably available. This guideline standard applies not merely to material published within the five years before the request but to the entire copyright period. The procedural standards set forth above apply here as well.

*Libraries in For-Profit Organizations.* As mentioned earlier in this chapter, the 1975 Senate report and the 1976 House report differed as to whether a library in a for-profit institution could use section 108 at all for its employees' research needs. The Senate-House Conference report generally sided with the House. However, the conference report sanctioned the for-profit library's use of section 108 if it occurred without "participation by such a library . . . in interlibrary arrangements. . . ."[20] The House report had explicitly stated such participation was permissible under section 108.[21]

The issue of how section 108 applies is significant enough that perhaps authoritative guidance will develop before too long. Meanwhile, libraries in for-profit institutions that plan to use section 108 should, at the very least, be sensitive to the following examples from the Senate report of subscription substitution situations.[22] The examples were developed before the interlibrary-arrangements proviso came into the legislative proceedings, but they are nonetheless worth noting.

(1) A library with a collection of journals in biology informs other libraries with similar collections that it will maintain and build its own collection and will make copies of articles from these journals available to them and their patrons on request. Accordingly, the other libraries discontinue or refrain from purchasing subscriptions to those journals and fulfill their patrons' requests for articles by obtaining photocopies from the source library.

(2) A research center employing a number of scientists and technicians subscribes to one or two copies of needed periodicals. By reproducing photocopies of articles the center is able to make the material in these periodicals available to its staff in the same manner which otherwise would have required multiple subscriptions.

(3) Several branches of a library system agree that one branch will subscribe to particular journals in lieu of each branch purchasing its own subscriptions, and the one subscribing branch will reproduce copies of articles from the publication for users of the other branches.

*The Supplying Library.* The subsection 108(g)(2) proviso speaks in terms of sanctioning a library's participation in an interlibrary arrangement if the receiving library is within the aggregate-quantity rule. Thus, the supplying library would seem to be protected when the receiving library is protected. It remains to be seen whether this interpretation will prevail. An unequivocal resolution favorable to the supplying library does not necessarily leave that library without other potential problems. Some concern would have to be given to exclusion of related and concerted copying of the same material on separate occasions in section 108(g)(1). Also, the following remark by

CONTU, prefatory to the guidelines themselves, should be kept in mind:

> The point has been made that the present practice on . . . use of photocopies in lieu of loans may be supplemented or even largely replaced by a system in which one or more agencies or institutions, public or private, exist for the specific purpose of providing a central source for photocopies. Of course, these guidelines would not apply to such a situation.[23]

## UNSUPERVISED REPRODUCING EQUIPMENT

According to one of its provisions, nothing in section 108 is to be construed to impose copyright liability upon a library for copyright infringement for the unsupervised use of reproducing equipment located in the library's premises *if* such equipment displays a notice that making a copy may be subject to the copyright law [108(f)(1)]. The individual using such equipment would not have the benefits of section 108 (unless by chance it happened that a library employee was using the equipment under section 108 circumstances).

The section includes an express provision stating that nothing in the section excuses a person who uses the unsupervised equipment from liability for any infringement that may be committed, the right of fair use, of course, being potentially applicable in some circumstances [108(f)(2)].

Unlike the "warning of copyright" statement noted earlier, no Copyright Office regulations set specific standards for the type of notice called for by this subsection.

Subsection 108(d) does not literally relieve a library from liability, as the provision relates only to the impact of section 108. However, both the House and Senate Judiciary Committee reports state that the clause "specifically exempts" the library and its employees.[24]

The House Judiciary Committee report states that a library in a for-profit organization could not avoid obligations under section 108 by installing reproducing equipment on its premises for unsupervised use by the organization's staff.[25]

## IMPORT PROVISIONS

The import provisions of the new law generally provide that it is an infringement of copyright to import a work that is protected by U.S. copyright without the copyright owner's consent [602]. The exceptions, some of which relate to libraries, are considered in Chapter 11.

## AUDIOVISUAL NEWS PROGRAMS

### Library of Congress

At the time the copyright law was passed, Congress also passed the American Television and Radio Archives Act [Transitional and Supplementary Provisions, Sec. 113]. Under the act, the Library of Congress is authorized to record broadcasts of news programs and to make compilations of them according to subject matter. The Library also is authorized to distribute a reproduction of such a newscast or compilation for deposit in a library whose collections meet the eligibility criteria of section 108(a). The distribution should be for use by researchers only in their research and not for further reproduction or performance. The library providing the recording to the researcher is supposed to lend it, not sell it.

### Other Libraries

As a companion provision to the act mentioned above, section 108 of the copyright law provides that nothing in section 108 shall be construed to limit the reproduction and distribution (through the lending of a limited number of copies and excerpts) of an audiovisual news program by a library [108(f)(3)]. According to the House Judiciary Committee report, it is intended to permit libraries to make off-the-air recordings of daily network newscasts for limited distribution for use in research.[26] The later Senate-House Conference report added that the term "audiovisual newscast program" was intended to include "local, regional, and network newscasts and also on-the-spot coverage of news events and interviews concerning news events."[27]

The copying and lending right is available to libraries that meet the collections accessibility criteria of section 108. Any reproduction should include a notice of copyright, and copies should be loaned without any purpose of commercial advantage [108(f)(3); 108(a)(1)–(3)].

## DEVELOPMENTS TO COME

The 1976 law was the first of the federal copyright statutes specifically to cover library reproduction and distribution rights. Congress, in passing the provision, also ruled that the Register of Copyrights report on it once it had been in operation for five years [108(i)]. The report is due at the beginning of 1983. In preparation for it, the Copyright Office has the benefit of related studies and considerations of CONTU, which issued its final report in 1978. In addition, the Copyright Office has held hearings throughout the country in order for interested parties to present their views. Also, surveys have been conducted to obtain information and reactions from publishers and libraries. And, beginning in 1982, representatives of authors and librarians entered into discussions concerning the photocopying provisions of the law.

The Register's report may also comment on the impact, in meeting the needs of copyright owners and libraries, of a not-for-profit organization that has been established—the Copyright Clearance Center. The CCC provides a system to facilitate copyright clearances and permissions payments for situations when the copying would go beyond what the statute authorizes without permission. The organization was founded in part pursuant to a

Senate committee recommendation that workable clearance and licensing procedures be established.[28] Participating libraries periodically submit to the center payments and related reports with respect to publications in the center's system. Participation in the CCC arrangements is voluntary for both librarians and publishers. Each publisher establishes the permission fees applicable to its publications, the center acting only as a facilitating operation to make it easier for libraries to obtain ready permission when needed and to distribute collected fees to the publishers.

At present, conclusions in the Register's report are unknown, as are any possible recommendations for legislative change. If substantial legislative changes are proposed, they are likely—based on the problems that developed over section 108 itself—to bring about considerable controversy. This is an area of public policy where, once past some high level of generalization, widely disparate opinions have often been intensely held concerning what is sound and equitable.

The interlibrary-arrangement guidelines are also scheduled, by their own terms, for reconsideration in 1983. No statutory provisions have been established for this review. Perhaps some informal arrangements will be made. In any event, some commentary about the guidelines presumably will be included in the Register's report, as they are integrally related to section 108.

The subject of corporate photocopying of others' copyrighted materials will receive increased attention in the years immediately ahead. At the time this edition was going to press, the Association of American Publishers announced that it had reached a settlement with one corporation. The corporation agreed, generally, to keep track of its copying of Copyright Clearance Center-registered material and to make appropriate royalty payments. (See *BP Reports*, May 3, 1982, p. 1.) The settlement, while not a binding court precedent for others, will cause some corporations to visit or revisit their own practices and make judgments anew as to what the copyright law's requirements are and what practical steps are needed in order to be in compliance.

# 16

# LIMITS ON RIGHTS OF PERFORMANCE AND DISPLAY

Two of the copyright owner's exclusive rights of copyright are the rights of public performance and public display [106]. The scope of these rights is considered in Chapter 5. Chapter 3 considers the performance right limitations with respect to sound recordings and, in Chapter 14, some performance right limitations relating to educational activities were discussed. In Chapter 17, we consider some special compulsory licensing provisions relating to performance or display rights and the making of recordings, jukeboxes, public broadcasting, and cable television systems. In this chapter, we consider a potpourri of other exceptions to the public performance and display rights.

## FREE PERFORMANCES

The statute authorizes certain noncommercial, nonprofit, free performances, other than by transmissions, of nondramatic literary works and nondramatic musical works [110(4)]. (A performance is "transmitted" when it is communicated "by any device or process whereby images or sounds are received beyond the place from which they are sent" [101 "transmit"].)

For a performance of the work to qualify under the subsection:

1. The performers and promoters must receive no compensation.
2. No admission may be charged.
3. There must be no purpose of direct or indirect commercial advantage.

The legislative history reports that, as a result of the last requirement, free public performances are not exempt from copyright liability if given, or sponsored in connection with a commercial or profit-making organization.[1]

## FUND-RAISING PERFORMANCES

In addition to exempting certain free performances, the statute exempts, in a qualified manner, certain fund-raising performances that take place other than by transmission [101 "transmit"; 110(4)]. This exemption also covers nondramatic literary and nondramatic musical works. In order for a performance to be eligible:

1. The funds, after reasonable production expenses, must be used exclusively for educational, religious, or charitable purposes and not for private financial gain.
2. The performers, promoters, and organizers must not be compensated.

The legislative history adds that the second rule is not considered violated if, for example, the performance is by a school orchestra conducted by a music teacher who receives an annual salary, or by members of a service band whose performance is part of their assigned duties and who receive military pay.[2]

By following certain procedures, the copyright owner has the power to remove his or her work from this exemption for a particular performance [110(4)].[3]

## RELIGIOUS SERVICES

A work performed or displayed during religious services is exempt from public performance and display rights [110(3)]. The performance exemption applies to nondramatic literary works, nondramatic musical works, and dramatic-musical works of a religious nature. The display exemption applies to all kinds of works.

The exemption covers performances and displays in the course of services at a place of worship or other religious assembly. The phrase "in the course of" is intended to exclude from the exemption those performances given at a place of worship for social, entertainment, or fund-raising purposes.[4] (Under some circumstances, performances for such purposes might be authorized under one of the provisions previously considered in this chapter.)

## AID FOR THE HANDICAPPED

### Nondramatic Literary Works

As an exemption to the copyright owner's public performance rights, nondramatic literary works may be transmitted on a noncommercial basis by specified classes of noncommercial entities under certain conditions.

The performance must be by or in the course of a transmission specifically designed for and primarily directed to: blind or other handicapped persons who are unable to read normal printed material as a result of their handicap, or deaf or other handicapped persons who are unable to hear the aural signals accompanying a transmission of visual signals.

In order for the performance to be exempt, it must be made without any intention to gain direct or indirect commercial advantage, and its transmission must be made through one of the following:

1. a governmental body;
2. a cable system;
3. a noncommercial educational broadcast station; or
4. a radio subcarrier authorization. [110(8)]

The second term is defined in the copyright law; the third and fourth are defined in the Communications Act [110(8); 111(f)].[5]

## Dramatic Literary Works

A dramatic literary work that is at least ten years old may be performed by transmission, through the facilities of a radio subcarrier authorization, if the transmission is specifically designed for and primarily directed to the blind or to other handicapped persons who are unable to read normal printed material as a result of their handicap [110(9)]. The performance must be made without any intention to gain direct or indirect commercial advantage.

The exemption provided under this subsection of the law is not applicable to more than one performance of the same work by the same performers or under the auspices of the same organization.

## Other Provisions for the Disabled

Chapter 14 considers a provision for certain instructional transmissions to aid the handicapped. Chapter 10 reports on a voluntary license arrangement that the Copyright Office seeks as part of the copyright registration process for nondramatic literary works [710].

## MISCELLANEOUS

### Annual Agricultural Fairs

Performance of a nondramatic musical work by a nonprofit agricultural or horticultural organization, in the course of its annual fair, is allowed as an exception to the copyright owner's public performance right [110(6)]. This provision protects the qualifying organization, but, as interpreted by the legislative history, the exception does not extend to such people as concessionaires who perform musical works.[6]

### Record Shops

The performance of a nondramatic musical work by a record shop, solely to promote retail sales of copies of the work or phonorecords of it, is authorized by the statute [110(7)].[7] One of the conditions is that the place of performance be open to the public. Another is that there be no admission charge.

## Home Receiving Apparatus

The ordinary use of home radio and television receivers is not a public performance and thus creates no need for any exception to be built into the copyright law. However, the law does authorize the use of such receivers in public places if no charge is made to see and hear the performance and if the transmission received on the set is not further transmitted [110(5); 101 "transmit"].[8]

## CERTAIN SECONDARY TRANSMISSIONS

These exceptions are concerned with secondary transmissions of primary transmissions that embody a performance or display of a copyrighted work.

A "primary transmission" is a transmission made to the public by the transmitting facility whose signals are being received and further transmitted by the secondary transmission service, regardless of where or when the performance or display was first transmitted [111(6)].

A "secondary transmission" is the further transmitting of a primary transmission simultaneously with the primary transmission, or nonsimultaneously with the primary transmission if by a "cable system" not located in whole or in part within the boundary of the 48 contiguous states, Hawaii, or Puerto Rico—provided, however, that a nonsimultaneous further transmission by a cable system located in Hawaii of a primary transmission shall be deemed to be a secondary transmission if the carriage of the television broadcast signal comprising such further transmission is permissible under the rules, regulations, or authorizations of the Federal Communications Commission [111(6)].

## Provisions Re Apartment Houses and So On

A secondary transmission is not an infringement where each of the following is the case:

1. The secondary transmission consists entirely of the relaying, by the management of a hotel, apartment house, or similar establishment, of signals transmitted by a broadcast station licensed by the Federal Communications Commission.
2. The transmission is within the local service area of such station.
3. The transmission is to the private lodgings of guests or residents of the establishment.
4. There is no direct charge made to see or hear the secondary transmission.
5. The secondary transmission is not made by a "cable system." [111(a)(1)]

A "cable system" is defined as:

> a facility, located in any State, Territory, Trust Territory, or Possession, that in whole or in part receives signals transmitted or programs broadcast by one or more television broadcast stations licensed by the Federal Communications Commission, and makes secondary transmissions of such signals or programs by wires, cables, or other communications channels to subscribing members of the public who pay for such service. [111(f)]

The legislative history adds the following comments concerning the exception:

> The exemption would not apply if the secondary transmission consists of anything other than the mere relay of ordinary broadcasts. The cutting out of advertising, the running in of new commercials, or any other change in the signal relayed would subject the secondary transmitter to full liability. Moreover, the term "private lodgings" is limited to rooms used as living quarters or for private parties, and does not include dining rooms, meeting halls, theatres, ballrooms, or similar places that are outside of a normal circle of a family and its social acquaintances.[9]

## Nonprofit Organizations

A secondary transmission made by a governmental body or other nonprofit organization is excepted from the copyright owner's public performance and display rights if:

1. The secondary transmission is made without any purpose of direct or indirect commercial advantage, and
2. It is made without charge to the recipients of the secondary transmission other than assessments necessary to defray the actual and reasonable costs of maintaining and operating the secondary transmission service. [110(a)(4)]

The legislative history indicates that this exemption serves to sanction certain "booster" and "translator" transmitters:

> [The clause] . . . would exempt the activities of secondary transmitters that operate on a completely nonprofit basis. The operations of nonprofit "translators" or "boosters," which do nothing more than amplify broadcast signals and retransmit them to everyone in an area for free reception, would be exempt . . . [if the "no commercial advantage" and "no charge" standards are met].[10]

## Certain Educational Transmissions

A secondary transmission is not an infringement if it is made solely for the purposes and under the conditions specified in subsection 110(2) of the statute [111(a)(2)]. (Subsection 110(2) is considered in Chapter 14.) The subsection concerns, generally, certain transmissions that constitute a regular part of the systematic instructional activities of a governmental body or nonprofit educational institution.

## CERTAIN SECONDARY TRANSMISSIONS BY PASSIVE CARRIERS

A secondary transmission of a primary transmission embodying a performance or display is not an infringement of copyright if:

1. It is made by a carrier who has no direct or indirect control over the content or selection of the primary transmission.
2. It is made by a carrier who has no direct or indirect control over the particular recipients of the primary transmission.
3. The activities of the carrier with respect to the secondary transmission consist solely of providing wires, cables, or other communications channels for the use of others. [111(a)(3)]

The exemption extends only to the activities of the carrier with respect to secondary transmissions. It does not exempt from liability the activities of others with respect to their own primary or secondary transmissions [111(a)(3)].

## FCC-MANDATED SECONDARY TRANSMISSIONS

When a primary transmission of copyrighted material is a controlled one, limited to reception by particular members of the public, it ordinarily is an infringement to make a secondary transmission of it unless copyright permission has been obtained [111(b)]. Examples of such primary transmissions are closed-circuit broadcasts to theaters and pay television and pay cable.[11]

The statute provides that the secondary transmission would not be an infringement if:

1. The primary transmission is made by an FCC-licensed broadcast station.
2. The carriage of the signals comprising the secondary transmission is required by the FCC.
3. The signal of the primary transmitter is not altered or changed in any way by the secondary transmitter. [111(b)(1)–(3)]

These exemption provisions take into account a possibility, envisioned as the 1976 Copyright Act was developing, that the FCC might at some time require, say, a cable system to carry a "scrambled" pay television signal.[12]

# 17

## COMPULSORY LICENSES

Under the copyright law, a person has a statutory right, in four copyright areas, to make certain designated uses of a copyrighted work if certain procedures are followed and statutorily established fees paid. The four areas, referred to as compulsory licenses, consist of:

1. cable system transmissions of broadcast programs;
2. noncommercial broadcasters' transmissions of published nondramatic musical works and of published pictorial, graphic, and sculptural works;
3. recording rights in nondramatic musical compositions; and
4. jukebox performances of nondramatic musical compositions.

## CABLE SYSTEM TRANSMISSIONS OF BROADCAST SIGNALS
### General

As the present copyright law was developing in Congress, cable television was developing as an industry. Cable systems were carrying broadcast programs of copyrighted material, commonly without the consent of either the broadcast station or the copyright owner. Over time, some of the cable systems went beyond carrying just the signals of local television stations and began to bring in programming from somewhat farther away, thus adding to the competition for viewers.

Eventually, some copyright infringement test cases were brought against cable systems to determine whether, under the then-applicable law, the 1909 Copyright Act, the cable systems' signal carriages constituted infringement. In the two leading cases, the cable systems were upheld, although the court in each case made it clear that the issues would be appropriately addressed in more modern legislation than that enacted near the turn of the century.[1]

As it turned out, the issues were addressed anew in two different forums—the Federal Communications Commission and Congress. The FCC stepped in by adopting a set of complex rules, which determined, for any particular cable system, what broadcast signals it must carry (generally, the regular television signals in the local area) and the additional, more distant, signals that it could carry if it wanted to.

In the context of those FCC rules, Congress dealt with the copyright issues. In general, the 1976 Copyright Act provided that a cable system may carry a broadcast signal without the necessity of obtaining copyright permission if the signal carriage is authorized by the FCC [111(c)(1)]. As the second step, Congress provided that the cable system would have to pay royalties for the privilege of carrying the nonlocal signals and would have to file certain signal carriage and accounting reports [111(d)(2)(B)]. The royalties were payable into a central pool, with the Copyright Royalty Tribunal to decide its division if the various claiming copyright owners could not reach agreement among themselves [111(d)(2),(3); 801(b)(3)]. Failure to file the required reports or to make the called-for royalty payments could mean that the carriage of the broadcast signals would constitute infringement of copyright [111(c)(2)].

The following material considers the current compulsory license provisions for cable systems in more detail. There are proposals pending to amend the law but it is too early to tell what or when Congress will enact. The leading proposal at the moment would codify, with some modifications, rules similar to the ones that the FCC repealed, thus in effect putting back limitations on the number of broadcast station signals that a cable system could carry without permission from the copyright owners. There also is some support for phasing out the compulsory license provision entirely but, at the moment, this does not seem likely.

## License Eligibility

The compulsory license applies to secondary transmissions to the public, by a cable system, of a primary transmission made by a broadcast station licensed by the FCC (or an appropriate government authority of Canada or Mexico) where the carriage of the broadcast signal is permissible under FCC standards [111(c)(1)]. Except in certain situations involving Alaska and Hawaii, the license relates only to transmissions that are simultaneous with the primary transmissions [111(f) "secondary transmission"].

The license generally does not apply in instances when the content of the broadcast program is willfully altered or where commercial advertisements or station announcements are changed or deleted. (A qualified exception covers certain market research situations [111(c)(3)].) The license also has some limitations with respect to carriage of Canadian and Mexican signals [111(c)(4)].

The terms "cable system," "primary transmission," and "secondary transmission" are defined in the statute [111(f)]. These definitions, quoted in Chapter 16 in regard to other statutory standards, are repeated here for convenience:

A "cable system" is a facility, located in any State, Territory, Trust Territory, or Possession, that in whole or in part receives signals transmitted or programs broadcast by one or more television broadcast stations licensed by the Federal Communications Commission, and makes secondary transmissions of such signals or programs by wires, cables, or other communications channels to subscribing members of the public who pay for such service.

A "primary transmission" is a transmission made to the public by the transmitting facility whose signals are being received and further transmitted by the secondary transmission service, regardless of where or when the performance or display was first transmitted.

A "secondary transmission" is the further transmitting of a primary transmission simultaneously with the primary transmission, or nonsimultaneously with the primary transmission if by a "cable system" not located in whole or in part within the boundary of the 48 contiguous states, Hawaii, or Puerto Rico—provided, however, that a nonsimultaneous further transmission by a cable system located in Hawaii of a primary transmission shall be deemed to be a secondary transmission if the carriage of the television broadcast signal comprising such further transmission is permissible under the rules, regulations, or authorizations of the Federal Communications Commission.

## How License Is Obtained and Maintained

For an eligible secondary transmission by the cable system to be covered by the compulsory license, the cable system must record, in the Copyright Office, a notice setting forth various ownership and signal-carriage information about the cable system. When there are changes, an update notice must be recorded [111(d)(1); 111(c)(2)(B)].

A second standard for the compulsory license is that the cable system file semiannual statements of account with the Copyright Office [111(d)(2)(A); 111(c)(2)(B)]. These statements report on the broadcast signals that the cable system has carried and on the gross amounts paid to the cable system for the basic service of providing secondary transmissions of primary broadcasting transmitters [111(d)(2)(A)]. The reporting requirements are quite complex. The information is submitted on the applicable Copyright Office form—CS/SA-1, 2, or 3—depending on the semiannual gross receipts of the system.

The third standard is that the applicable royalty amounts, which are calculated using the above forms, be paid to the Copyright Office [111(c)(2)(B)–(D)].

## Royalty Rates

When the 1976 Copyright Act took effect, a general royalty rate structure was established and some modifications were included for some smaller cable systems.

A key figure for royalty calculations is the cable system's "gross receipts from subscribers for the basic service of providing secondary transmissions of primary broadcast transmitters." (That amount will typically be less than the cable system's total payments from subscribers.) For convenience, we will note the amount as "section 111 receipts." The basic rules established in the statute are that the cable system would pay a basic semiannual royalty calculated on "section 111 receipts" [111(d)(2)(B)(i)]. The payment can be higher than the basic semiannual royalty depending on how many "distant signal equivalents" the cable system actually carries. The general payment rules initially applied to systems with semiannual "section 111 receipts" of $160,000 or more. That figure was raised to $214,000 for 1981 and later.[2] There are provisions for lesser payments in the cases of systems with lower semiannual gross receipts [111(d)(2)(C)(D)]. The cutoff points were initially at semiannual "section 111 receipts" of 0–$80,000 and $80,000–$160,000; raised for 1981 and later to 0–$107,000 and $107,000–$214,000.[3]

Table 19 shows, for a system with semiannual "section 111 receipts" of $160,000 or more, the applicable royalty rates, expressed in terms of amounts per thousand dollars of semiannual "section 111 receipts." The table includes the rates as initially set by the statute and the higher rates established by the Tribunal beginning with 1981 receipts. (The Copyright Royalty Tribunal's decision on the higher rates is now under court review.) An allocation is made when the calculations for "distant signal equivalents" result in something other than a whole number [111(d)(2)(B)]. For purposes of the calculations, a "distant signal equivalent" is defined by the statute in part as:

> the value assigned to the secondary transmission of any nonnetwork television programming carried by a cable system in whole or in part beyond the local service area of a primary transmitter of such programming. It is computed by assigning a value of one to each independent station and a value of one-quarter to each network station and noncommercial educational station for the nonnetwork programming so carried pursuant to the rules . . . of the Federal Communications Commission. [111(f)]

This subsection adds some qualifications to the above and establishes definitions for some of the included terms—"local service area of a primary transmitter," "network station," "independent station," and "noncommercial educational station" [see also 111(d)(2)(B)].

## Royalty Rate Adjustments

Subject to meeting some threshold criteria, the statute authorizes further changes in the above royalty rate structure by means of Copyright Royalty Tribunal proceedings beginning in 1985 [801(b)(2)(A); 804(a)(2)(A)].

When the royalty rate structure was established in the statute, the context included not only the FCC's general signal carriage rules already noted (that

TABLE 19   SYSTEM WITH SEMIANNUAL SECTION III RECEIPTS

|  | Initial Statutory Rates* | Tribunal Rates for 1981 et seq.* |
|---|---|---|
| Base figure | $6.25 | $8.17 |
| If one distant signal equivalent is carried, an additional | — | — |
| If a 2nd, 3rd, or 4th distant signal equivalent is carried, an additional amount per such signal equivalent, of | $4.25 | $5.141 |
| If a 5th or more distant signal equivalent is carried, an additional amount per such signal equivalent, of | $2.00 | $2.42 |

* Per thousand dollars of semiannual section III receipts.

is, criteria as to local and distant signals) but also FCC rules that modified those general standards to sometimes require the deletion of particular broadcast program signals in the case of some sports programs and in the case of some syndicated programs where a local broadcaster had obtained exclusive rights. The statute provides that, subject to certain threshold criteria, there can be royalty rate adjustment proceedings should the FCC change such rules [801(b)(2)(B),(C); 804(b)]. The FCC has, in fact, changed the rules, but no rate modification proceedings have yet been started.

## Allocation and Distribution of Collected Royalties

The royalty payments under the compulsory license are paid into the Copyright Office and distributed by the Copyright Royalty Tribunal to eligible copyright owners or their representatives [111(d)(3); 801(b)(3)]. Certain administrative charges are deducted before distribution, but the distribution figure is higher than the amount collected because, pending distribution, considerable interest is earned on the funds [111(d)(3); 807].[4]

When copyright owners cannot agree on how the amounts should be allocated among them, the Copyright Royalty Tribunal decides [801(b)(3); 804(d)]. Because cable systems' payments are not tied to specific copyrighted material, and because a great number and variety of copyrighted materials are involved, it is not surprising that the Tribunal has many issues to resolve. In its first "final determination" under the compulsory license system, the Tribunal established some general criteria for allocating the funds among eligible copyright claimants and also made a number of decisions concerning eligibility.[5]

As for general allocation criteria, the Tribunal determined three primary factors: (1) the harm caused to copyright owners by secondary transmissions of copyrighted works by cable systems, (2) the benefit derived by cable systems from the secondary transmission of certain copyrighted works, and (3) the marketplace value of the works transmitted. In addition, the Tribunal adopted two secondary criteria: quality of copyrighted program material and time-related considerations.

Regarding the actual application of the preceding criteria, the Tribunal noted that, with respect to the first year, 1978, it did not give any significant weight to the quality factor and did give "some limited weight" to time-related considerations. Regarding the latter, the Tribunal noted: "We conclude that an allocation of royalties mainly based on the amount of time occupied by particular categories of programming would ignore market considerations and produce a distorted value of programming."

After applying the criteria and making some eligibility decisions, the Tribunal's allocation results were:

| | |
|---|---|
| Motion Picture Association of America, Christian Broadcasting Network, and other program syndicators | 75% |
| Joint Sports Claimants and NCAA | 12% |
| Public Broadcasting Service | 5.25% |
| Music performing rights societies (The suballocation of that percentage was 54% to ASCAP, 43% to BMI, and 3% to SESAC) | 4.50% |
| U.S. and Canadian Television Broadcasters | 3.25% |

Approximately $12.8 million in statutory royalties was paid in 1978. The comparable figures for 1979 and 1980 were approximately $15.8 million and $19.1 million, respectively.

Following in abbreviated form are some of the decisions in the final report concerning eligibility:

Some broadcaster interests claimed royalty sharing in part on the theory that a "broadcast day" of programming constituted a copyrighted compilation. The Tribunal ruled that Congress did not intend section 111 compensation on that basis.

With respect to syndicated programming, the Tribunal ruled the general congressional intent to be that television stations would be compensated under section 111 only for eligible locally produced programs and that, with respect to syndicated programming, the royalties should be distributed to program syndicators. (The Tribunal, considering this issue in the context of its own role, was not addressing the validity of contractual provisions under which a broadcaster and a syndicator might agree to allocate among themselves the syndicator's royalty, where, say, the broadcaster carries a syndicated program and the same program shows up in the market as the result of the cable importation of a distant signal.)

The statute speaks of royalty fees with respect to a "nonnetwork television program" [111(d)(4)(A)]. The Public Broadcasting Service successfully argued that the operation of PBS should be equated to that of a program syndicator and not to network programming.

Copyright owners of characters such as "Bugs Bunny" made claims, but the Tribunal rejected them, concluding that Congress did not contemplate the awarding of section 111 royalty fees to the copyright owners of individual components of programs other than music. (The Tribunal ruled, in the alternative, that even if it were wrong on the legal point, the evidentiary record did not justify the distribution of any royalties to the copyright owners.)

As for sports programming, the Tribunal concluded that royalties belonged to the sports leagues, absent contractual arrangements specifically providing that such royalties be distributed to broadcaster claimants.

Concerning commercial radio, the Tribunal concluded that the record before it provided no basis for an allocation of royalty fees.

In April 1982 a federal appeals court upheld, generally, the Tribunal's percentage allocations, though not agreeing entirely with all of the Tribunal's rationale.

## NONCOMMERCIAL BROADCASTING

### Scope of Compulsory License

This category of compulsory licensing, also new with the 1976 Copyright Act, concerns program productions by public broadcasting entities and the following types of works: published nondramatic musical works and published pictorial, graphic, and sculptural works [118(b),(e)]. Specifically excluded from the license are dramatizations of nondramatic musical works, the unauthorized use of any portion of an audiovisual work, and the production of a transmission program drawn to any substantial extent from a published compilation of pictorial, graphic, or sculptural works [118(f)].

The license covers use as part of programs for noncommercial educational broadcast station transmissions [108(d)(1),(g)]. It also authorizes reproductions, distributions, and performances of those programs by a nonprofit institution solely for the purpose of performance transmission or display as part of programs for noncommercial educational broadcast station transmissions [118(d)(2)].

When a covered program is transmitted in accordance with the license, a government body or a nonprofit institution may make simultaneous reproductions, which may be used, for a limited period, just as the original authorized transmission for noncommercial educational broadcast station transmissions [118(d)(1),(3)]. Also, the license coverage would apply, for a limited period, if the reproduction were used for the performance or display of a covered work by instructors or pupils in the course of face-to-face teaching activities of a nonprofit educational institution, in a classroom, or a similar place devoted to instruction [118(d)(3); 110(1)].

The limited period referred to above is no more than seven days from the date of the initial transmission. Also, for the license to apply, the reproduction must be destroyed by the end of that period [118(d)(3)]. If it is not destroyed, an authorized entity who supplied the reproduction will not be subject to an infringement claim if the entity informed the recipient of the destruction requirement [118(d)(3)].

## Royalty Terms

When the compulsory license was enacted, no licensing rates had been established. The statute encouraged voluntary agreements to be reached and filed with the Copyright Office [118(b)]. When such agreements were not reached, the Copyright Royalty Tribunal was authorized to establish licensing rates [118(b)(3),(4)]. Copyright Royalty Tribunal regulations now cover a whole series of rates.[6] For example, one regulation requires the Public Broadcasting Service, National Public Radio, and their stations to pay a total of $1,584,440 per year to the American Society of Composers, Authors, and Publishers (ASCAP), with provisions for adjustments up or down if stations are added or deleted.[7] Other topics covered by the regulations include performances of musical compositions not in ASCAP's repertoire; performances of musical compositions by public broadcast entities licensed to colleges and universities; rights, rates, and terms for recording musical works to be transmitted pursuant to the compulsory license; and terms and rates of royalty payments for the use of published pictorial, graphic, and sculptural works.

The statute requires licensing terms and royalty rates under the compulsory license to be reconsidered by the Tribunal beginning in 1982 and at five-year intervals thereafter [118(c)].

## Nondramatic Literary Works Not Covered

Nondramatic literary works are not covered by the compulsory license. However, when Congress enacted the 1976 Copyright Act, it encouraged copyright owners and public broadcasting entities to agree among themselves as to terms and royalty payments [118(e)(1)]. In 1979, various parties—the Association of American Publishers, the Authors League, the Public Broadcasting Service, and National Public Radio—agreed on a recommended license form and fee schedule. Initially, they approved the arrangement for a two-year period; in 1981, it was approved for another two years. The form—Public Broadcasting License, Nondramatic Literary Works—includes the schedule of recommended fees and may be obtained from the Public Broadcasting Expediting Center, 2005 Massachusetts Avenue, N.W., Washington, D.C. 20036.

Neither the licensing terms on the form nor the fee schedule is mandatory. (An example of a recommended fee would be $25 for 101 to 250 words in a national television broadcast.) Using the license form, the public broadcasting entity ordinarily works directly with the permissions department of the relevant publisher. However, the Expediting Center mentioned above was established to offer assistance when needed.

In addition to agreeing on the form and fee schedule, the parties agreed that, for nondramatic uses of nondramatic literary works in public broadcasting programs, the following generally should be considered fair use:

1. all works, except those covered by (2) below: use of up to 100 words;
2. a complete poem of between 50 and 100 words or a complete children's book of between 50 and 100 words; use of less than the complete or substantially complete work generally should be considered fair use.

Part of the background facts for the licensing and fair-use agreements, of course, was the nonprofit nature of public broadcasting and the fact that commercials are not carried. To the extent that public broadcasting shifts to carrying commercials on a regular and long-term basis, the interested parties may wish to revise their arrangements.

## MUSICAL COMPOSITIONS: RECORDING RIGHTS

### General

This category of the compulsory license has been a part of U.S. copyright law since 1909. It covers, under defined circumstances, rights to reproduce and distribute phonorecords of nondramatic musical compositions [115].

The license does not include the right of public performance [106, 115]. Thus when, say, a radio station acquires a recording made under a compulsory license, the station is not free of an obligation to obtain a license to perform the musical composition publicly. Such licenses ordinarily are obtained from the three performing rights societies noted in Chapter 5—ASCAP, BMI, and SESAC.

The compulsory license covers rights to record nondramatic musical compositions and does not cover the right to duplicate others' recordings of such compositions [115(a)(1)].[8] In order to duplicate another's recording, permission ordinarily would have to be obtained [115(a)(1)]. If so, the permission would cover the sound recording, and the compulsory license then could be used, if otherwise applicable, to cover the underlying musical composition.

### When License Is Available

The right to the compulsory license becomes available, as to a particular musical work, once phonorecords of the work have been distributed to the public in the United States by authority of the copyright owner [115(a)(1)]. (Note: The soundtrack accompanying a motion picture or other audiovisual work is not a "phonorecord" [101 "phonorecord"].)

The compulsory license may be obtained only if the primary purpose in making the phonorecords is to distribute them to the public for private use

[115(a)(1)]. Thus, for example, the license would not apply if the primary purpose was to distribute for commercial uses such as jukeboxes or background music services.[9]

The license includes a right of making musical arrangements of the work for recording purposes. However, Congress did not want the compulsory license to allow the music to be "perverted, distorted, or travestied."[10] Thus, the statute does not allow unlimited leeway, but instead authorizes the making of musical arrangements:

> to the extent necessary to conform it to the style or manner of interpretation of the performance involved, but the arrangement shall not change the basic melody or fundamental character of the work. . . . [115(a)(2)]

When the arrangement constitutes new copyrightable material as a derivative work, the arrangement is not entitled to protection as a derivative work except with the express consent of the copyright owner of the underlying musical work [115(a)(2)].

## How License Is Obtained

The license can be obtained by serving notice of intention to do so on the copyright owner [115(b)(1)]. In the case of co-owners, service on any one of them suffices.[11]

If the registration or other public records of the Copyright Office do not identify the copyright owner and include an address at which notice can be served, the license can be obtained by filing the notice of intent with the Copyright Office [115(b)(1)].

The notice must be served (or, in the second case above, filed) before, or within 30 days after, making the phonorecords, but, in any event, before distributing them [115(b)(1)].

If the notice is sent by certified or registered mail to the last known address for the copyright owner shown by the records of the Copyright Office and is returned to the sender because the copyright owner is no longer located there or refuses to accept delivery, the original notice, as sent, may be recorded in the Copyright Office and the sender credited as having sent the notice on the date it was mailed to the copyright owner.[12]

There is no standard Copyright Office form to provide the required notice. However, there are Copyright Office regulations that spell out in detail the information the notice should contain.[13]

Failure to serve or file the notice of intention to use "forecloses the possibility of a compulsory license and, in the absence of a negotiated license, renders the making and distributing of phonorecords actionable as acts of infringement. . . " [115(b)(2)].

In practice, the compulsory license is not regularly obtained. It is more typical for the parties to reach a voluntary licensing agreement, the Harry Fox Agency being the leading representative of copyright owners in this area of licensing activities. However, the compulsory licensing system is an available alternative to these private arrangements, and thus it plays a major role in determining the terms of the private license, including royalties.

## Royalties

The licensee under a compulsory license is obligated to pay royalties with respect to phonorecords made and distributed under the license at any time after the copyright owner is identified in the registration or other public records of the Copyright Office [115(c)].

The statutory royalties apply to those phonorecords made and distributed under the compulsory license. When the current law took effect, in 1978, the rates were $.0275 for playing times of five minutes or less and, for playing times of more than five minutes, $.005 per minute or fraction thereof [115(c)(2)]. Subsequently, the Copyright Royalty Tribunal increased these rates to the following:

1. for playing times of five minutes or less—$.04;
2. for playing times of more than five minutes—$.0075 per minute or fraction thereof.[14]

Beginning with the years indicated below, the rates are scheduled to be as indicated:

|  | 1983 | 1984 | 1986 |
|---|---|---|---|
| 1. for playing time of five minutes or less | $.0425 | $.045 | $.05 |
| 2. for playing time of more than five minutes, per minute or fraction thereof | $.008 | $.0085 | $.0095 |

The statute authorizes new royalty rate adjustment proceedings to begin in 1987 [801(b)(1); 804(a)(2)(B)].

## Royalty Payment Procedures

Royalty payments under the compulsory license procedures are due monthly (by the 20th) for the previous month and are required to be made under oath [115(c)(3)]. Copyright Office regulations govern the required monthly and annual statements of account, and Copyright Office forms are to be used [115(c)].[15] The statements and payments are made directly to the copyright owner. When for some reason they are not deliverable, the statements may be filed with the Copyright Office, but it will not accept the related fees.

If the payments and statements are not provided on time, as called for by the statute and regulations, the copyright owner may give notice of default and a 30-day termination notice to the licensee. If the default is not remedied within 30 days of the date of the notice, the compulsory license terminates. Those phonorecords not covered by paid royalties are infringing phonorecords [115(c)(4)].

As a general rule, the royalty payments under the compulsory license relate only to phonorecords made and distributed [115(c)(2)]. The statute provides that "[f]or this purpose, a phonorecord is considered 'distributed' if the person exercising the compulsory license has voluntarily and permanently parted with its possession" [115(c)(2)].

The legislative history notes that the recording industry's practice is to distribute phonorecords to wholesalers and retailers with the privilege of returning unsold copies for credit or exchange and that, as a result, the number of phonorecords "permanently" distributed is not known until a period of time has passed after they have entered the chain of distribution.[16] Therefore, on occasion it may be uncertain, for a long time, whether the licensee has "permanently" parted with possession. This problem was addressed in the legislative history by noting that the regulations implementing the law should prescribe a point in time when a phonorecord will be considered "permanently distributed" and should prescribe the situations in which a compulsory licensee should be barred from maintaining reserves against the possibility of returns of phonorecords.[17]

Current Copyright Office regulations require that when phonorecords are sold with a privilege of returning unsold ones, the compulsory licensee will be considered to have permanently parted with possession at the time the licensee recognizes revenue from the sale—a standard further developed in the regulations—or, in any event, nine months from the month in which the licensee actually parted with possession.[18]

## JUKEBOX PERFORMANCES

### General

This category of compulsory license is new with the 1976 Copyright Act. Under the 1909 Copyright Act, no licenses were required for records played on jukeboxes.

The compulsory license covers the public performance of nondramatic musical works by means of a "coin-operated phonorecord player" [116(a)]. Such a player is defined as a machine or device that:

1. is employed solely for the performance of nondramatic musical works by means of phonorecords upon being activated by insertion of coins, currency, tokens, or other monetary units or their equivalent;
2. is located in an establishment making no direct or indirect charge for admission;
3. is accompanied by a list of the titles of all the musical works

available for performance on it, which list is affixed to the phono-record player or posted in the establishment in a prominent position where it can be readily examined by the public; and

4. affords a choice of works available for performance and permits the choice to be made by the patrons of the establishment in which it is located. [116(e)(1)]

All four criteria must apply. Thus, for example, the compulsory license would not be available for a machine that performs audiovisual works, as the recording used would not be a phonorecord [101 "copies," "phono-records," "audiovisual work"].[19] Also, a machine would not qualify if it were located in an establishment that required membership fees for admission or if it provided music without giving the choice of the specific composition to be played at a particular time.[20]

Copyright Office regulations interpreting the definitions established that a coin-operated phonorecord system using multiple wall boxes operating from a remote master unit constitutes only one player for purposes of the statute.[21]

## Who Obtains the License

The compulsory license is obtained by the operator of the coin-operated record player (henceforth called the jukebox). The operator can be the person who owns the jukebox, or the person, such as a jukebox distributor, who has the power to make the jukebox available for placement. The operator also can be the person who has the power to exercise primary control over the selection of musical works to be included in the jukebox repertoire [116(e)(2)].

The proprietor of the establishment where the jukebox is located will ordinarily not be considered the operator nor be liable for any infringement by performances on the equipment should the compulsory license provisions not be followed [116(a)(1); 116(b)(2)].[22] That assumes, of course, that the equipment falls within the definition of a "coin-operated phonorecord player." If it does not, public performances on the equipment will be governed by the general principles of copyright law, and the proprietor can be liable for infringement of the musical works involved.

## How License Is Obtained

A jukebox operator obtains an annual jukebox license by:

1. filing an application with the Copyright Office;
2. affixing to the jukebox the certificate that the Copyright Office issues pursuant to the application; and
3. paying a royalty fee to the Copyright Office. [116(b)(1)]

Failure to comply with those requirements can render the public performance of the nondramatic musical work an infringement [116(b)(2)].

The Copyright Office is supposed to issue a certificate within 20 days of receipt of an application and royalty fee [116(b)(1)(B)]. The operator is supposed to affix the certificate to the phonorecord player where it can be readily examined by the public [116(b)(1)(C)].

There can be a fine of as much as $2,500 for knowingly making a false representation of a material fact in an application for a certificate, or for knowingly altering a certificate issued by the Copyright Office, or for knowingly affixing a certificate to a phonorecord player other than the one it covers [116(d)].

## Royalties

When the current copyright law took effect, the jukebox royalty was established at $8 per year, payable each January [116(b)(1)(A)]. The Copyright Royalty Tribunal subsequently raised the rate to $25 per year, effective January 1, 1982, and to $50 per year, effective January 1, 1984.[23] A provision was also made for a cost of living increase in the rate, the increase to be determined in 1986 and to go into effect in 1987.

The Tribunal is empowered to consider a general adjustment to the jukebox royalty rate in 1990 [804(a)(2)(c)].

## Distribution of Royalties Collected

The royalty payments are per jukebox, but the royalty recipients are the copyright owners of the musical works on the recordings played [116(b)(1)(A); 116(c)]. The statutory arrangement for allocating the collected royalties takes into account that most of the royalty claimants will be represented by performing rights societies such as ASCAP, BMI (Broadcast Music, Inc.), and SESAC, Inc. [116(c)(4)]. The Copyright Royalty Tribunal determines how much should go to these societies and what to other claimants [116(c)(4)]. If the societies cannot agree among themselves on the allocation of their total share, the Tribunal can decide [116(c)(2),(3); 801(b)(3)]. For the royalties collected in 1978, three performing rights societies agreed to the following split: ASCAP and BMI 47.5 percent each and SESAC 5 percent. They have not reached a similar agreement for later years.

# NOTES AND REFERENCES

## LIST OF CASES

Following is a listing of the cases cited in the chapter notes. For the citation to the case itself, see the chapter and note referred to in each case. The chapter notes and references follow this listing.

ABKCO Music, Inc. v. Harrisongs Music, Ltd. (Ch 5, n. 2)
A&M Records, Inc. v. M.V.C. Distributing Corp. (Ch 2, n. 14)
Alexander v. Haley (Ch 3, n. 9)
Allied Artists Pictures Corp. v. Rhodes (Ch 5, n. 30)
Amana Refrigeration, Inc. v. Consumers Union of United States, Inc. (Ch 13, n. 9)
American Vitagraph, Inc. v. Levy (Ch 7, n. 25)
Associated Film Distribution Corp. v. Thornburgh (Ch 5, n. 30)
Association of American Medical Colleges v. Carey (Ch 5, n. 30)
Avco Corp. v. Precision Air Part, Inc. (Ch 5, n. 31)
Basic Books, Inc. v. The Gnomon Corp. (Ch 13, n. 34)
Best Medium Pub. Co. v. National Insider, Inc. (Ch 6, n. 3)
Bruzzone v. Miller Brewing Co. (Ch 13, n. 13)
Building Officials & Code Adm. v. Code Technology, Inc. (Ch 3, n. 12)
Burke v. National Broadcasting Co. (Ch 7, n. 26)
Burwood Products Co. v. Marsel Mirror and Glass Products, Inc. (Ch 5, n. 8)
Classic Film Museum, Inc. v. Warner Bros., Inc. (Ch 4, n. 14)
Coin-Operated Audiovisual Games and Components Thereof; In the Matter of Certain (Ch 5, n. 21)
Custom Decor, Inc. v. Nautical Crafts, Inc. (Ch 3, n. 3)
Dallas Cowboy Cheerleaders, Inc. v. Scoreboard Posters, Inc. (Ch 13, n. 19)
Data Cash Systems, Inc. v. JS&A Group, Inc. (Ch 2, n. 21)
DC Comics Inc. v. Crazy Eddie, Inc. (Ch 13, n. 11)
Diamond v. Diehr (Ch 5, n. 10)

National Conference of Bar Examiners v. Multistate Legal Studies, Inc. (Ch 12, n. 12)

National Research Bureau, Inc. v. Kucker (Ch 7, n. 27)

New Boston Television, Inc. v. Entertainment Sports Programming Network, Inc. (Ch 13, n. 12)

Nichols v. Universal Pictures Corp. (Ch 2, n. 5; Ch 3, n. 2)

Norris Industries, Inc. v. International Telephone and Telegraph Corp. (Ch 3, n. 17)

Northwestern Bell Telephone Co. v. Bedco of Minnesota, Inc. (Ch 13, n. 32)

P. Kaufman, Inc. v. Rex Curtain Corp. (Ch 7, n. 7)

Pillsbury Co. v. Milky Way Productions (Ch 13, n. 20)

Quinto v. Legal Times of Washington, Inc. (Ch 3, n. 8; Ch 7, n. 19)

Rosemont Enterprises, Inc. v. Random House, Inc. (Ch 13, n. 10)

Roy Export Co. v. Columbia Broadcast System, Inc. (Ch 13, n. 24)

Rubin v. Boston Magazine Co. (Ch 13, n. 8)

Russ Berrie & Co. v. Jerry Eisner Co. (Ch 10, n. 6)

Russell v. Price (Ch 4, n. 14)

Sailor Music v. The Gap Stores, Inc. (Ch 16, n. 8)

Schnapper v. Foley (Ch 3, n. 11)

Schroeder v. William Morrow & Co. (Ch 3, n. 8)

Stern Electronics v. Kaufman (Ch 2, n. 22)

Stonehill Communications, Inc. v. Martuge (Ch 11, n. 4)

Streeter v. Rolfe (Ch 3, n. 3)

Suid v. Newsweek Magazine (Ch 3, n. 8; Ch 13, n. 23)

Tandy Corp. v. Personal Microcomputers, Inc. (Ch 2, n. 21)

Technicon Medical Information Systems Corp. v. Green Bay Packaging Inc. (Ch 5, n. 31)

Teleprompter Corp. v. Columbia Broadcasting System, Inc. (Ch 17, n. 1)

Testa v. Janssen (Ch 10, n. 5)

Time, Inc. v. Bernard Geis Assoc. (Ch 13, n. 10)

Triangle Publications, Inc. v. Knight-Ridder Newspapers, Inc. (Ch 13, n. 10, 14)

Twentieth Century-Fox Film Corp. v. MCA, Inc. (Ch 3, n. 4)

Twentieth Century Music Corp. v. Aiken (Ch 1, n. 1)

Twentieth Century Music Corp. v. Frith (Ch 12, n. 10)

United Artists Corp. v. Ford Motor Co. (Ch 3, n. 4)

Universal City Studios, Inc. v. Sony Corp. of America (Ch 12, n. 2, 3; Ch 13, n. 38, 39)

Wainwright Securities Inc. v. Wall Street Transcript Corp. (Ch 13, n. 21)

Walt Disney Productions v. The Air Pirates (Ch 13, n. 19)

Warner Bros., Inc. v. American Broadcasting Cos. (Ch 3, n. 4; Ch 13, n. 18)

Warrington Associates, Inc. v. Kellog Citizens National Bank, Inc. (Ch 5, n. 31)

Warrington Associates, Inc. v. Real-Time Engineering Systems, Inc. (Ch 5, n. 31)
Weisberg v. U.S. (Ch 5, n. 19)
White v. Kimmell (Ch 7, n. 24)
White-Smith Publishing Co. v. Apollo Co. (Ch 2, n. 13)
Wihtol v. Crow (Ch 13, n. 25)
Williams & Wilkins Co. v. U.S. (Ch 13, n. 26)

## CHAPTER NOTES

In the notes that follow, the abbreviations below are used for frequently cited reports.

"1909 Act." The Copyright Act of 1909, as amended up to the enactment of the 1976 Copyright Act. The text of the 1909 Act is set forth in Appendix 5.

"1975 Senate Report." The November 20, 1975 copyright law revision report of the Senate Committee on the Judiciary, 94th Cong., 1st sess., 1975, S. Rept. No. 94-473.

"1976 House Report." The September 22, 1976 copyright law revision report of the House Committee on the Judiciary, 94th Cong., 2d sess., 1976, H.R. Rept. No. 94-1476.

"1976 Conference Report." The September 29, 1976 Senate-House Conference Report on the copyright law, 94th Cong., 2d sess., 1976, H.R. No. 94-1733.

"1978 CONTU Report." The Final Report of the National Commission of New Technological Uses of Copyrighted Works.

### Preface

1. Article I, Section 1, clause 8. The clause is also authority for patent law. It provides in full: "To promote the Progress of Science and useful Arts, by securing for limited Times to Authors and Inventors the exclusive Right to their Writings and Discoveries."
2. See 1976 House Report, p. 47. See also *Copyright Enactments, Laws Passed in the United States Since 1783 Relating to Copyright,* 3 C.O. Bull. (Revised).

### Chapter 1. Introduction

1. Gilbert & Sullivan v. Bacher & Boner, 14 C.O. Bull. 1068 (Phila. Common Pleas, 1880).
2. Twentieth Century Music Corp. v. Aiken, 422 U.S. 151, 40 C.O. Bull. 1206 (1975).

## Chapter 2. Copyrightable Subject Matter, Part I: Basic Standards

1. Although the statute does not attempt to list, at any level of detail, all the types of works that may qualify for copyright protection, it does mention many of them, either for illustrative purposes (especially in section 101 definitions) or in connection with special rules.

2. The statute introduces the list with the word "include." The legislative history states:

> The use of the word "include," as defined in section 101, makes clear that the listing is "illustrative and not limitative," and that the seven categories do not necessarily exhaust the scope of "original works of authorship," that the bill is intended to protect. Rather, the list sets out the general area of copyrightable subject matter, but with sufficient flexibility to free the courts from rigid or outmoded concepts of the scope of particular categories. The items are also overlapping in the sense that a work falling within one class may encompass works coming within some or all of the other categories. In the aggregate, the list covers all classes of works now specified in section 5 of . . . [the 1909 Copyright Act]; in addition, it specifically enumerates "pantomimes and choreographic works" (1976 House Report, p. 53).

3. 1976 House Report, p. 51. The phrase "original works of authorship" in the 1976 law replaces the phrase "all the writings of an author" of the Copyright Act of 1909. The legislative history reports:

> Since the [1909 Act's] . . . language is substantially the same as the empowering language of the Constitution, a recurring question has been whether the statute and the constitutional powers are coextensive. If so, the courts would be faced with the alternative of holding copyrightable something that Congress clearly did not intend to protect, or of holding constitutionally incapable of copyright something that Congress might one day want to protect. To avoid these equally undesirable results, the courts have indicated that "all the writings of an author" under the . . . [1909 Act] is narrower in scope than the "writings" of "authors" referred to in the Constitution. The bill avoids this dilemma by using a different phrase—"original works of authorship"—in characterizing the general subject matter of statutory copyright protection. . . .
>
> Authors are continually finding new ways of expressing themselves, but it is impossible to foresee the forms that these new expressive methods will take. The bill does not intend either to freeze the scope of copyrightable technology or to allow unlimited expansion into areas completely outside the present congressional intent.

4. 1976 House Report, p. 51.

5. Nichols v. Universal Pictures Corp., 45 F.2d 119, 20 C.O. Bull. 528 (2d Cir. 1930), cert. denied, 282 U.S. 902 (1931).

6. See, e.g., Morrison v. Solomons, 494 F.Supp. 218, 210 USPQ 121, 1978–81 Copyright Law Decisions ¶ 25,171 (S.D.N.Y. 1980).

7. E.H. Tate Co. v. Jiffy Enterprises, Inc., 16 F.R.D. 571, 103 USPQ 178 (E.D. Pa. 1954).

8. Donald v. Zack Meyer's T.V. Sales and Services, 426 F.2d 1027, 165 USPQ 751 (5th Cir. 1970), *cert.* denied, 400 U.S. 992 (1971).

9. Morrissey v. Procter & Gamble Co., 379 F.2d 675, 154 USPQ 193, 36 C.O. Bull. 369 (1st Cir. 1967).

10. "The term 'literary works' does not connote any criterion of literary merit or qualitative value: it includes catalogs, directories, and similar factual, reference, or instructional works and compilations of data. It also includes computer data bases, and computer programs to the extent that they incorporate authorship in the programmer's expression of original ideas, as distinguished from the ideas themselves" (1976 House Report, p. 54).

11. 1976 House Report, p. 54.

12. 1976 House Report, pp. 53–54.

13. White-Smith Publishing Co. v. Apollo Co., 209 U.S. 1, 15 C.O. Bull. 2978 (1908).

14. See, e.g., the 5-4 decision in Goldstein v. California, 412 U.S. 546 (1973). For a recent decision on the scope of protection, see A&M Records, Inc. v. M.V.C. Distributing Corp., 574 F.2d 312, 197 USPQ 598, 1978–81 Copyright Law Decisions ¶ 25,013 (6th Cir. 1978).

15. Public Law 92–140.

16. 1976 House Report, p. 56.

17. See 43 *Federal Register* 12763, CCH Copr. L. Rptr. ¶ 16,044 (March 27, 1978).

18. 1976 House Report, pp. 57–58.

19. 1976 House Report, p. 54.

20. 1978 CONTU Report, pp. 1, 9–27. Commissioner John Hersey dissented, taking "the view that copyright is an inappropriate, as well as an unnecessary, way of protecting the usable forms of computer programs" (1978 CONTU Report, pp. 27–37). Commissioner Rhoda Karpatkin stated: "Without agreeing with the entire text of Commissioner Hersey's dissent I share his doubts and concerns sufficiently to lead me to add my dissent to his" (1978 CONTU Report, p. 38). Commissioner Melville Nimmer concurred "in the Commission's opinion and in its recommendations regarding software" but shared "in a number of the doubts and concerns expressed in Commissioner Hersey's thoughtful dissenting opinion" (1978 CONTU Report, pp. 26–27).

21. Tandy Corp. v. Personal Microcomputers, Inc., CCH Copr. L. Rptr. ¶ 25,303 (N.D. Cal. 1981). The court disagreed with a decision of another district court, Data Cash Systems, Inc. v. JS&A Group, Inc., 480 F.Supp. 1063, 203 USPQ 735, 1978–81 Copyright Law Decisions ¶ 25,109 (N.D. Ill. 1979), affirmed on other grounds, 628 F.2d 1038, 208 USPQ 197, 1978–81 Copyright Law Decisions ¶ 25,183 (7th Cir. 1980) (absence of copyright notice). For a discussion concerning the copyrightability of computer programs in the form of object codes, see Richard H. Stern, "Another Look at Copyright Protection of Software: Did the 1980 Act Do Anything for Object Code?" III *Computer/Law Journal* 1 (1981).

22. Stern Electronics v. Kaufman, *BNA Patent, Trademark, & Copyright Journal* 565 (February 4, 1982): A-1. In Midway Mfg. Co. v. Artic International, Inc., CCH Copr. L. Rptr. ¶ 25,337 (N.D. Ill. 1981), the court noted, but did not resolve,

the question of what the copyright covers in the case where registration was made using deposits of videotapes of an electronic game.

23. This provision was section 117 of the 1976 Copyright Law as originally enacted. It was deleted by legislation in 1980, Public Law 96-517, and replaced in that legislation by a new section 117.

24. 1978 CONTU Report, pp. 1, 38–46.

25. 1909 Act, §§10, 12; 1976 House Report, pp. 129–130.

## Chapter 3. Copyrightable Subject Matter, Part II: Copyrightability Limits

1. The legislative history notes that the section was not intended either to enlarge or contract the scope of copyright protection as it applied under the 1909 Copyright Act. 1976 House Report, p. 57. Copyright Office regulations (37 CFR §202.1) elaborate on the "ideas, etc." category and include some others as well, which come up in Chapter 3. The regulations include the following as examples of works not subject to copyright:

   (a) Words and short phrases such as names, titles, and slogans; familiar symbols or designs; mere variations of typographic ornamentation, lettering or coloring; mere listing of ingredients or contents;

   (b) Ideas, plans, methods, systems, or devices, as distinguished from the particular manner in which they are expressed or described in writing;

   (c) Blank forms, such as time cards, graph paper, account books, diaries, bank checks, scorecards, address books, report forms, order forms and the like, which are designed for recording information and do not in themselves convey information;

   (d) Works consisting entirely of information that is common property containing no original work of authorship, such as, for example: standard calendars, height and weight charts, tape measures and rulers, schedules of sporting events, and lists of tables taken from public documents or other common sources.

2. Nichols v. Universal Pictures Corp., 45 F.2d 119, 20 C.O. Bull. 528 (2d Cir. 1930), cert. denied, 282 U.S. 902 (1931).

3. Streeter v. Rolfe, 491 F.Supp. 416, 209 USPQ 918, 1978–81 Copyright Law Decisions ¶ 25,184 (W.D. La. 1980) (turkey decoys); Custom Decor, Inc. v. Nautical Crafts, Inc., 502 F.Supp. 154, 1978–81 Copyright Law Decisions ¶ 25,206 (E.D. Pa. 1980) (duck's heads) (preliminary injunction granted); Gibson v. CBS, Inc., 491 F.Supp. 583, 211 USPQ 262, 1978–81 Copyright Law Decisions ¶ 25,164 (S.D.N.Y. 1980) (eggs talking) (summary judgment granted, complaint dismissed).

4. Twentieth Century-Fox Film Corp. v. MCA, Inc., 1978–81 Copyright Law Decisions ¶ 25,267 (C.D. Calif. 1980) (Battlestar Gallactica); United Artists Corp. v. Ford Motor Co., 483 F.Supp. 89, 209 USPQ 227, 1978–81 Copyright Law Decisions ¶ 25,128 (S.D.N.Y. 1980) (Pink Panther); Warner Bros., Inc. v. American Broadcasting Cos., 654 F.2d 204, 211 USPQ 97, CCH Copr. L. Rptr. ¶ 25,284 (2d Cir. 1981) (Superman) (affirmance of denial of preliminary injunction).

5. 1976 House Report, p. 61.

6. *Notice of Inquiry, Registration of Claims to Copyright; Inquiry—Blank Form,* 44 Federal Register 69977–69978 (12/5/79), *Notice of Termination of Inquiry,* 45 Federal Register 63297–63330 (9/24/80). The latter document reviews a number of the cases in this area. The existing regulations, which the Copyright Office decided not to modify, are included in note 1 above. *Advance Notice of Proposed Rulemaking, Registration of Claims to Copyright in the Graphic Elements Involved in the Design of Books and Other Printed Publications,* 44 Federal Register 47555–47557 (8/14/79); *Extension of Comment Period,* 44 Federal Register 62913–62914 (11/1/79); *Notice of Termination of Proposed Rulemaking,* 46 Federal Register 30651–30653 (6/10/81).

7. 1978 CONTU Report, pp. 20, 22–23. In a concurring opinion to the commission majority's recommendation for computer program protection under copyright, Commissioner Melville Nimmer, who is the author of a widely used and acclaimed treatise on copyright law, stated in part:

> What is most troubling about the Commission's recommendation of open-ended copyright protection for all computer software is its failure to articulate any rationale which would not equally justify copyright protection for the tangible expression of any and all original ideas (whether or not computer technology, business, or otherwise). . . . Apart from the constitutional issues, it raises policy questions, the full implications of which remain murky at best. Still, at this time, knowing what we know about the nature of the computer industry, its needs, and its potential for great contributions to the public welfare, I am prepared, on balance, to support the Commission's conclusions and recommendations (1978 CONTU Report, pp. 26–27).

8. World War II stories: Mosley v. Follett, 1978–81 Copyright Law Decisions ¶ 25,202 (S.D.N.Y. 1980) (preliminary injunction denied); A zeppelin: Hoehling v. Universal City Studios, Inc., 618 F.2d 982, 1978–81 Copyright Law Decisions ¶ 25,146 (2d Cir. 1980); A kidnapping: Miller v. Universal City Studios, Inc., 650 F.2d 1365, CCH Copr. L. Rptr. ¶ 25,285 (5th Cir. 1981); John Wayne: Suid v. Newsweek Magazine, 503 F.Supp. 146, 211 USPQ 898, 1978–81 Copyright Law Decisions ¶ 25,205 (D.D.C. 1980); Gardening data: Schroeder v. William Morrow & Co., 566 F.2d 3, 198 USPQ 143 (7th Cir. 1977) (For discussions of compilations, etc., see Denicola, "Copyright in Collection of Facts: A Theory for the Protection of Nonfiction Literary Works," 81 *Columbia Law Review* 516 [1981]); Law students: Quinto v. Legal Times of Washington, Inc., 506 F.Supp. 554, 1978–81 Copyright Law Decisions ¶ 25,220 (D.D.C. 1981).

9. Alexander v. Haley, 460 F.Supp. 40, 200 USPQ 239, 1978–81 Copyright Law Decisions ¶ 25,036 (S.D.N.Y. 1980).

10. See Note 1.

11. 1976 House Report, p. 59. The report adds the caveat: ". . . it can be assumed that, where a Government agency commissions a work for its own use merely as an alternative to having one of its own employees prepare the work, the right to secure a copyright would be withheld." A recent case noted the same consideration but found it not applicable in the circumstances. Schnapper v.

Foley, 471 F.Supp. 426, 202 USPQ 699, 1978–81 Copyright Law Decisions ¶ 25,082 (D.D.C. 1979), aff'd, CCH Copr. L. Rptr. ¶ 25,315 (D.C. Cir. 1981).

12. See the cases cited in Building Officials & Code Adm. v. Code Technology, Inc., 628 F.2d 730, 207 USPQ 81, 1978–81 Copyright Law Decisions ¶ 25,180 (1st Cir. 1980). After the case went back to the district court, a further opinion was issued, but it did not definitively resolve the legal issue. Building Officials & Code Administrators International, Inc. v. Code Technology, Inc., 1978–81 Copyright Law Decisions ¶ 25,199 (D. Mass. 1980).

13. 1976 House Report, p. 54.

14. Mazer v. Stein, 347 U.S. 201, 100 USPQ 325, 29 C.O. Bull. 239 (1954).

15. 1976 House Report, p. 55.

16. Folsom v. Marsh, 9 Fed. Cas. 342, No. 4901, 13 C.O. Bull. 991 (C.C.D. Mass. 1841).

17. Kieselstein-Cord v. Accessories by Pearl, Inc., 632 F.2d 989, 208 USPQ 1, 1978–81 Copyright Law Decisions ¶ 25,189 (2nd Cir. 1980). For other recent cases, see: Esquire, Inc. v. Ringer, 591 F.2d 796, 1978–81 Copyright Law Decisions ¶ 25,029 (D.C. Cir. 1978); Norris Industries, Inc. v. International Telephone and Telegraph Corp., 1978–81 Copyright Law Decisions ¶ 25,310 (N.D. Fla. 1981), Gay Toys, Inc. v. Buddy L Corp., CCH Copr. L. Rptr. ¶ 25,342 (E.D. Mich. 1981).

18. 1976 House Report, p. 55; Eltra Corp. v. Ringer, 579 F.2d 294, 198 USPQ 321, 1978–81 Copyright Law Decisions ¶ 25,015 (4th Cir. 1978).

19. 1976 House Report, p. 105.

20. 1976 House Report, p. 55.

## Chapter 4. Copyright Duration

1. See, e.g., 1976 House Report, p. 139.

2. A compilation of various nations' general duration rules appears at pages 123–124 of the Hearings Before the Subcommittee on Court, Civil Liberties, and the Administration of Justice of the House Committee on the Judiciary, 94th Cong., 1st Sess., 1975, ser. 36, pt. 1. The adoption of the life-plus-50 rule removed one of the barriers that makes the United States ineligible to join the Berne Convention (discussed briefly in Chapter 11).

3. The table is based on information in The New Columbia Encyclopedia (Columbia University Press, 1975). Edgar Allen Poe's The Raven was published by 1845, four years before Poe's death at the age of 40. Elizabeth Barrett Browning's Sonnets from the Portuguese was published in 1850, when she was 44. She died 11 years later. Leonardo's The Last Supper was finished by 1498; Leonardo himself died in 1519, at 67. Herman Melville's Moby Dick was published in 1851, when he was 33; he died at 72. Harriet Beecher Stowe was born in 1811 and died in 1896; her Uncle Tom's Cabin was published in 1852. Verdi set down La Traviata by 1853; he died in 1901 at the age of 78. Michelangelo's Sistine ceiling was executed by 1512, when he was 37 years old, 52 years before his death.

4. 1976 House Report, p. 135.

5. The phrase "two or more joint authors who did not work for hire" makes sense

as a lead-in to the life-plus-50 standard but it would have been nice, for the sake of comprehensiveness, to have gone on to the other possibilities. In figuring out the answer, it should be noted that the duration rule for a work for hire, by itself, was selected as being more or less the equivalent of life-plus-50. The legislative history, in speaking of the duration rules for anonymous and pseudonymous works and works for hire, states: "In general the terms . . . approximate, on the average, the term of life plus 50 years established for other works" (1976 House Report, p. 138). The reference apparently is to the 75-year component since elsewhere the report states: "If life expectancy in 1909, which was in the neighborhood of 56 years, offered a rough guide to the length of copyright protection, then life expectancy in the 1970's, which is well over 70 years, should offer a similar guide . . ." (1976 House Report, p. 135).

6. In August 1979, the Copyright Office promulgated a draft of some regulations for implementing this part of the law. Proposed Rule, *Statements Identifying One or More Authors of an Anonymous or Pseudonymous Work; Statements of the Date of Death of an Author, or That an Author Is Still Living; Registry of Vital Information Concerning Authors,* 44 *Federal Register* 158, at 47550–47554 (August 14, 1979). As of this writing, regulations have not yet been issued.

7. Some works that were works for hire under the 1909 Act could not qualify as such under the current statute. We assume that Congress did not intend to change the ownership status of those old works and that the current duration rules for works for hire will apply to all old law works for hire.

8. See note 6.

9. 1909 Act, §12. The provision speaks of works not reproduced for sale, but was interpreted to cover unpublished works. The provision was construed to cover only the types of works mentioned in it, i.e., "lecture or similar production or a dramatic, musical, or dramatico-musical composition; . . . motion-picture photoplay; . . . photograph; . . . motion picture other than a photoplay; . . . work of art or a plastic work or drawing."

10. 1909 Act, §24.

11. Ibid.

12. See 1976 House Report, pp. 139–140.

13. Russell v. Price, 612 F.2d 1123, 205 USPQ 206, 1978–81 Copyright Law Decisions ¶ 25,125 (9th Cir. 1979) (1909 Act) (Shaw's *Pygmalion* and a 1938 movie of the same name), *cert.* denied, 446 U.S. 952 (1980); see also Filmvideo Releasing Corp. v. Hastings, 509 F.Supp. 60, 1978–81 Copyright Law Decisions ¶ 25,222 (S.D.N.Y. 1981), *aff'd* on the point cited for, CCH Copr. L. Rptr. ¶ 25,339 (2d Cir. 1981). Another recent case where the film copyright had not been renewed did not involve an underlying copyright in a *published* work. Instead, the contention was that the underlying unpublished filmscript (and other related unpublished material) was still in copyright because it had never been "published" in the copyright law sense. The court ruled that the film could be publicly performed without having to obtain permission from the owner of the copyright (state law) in the script. Classic Film Museum, Inc. v. Warner Bros., Inc., 597 F.2d 13, 202 USPQ 467, 1978–81 Copyright Law Decisions ¶ 25,022 (1st Cir. 1979) (1909 Act) (1937 film *A Star Is Born*). At the time, the state law copyright in the unpublished script could have lasted in-

definitely. The court did not want that possibility to operate so as to keep the film subject to copyright control indefinitely also.

14. Frederick Warne & Co. v. Book Sales, Inc., 481 F.Supp. 1191, 205 USPQ 444, 1978–81 Copyright Law Decisions ¶ 25,127 (S.D.N.Y. 1979) (illustrations from Beatrix Potter's works). The court left to a later time the issues of whether plaintiff's claimed marks derived from the public domain illustrations functioned as valid trademarks and, if so, whether defendant's uses constituted trademark infringement.

15. 1909 Act, §§16, 22, 23.

## Chapter 5. Exclusive Rights of Copyright

1. Franklin Mint Corp. v. National Wildlife Art Exchange, Inc., 575 F.2d 62, 197 USPQ 721, 1978–81 Copyright Law Decisions ¶ 25,004 (3rd Cir. 1978), cert. denied, 1439 U.S. 880 (1978).

2. ABKCO Music, Inc. v. Harrisongs Music, Ltd., 508 F.Supp. 798, 1978–81 Copyright Law Decisions ¶ 25,235 (S.D.N.Y. 1981).

3. 1976 House Report, p. 130.

4. 1976 House Report, p. 64. A California attorney general's ruling recently concluded that the showing of videocassette tapes of movies to state prison inmates constitutes a public performance. Fair use was found inapplicable. BNA Patent, Trademark, & Copyright Journal 567 (February 18, 1982): A-1.

5. Ibid.

6. Ibid.

7. 1976 House Report, p. 63.

8. Burwood Products Co. v. Marsel Mirror and Glass Products, Inc., 468 F.Supp. 1215, 202 USPQ 813, 1978–81 Copyright Law Decisions ¶ 25,090 (N.D. Ill. 1979).

9. Title 35, United States Code.

10. See, e.g., Diamond v. Diehr, 450 U.S. 175, 209 USPQ 1 (1981).

11. Title 35, United States Code.

12. Title 15, United States Code.

13. Section 43(a) of the Lanham Act, 15 U.S.C.A. §1125(a). The case is Follett v. New American Library, Inc., 497 F.Supp. 304, 1978–81 Copyright Law Decisions ¶ 25,175 (S.D.N.Y. 1980). It should also be noted that section 43(a) of the Lanham Act is one of the means—as is contract law—which courts sometimes are able to use to provide protection under U.S. law in cases where the court perceives that someone has improperly affected the artistic integrity of an author's works. See Note, "Protection of Artistic Integrity," 90 Harvard Law Review 473 (1976). In some countries, rights such as these are protected directly under what is called "droit moral." Such rights are not given express protection under the U.S. copyright statute although, of course, control of the rights of copyright sometimes permits the author, through contractual provisions, to obtain some of the rights. For a discussion of droit moral, in the context of English copyright law, see G. Dworkin, "The Moral Right and English Copyright Law," 12 IIC 476 (1981).

One of the potential barriers to the U.S. becoming a member of the Berne Union (see Chapter 11) is the requirement of protection of moral rights. For a discussion of whether the law in the U.S meets the requirement in practice, see 1980 Committee Reports section of *Patent, Trademark and Copyright Law* (American Bar Association, 1980), p. 140.

14. Flashmaps Publications, Inc. v. Geographia Map Co., 204 USPQ 552, 1978–81 Copyright Law Decisions ¶ 25,129 (S.D.N.Y. 1979), *aff'd*, 1978–81 Copyright Law Decisions ¶ 25,130 (2d Cir. 1979).

15. The federal antitrust laws are set forth in Title 15 of the *United States Code,* principally in the first 77 sections.

16. Federal communications law is in Title 47 of the *United States Code.*

17. See Home Box Office, Inc. v. Pay TV of Greater New York, Inc., 467 F.Supp. 525, 1978–81 Copyright Law Decisions ¶ 25,088 (E.D.N.Y. 1979).

18. Title 15 *United States Code,* section 552.

19. Weisberg v. U.S., 631 F.2d 824, 207 USPQ 1080, 1978–81 Copyright Law Decisions ¶ 25,169 (D.C. Cir. 1980).

20. Title 19 *United States Code,* section 1337.

21. *In the Matter of Certain Coin-Operated Audiovisual Games and Components Thereof,* CCH Copr. L. Rptr. ¶ 25,299 (United States International Trade Commission, 1981).

22. See, e.g., the 5-4 decision in Goldstein v. California, 412 U.S. 546, 178 USPQ 129 (1973).

23. 1976 House Report, p. 130.

24. Although not limited by the 1976 Act, such rights may be limited by the judge-made provisions in effect during the reign of the 1909 Act. See the case cited in note 22, above.

25. 1976 House Report, p. 131.

26. Ibid.

27. 1976 House Report, p. 24.

28. 122 *Congressional Record* H10910 (daily ed., Sept. 22, 1976).

29. 1976 House Report, p. 132.

30. New York's "truth in testing" statute: Association of American Medical Colleges v. Carey, 482 F.Supp. 1358, 205 USPQ 42, 1978–81 Copyright Law Decisions ¶ 25,138 (N.D.N.Y. 1980). Ohio and Pennsylvania "blind bidding" statutes: Allied Artists Pictures Corp. v. Rhodes, 496 F.Supp. 408, 207 USPQ 630, 1978–81 Copyright Law Decisions ¶ 25,209 (S.D. Ohio 1980); Associated Film Distribution Corp. v. Thornburgh, 520 F.Supp. 971, 1978–81 Copyright Law Decisions ¶ 25,300 (E.D. Pa. 1981). California's resale royalties act (the district court found no preemption under either the 1909 or 1976 Acts; the appeals court agreed as to the 1909 Act and concluded it was unnecessary to decide about the 1976 Act): Morseburg v. Balyon, 201 USPQ 518, 1978–81 Copyright Law Decisions ¶ 25,077 (C.D. Cal. 1978), *aff'd,* 621 F.2d 972, 207 USPQ 183, 1978–81 Copyright Law Decisions ¶ 25,061 (9th Cir. 1980), *cert.* denied, 449 U.S. 983 (1980). The Massachusetts statute: Massachusetts v. Rizzuto, 1978–81 Copyright Law Decisions ¶ 25,233 (Super. Ct. Mass. 1980). Tortious interference with contractual relations: Harper & Row, Publishers, Inc. v. Nation

Enterprises, 501 F.Supp. 848, 1978–81 Copyright Law Decisions ¶ 25,221 (S.D.N.Y. 1980). Right of publicity case: Factors Etc., Inc. v. Pro Arts, Inc., 496 F.Supp. 1090, 208 USPQ 529, 1978–81 Copyright Law Decisions ¶ 25,176 (S.D.N.Y. 1980), rev'd. 652 F.2d 278, 211 USPQ 1 (2nd Cir. 1980).

31. Avco Corp. v. Precision Air Part, Inc., 210 USPQ 894, 1978–81 Copyright Law Decisions ¶ 25,207 (M.D. Ala. 1980); Technicon Medical Information Systems Corp. v. Green Bay Packaging Inc., 211 USPQ 343, 1978–81 Copyright Law Decisions ¶ 25,255 (E.D. Wis. 1980), 1978–81 Copyright Law Decisions ¶ 25,261 (E.D. Wis. 1981) (the case concerns the issue of what legal effect, under the 1909 Act, the use of a statutory copyright notice has on trade secrecy protection, with the federal district court concluding that the notice did not destroy trade secrecy protection if there was only a limited publication of the work); Warrington Associates, Inc. v. Real-Time Engineering Systems, Inc., 522 F.Supp. 367, CCH Copr. L. Rptr. ¶ 25,316 (N.D. Ill. 1981) (registration of a computer program manual as an unpublished work found not to preclude trade secrecy protection). For a companion case to the last case cited, see Warrington Associates, Inc. v. Kellog Citizens National Bank, Inc., BNA Patent, Trademark, & Copyright Journal 566 (February 11, 1982); A-13.

## Chapter 6. Copyright Ownership, Transfers, and Licenses

1. 1976 House Report, p. 120.
2. 1976 House Report, p. 121.
3. See Best Medium Pub. Co. v. National Insider, Inc., 259 F.Supp. 433, 152 USPQ 56 (N.D. Ill. 1966), aff'd 385 F.2d 384, 155 USPQ 550 (7th Cir. 1967), cert. denied, 390 U.S. 955 (1968).
4. For a discussion of when a person is considered an "employee" for work made for hire, see Angel and Tannenbaum, "Works Made for Hire Under S. 22," 22 New York Law School Law Review 209 (1976): 221–225. ("S. 22" was the number assigned to the Senate version of what eventually became the 1976 Copyright Law.)
5. 1976 House Report, p. 124.
6. This rule combined with the old law's notice rules to create quite a mess. For example, under the old law, an error in the name of the copyright owner could make the notice defective and put the work in the public domain. Thus a magazine that printed an article that it did not own (but only had permission to use) could place copyright in the article in the public domain if only the magazine's own name showed up as copyright owner. To avoid such a result, the law sometimes construed the article author's transfer to the magazine as a transfer of all the rights under copyright. Another device was to treat the transfer as a transfer of legal title to all of the rights, under an equitable trust obligation to administer the copyright in the interest of the article author.
7. See 1976 House Report, p. 124.
8. See 1976 House Report, p. 79.
9. See 1976 House Report, p. 127.
10. 1976 House Report, p. 140.

## Chapter 7. Copyright Notices

1. Concerning works published outside of the United States, the legislative history states: "The values of notice are fully applicable to foreign editions of works copyrighted in the United States, especially with the increased flow of intellectual materials across national boundaries, and the gains in the use of notice on editions published abroad under the Universal Copyright Convention should not be wiped out" (1976 House Report, p. 144).

2. 1976 House Report, p. 138.

3. Ibid.

4. 1976 House Report, pp. 143–144.

5. 1976 House Report, p. 149.

6. One court recently expressed the view that the statutory provision relating to express, written conditions eliminates consideration of implied conditions. Fantastic Fakes, Inc. v. Pickwick International, Inc., CCH Copr. L. Rptr. ¶ 25,332 (5th Cir. 1981).

7. P. Kaufman, Inc. v. Rex Curtain Corp., 1978–81 Copyright Law Decisions ¶ 25,264 (S.D.N.Y. 1978).

8. See, e.g., Florists' Transworld Delivery Assoc. v. Reliable Glassware and Pottery Co., CCH Copr. L. Rptr. ¶ 25,301 (N.D. Ill. 1981).

9. Cf. section 402(b)(3).

10. The use of the symbol may be of less practical value to U.S. authors than is generally supposed. A recent study indicates that the domestic laws of only three countries—Chile, Italy, and Nicaragua—require that U.S. authors place copyright notices on their works. See Report of Committee No. 302 (International Copyright Treaties and Laws), Committee Reports section of *Patent, Trademark, and Copyright Law*, American Bar Association, pp. 138–139 (1980). The report also notes: "The use of the U.C.C. copyright notice does not under the Convention avoid the necessity of complying with formalities required to enforce or exercise the copyright protection for a work in a U.C.C. country . . . but its use does eliminate the need to comply with formalities which, if not fulfilled, would prevent the acquisition of copyright or would result in the loss of the once acquired copyright before the expiration of the applicable term. . . . After careful study, the subcommittee was not able to discover in the law of any U.C.C. country even one formality that attained the status of a 'condition of copyright' which would apply to a U.S. authored work first published in a U.C.C. country. Hence, the Subcommittee has concluded that U.S. authors receive absolutely no legal benefit from Article III of the Convention by using the U.C.C. copyright notice."

11. But see Rinaldo, "The Scope of Copyright Protection in the United States Under Existing Inter-American Relations: Abrogation for the Need for U.S. Protection Under the Buenos Aires Convention by Reliance Upon the U.C.C.," 22 *Bulletin of the Copyright Society of the USA* 417 (1975).

12. The letter P within a circle is the international symbol for the protection of sound recordings by the Convention for the Protection of Producers of Phonograms Against Unauthorized Duplication of Their Phonograms.

13. "Since 'phonorecords' are not 'copies,' there is no need to place a section 401

notice on 'phonorecords' to protect the literary or muscial works embodied in the records" (1976 House Report, p. 145).

14. See Copyright Office, *Compendium of Copyright Office Practices* §4.2.2. (1973 ed.). It was suggested to the Copyright Office that its regulations allow a "(c)" as an acceptable substitute for the letter c within a circle. Such an option is not provided for in the statute and the Copyright Office concluded it had no authority to alter the statutory requirements in the regulations. *Methods of Affixation and Positions of the Copyright Notice: Comments Accompanying §201.20, 46 Federal Register 58307,* CCH Copr. L. Rptr. ¶ 13,049 (December 1, 1981).

15. 1909 Act, §12.

16. A recent report suggests that the omission of the section 401 language from section 402 was inadvertent. Nonetheless, because of the negative implication that arguably arises from the difference, the report proposed an amendment to the statute to clarify the matter. See Report of Committee No. 301 (Copyright Legislation), Committee Reports section of *Patent, Trademark, and Copyright Law,* American Bar Association (1980), p. 133.

17. 1909 Act, §19.

18. 1976 House Report, pp. 148–149.

19. Quinto v. Legal Times of Washington, Inc., 506 F.Supp. 554, 1978–81 Copyright Law Decisions ¶ 25,220 (D. D.C. 1981).

20. 1976 House Report, p. 146.

21. 1976 House Report, p. 143.

22. See the discussion in the case cited in note 6.

23. 1 *Nimmer on Copyright* §4.04 at 4-18–4-19.

24. White v. Kimmell, 193 F.2d 744 (9th Cir. 1952).

25. American Vitagraph, Inc. v. Levy, 659 F.2d 1023, CCH Copr. L. Rptr. ¶ 25,320 (9th Cir. 1981).

26. Burke v. National Broadcasting Co., 598 F.2d 688, 202 USPQ 531, 1978–81 Copyright Law Decisions ¶ 25,075 (1st Cir. 1979), cert. denied (1979)

27. National Research Bureau, Inc. v. Kucker, 481 F. Supp. 612, 1978–81 Copyright Law Decisions ¶ 25,080 (S.D.N.Y. 1979); Kisling v. Rothschild, 388 So.2d 1310, 1978–81 Copyright Law Decisions ¶ 25,196 (Fla. D. Ct. App. 1980).

28. Goldsmith v. Max, 1978–81 Copyright Law Decisions ¶ 25,248 (S.D.N.Y. 1981).

29. See 1 *Nimmer on Copyright* §4.13 at 4-70–4-71.

30. See Copyright Office Bulletin No. 3, *Copyright Enactments — Laws Passed in the United States Since 1783 Relating to Copyright* (1973), p. 71.

31. Fantastic Fakes, Inc. v. Pickwick International, Inc., CCH Copr. L. Rptr. ¶ 25,332 (5th Cir. 1981).

## Chapter 8. Deposits for the Library of Congress: Section 407

1. In 1980, the Copyright Office announced that it "has decided to resume a policy of enforcing the deposit requirements against foreign books and other printed works published in the United States with notice of copyright since the statutory policy is clear, and the potential benefits to the Library of Congress

of enforcing the mandatory deposit provisions against foreign works are large" (45 *Federal Register* 49721, CCH Copr. L. Rptr. ¶ 20,079).

2. 47 *Federal Register* 5259 (Feb. 4, 1982), reproduced at *BNA Patent, Trademark & Copyright Journal* 566 (February 11, 1982), p. D-1.

## Chapter 9. Copyright Registrations, Part I: Registration Advantages

1. 37 *Code of Federal Regulations* §201.8, CCH Copr. L. Rptr. ¶ 12,015.

## Chapter 10. Copyright Registrations, Part II: How to Register

1. 37 *Code of Federal Regulations* §202.3, CCH Copr. L. Rptr. ¶ 12,054.

2. The Copyright Office also concluded that "the allowance of multiple registrations could be taken to suggest that, in view of the inducements to registration offered by that statute, the owner of each particular right would be forced, as a practical matter, to make registration to enforce that right. This was certainly not the intent of the statute." Comments accompanying final regulations, 46 *Federal Register* 965, CCH Copr. L. Rptr. ¶ 13,013.

3. Ibid.

4. Ibid.

5. Ibid.

6. Testa v. Janssen, 492 F.Supp. 198, 208 USPQ 213, 1978–81 Copyright Law Decisions ¶ 25,190 (W.D.Pa. 1980).

7. Russ Berrie & Co. v. Jerry Elsner Co., 482 F.Supp. 980, 205 USPQ 320, 1978–81 Copyright Law Decisions ¶ 25,141 (S.D.N.Y. 1980). The court also ruled against the registered gorilla because, in the judge's view, the differences between it and the public domain stuffed toy gorilla were not sufficient to constitute copyrightable subject matter. In ruling on the significance of the nondisclosure in the registration, the court in part reasoned that, had the public domain gorilla been disclosed in the registration application, registration might have been denied. It may be, however, that the Copyright Office would have accepted, on face value, the applicant's statements about new matter added and granted registration. The Office has hundreds of thousands of applications a year and, because of that and because of the nature of copyright, it does not carry out a complete check on each statement made.

## Chapter 11. Transnational Aspects of U.S. Copyright Law

1. The text of the U.S. copyright statute for any given time between 1909 and 1952 may be found in the 1952 edition of Title 17, *United States Code Annotated*, published by West Publishing Company. The statute was further amended, effective September 16, 1955. The law as so amended remained in force until January 1, 1978, when the current copyright law took effect. The text of the statute for the 1955–1977 period may be found in the 1976 edition of the Cumulative Annual Pocket Part to Title 17, *United States Code Annotated*.

2. Ibid.

3. *Congressional Record* 122 (daily ed., Sept. 30, 1976): S17253.

4. Stonehill Communications, Inc. v. Martuge, 512 F.Supp. 349, 1978–81 Copyright Law Decisions ¶ 25,254 (S.D.N.Y. 1981).

5. The term "domestic corporation or enterprise" is intended also to cover such entities as a foreign subsidiary formed primarily for the purpose of obtaining the exemption. See 1976 House Report, p. 167.

6. 1976 House Report, p. 168.

7. See sections 16, 17, 21, and 22, 1909 Act.

8. For recent comments re the United States and the Berne Convention, see 1981 Committee Reports section of *Patent, Trademark, and Copyright Law* (American Bar Association): 103–106.

## Chapter 12. Remedies for Copyright Infringement

1. 1976 House Report, pp. 159–160.

2. Universal City Studios, Inc. v. Sony Corp. of America, 480 F.Supp. 429, 203 USPQ 656, 1978–81 Copyright Law Decisions ¶ 25,106 (C.D. Cal. 1979).

3. Universal City Studios, Inc. v. Sony Corp. of America, 659 F.2d 953, 211 USPQ 761, CCH Copr. L. Rptr. ¶ 25,308 (9th Cir. 1981).

4. See 1976 House Report, p. 162.

5. Title 28 *United States Code* §1498.

6. 1976 House Report, p. 161.

7. 1976 House Report, p. 162.

8. Ibid.

9. Ibid.

10. See Twentieth Century Music Corp. v. Frith, 645 F.2d 6, 1978–81 Copyright Law Decisions ¶ 25,260 (5th Cir. 1981); National Conference of Bar Examiners v. Multistate Legal Studies, Inc., 1978–81 Copyright Law Decisions ¶ 25,266 (N.D. Ill. 1981).

## Chapter 13. Fair Use: Section 107

1. 1976 House Report, p. 65. See also Jartech, Inc. v. Clancy, *BNA Patent, Trademark, & Copyright Journal* 566 (February 11, 1982): A-1 (9th Cir. 1982) (City Council's making of abbreviated copies of films, for evidence in nuisance abatement proceedings, not an infringement).

2. Folsom v. Marsh, 9 Fed.Cas. 342, No. 4901, 13 C.O. Bull. 991 (C.C.D. 1841) (opinion by Justice Story). In setting forth the applicable criteria for deciding the case, the court stated: ". . . we must often, in deciding questions of this sort, look to the nature and objects of the selections made, the quantity and value of the materials used, and the degree in which the use may prejudice the sale, or diminish the profits, or supersede the objects, of the original work." That is pretty much the same general standard we have today.

3. Lawrence v. Dana, 15 Fed.Cas. 26, No. 8136, 14 C.O. Bull. 1545 (C.C.D. Mass. 1869). The Dana in the case was Richard Henry Dana, of *Two Years Before the Mast* fame. He had prepared a new edition of a book, *Elements of International Law*, and the court found that he had taken too much from one of the earlier editions without permission.

4. 1976 House Report, p. 66.

5. 1976 House Report, p. 65.

6. The text of section 107 introduces the four criteria with the phrase "shall include." The definitions section of the statute declares that the terms "including" and "such as" are illustrative and not limitative [101].

7. 1975 Senate Report, p. 65.

8. Rubin v. Boston Magazine Co., 645 F.2d 80, 1978–81 Copyright Law Decisions ¶ 25,243 (1st Cir. 1981).

9. Amana Refrigeration, Inc. v. Consumers Union of United States, Inc., 431 F.Supp. 324 (D. Iowa 1977).

10. The First Amendment provides in full: "Congress shall make no law respecting an establishment of religion, or prohibiting the free exercise thereof; or abridging the freedom of speech, or of the press; or the right of the people peaceably to assemble and to petition the Government for a redress of grievances." A leading case relating the First Amendment to copyright is Time Inc. v. Bernard Geis Assoc., 293 F.Supp. 130 (S.D.N.Y. 1968). See also Rosemont Enterprises, Inc. v. Random House, Inc., 366 F.2d 303, 150 USPQ 517 (2d Cir. 1966), cert. denied, 385 U.S. 1009 (1967). For a more recent case, see Triangle Publications, Inc. v. Knight-Ridder Newspapers, Inc., 621 F.2d 1318, 626 F.2d 1171, 207 USPQ 977, 1978–81 Copyright Law Decisions ¶ 25,174 (5th Cir. 1980). See also R. C. Denicola, "Copyright and Free Speech: Constitutional Limitations on the Protection of Expression," 67 California Law Review 283 (1979).

11. DC Comics Inc. v. Crazy Eddie, Inc., 205 USPQ 1177, 1978–81 Copyright Law Decisions ¶ 25,096 (S.D.N.Y. 1979) (preliminary injunction granted).

12. New Boston Television, Inc. v. Entertainment Sports Programming Network, Inc., CCH Copr. L. Rptr. ¶ 25,293 (D. Mass. 1981) (preliminary injunction granted).

13. Bruzzone v. Miller Brewing Co., 202 USPQ 809, 1978–81 Copyright Law Decisions ¶ 25,105 (N.D. Calif. 1979).

14. Triangle Publications, Inc. v. Knight-Ridder Newspapers, Inc., 621 F.2d 1318, 626 F.2d 1171, 207 USPQ 977, 1978–81 Copyright Law Decisions ¶ 25,174 (5th Cir. 1980).

15. Elsmere Music, Inc. v. National Broadcasting Co., 482 F.Supp. 741, 206 USPQ 913, 1978–81 Copyright Law Decisions ¶ 25,140 (S.D.N.Y. 1980).

16. Elsmere Music, Inc. v. National Broadcasting Co., 623 F.2d 252, 207 USPQ 277, 1978–81 Copyright Law Decisions ¶ 25,170 (2nd Cir. 1980).

17. Metro-Goldwyn-Mayer Inc. v. Showcase Atlanta Cooperative Productions, Inc., CCH Copr. L. Rptr. ¶ 25,313 (N.D. Ga. 1981).

18. Warner Bros., Inc. v. American Broadcasting Cos., 654 F.2d 204, CCH Copr. L. Rptr. ¶ 25,284 (2nd Cir. 1981).

19. See, e.g., Walt Disney Productions v. The Air Pirates, 581 F.2d 751, 199 USPQ 769, 1978–81 Copyright Law Decisions ¶ 25,032 (9th Cir. 1978), cert. denied, 439 U.S. 1132 (1979); Dallas Cowboy Cheerleaders, Inc. v. Scoreboard Posters, Inc., 600 F.2d 1184, 203 USPQ 321, 1978–81 Copyright Law Decisions ¶ 25,101 (5th Cir. 1979); Metro-Goldwyn-Mayer, Inc. v. Showcase Atlanta Cooperative Productions, Inc., 479 F.Supp. 351, 203 USPQ 822, 1978–81 Copy-

right Law Decisions ¶ 25,122 (N.D. Ga. 1979); MCA, Inc. v. Earl Wilson, Jr., 211 USPQ 577, CCH Copr. L. Rptr. ¶ 25,287 (2nd Cir. 1981).

20. See some of the cases cited in note 19. In a dissenting opinion in the MCA, Inc. case, Judge Mansfield stated:

> The majority implies that to "substitute dirty lyrics" should not permit a person to "escape liability by calling the end result a parody or satire on the mores of society." . . . In my view the defendants' use of "dirty lyrics'" or of language or allusions that I might personally find distasteful or even offensive is wholly irrelevant to the issue before us. . . . We cannot, under the guise of deciding a copyright issue, act as a board of censors outlawing X-rated performances.

Recently a federal district court in Georgia upheld a fair-use defense in the case of a pornographic adaptation of a copyrighted work, finding that the defendant's use was in the nature of an editorial or social commentary as contrasted with an attempt to capitalize financially on plaintiff's original work. Pillsbury Co. v. Milky Way Productions, BNA Patent, Trademark, & Copyright Journal 566 (Feb. 11, 1982): A-3 (N.D.Ga. 1981).

On the subject of whether a work is ineligible for copyright protection if it is obscene, two federal appeals courts have recently said no. Mitchell Brothers Film Group v. Cinema Adult Theatre, 604 F.2d 852, 203 USPQ 1041, 1978–81 Copyright Law Decisions ¶ 25,110 (5th Cir. 1979); Jartech, Inc. v. Clancy, BNA Patent, Trademark, & Copyright Journal 566 (Feb. 11, 1982): A-1 (9th Cir. 1982).

21. Wainwright Securities Inc. v. Wall Street Transcript Corp., 558 F.2d 91, 194 USPQ 401 (2d Cir. 1977) (preliminary injunction affirmed), cert. denied, 434 U.S. 1014 (1978). Subsequent to the appellate court decision, the brokerage firm ceased doing business and commenced liquidation. It moved to dismiss the suit, which was still pending, with prejudice. The Transcript opposed the motion because the discontinuance would deprive it of the opportunity to vindicate its position at a trial. Nonetheless, the court allowed the suit to be dismissed. Wainwright Securities Inc. v. Wall Street Transcript Corp., 80 F.R.D. 103, 204 USPQ 217, 1978–81 Copyright Law Decisions ¶ 25,039 (S.D.N.Y. 1978).

22. Italian Book Corp. v. American Broadcasting Cos., 458 F.Supp. 65, 200 USPQ 312, 1978–81 Copyright Law Decisions ¶ 25,032 (S.D.N.Y. 1978).

23. Suid v. Newsweek Magazine, 503 F.Supp. 146, 211 USPQ 898, 1978–81 Copyright Law Decisions ¶ 25,205 (D.D.C. 1980). The case not only involved the fair-use defense but also the issue of what is copyrightable.

24. Roy Export Co. v. Columbia Broadcast System, Inc., 503 F.Supp. 1137, 208 USPQ 580, 1978–81 Copyright Law Decisions ¶ 25,212 (S.D.N.Y. 1980); Iowa State Research Foundation, Inc. v. American Broadcasting Cos., 621 F.2d 57, 207 USPQ 97, 1978–81 Copyright Law Decisions ¶ 25,156 (2d Cir. 1980).

25. Wihtol v. Crow, 309 F.2d 777, 135 USPQ 385, 33 C.O. Bull. 669 (8th Cir. 1962).

26. Williams & Wilkins Co. v. U.S., 487 F.2d 1345, 180 USPQ 49, 39 C.O. Bull. 967 (Ct. Claims, 1974), aff'd by an equally divided court, 420 U.S. 376 (1975).

27. 1975 Senate Report, p. 71.
28. P.L. 93-573 and P.L. 95-146.
29. *Final Report of the National Commission on New Technological Uses of Copyrighted Works* (Library of Congress ed. 1979, Government Printing Office). Under the CONTU proposal, which is at p. 50 of its final report, the term "commercial copier" was used to mean "those who make or supply copies or phonorecords to customers in the regular course of their commercial business activity. . . ." The proposal would require commercial copiers to display a warning sign; failure to do so could result in the denial of the defense of fair use to the commercial copier and, also, to the trebling of copyright infringement damages that might be awarded. The proposed text of the warning sign stated, in part: "If a work is protected by copyright, in most cases it is copyright infringement, even for purposes of private study, to reproduce more than one article or other contribution to a copyrighted collection or periodical . . . or to make at the same time or at different times, more than one copy of any such article. . . ." Congress has not acted on the proposal.
30. Ibid., p. 48.
31. Ibid., pp. 50–51.
32. Northwestern Bell Telephone Co. v. Bedco of Minnesota, Inc., 501 F.Supp. 299, 210 USPQ 564, 1978–81 Copyright Law Decisions ¶ 25,245 (D. Minn. 1980) (preliminary injunction granted).
33. "Va. College, 3 Pubberies Settle Photocopying Suit," *Variety,* November 4, 1981, p. 65.
34. Basic Books, Inc. v. The Gnomon Corp., 1978–81 Copyright Law Decisions ¶ 25,145 (D. Conn. 1980) (consent judgment); Harper & Row, Publishers, Inc. v. Tyco Copy Service, Inc., 1978–81 Copyright Law Decisions ¶ 25,230 (1981) (consent judgment).
35. F.E.L. Publications, Ltd. v. Catholic Bishop of Chicago, 506 F.Supp. 1127, 210 USPQ 403, 1978–81 Copyright Law Decisions ¶ 25,223 (N.D. Ill. 1981), reversed, CCH Regs. ¶ 64,632 (7th Cir. 1982).
36. *Final Report of the National Commission on New Technological Uses of Copyrighted Works,* pp. 39, 40, 42.
37. Ibid., p. 79.
38. Universal City Studios, Inc. v. Sony Corp. of America, 480 F.Supp. 429, 203 USPQ 656, 1978–81 Copyright Law Decisions ¶ 25,106 (C.D. Cal. 1979).
39. Universal City Studios, Inc. v. Sony Corp. of America, 659 F.2d 953, 211 USPQ 761, CCH Copr. L. Rptr. ¶ 25,308 (9th Cir. 1981).

## Chapter 14. Copyrights and Teaching Activities

1. 1976 House Report, p. 66.
2. 1975 Senate Report, pp. 63–67.
3. The 1975 Senate Committee Report's language traces fairly closely the text of a 1967 House Committee Report. The 1976 House Committee Report, at p. 67, refers to both earlier reports as follows: "In 1967 the Committee also sought

to approach this problem by including, in its report, a very thorough discussion of 'the considerations lying behind the four criteria listed in the amended section 107, in the context of typical classroom situations arising today.' This discussion appeared on pp. 32–35 of the 1967 report, and with some changes has been retained in the Senate Report on S. 22 (S.Rep. No. 94-473, pp. 63–65). The Committee has reviewed this discussion, and considers that it still has value as an analysis of various aspects of the problem."

4. 1976 House Report, pp. 67–72.

5. 1976 House Report, p. 72.

6. 1976 Conference Report, p. 70.

7. 122 *Congressional Record* H10875 (daily ed., Sept. 22, 1976). This interpretation of "teacher" is not a part of the guidelines that were developed by the parties, but was incorporated in the *Congressional Record* prior to the 1976 Conference Report. The Senate-House Conference Committee Report states that the conferees endorsed the interpretation. 1976 Conference Report, p. 70.

8. 122 *Congressional Record* H10875 (daily ed., Sept. 22, 1976).

9. 122 *Congressional Record* H10881 (daily ed., Sept. 22, 1976); 1976 House Report, p. 72.

10. Harper & Row, Publishers, Inc. v. Tyco Copy Service, Inc., 1978–81 Copyright Law Decisions ¶ 25,230 (D. Conn. 1980); Basic Books Inc. v. The Gnomon Corp., 1978–81 Copyright Law Decisions ¶ 25,145 (D.Conn. 1980).

11. 1978–81 Copyright Law Decisions ¶ 25,331 (1981).

12. 1976 House Report, pp. 71–72.

13. 127 *Congressional Record* E4751 (October 14, 1981). See Appendix 4.

14. See citation in note 13. The motion picture companies are Avco Embassy Pictures Corp.; Columbia Pictures Industries, Inc.; Filmways Pictures, Inc.; Metro-Goldwyn-Mayer Film Co.; Paramount Pictures Corp.; Twentieth Century-Fox Film Corp.; and Universal Pictures, a division of Universal City Studios, Inc.

15. See citation in note 13.

16. Encyclopaedia Brittanica Educational Corp. v. Crooks, 447 F.Supp. 243, 197 USPQ 280, 1978–81 Copyright Law Decisions ¶ 25,006 (W.D.N.Y. 1978) (preliminary injunction granted).

17. 1976 Conference Report, p. 70. See also 122 *Congressional Record* H10875 (daily ed. Sept. 22, 1976).

18. 1975 Senate Report, p. 66.

19. 1976 House Report, pp. 71–72.

20. 1976 House Report, p. 83.

21. 1976 House Report, p. 82.

22. 1976 House Report, p. 83.

23. 1976 House Report, p. 83.

24. 1976 House Report, p. 83.

25. See 1976 Conference Report, p. 78. See also subsection 118(e) of the 1976 Copyright Act.

## Chapter 15. Library Reproductions: Section 108

1. See 1975 Senate Report, p. 64.
2. 1976 House Report, p. 74.
3. 1975 Senate Report, p. 67.
4. 1976 House Report, p. 75.
5. 1976 House Report, p. 74.
6. 1975 Senate Report, p. 67.
7. 1976 House Report, p. 75.
8. 1976 Conference Report, pp. 73–74.
9. 1976 House Report, p. 76.
10. 1975 Senate Report, p. 70.
11. This form of notice was recommended by the Council of National Library Associations, Inc.
12. 1976 House Report, p. 77.
13. 1976 House Report, p. 75.
14. Ibid.
15. 1976 House Report, pp. 75–76, 78–79.
16. Ibid.
17. 37 CFR §201.14. The notice for display use should be "printed on heavy paper or other durable material in type at least 18 points in size, and shall be displayed prominently, in such manner and location as to be clearly visible, legible, and comprehensible to a casual observer within the immediate vicinity of the place where orders are accepted." The notice on the order form "shall be printed within a box located prominently on the order form itself, either on the front side of the form or immediately adjacent to the space calling for the name or signature of the person using the form. The notice shall be printed in type size no smaller than that used predominantly throughout the form, and in no case shall the type size be smaller than 8 points. The notice shall be printed in such manner as to be clearly legible, comprehensible, and readily apparent to a casual reader of the form."
18. 1975 Senate Report, p. 70.
19. 1976 Conference Report, pp. 71–72.
20. 1976 Conference Report, p. 74.
21. 1976 House Report, p. 75.
22. 1975 Senate Report, p. 70. The 1976 House Report, though it often repeats the Senate report's language, did not repeat any of the three examples or comment as to why they were excluded. A reasonable conjecture, but only that, is that two of the three examples involved, or arguably involved, interlibrary transactions and the committee did not wish to reevaluate the examples in the context of the newly added proviso in subsection (g)(2). To have repeated the examples without any comment, or with comment—either might have upset the delicate compromise that had been reached on subsection (g)(2).
23. 1976 Conference Report, p. 72.
24. 1975 Senate Report, p. 69; 1976 House Report, p. 76.

25. 1976 House Report, p. 75.
26. 1976 House Report, p. 169.
27. 1976 Conference Report, p. 73.
28. 1975 Senate Report, p. 71.

## Chapter 16. Limitations on Rights of Performance and Display

1. 1976 House Report, p. 85.
2. 1976 House Report, p. 85.
3. 1976 House Report, p. 86.
4. 1976 House Report, p. 84.
5. 47 U.S.C. §397; 47 CFR §§73.293–73.295 and 47 CFR §§73.593–73.595.
6. 1976 House Report, p. 87.
7. 1976 House Report, pp. 87–88.
8. For a recent decision interpreting this rule and finding it inapplicable in particular circumstances involving a retail store, see Sailor Music v. The Gap Stores, Inc., CCH Copr. L. Rptr. ¶ 25,340 (2d Cir. 1981).
9. 1976 House Report, p. 91.
10. 1976 House Report, p. 92.
11. 1976 House Report, p. 92.
12. 1976 House Report, p. 92.

## Chapter 17. Compulsory Licenses

1. Fortnightly Corp. v. United Artists, Inc., 392 U.S. 390 (1968); Teleprompter Corp. v. Columbia Broadcasting System, Inc., 415 U.S. 394 (1974).
2. 46 Federal Register 897 (1980).
3. Ibid.
4. For example, a little less than $13 million was paid with respect to 1978 and, as of October 1980, it had aggregated to a little less than $15 million. 45 Federal Register 50621 (1980).
5. Ibid.
6. See 37 CFR §§304.3–304.8.
7. 37 CFR §304.3.
8. 1976 House Report, p. 108.
9. Ibid.
10. 1976 House Report, p. 109.
11. 37 CFR §201.18(a)(3).
12. 37 CFR §201.18(e)(3).
13. 37 CFR §201.18(b)–(d).
14. 37 CFR §§307.2–307.3.
15. 37 CFR §201.19.
16. 1976 House Report, p. 110.
17. Ibid.

18. 37 CFR §201.19(a)(5)(iii).
19. 1976 House Report, p. 114.
20. Ibid.
21. 37 CFR §201.16.
22. 1976 House Report, pp. 113–114.
23. 37 CFR §§306.3–306.4.

# Appendix 1
# TEXT OF THE 1976 COPYRIGHT ACT, AS AMENDED

## TITLE I—GENERAL REVISION OF COPYRIGHT LAW

SEC. 101. Title 17 of the United States Code, entitled "Copyrights", is hereby amended in its entirety to read as follows:

## TITLE 17—COPYRIGHTS

### Chapter 1.—SUBJECT MATTER AND SCOPE OF COPYRIGHT

### § 101. Definitions

As used in this title, the following terms and their variant forms mean the following:

An "anonymous work" is a work on the copies or phonorecords of which no natural person is identified as author.

"Audiovisual works" are works that consist of a series of related images which are intrinsically intended to be shown by the use of machines or devices such as projectors, viewers, or electronic equipment, together with accompanying sounds, if any, regardless of the nature of the material objects, such as films or tapes, in which the works are embodied.

The "best edition" of a work is the edition, published in the United States at any time before the date of deposit, that the Library of Congress determines to be most suitable for its purposes.

A person's "children" are that person's immediate offspring, whether legitimate or not, and any children legally adopted by that person.

A "collective work" is a work, such as a periodical issue, anthology, or encyclopedia, in which a number of contributions, constituting separate and independent works in themselves, are assembled into a collective whole.

A "compilation" is a work formed by the collection and assembling of preexisting materials or of data that are selected, coordinated, or arranged in such a way that the resulting work as a whole constitutes an original work of authorship. The term "compilation" includes collective works.

"Copies" are material objects, other than phonorecords, in which a work is fixed by any method now known or later developed, and from which the work can be perceived, reproduced, or otherwise communicated, either directly or with the aid of a machine or device. The term "copies" includes the material object, other than a phonorecord, in which the work is first fixed.

A "computer program" is a set of statements or instructions to be used directly or indirectly in a computer in order to bring about a certain result.*[1]

"Copyright owner", with respect to any one of the exclusive rights comprised in a copyright, refers to the owner of that particular right.

A work is "created" when it is fixed in a copy or phonorecord for the first time; where a work is prepared over a period of time, the portion of it that has been fixed at any particular time constitutes the work as of that time, and where the work has been prepared in different versions, each version constitutes a separate work.

A "derivative work" is a work based upon one or more preexisting works, such as a translation, musical arrangement, dramatization, fictionalization, motion picture version, sound recording, art reproduction, abridgment, condensation, or any other form in which a work may be recast, transformed, or adapted. A work consisting of editorial revisions, annotations, elaborations, or other modifications which, as a whole, represent an original work of authorship, is a "derivative work".

A "device", "machine", or "process" is one now known or later developed.

To "display" a work means to show a copy of it, either directly or by means of a film, slide, television image, or any other device or process or, in the case of a motion picture or other audiovisual work, to show individual images nonsequentially.

A work is "fixed" in a tangible medium of expression when its embodiment in a copy or phonorecord, by or under the authority of the author, is sufficiently permanent or stable to permit it to be perceived, reproduced, or otherwise communicated for a period of more than transitory duration. A work consisting of sounds, images, or both, that are being transmitted, is "fixed" for purposes of this title if a fixation of the work is being made simultaneously with its transmission.

*See Note 1, page 284.

The terms "including" and "such as" are illustrative and not limitative.

A "joint work" is a work prepared by two or more authors with the intention that their contributions be merged into inseparable or interdependent parts of a unitary whole.

"Literary works" are works, other than audiovisual works, expressed in words, numbers, or other verbal or numerical symbols or indicia, regardless of the nature of the material objects, such as books, periodicals, manuscripts, phonorecords, film, tapes, disks, or cards, in which they are embodied.

"Motion pictures" are audiovisual works consisting of a series of related images which, when shown in succession, impart an impression of motion, together with accompanying sounds, if any.

To "perform" a work means to recite, render, play, dance, or act it, either directly or by means of any device or process or, in the case of a motion picture or other audiovisual work, to show its images in any sequence or to make the sounds accompanying it audible.

"Phonorecords" are material objects in which sounds, other than those accompanying a motion picture or other audiovisual work, are fixed by any method now known or later developed, and from which the sounds can be perceived, reproduced, or otherwise communicated, either directly or with the aid of a machine or device. The term "phonorecords" includes the material object in which the sounds are first fixed.

"Pictorial, graphic, and sculptural works" include two-dimensional and three-dimensional works of fine, graphic, and applied art, photographs, prints and art reproductions, maps, globes, charts, technical drawings, diagrams, and models. Such works shall include works of artistic craftsmanship insofar as their form but not their mechanical or utilitarian aspects are concerned; the design of a useful article, as defined in this section, shall be considered a pictorial, graphic, or sculptural work only if, and only to the extent that, such design incorporates pictorial, graphic, or sculptural features that can be identified separately from, and are capable of existing independently of, the utilitarian aspects of the article.

A "pseudonymous work" is a work on the copies or phonorecords of which the author is identified under a fictitious name.

"Publication" is the distribution of copies or phonorecords of a work to the public by sale or other transfer of ownership, or by rental, lease, or lending. The offering to distribute copies or phonorecords to a group of persons for purposes of further distribution, public performance, or public display, constitutes publication. A public performance or display of a work does not of itself constitute publication.

To perform or display a work "publicly" means—

 (1) to perform or display it at a place open to the public or at any place where a substantial number of persons outside of a normal circle of a family and its social acquaintances is gathered; or

 (2) to transmit or otherwise communicate a performance or display of the work to a place specified by clause (1) or to the public, by means of any device or processs, whether the members of the public capable of receiving the performance or display receive it in the same place or in separate places and at the same time or at different times.

"Sound recordings" are works that result from the fixation of a series of musical, spoken, or other sounds, but not including the sounds accompanying a motion picture or other audiovisual work, regardless of the nature of the material objects, such as disks, tapes, or other phonorecords, in which they are embodied.

"State" includes the District of Columbia and the Commonwealth of Puerto Rico, and any territories to which this title is made applicable by an Act of Congress.

A "transfer of copyright ownership" is an assignment, mortgage, exclusive license, or any other conveyance, alienation, or hypothecation of a copyright or of any of the exclusive rights comprised in a copyright, whether or not it is limited in time or place of effect, but not including a nonexclusive license.

A "transmission program" is a body of material that, as an aggregate, has been produced for the sole purpose of transmission to the public in sequence and as a unit.

To "transmit" a performance or display is to communicate it by any device or process whereby images or sounds are received beyond the place from which they are sent.

The "United States", when used in a geographical sense, comprises the several States, the District of Columbia and the Commonwealth of Puerto Rico, and the organized territories under the jurisdiction of the United States Government.

A "useful article" is an article having an intrinsic utilitarian function that is not merely to portray the appearance of the article or to convey information. An article that is normally a part of a useful article is considered a "useful article".

The author's "widow" or "widower" is the author's surviving spouse under the law of the author's domicile at the time of his or her death, whether or not the spouse has later remarried.

A "work of the United States Government" is a work prepared by an officer or employee of the United States Government as part of that person's official duties.

A "work made for hire" is—

    (1) a work prepared by an employee within the scope of his or her employment; or

    (2) a work specially ordered or commissioned for use as a contribution to a collective work, as a part of a motion picture or other audiovisual work, as a translation, as a supplementary work, as a compilation, as an instructional text, as a test, as answer material for a test, or as an atlas, if the parties expressly agree in a written instrument signed by them that the work shall be considered a work made for hire. For the purpose of the foregoing sentence, a "supplementary work" is a work prepared for publication as a secondary adjunct to a work by another author for the purpose of introducing, concluding, illustrating, explaining, revising, commenting upon, or assisting in the use of the other work, such as forewords, afterwords, pictorial illustrations, maps, charts, tables, editorial notes, musical arrangements, answer material for tests, bibliographies, appendixes, and indexes, and an "instructional text" is a literary, pictorial, or graphic work prepared for publication and with the purpose of use in systematic instructional activities.

## § 102. Subject matter of copyright: In general

(a) Copyright protection subsists, in accordance with this title, in original works of authorship fixed in any tangible medium of expression, now known or later developed, from which they can be perceived, reproduced, or otherwise communicated, either directly or with the aid of a machine or device. Works of authorship include the following categories:

(1) literary works;
(2) musical works, including any accompanying words;
(3) dramatic works, including any accompanying music;
(4) pantomimes and choreographic works;
(5) pictorial, graphic, and sculptural works;
(6) motion pictures and other audiovisual works; and
(7) sound recordings.

(b) In no case does copyright protection for an original work of authorship extend to any idea, procedure, process, system, method of operation, concept, principle, or discovery, regardless of the form in which it is described, explained, illustrated, or embodied in such work.

## § 103. Subject matter of copyright: Compilations and derivative works

(a) The subject matter of copyright as specified by section 102 includes compilations and derivative works, but protection for a work employing preexisting material in which copyright subsists does not extend to any part of the work in which such material has been used unlawfully.

(b) The copyright in a compilation or derivative work extends only to the material contributed by the author of such work, as distinguished from the preexisting material employed in the work, and does not imply any exclusive right in the preexisting material. The copyright in such work is independent of, and does not affect or enlarge the scope, duration, ownership, or subsistence of, any copyright protection in the preexisting material.

## § 104. Subject matter of copyright: National origin

(a) UNPUBLISHED WORKS.—The works specified by sections 102 and 103, while unpublished, are subject to protection under this title without regard to the nationality or domicile of the author.

(b) PUBLISHED WORKS.—The works specified by sections 102 and 103, when published, are subject to protection under this title if—

(1) on the date of first publication, one or more of the authors is a national or domiciliary of the United States, or is a national, domiciliary, or sovereign authority of a foreign nation that is a party to a copyright treaty to which the United States is also a party, or is a stateless person, wherever that person may be domiciled; or

(2) the work is first published in the United States or in a foreign nation that, on the date of first publication, is a party to the Universal Copyright Convention; or

(3) the work is first published by the United Nations or any of its specialized agencies, or by the Organization of American States; or

(4) the work comes within the scope of a Presidential proclamation. Whenever the President finds that a particular foreign nation extends, to works by authors who are nationals or domiciliaries of the United States or to works that are first published in the United States, copyright protection on substantially the same basis as that on which the foreign nation extends protection to works of its own nationals and domiciliaries and works first published in that nation, the President may by proclamation extend protection under this title to works of which one or more

of the authors is, on the date of first publication, a national, domiciliary, or sovereign authority of that nation, or which was first published in that nation. The President may revise, suspend, or revoke any such proclamation or impose any conditions or limitations on protection under a proclamation.

## § 105. Subject matter of copyright: United States Government works

Copyright protection under this title is not available for any work of the United States Government, but the United States Government is not precluded from receiving and holding copyrights transferred to it by assignment, bequest, or otherwise.

## § 106. Exclusive rights in copyrighted works

Subject to sections 107 through 118, the owner of copyright under this title has the exclusive rights to do and to authorize any of the following:

(1) to reproduce the copyrighted work in copies or phonorecords;

(2) to prepare derivative works based upon the copyrighted work;

(3) to distribute copies or phonorecords of the copyrighted work to the public by sale or other transfer of ownership, or by rental, lease, or lending;

(4) in the case of literary, musical, dramatic, and choreographic works, pantomimes, and motion pictures and other audiovisual works, to perform the copyrighted work publicly; and

(5) in the case of literary, musical, dramatic, and choreographic works, pantomimes, and pictorial, graphic, or sculptural works, including the individual images of a motion picture or other audiovisual work, to display the copyrighted work publicly.

## § 107. Limitations on exclusive rights: Fair use

Notwithstanding the provisions of section 106, the fair use of a copyrighted work, including such use by reproduction in copies or phonorecords or by any other means specified by that section, for purposes such as criticism, comment, news reporting, teaching (including multiple copies for classroom use), scholarship, or research, is not an infringement of copyright. In determining whether the use made of a work in any particular case is a fair use the factors to be considered shall include—

(1) the purpose and character of the use, including whether such use is of a commercial nature or is for nonprofit educational purposes;

(2) the nature of the copyrighted work;

(3) the amount and substantiality of the portion used in relation to the copyrighted work as a whole; and

(4) the effect of the use upon the potential market for or value of the copyrighted work.

## § 108. Limitations on exclusive rights: Reproduction by libraries and archives

(a) Notwithstanding the provisions of section 106, it is not an infringement of copyright for a library or archives, or any of its employees acting within the scope of their employment, to reproduce no more than one copy or phonorecord of a work, or to distribute such copy or phonorecord, under the conditions specified by this section, if—

(1) the reproduction or distribution is made without any purpose of direct or indirect commercial advantage;

(2) the collections of the library or archives are (i) open to the public, or (ii) available not only to researchers affiliated with the library or archives or with the institution of which it is a part, but also to other persons doing research in a specialized field; and

(3) the reproduction or distribution of the work includes a notice of copyright.

(b) The rights of reproduction and distribution under this section apply to a copy or phonorecord of an unpublished work duplicated in facsimile form solely for purposes of preservation and security or for deposit for research use in another library or archives of the type described by clause (2) of subsection (a), if the copy or phonorecord reproduced is currently in the collections of the library or archives.

(c) The right of reproduction under this section applies to a copy or phonorecord of a published work duplicated in facsimile form solely for the purpose of replacement of a copy or phonorecord that is damaged, deteriorating, lost, or stolen, if the library or archives has, after a reasonable effort, determined that an unused replacement cannot be obtained at a fair price.

(d) The rights of reproduction and distribution under this section apply to a copy, made from the collection of a library or archives where the user makes his or her request or from that of another library or archives, of no more than one article or other contribution to a copyrighted collection or periodical issue, or to a copy or phonorecord of a small part of any other copyrighted work, if—

(1) the copy or phonorecord becomes the property of the user, and the library or archives has had no notice that the copy or phonorecord would be used for any purpose other than private study, scholarship, or research; and

(2) the library or archives displays prominently, at the place where orders are accepted, and includes on its order form, a warning of copyright in accordance with requirements that the Register of Copyrights shall prescribe by regulation.

(e) The rights of reproduction and distribution under this section apply to the entire work, or to a substantial part of it, made from the collection of a library or archives where the user makes his or her request or from that of another library or archives, if the library or archives has first determined, on the basis of a reasonable investigation, that a copy or phonorecord of the copyrighted work cannot be obtained at a fair price, if—

(1) the copy or phonorecord becomes the property of the user, and the library or archives has had no notice that the copy or phonorecord would be used for any purpose other than private study, scholarship, or research; and

(2) the library or archives displays prominently, at the place where orders are accepted, and includes on its order form, a warning of copyright in accordance with requirements that the Register of Copyrights shall prescribe by regulation.

(f) Nothing in this section—

(1) shall be construed to impose liability for copyright infringement upon a library or archives or its employees for the unsupervised use of reproducing equipment located on its premises: *Provided*, That such equipment displays a notice that the making of a copy may be subject to the copyright law;

(2) excuses a person who uses such reproducing equipment or who requests a copy or phonorecord under subsection (d) from liability for copyright infringement for any such act, or for any later use of such copy or phonorecord, if it exceeds fair use as provided by section 107;

(3) shall be construed to limit the reproduction and distribution by lending of a limited number of copies and excerpts by a library or archives of an audiovisual news program, subject to clauses (1), (2), and (3) of subsection (a) ; or

(4) in any way affects the right of fair use as provided by section 107, or any contractual obligations assumed at any time by the library or archives when it obtained a copy or phonorecord of a work in its collections.

(g) The rights of reproduction and distribution under this section extend to the isolated and unrelated reproduction or distribution of a single copy or phonorecord of the same material on separate occasions, but do not extend to cases where the library or archives, or its employee—

(1) is aware or has substantial reason to believe that it is engaging in the related or concerted reproduction or distribution of multiple copies or phonorecords of the same material, whether made on one occasion or over a period of time, and whether intended for aggregate use by one or more individuals or for separate use by the individual members of a group; or

(2) engages in the systematic reproduction or distribution of single or multiple copies or phonorecords of material described in subsection (d) : *Provided,* That nothing in this clause prevents a library or archives from participating in interlibrary arrangements that do not have, as their purpose or effect, that the library or archives receiving such copies or phonorecords for distribution does so in such aggregate quantities as to substitute for a subscription to or purchase of such work.

(h) The rights of reproduction and distribution under this section do not apply to a musical work, a pictorial, graphic or sculptural work, or a motion picture or other audiovisual work other than an audiovisual work dealing with news, except that no such limitation shall apply with respect to rights granted by subsections (b) and (c), or with respect to pictorial or graphic works published as illustrations, diagrams, or similar adjuncts to works of which copies are reproduced or distributed in accordance with subsections (d) and (e).

(i) Five years from the effective date of this Act, and at five-year intervals thereafter, the Register of Copyrights, after consulting with representatives of authors, book and periodical publishers, and other owners of copyrighted materials, and with representatives of library users and librarians, shall submit to the Congress a report setting forth the extent to which this section has achieved the intended statutory balancing of the rights of creators, and the needs of users. The report should also describe any problems that may have arisen, and present legislative or other recommendations, if warranted.

## § 109. Limitations on exclusive rights: Effect of transfer of particular copy or phonorecord

(a) Notwithstanding the provisions of section 106(3), the owner of a particular copy or phonorecord lawfully made under this title, or any person authorized by such owner, is entitled, without the authority of the copyright owner, to sell or otherwise dispose of the possession of that copy or phonorecord.

(b) Notwithstanding the provisions of section 106(5), the owner of a particular copy lawfully made under this title, or any person authorized by such owner, is entitled, without the authority of the copyright owner, to display that copy publicly, either directly or by the projection of no more than one image at a time, to viewers present at the place where the copy is located.

(c) The privileges prescribed by subsections (a) and (b) do not, unless authorized by the coyright owner, extend to any person who has acquired possession of the copy or phonorecord from the copyright owner, by rental, lease, loan, or otherwise, without acquiring ownership of it.

## § 110. Limitations on exclusive rights: Exemption of certain performances and displays

Notwithstanding the provisions of section 106, the following are not infringements of copyright:

(1) performance or display of a work by instructors or pupils in the course of face-to-face teaching activities of a nonprofit educational institution, in a classroom or similar place devoted to instruction, unless, in the case of a motion picture or other audiovisual work, the performance, or the display of individual images, is given by means of a copy that was not lawfully made under this title, and that the person responsible for the performance knew or had reason to believe was not lawfully made;

(2) performance of a nondramatic literary or musical work or display of a work, by or in the course of a transmission, if—

(A) the performance or display is a regular part of the systematic instructional activities of a governmental body or a nonprofit educational institution; and

(B) the performance or display is directly related and of material assistance to the teaching content of the transmission; and

(C) the transmission is made primarily for—

(i) reception in classrooms or similar places normally devoted to instruction, or

(ii) reception by persons to whom the transmission is directed because their disabilities or other special circumstances prevent their attendance in classrooms or similar places normally devoted to instruction, or

(iii) reception by officers or employees of governmental bodies as a part of their official duties or employment;

(3) performance of a nondramatic literary or musical work or of a dramatico-musical work of a religious nature, or display of a work, in the course of services at a place of worship or other religious assembly;

(4) performance of a nondramatic literary or musical work otherwise than in a transmission to the public, without any purpose of direct or indirect commercial advantage and without payment of any fee or other compensation for the performance to any of its performers, promoters, or organizers, if—

(A) there is no direct or indirect admission charge; or

(B) the proceeds, after deducting the reasonable costs of producing the performance, are used exclusively for educational, religious, or charitable purposes and not for private financial gain, except where the copyright owner has served notice of objection to the performance under the following conditions;

(i) the notice shall be in writing and signed by the copyright owner or such owner's duly authorized agent; and

(ii) the notice shall be served on the person responsible for the performance at least seven days before the date of the performance, and shall state the reasons for the objection; and

(iii) the notice shall comply, in form, content, and manner of service, with requirements that the Register of Copyrights shall prescribe by regulation;

(5) communication of a transmission embodying a performance or display of a work by the public reception of the transmission on a single receiving apparatus of a kind commonly used in private homes, unless—

(A) a direct charge is made to see or hear the transmission; or

(B) the transmission thus received is further transmitted to the public;

(6) performance of a nondramatic musical work by a governmental body or a nonprofit agricultural or horticultural organization, in the course of an annual agricultural or horticultural fair or exhibition conducted by such body or organization; the exemption provided by this clause shall extend to any liability for copyright infringement that would otherwise be imposed on such body or organization, under doctrines of vicarious liability or related infringement, for a performance by a concessionnaire, business establishment, or other person at such fair or exhibition, but shall not excuse any such person from liability for the performance;

(7) performance of a nondramatic musical work by a vending establishment open to the public at large without any direct or indirect admission charge, where the sole purpose of the performance is to promote the retail sale of copies or phonorecords of the work, and the performance is not transmitted beyond the place where the establishment is located and is within the immediate area where the sale is occurring;

(8) performance of a nondramatic literary work, by or in the course of a transmission specifically designed for and primarily directed to blind or other handicapped persons who are unable to read normal printed material as a result of their handicap, or deaf or other handicapped persons who are unable to hear the aural signals accompanying a transmission of visual signals, if the performance is made without any purpose of direct or indirect commercial advantage and its transmission is made through the facilities of: (i) a governmental body; or (ii) a noncommercial educational broadcast station (as defined in section 397 of title 47); or (iii) a radio subcarrier authorization (as defined in 47 CFR 73.293–73.295 and 73.593–73.595); or (iv) a cable system (as defined in section 111(f)).

(9) performance on a single occasion of a dramatic literary work published at least ten years before the date of the performance, by or in the course of a transmission specifically designed for and primarily directed to blind or other handicapped persons who are unable to read normal printed material as a result of their handicap, if the performance is made without any purpose of direct or indirect commercial advantage and its transmission is made through the facilities of a radio subcarrier authorization referred to in clause (8)(iii), *Provided*, That the provisions of this clause shall not be applicable to more than one performance of the same work by the same performers or under the auspices of the same organization.

## § 111. Limitations on exclusive rights: Secondary transmissions

(a) CERTAIN SECONDARY TRANSMISSIONS EXEMPTED.—The secondary transmission of a primary transmission embodying a performance or display of a work is not an infringement of copyright if—

(1) the secondary transmission is not made by a cable system, and consists entirely of the relaying, by the management of a hotel, apartment house, or similar establishment, of signals transmitted by a broadcast station licensed by the Federal Communications Commission, within the local service area of such station, to the private lodgings of guests or residents of such establishment, and no direct charge is made to see or hear the secondary transmission; or

(2) the secondary transmission is made solely for the purpose and under the conditions specified by clause (2) of section 110; or

(3) the secondary transmission is made by any carrier who has no direct or indirect control over the content or selection of the primary transmission or over the particular recipients of the secondary transmission, and whose activities with respect to the secondary transmission consist solely of providing wires, cables, or other communications channels for the use of others: *Provided*, That the provisions of this clause extend only to the activities of said carrier with respect to secondary transmissions and do not exempt from liability the activities of others with respect to their own primary or secondary transmissions; or

(4) the secondary transmission is not made by a cable system but is made by a governmental body, or other nonprofit organization, without any purpose of direct or indirect commercial advantage, and without charge to the recipients of the secondary transmission other than assessments necessary to defray the actual and reasonable costs of maintaining and operating the secondary transmission service.

(b) SECONDARY TRANSMISSION OF PRIMARY TRANSMISSION TO CONTROLLED GROUP.—Notwithstanding the provisions of subsections (a) and (c), the secondary transmission to the public of a primary transmission embodying a performance or display of a work is actionable as an act of infringement under section 501, and is fully subject to the remedies provided by sections 502 through 506 and 509, if the primary transmission is not made for reception by the public at large but is controlled and limited to reception by particular members of the public: *Provided*, however, That such secondary transmission is not actionable as an act of infringement if—

(1) the primary transmission is made by a broadcast station licensed by the Federal Communications Commission; and

(2) the carriage of the signals comprising the secondary transmission is required under the rules, regulations, or authorizations of the Federal Communications Commission; and

(3) the signal of the primary transmitter is not altered or changed in any way by the secondary transmitter.

(c) SECONDARY TRANSMISSIONS BY CABLE SYSTEMS.—

(1) Subject to the provisions of clauses (2), (3), and (4) of this subsection, secondary transmissions to the public by a cable system of a primary transmission made by a broadcast station licensed by the Federal Communications Commission or by an appropriate governmental authority of Canada or Mexico and embodying a performance or display of a work shall be subject to compulsory licensing upon compliance with the requirements of subsection (d) where the carriage of the signals comprising the secondary transmission is permissible under the rules, regulations, or authorizations of the Federal Communications Commission.

(2) Notwithstanding the provisions of clause (1) of this subsection, the willful or repeated secondary transmission to the public by a cable system of a primary transmission made by a

broadcast station licensed by the Federal Communications Commission or by an appropriate governmental authority of Canada or Mexico and embodying a performance or display of a work is actionable as an act of infringement under section 501, and is fully subject to the remedies provided by sections 502 through 506 and 509, in the following cases:

(A) where the carriage of the signals comprising the secondary transmission is not permissible under the rules, regulations, or authorizations of the Federal Communications Commission; or

(B) where the cable system has not recorded the notice specified by subsection (d) and deposited the statement of account and royalty fee required by subsection (d).

(3) Notwithstanding the provisions of clause (1) of this subsection and subject to the provisions of subsection (e) of this section, the secondary transmission to the public by a cable system of a primary transmission made by a broadcast station licensed by the Federal Communications Commission or by an appropriate governmental authority of Canada or Mexico and embodying a performance or display of a work is actionable as an act of infringement under section 501, and is fully subject to the remedies provided by sections 502 through 506 and sections 509 and 510, if the content of the particular program in which the performance or display is embodied, or any commercial advertising or station announcements transmitted by the primary transmitter during, or immediately before or after, the transmission of such program, is in any way willfully altered by the cable system through changes, deletions, or additions, except for the alteration, deletion, or substitution of commercial advertisements performed by those engaged in television commercial advertising market research: *Provided*, That the research company has obtained the prior consent of the advertiser who has purchased the original commercial advertisement, the television station broadcasting that commercial advertisement, and the cable system performing the secondary transmission: *And provided further*, That such commercial alteration, deletion, or substitution is not performed for the purpose of deriving income from the sale of that commercial time.

(4) Notwithstanding the provisions of clause (1) of this subsection, the secondary transmission to the public by a cable system of a primary transmission made by a broadcast station licensed by an appropriate governmental authority of Canada or Mexico and embodying a performance or display of a work is actionable as an act of infringement under section 501, and is fully subject to the remedies provided by sections 502 through 506 and section 509, if (A) with respect to Canadian signals, the community of the cable system is located more than 150 miles from the United States-Canadian border and is also located south of the forty-second parallel of latitude, or (B) with respect to Mexican signals, the secondary transmission is made by a cable system which received the primary transmission by means other than direct interception of a free space radio wave emitted by such broadcast television station, unless prior to April 15, 1976, such cable system was actually carrying, or was specifically authorized to carry, the signal of such foreign station on the system pursuant to the rules, regulations, or authorizations of the Federal Communications Commission.

(d) Compulsory License for Secondary Transmissions by Cable Systems.—

(1) For any secondary transmission to be subject to compulsory licensing under subsection (c), the cable system shall, at least one month before the date of the commencement of operations of the cable system or within one hundred and eighty days after the enactment of this Act, whichever is later, and thereafter within thirty days after each occasion on which the ownership or control or the signal carriage complement of the cable system changes, record in the Copyright Office a notice including a statement of the identity and address of the person who owns or operates the secondary transmission service or has power to exercise primary control over it, together with the name and location of the primary transmitter or primary transmitters whose signals are regularly carried by the cable system, and thereafter, from time to time, such further information as the Register of Copyrights, after consultation with the Copyright Royalty Tribunal (if and when the Tribunal has been constituted), shall prescribe by regulation to carry out the purpose of this clause.

(2) A cable system whose secondary transmissions have been subject to compulsory licensing under subsection (c) shall, on a semiannual basis, deposit with the Register of Copyrights, in accordance with requirements that the Register shall, after consultation with the Copyright Royalty Tribunal (if and when the Tribunal has been constituted), prescribe by regulation—

(A) a statement of account, covering the six months next preceding, specifying the number of channels on which the cable system made secondary transmissions to its subscribers, the names and locations of all primary transmitters whose transmissions were further transmitted by the cable system, the total number of subscribers, the gross amounts paid to the cable system for the basic service of providing secondary transmissions of primary broadcast transmitters, and such other data as the Register of Copyrights may, after consultation with the Copyright Royalty Tribunal (if and when the Tribunal has been constituted), from time to time prescribe by regulation. Such statement shall also include a special statement of account covering any nonnetwork television programming that was carried by the cable system in whole or in part beyond the local service area of the primary transmitter, under rules, regulations, or authorizations of the Federal Communications Commission permitting the substitution or addition of signals under certain circumstances, together with logs showing the times, dates, stations, and programs involved in such substituted or added carriage; and

(B) except in the case of a cable system whose royalty is specified in subclause (C) or (D), a total royalty fee for the period covered by the statement, computed on the basis of specified percentages of the gross receipts from subscribers to the cable service during said period for the basic service of providing secondary transmissions of primary broadcast transmitters, as follows:

(i) 0.675 of 1 per centum of such gross receipts for the privilege of further transmitting any nonnetwork programing of a primary transmitter in whole or in part beyond the local service area of such primary transmitter, such amount to be applied against the fee, if any, payable pursuant to paragraphs (ii) through (iv);

(ii) 0.675 of 1 per centum of such gross receipts for the first distant signal equivalent;

(iii) 0.425 of 1 per centum of such gross receipts for each of the second, third, and fourth distant signal equivalents;

(iv) 0.2 of 1 per centum of such gross receipts for the fifth distant signal equivalent and each additional distant signal equivalent thereafter; and

in computing the amounts payable under paragraph (ii) through (iv), above, any fraction of a distant signal equivalent shall be computed at its fractional value and, in the case of any cable system located partly within and partly without the local service area of a primary transmitter, gross receipts shall be limited to those gross receipts derived from subscribers located without the local service area of such primary transmitter; and

(C) if the actual gross receipts paid by subscribers to a cable system for the period covered by the statement for the basic service of providing secondary transmissions of primary broadcast transmitters total $80,000 or less, gross receipts of the cable system for the purpose of this subclause shall be computed by subtracting from such actual gross receipts the amount by which $80,000 exceeds such actual gross receipts, except that in no case shall a cable system's gross receipts be reduced to less than $3,000. The royalty fee payable under this subclause shall be 0.5 of 1 per centum, regardless of the number of distant signal equivalents, if any; and

(D) if the actual gross receipts paid by subscribers to a cable system for the period covered by the statement, for the basic service of providing secondary transmissions of primary broadcast transmitters, are more than $80,000 but less than $160,000, the royalty fee payable under this subclause shall be (i) 0.5 of 1 per centum of any gross receipts up to $80,000; and (ii) 1 per centum of any gross receipts in excess of $80,000 but less than $160,000, regardless of the number of distant signal equivalents, if any.

(3) The Register of Copyrights shall receive all fees deposited under this section and, after deducting the reasonable costs incurred by the Copyright Office under this section, shall deposit the balance in the Treasury of the United States, in such manner as the Secretary of the Treasury directs. All funds held by the Secretary of the Treasury shall be invested in interest-bearing United States securities for later distribution with interest by the Copyright Royalty Tribunal as provided by this title. The Register shall submit to the Copyright Royalty Tribunal, on a semiannual basis, a compilation of all statements of account covering the relevant six-month period provided by clause (2) of this subsection.

(4) The royalty fees thus deposited shall, in accordance with the procedures provided by clause (5), be distributed to those among the following copyright owners who claim that their works were the subject of secondary transmissions by cable systems during the relevant semiannual period:

(A) any such owner whose work was included in a secondary transmission made by a cable system of a nonnetwork television program in whole or in part beyond the local service area of the primary transmitter; and

(B) any such owner whose work was included in a secondary transmission identified in a special statement of account deposited under clause (2)(A); and

(C) any such owner whose work was included in nonnetwork programing consisting exclusively of aural signals carried by a cable system in whole or in part beyond the local service area of the primary transmitter of such programs.

(5) The royalty fees thus deposited shall be distributed in accordance with the following procedures:

(A) During the month of July in each year, every person claiming to be entitled to compulsory license fees for secondary transmissions shall file a claim with the Copyright Royalty Tribunal, in accordance with requirements that the Tribunal shall prescribe by regulation. Notwithstanding any provisions of the antitrust laws, for purposes of this clause any claimants may agree among themselves as to the proportionate division of compulsory licensing fees among them, may lump their claims together and file them jointly or as a single claim, or may designate a common agent to receive payment on their behalf.

(B) After the first day of August of each year, the Copyright Royalty Tribunal shall determine whether there exists a controversy concerning the distribution of royalty fees. If the Tribunal determines that no such controversy exists, it shall, after deducting its reasonable administrative costs under this section, distribute such fees to the copyright owners entitled, or to their designated agents. If the Tribunal finds the existence of a controversy, it shall, pursuant to chapter 8 of this title, conduct a proceeding to determine the distribution of royalty fees.

(C) During the pendency of any proceeding under this subsection, the Copyright Royalty Tribunal shall withhold from distribution an amount sufficient to satisfy all claims with respect to which a controversy exists, but shall have discretion to proceed to distribute any amounts that are not in controversy.

(e) NONSIMULTANEOUS SECONDARY TRANSMISSIONS BY CABLE SYSTEMS.—

(1) Notwithstanding those provisions of the second paragraph of subsection (f) relating to nonsimultaneous secondary transmissions by a cable system, any such transmissions are actionable as an act of infringement under section 501, and are fully subject to the remedies provided by sections 502 through 506 and sections 509 and 510, unless—

(A) the program on the videotape is transmitted no more than one time to the cable system's subscribers; and

(B) the copyrighted program, episode, or motion picture videotape, including the commercials contained within such program, episode, or picture, is transmitted without deletion or editing; and

(C) an owner or officer of the cable system (i) prevents the duplication of the videotape while in the possession of the system, (ii) prevents unauthorized duplication while in the possession of the facility making the videotape for the system if the system owns or controls the facility, or takes reasonable precautions to prevent such duplication if it does not own or control the facility, (iii) takes adequate precautions to prevent duplication while the tape is being transported, and (iv) subject to clause (2), erases or destroys, or causes the erasure or destruction of, the videotape; and

(D) within forty-five days after the end of each calendar quarter, an owner or officer of the cable system executes an affidavit attesting (i) to the steps and precautions taken to prevent duplication of the videotape, and (ii) subject to clause (2), to the erasure or destruction of all videotapes made or used during such quarter; and

(E) such owner or officer places or causes each such affidavit, and affidavits received pursuant to clause (2)(C), to be placed in a file, open to public inspection, at such system's main office in the community where the transmission is made or in the nearest community where such system maintains an office; and

(F) the nonsimultaneous transmission is one that the cable system would be authorized to transmit under the rules, regulations, and authorizations of the Federal Communications Commission in effect at the time of the nonsimultaneous transmission if the transmission had been made simultaneously, except that this subclause shall not apply to inadvertent or accidental transmissions.

(2) If a cable system transfers to any person a videotape of a program nonsimultaneously transmitted by it, such transfer is actionable as an act of infringement under section 501, and is fully subject to the remedies provided by sections 502 through 506 and 509, except that, pursuant to a written, nonprofit contract providing for the equitable sharing of the costs of such videotape and its transfer, a videotape nonsimultaneously transmitted by it, in accordance with clause (1), may be transferred by one cable system in Alaska to another system in Alaska, by one cable system in Hawaii permitted to make such nonsimultaneous transmissions to another such cable system in Hawaii, or by one cable system in Guam, the Northern Mariana Islands, or the Trust Territory of the Pacific Islands, to another cable system in any of those three territories, if—

(A) each such contract is available for public inspection in the offices of the cable systems involved, and a copy of such contract is filed, within thirty days after such contract is entered into, with the Copyright Office (which Office shall make each such contract available for public inspection); and

(B) the cable system to which the videotape is transferred complies with clause (1)(A), (B), (C)(i), (iii), and (iv), and (D) through (F); and

(C) such system provides a copy of the affidavit required to be made in accordance with clause (1)(D) to each cable system making a previous nonsimultaneous transmission of the same videotape.

(3) This subsection shall not be construed to supersede the exclusivity protection provisions of any existing agreement, or any such agreement hereafter entered into, between a cable system and a television broadcast station in the area in which the cable system is located, or a network with which such station is affiliated.

(4) As used in this subsection, the term "videotape", and each of its variant forms, means the reproduction of the images and

sounds of a program or programs broadcast by a television broadcast station licensed by the Federal Communications Commission, regardless of the nature of the material objects, such as tapes or films, in which the reproduction is embodied.

(f) DEFINITIONS.—As used in this section, the following terms and their variant forms mean the following:

A "primary transmission" is a transmission made to the public by the transmitting facility whose signals are being received and further transmitted by the secondary transmission service, regardless of where or when the performance or display was first transmitted.

A "secondary transmission" is the further transmitting of a primary transmission simultaneously with the primary transmission, or nonsimultaneously with the primary transmission if by a "cable system" not located in whole or in part within the boundary of the forty-eight contiguous States, Hawaii, or Puerto Rico: *Provided, however,* That a nonsimultaneous further transmission by a cable system located in Hawaii of a primary transmission shall be deemed to be a secondary transmission if the carriage of the television broadcast signal comprising such further transmission is permissible under the rules, regulations, or authorizations of the Federal Communications Commission.

A "cable system" is a facility, located in any State, Territory, Trust Territory, or Possession, that in whole or in part receives signals transmitted or programs broadcast by one or more television broadcast stations licensed by the Federal Communications Commission, and makes secondary transmissions of such signals or programs by wires, cables, or other communications channels to subscribing members of the public who pay for such service. For purposes of determining the royalty fee under subsection (d)(2), two or more cable systems in contiguous communities under common ownership or control or operating from one headend shall be considered as one system.

The "local service area of a primary transmitter", in the case of a television broadcast station, comprises the area in which such station is entitled to insist upon its signal being retransmitted by a cable system pursuant to the rules, regulations, and authorizations of the Federal Communications Commission in effect on April 15, 1976, or in the case of a television broadcast station licensed by an appropriate governmental authority of Canada or Mexico, the area in which it would be entitled to insist upon its signal being retransmitted if it were a television broadcast station subject to such rules, regulations, and authorizations. The "local service area of a primary transmitter", in the case of a radio broadcast station, comprises the primary service area of such station, pursuant to the rules and regulations of the Federal Communications Commission.

A "distant signal equivalent" is the value assigned to the secondary transmission of any nonnetwork television programing carried by a cable system in whole or in part beyond the local service area of the primary transmitter of such programing. It is computed by assigning a value of one to each independent station and a value of one-quarter to each network station and noncommercial educational station for the nonnetwork programing so carried pursuant to the rules, regulations, and authorizations of the Federal Communications Commission. The foregoing values for independent, network, and noncommercial educational stations are subject, however, to the following exceptions and limitations. Where the rules and regulations of the Federal Communications Commission require a cable system to omit the further transmission of a particular program and such rules and regulations also permit the substitution of another program embodying a performance or display of a work in place of the omitted transmission, or where such rules and regulations in effect on the date of enactment of this Act permit a cable system, at its election, to effect such deletion and substitution of a nonlive program or to carry additional programs not transmitted by primary transmitters within whose local service area the cable system is located, no value shall be assigned for the substituted or additional program; where the rules, regulations, or authorizations of the Federal Communications Commission in effect on the date of enactment of this Act permit a cable system, at its election, to omit the further transmission of a particular program and such rules, regulations, or authorizations also permit the substitution of another program embodying a performance or display of a work in place of the omitted transmission, the value assigned for the substituted or additional program shall be, in the case of a live program, the value of one full distant signal equivalent multiplied by a fraction that has as its numerator the number of days in the year in which such substitution occurs and as its denominator the number of days in the year. In the case of a station carried pursuant to the late-night or specialty programing rules of the Federal Communications Commission, or a station carried on a part-time basis where full-time carriage is not possible because the cable system lacks the activated channel capacity to retransmit on a full-time basis all signals which it is authorized to carry, the values for independent, network, and noncommercial educational stations set forth above, as the case may be, shall be multiplied by a fraction which is equal to the ratio of the broadcast hours of such station carried by the cable system to the total broadcast hours of the station.

A "network station" is a television broadcast station that is owned or operated by, or affiliated with, one or more of the television networks in the United States providing nationwide transmissons, and that transmits a substantial part of the programing supplied by such networks for a substantial part of that station's typical broadcast day.

An "independent station" is a commercial television broadcast station other than a network station.

A "noncommercial educational station" is a television station that is a noncommercial educational broadcast station as defined in section 397 of title 47.

## § 112. Limitations on exclusive rights: Ephemeral recordings

(a) Notwithstanding the provisions of section 106, and except in the case of a motion picture or other audiovisual work, it is not an infringement of copyright for a transmitting organization entitled to transmit to the public a performance or display of a work, under a license or transfer of the copyright or under the limitations on exclusive rights in sound recordings specified by section 114(a), to make no more than one copy or phonorecord of a particular transmission program embodying the performance or display, if—

(1) the copy or phonorecord is retained and used solely by the transmitting organization that made it, and no further copies or phonorecords are reproduced from it; and

(2) the copy or phonorecord is used solely for the transmitting organization's own transmissions within its local service area, or for purposes of archival preservation or security; and

(3) unless preserved exclusively for archival purposes, the copy or phonorecord is destroyed within six months from the date the transmission program was first transmitted to the public.

(b) Notwithstanding the provisions of section 106, it is not an infringement of copyright for a governmental body or other nonprofit organization entitled to transmit a performance or display of a work, under section 110(2) or under the limitations on exclusive rights in sound recordings specified by section 114(a), to make no more than thirty copies or phonorecords of a particular transmission program embodying the performance or display, if—

(1) no further copies or phonorecords are reproduced from the copies or phonorecords made under this clause; and

(2) except for one copy or phonorecord that may be preserved exclusively for archival purposes, the copies or phonorecords are destroyed within seven years from the date the transmission program was first transmitted to the public.

(c) Notwithstanding the provisions of section 106, it is not an infringement of copyright for a governmental body or other nonprofit organization to make for distribution no more than one copy or phonorecord, for each transmitting organization specified in clause (2) of this subsection, of a particular transmission program embodying a performance of a nondramatic musical work of a religious nature, or of a sound recording of such a musical work, if—

(1) there is no direct or indirect charge for making or distributing any such copies or phonorecords; and

(2) none of such copies or phonorecords is used for any performance other than a single transmission to the public by a transmitting organization entitled to transmit to the public a performance of the work under a license or transfer of the copyright; and

(3) except for one copy or phonorecord that may be preserved exclusively for archival purposes, the copies or phonorecords are all destroyed within one year from the date the transmission program was first transmitted to the public.

(d) Notwithstanding the provisions of section 106, it is not an infringement of copyright for a governmental body or other nonprofit organization entitled to transmit a performance of a work under section 110(8) to make no more than ten copies or phonorecords embodying the performance, or to permit the use of any such copy or phonorecord by any governmental body or nonprofit organization entitled to transmit a performance of a work under section 110(8), if—

(1) any such copy or phonorecord is retained and used solely by the organization that made it, or by a governmental body or nonprofit organization entitled to transmit a performance of a work under section 110(8), and no further copies or phonorecords are reproduced from it; and

(2) any such copy or phonorecord is used solely for transmissions authorized under section 110(8), or for purposes of archival preservation or security; and

(3) the governmental body or nonprofit organization permitting any use of any such copy or phonorecord by any governmental body or nonprofit organization under this subsection does not make any charge for such use.

(e) The transmission program embodied in a copy or phonorecord made under this section is not subject to protection as a derivative work under this title except with the express consent of the owners of copyright in the preexisting works employed in the program.

## § 113. Scope of exclusive rights in pictorial, graphic, and sculptural works

(a) Subject to the provisions of subsections (b) and (c) of this section, the exclusive right to reproduce a copyrighted pictorial, graphic, or sculptural work in copies under section 106 includes the right to reproduce the work in or on any kind of article, whether useful or otherwise.

(b) This title does not afford, to the owner of copyright in a work that portrays a useful article as such, any greater or lesser rights with respect to the making, distribution, or display of the useful article so portrayed than those afforded to such works under the law, whether title 17 or the common law or statutes of a State, in effect on December 31, 1977, as held applicable and construed by a court in an action brought under this title.

(c) In the case of a work lawfully reproduced in useful articles that have been offered for sale or other distribution to the public, copyright does not include any right to prevent the making, distribution, or display of pictures or photographs of such articles in connection with advertisements or commentaries related to the distribution or display of such articles, or in connection with news reports.

## § 114. Scope of exclusive rights in sound recordings

(a) The exclusive rights of the owner of copyright in a sound recording are limited to the rights specified by clauses (1), (2), and (3) of section 106, and do not include any right of performance under section 106(4).

(b) The exclusive right of the owner of copyright in a sound recording under clause (1) of section 106 is limited to the right to duplicate the sound recording in the form of phonorecords, or of copies of motion pictures and other audiovisual works, that directly or indirectly recapture the actual sounds fixed in the recording. The exclusive right of the owner of copyright in a sound recording under clause (2) of section 106 is limited to the right to prepare a derivative work in which the actual sounds fixed in the sound recording are rearranged, remixed, or otherwise altered in sequence or quality. The exclusive rights of the owner of copyright in a sound recording under clauses (1) and (2) of section 106 do not extend to the making or duplication of another sound recording that consists entirely of an independent fixation of other sounds, even though such sounds imitate or simulate those in the copyrighted sound recording. The exclusive rights of the owner of copyright in a sound recording under clauses (1), (2), and (3) of section 106 do not apply to sound recordings included in educational television and radio programs (as defined in section 397 of title 47) distributed or transmitted by or through public broadcasting entities (as defined by section 118(g)) : *Provided*, That copies or phonorecords of said programs are not commercially distributed by or through public broadcasting entities to the general public.

(c) This section does not limit or impair the exclusive right to perform publicly, by means of a phonorecord, any of the works specified by section 106(4).

(d) On January 3, 1978, the Register of Copyrights, after consulting with representatives of owners of copyrighted materials, representatives of the broadcasting, recording, motion picture, entertainment industries, and arts organizations, representatives of organized labor and performers of copyrighted materials, shall submit to the Congress a report setting forth recommendations as to whether this section should be amended to provide for performers and copyright owners of copyrighted material any performance rights in such material. The report should describe the status of such rights in foreign countries, the views of major interested parties, and specific legislative or other recommendations, if any.

## § 115. Scope of exclusive rights in nondramatic musical works: Compulsory license for making and distributing phonorecords

In the case of nondramatic musical works, the exclusive rights provided by clauses (1) and (3) of section 106, to make and to distribute phonorecords of such works, are subject to compulsory licensing under the conditions specified by this section.

(a) AVAILABILITY AND SCOPE OF COMPULSORY LICENSE.—

(1) When phonorecords of a nondramatic musical work have been distributed to the public in the United States under the authority of the copyright owner, any other person may, by complying with the provisions of this section, obtain a compulsory license to make and distribute phonorecords of the work. A person may obtain a compulsory license only if his or her primary purpose in making phonorecords is to distribute them to the public for private use. A person may not obtain a compulsory license for use of the work in the making of phonorecords duplicating a sound recording fixed by another, unless: (i) such sound recording was fixed lawfully; and (ii) the making of the phonorecords was authorized by the owner of copyright in the sound recording or, if the sound recording was fixed before February 15, 1972, by any person who fixed the sound recording pursuant to an express license from the owner of the copyright in the musical work or pursuant to a valid compulsory license for use of such work in a sound recording.

(2) A compulsory license includes the privilege of making a musical arrangement of the work to the extent necessary to conform it to the style or manner of interpretation of the performance involved, but the arrangement shall not change the basic melody or fundamental character of the work, and shall not be subject to protection as a derivative work under this title, except with the express consent of the copyright owner.

(b) NOTICE OF INTENTION TO OBTAIN COMPULSORY LICENSE.—

(1) Any person who wishes to obtain a compulsory license under this section shall, before or within thirty days after making, and before distributing any phonorecords of the work, serve notice of intention to do so on the copyright owner. If the registration or other public records of the Copyright Office do not identify the copyright owner and include an address at which notice can be served, it shall be sufficient to file the notice of intention in the Copyright Office. The notice shall comply, in form, content, and manner of service, with requirements that the Register of Copyrights shall prescribe by regulation.

(2) Failure to serve or file the notice required by clause (1) forecloses the possibility of a compulsory license and, in the absence of a negotiated license, renders the making and distribution of phonorecords actionable as acts of infringement under section 501 and fully subject to the remedies provided by sections 502 through 506 and 509.

(c) ROYALTY PAYABLE UNDER COMPULSORY LICENSE.—

(1) To be entitled to receive royalties under a compulsory license, the copyright owner must be identified in the registration or other public records of the Copyright Office. The owner is entitled to royalties for phonorecords made and distributed after

being so identified, but is not entitled to recover for any phonorecords previously made and distributed.

(2) Except as provided by clause (1), the royalty under a compulsory license shall be payable for every phonorecord made and distributed in accordance with the license. For this purpose, a phonorecord is considered "distributed" if the person exercising the compulsory license has voluntarily and permanently parted with its possession. With respect to each work embodied in the phonorecord, the royalty shall be either two and three-fourths cents, or one-half of one cent per minute of playing time or fraction thereof, whichever amount is larger.

(3) Royalty payments shall be made on or before the twentieth day of each month and shall include all royalties for the month next preceding. Each monthly payment shall be made under oath and shall comply with requirements that the Register of Copyrights shall prescribe by regulation. The Register shall also prescribe regulations under which detailed cumulative annual statements of account, certified by a certified public accountant, shall be filed for every compulsory license under this section. The regulations covering both the monthly and the annual statements of account shall prescribe the form, content, and manner of certification with respect to the number of records made and the number of records distributed.

(4) If the copyright owner does not receive the monthly payment and the monthly and annual statements of account when due, the owner may give written notice to the licensee that, unless the default is remedied within thirty days from the date of the notice, the compulsory license will be automatically terminated. Such termination renders either the making or the distribution, or both, of all phonorecords for which the royalty has not been paid, actionable as acts of infringement under section 501 and fully subject to the remedies provided by sections 502 through 506 and 509.

## § 116. Scope of exclusive rights in nondramatic musical works: Public performances by means of coin-operated phonorecord players

(a) LIMITATION ON EXCLUSIVE RIGHT.—In the case of a nondramatic musical work embodied in a phonorecord, the exclusive right under clause (4) of section 106 to perform the work publicly by means of a coin-operated phonorecord player is limited as follows:

(1) The proprietor of the establishment in which the public performance takes place is not liable for infringement with respect to such public performance unless—

(A) such proprietor is the operator of the phonorecord player; or

(B) such proprietor refuses or fails, within one month after receipt by registered or certified mail of a request, at a time during which the certificate required by clause (1)(C) of subsection (b) is not affixed to the phonorecord player, by the copyright owner, to make full disclosure, by registered or certified mail, of the identity of the operator of the phonorecord player.

(2) The operator of the coin-operated phonorecord player may obtain a compulsory license to perform the work publicly on that phonorecord player by filing the application, affixing the certificate, and paying the royalties provided by subsection (b).

(b) RECORDATION OF COIN-OPERATED PHONORECORD PLAYER, AFFIXATION OF CERTIFICATE, AND ROYALTY PAYABLE UNDER COMPULSORY LICENSE.—

(1) Any operator who wishes to obtain a compulsory license for the public performance of works on a coin-operated phonorecord player shall fulfill the following requirements:

(A) Before or within one month after such performances are made available on a particular phonorecord player, and during the month of January in each succeeding year that such performances are made available on that particular phonorecord player, the operator shall file in the Copyright Office, in accordance with requirements that the Register of Copyrights, after consultation with the Copyright Royalty Tribunal (if and when the Tribunal has been constituted), shall prescribe by regulation, an application containing the name and address of the operator of the phonorecord player and the manufacturer and serial number or other explicit identification of the phonorecord player, and deposit with the Register of Copyrights a royalty fee for the current calendar year of $8 for that particular phonorecord player. If such performances are made available on a particular phonorecord player for the first time after July 1 of any year, the royalty fee to be deposited for the remainder of that year shall be $4.

(B) Within twenty days of receipt of an application and a royalty fee pursuant to subclause (A), the Register of Copyrights shall issue to the applicant a certificate for the phonorecord player.

(C) On or before March 1 of the year in which the certificate prescribed by subclause (B) of this clause is issued, or within ten days after the date of issue of the certificate, the operator shall affix to the particular phonorecord player, in a position where it can be readily examined by the public, the certificate, issued by the Register of Copyrights under subclause (B), of the latest application made by such operator under subclause (A) of this clause with respect to that phonorecord player.

(2) Failure to file the application, to affix the certificate, or to pay the royalty required by clause (1) of this subsection renders the public performance actionable as an act of infringement under section 501 and fully subject to the remedies provided by sections 502 through 506 and 509.

(c) DISTRIBUTION OF ROYALTIES.—

(1) The Register of Copyrights shall receive all fees deposited under this section and, after deducting the reasonable costs incurred by the Copyright Office under this section, shall deposit the balance in the Treasury of the United States, in such manner as the Secretary of the Treasury directs. All funds held by the Secretary of the Treasury shall be invested in interest-bearing United States securities for later distribution with interest by the Copyright Royalty Tribunal as provided by this title. The Register shall submit to the Copyright Royalty Tribunal, on an annual basis, a detailed statement of account covering all fees received for the relevant period provided by subsection (b).

(2) During the month of January in each year, every person claiming to be entitled to compulsory license fees under this section for performances during the preceding twelve-month period shall file a claim with the Copyright Royalty Tribunal, in accordance with requirements that the Tribunal shall prescribe by regulation. Such claim shall include an agreement to accept as final,

except as provided in section 810 of this title, the determination of the Copyright Royalty Tribunal in any controversy concerning the distribution of royalty fees deposited under subclause (A) of subsection (b)(1) of this section to which the claimant is a party. Notwithstanding any provisions of the antitrust laws, for purposes of this subsection any claimants may agree among themselves as to the proportionate division of compulsory licensing fees among them, may lump their claims together and file them jointly or as a single claim, or may designate a common agent to receive payment on their behalf.

(3) After the first day of October of each year, the Copyright Royalty Tribunal shall determine whether there exists a controversy concerning the distribution of royalty fees deposited under subclause (A) of subsection (b)(1). If the Tribunal determines that no such controversy exists, it shall, after deducting its reasonable administrative costs under this section, distribute such fees to the copyright owners entitled, or to their designated agents. If it finds that such a controversy exists, it shall, pursuant to chapter 8 of this title, conduct a proceeding to determine the distribution of royalty fees.

(4) The fees to be distributed shall be divided as follows:

(A) to every copyright owner not affiliated with a performing rights society, the pro rata share of the fees to be distributed to which such copyright owner proves entitlement.

(B) to the performing rights societies, the remainder of the fees to be distributed in such pro rata shares as they shall by agreement stipulate among themselves, or, if they fail to agree, the pro rata share to which such performing rights societies prove entitlement.

(C) during the pendency of any proceeding under this section, the Copyright Royalty Tribunal shall withhold from distribution an amount sufficient to satisfy all claims with respect to which a controversy exists, but shall have discretion to proceed to distribute any amounts that are not in controversy.

(5) The Copyright Royalty Tribunal shall promulgate regulations under which persons who can reasonably be expected to have claims may, during the year in which performances take place, without expense to or harassment of operators or proprietors of establishments in which phonorecord players are located, have such access to such establishments and to the phonorecord players located therein and such opportunity to obtain information with respect thereto as may be reasonably necessary to determine, by sampling procedures or otherwise, the proportion of contribution of the musical works of each such person to the earnings of the phonorecord players for which fees shall have been deposited. Any person who alleges that he or she has been denied the access permitted under the regulations prescribed by the Copyright Royalty Tribunal may bring an action in the United States District Court for the District of Columbia for the cancellation of the compulsory license of the phonorecord player to which such access has been denied, and the court shall have the power to declare the compulsory license thereof invalid from the date of issue thereof.

(d) CRIMINAL PENALTIES.—Any person who knowingly makes a false representation of a material fact in an application filed under clause (1)(A) of subsection (b), or who knowingly alters a certificate issued under clause (1)(B) of subsection (b) or knowingly affixes such a certificate to a phonorecord player other than the one it covers, shall be fined not more than $2,500.

(e) DEFINITIONS.—As used in this section, the following terms and their variant forms mean the following:

(1) A "coin-operated phonorecord player" is a machine or device that—

(A) is employed solely for the performance of nondramatic musical works by means of phonorecords upon being activated by insertion of coins, currency, tokens, or other monetary units or their equivalent;

(B) is located in an establishment making no direct or indirect charge for admission;

(C) is accompanied by a list of the titles of all the musical works available for performance on it, which list is affixed to the phonorecord player or posted in the establishment in a prominent position where it can be readily examined by the public; and

(D) affords a choice of works available for performance and permits the choice to be made by the patrons of the establishment in which it is located.

(2) An "operator" is any person who, alone or jointly with others:

(A) owns a coin-operated phonorecord player; or

(B) has the power to make a coin-operated phonorecord player available for placement in an establishment for purposes of public performance; or

(C) has the power to exercise primary control over the selection of the musical works made available for public performance on a coin-operated phonorecord player.

(3) A "performing rights society" is an association or corporation that licenses the public performance of nondramatic musical works on behalf of the copyright owners, such as the American Society of Composers, Authors and Publishers, Broadcast Music, Inc., and SESAC, Inc.

## §117. Limitations on exclusive rights: Computer programs

Notwithstanding the provisions of section 106, it is not an infringement for the owner of a copy of a computer program to make or authorize the making of another copy or adaptation of that computer program provided:

(1) that such a new copy or adaptation is created as an essential step in the utilization of the computer program in conjunction with a machine and that it is used in no other manner, or

(2) that such new copy or adaptation is for archival purposes only and that all archival copies are destroyed in the event that continued possession of the computer program should cease to be rightful.

Any exact copies prepared in accordance with the provisions of this section may be leased, sold, or otherwise transferred, along with the copy from which such copies were prepared, only as part of the lease, sale, or other transfer of all rights in the program. Adaptations so prepared may be transferred only with the authorization of the copyright owner.*[2]

## § 118. Scope of exclusive rights: Use of certain works in connection with noncommercial broadcasting

(a) The exclusive rights provided by section 106 shall, with respect to the works specified by subsection (b) and the activities specified by subsection (d), be subject to the conditions and limitations prescribed by this section.

*See Note 2, page 284, for text of the old section 117.

(b) Not later than thirty days after the Copyright Royalty Tribunal has been constituted in accordance with section 802, the Chairman of the Tribunal shall cause notice to be published in the Federal Register of the initiation of proceedings for the purpose of determining reasonable terms and rates of royalty payments for the activities specified by subsection (d) with respect to published nondramatic musical works and published pictorial, graphic, and sculptural works during a period beginning as provided in clause (3) of this subsection and ending on December 31, 1982. Copyright owners and public broadcasting entities shall negotiate in good faith and cooperate fully with the Tribunal in an effort to reach reasonable and expeditious results. Notwithstanding any provision of the antitrust laws, any owners of copyright in works specified by this subsection and any public broadcasting entities, respectively, may negotiate and agree upon the terms and rates of royalty payments and the proportionate division of fees paid among various copyright owners, and may designate common agents to negotiate, agree to, pay, or receive payments.

(1) Any owner of copyright in a work specified in this subsection or any public broadcasting entity may, within one hundred and twenty days after publication of the notice specified in this subsection, submit to the Copyright Royalty Tribunal proposed licenses covering such activities with respect to such works. The Copyright Royalty Tribunal shall proceed on the basis of the proposals submitted to it as well as any other relevant information. The Copyright Royalty Tribunal shall permit any interested party to submit information relevant to such proceedings.

(2) License agreements voluntarily negotiated at any time between one or more copyright owners and one or more public broadcasting entities shall be given effect in lieu of any determination by the Tribunal: *Provided*, That copies of such agreements are filed in the Copyright Office within thirty days of execution in accordance with regulations that the Register of Copyrights shall prescribe.

(3) Within six months, but not earlier than one hundred and twenty days, from the date of publication of the notice specified in this subsection the Copyright Royalty Tribunal shall make a determination and publish in the Federal Register a schedule of rates and terms which, subject to clause (2) of this subsection, shall be binding on all owners of copyright in works specified by this subsection and public broadcasting entities, regardless of whether or not such copyright owners and public broadcasting entities have submitted proposals to the Tribunal. In establishing such rates and terms the Copyright Royalty Tribunal may consider the rates for comparable circumstances under voluntary license agreements negotiated as provided in clause (2) of this subsection. The Copyright Royalty Tribunal shall also establish requirements by which copyright owners may receive reasonable notice of the use of their works under this section, and under which records of such use shall be kept by public broadcasting entities.

(4) With respect to the period beginning on the effective date of this title and ending on the date of publication of such rates and terms, this title shall not afford to owners of copyright or public broadcasting entities any greater or lesser rights with respect to the activities specified in subsection (d) as applied to works specified in this subsection than those afforded under the law in effect on December 31, 1977, as held applicable and construed by a court in an action brought under this title.

(c) The initial procedure specified in subsection (b) shall be repeated and concluded between June 30 and December 31, 1982, and at five-year intervals thereafter, in accordance with regulations that the Copyright Royalty Tribunal shall prescribe.

(d) Subject to the transitional provisions of subsection (b) (4), and to the terms of any voluntary license agreements that have been negotiated as provided by subsection (b) (2), a public broadcasting entity may, upon compliance with the provisions of this section, including the rates and terms established by the Copyright Royalty Tribunal under subsection (b) (3), engage in the following activities with respect to published nondramatic musical works and published pictorial, graphic, and sculptural works:

(1) performance or display of a work by or in the course of a transmission made by a noncommercial educational broadcast station referred to in subsection (g) ; and

(2) production of a transmission program, reproduction of copies or phonorecords of such a transmission program, and distribution of such copies or phonorecords, where such production, reproduction, or distribution is made by a nonprofit institution or organization solely for the purpose of transmissions specified in clause (1) ; and

(3) the making of reproductions by a governmental body or a nonprofit institution of a transmission program simultaneously with its transmission as specified in clause (1), and the performance or display of the contents of such program under the conditions specified by clause (1) of section 110, but only if the reproductions are used for performances or displays for a period of no more than seven days from the date of the transmission specified in clause (1), and are destroyed before or at the end of such period. No person supplying, in accordance with clause (2), a reproduction of a transmission program to governmental bodies or nonprofit institutions under this clause shall have any liability as a result of failure of such body or institution to destroy such reproduction: *Provided*, That it shall have notified such body or institution of the requirement for such destruction pursuant to this clause: *And provided further*, That if such body or institution itself fails to destroy such reproduction it shall be deemed to have infringed.

(e) Except as expressly provided in this subsection, this section shall have no applicability to works other than those specified in subsection (b).

(1) Owners of copyright in nondramatic literary works and public broadcasting entities may, during the course of voluntary negotiations, agree among themselves, respectively, as to the terms and rates of royalty payments without liability under the antitrust laws. Any such terms and rates of royalty payments shall be effective upon filing in the Copyright Office, in accordance with regulations that the Register of Copyrights shall prescribe.

(2) On January 3, 1980, the Register of Copyrights, after consulting with authors and other owners of copyright in nondramatic literary works and their representatives, and with public broadcasting entities and their representatives, shall submit to the Congress a report setting forth the extent to which voluntary licensing arrangements have been reached with respect to the use of nondramatic literary works by such broadcast stations. The report should also describe any problems that may have arisen, and present legislative or other recommendations, if warranted.

(f) Nothing in this section shall be construed to permit, beyond the limits of fair use as provided by section 107, the unauthorized dramatization of a nondramatic musical work, the production of a transmission program drawn to any substantial extent from a published compilation of pictorial, graphic, or sculptural works, or the unauthorized use of any portion of an audiovisual work.

(g) As used in this section, the term "public broadcasting entity" means a noncommercial educational broadcast station as defined in section 397 of title 47 and any nonprofit institution or organization engaged in the activities described in clause (2) of subsection (d).

## Chapter 2.—COPYRIGHT OWNERSHIP AND TRANSFER

### § 201. Ownership of copyright

(a) INITIAL OWNERSHIP.—Copyright in a work protected under this title vests initially in the author or authors of the work. The authors of a joint work are coowners of copyright in the work.

(b) WORKS MADE FOR HIRE.—In the case of a work made for hire, the employer or other person for whom the work was prepared is considered the author for purposes of this title, and, unless the parties have expressly agreed otherwise in a written instrument signed by them, owns all of the rights comprised in the copyright.

(c) CONTRIBUTIONS TO COLLECTIVE WORKS.—Copyright in each separate contribution to a collective work is distinct from copyright in the collective work as a whole, and vests initially in the author of the contribution. In the absence of an express transfer of the copyright or of any rights under it, the owner of copyright in the collective work is presumed to have acquired only the privilege of reproducing and distributing the contribution as part of that particular collective work, any revision of that collective work, and any later collective work in the same series.

(d) TRANSFER OF OWNERSHIP.—

    (1) The ownership of a copyright may be transferred in whole or in part by any means of conveyance or by operation of law, and may be bequeathed by will or pass as personal property by the applicable laws of intestate succession.

    (2) Any of the exclusive rights comprised in a copyright, including any subdivision of any of the rights specified by section 106, may be transferred as provided by clause (1) and owned separately. The owner of any particular exclusive right is entitled, to the extent of that right, to all of the protection and remedies accorded to the copyright owner by this title.

(e) INVOLUNTARY TRANSFER.—When an individual author's ownership of a copyright, or of any of the exclusive rights under a copyright, has not previously been transferred voluntarily by that individual author, no action by any governmental body or other official or organization purporting to seize, expropriate, transfer, or exercise rights of ownership with respect to the copyright, or any of the exclusive rights under a copyright, shall be given effect under this title.

### § 202. Ownership of copyright as distinct from ownership of material object

Ownership of a copyright, or of any of the exclusive rights under a copyright, is distinct from ownership of any material object in which the work is embodied. Transfer of ownership of any material object, including the copy or phonorecord in which the work is first fixed, does not of itself convey any rights in the copyrighted work embodied in the object; nor, in the absence of an agreement, does transfer of ownership of a copyright or of any exclusive rights under a copyright convey property rights in any material object.

### § 203. Termination of transfers and licenses granted by the author

(a) CONDITIONS FOR TERMINATION.—In the case of any work other than a work made for hire, the exclusive or nonexclusive grant of a transfer or license of copyright or of any right under a copyright, executed by the author on or after January 1, 1978, otherwise than by will, is subject to termination under the following conditions:

(1) In the case of a grant executed by one author, termination of the grant may be effected by that author or, if the author is dead, by the person or persons who, under clause (2) of this subsection, own and are entitled to exercise a total of more than one-half of that author's termination interest. In the case of a grant executed by two or more authors of a joint work, termination of the grant may be effected by a majority of the authors who executed it; if any of such authors is dead, the termination interest of any such author may be exercised as a unit by the person or persons who, under clause (2) of this subsection, own and are entitled to exercise a total of more than one-half of that author's interest.

(2) Where an author is dead, his or her termination interest is owned, and may be exercised, by his widow or her widower and his or her children or grandchildren as follows:

(A) the widow or widower owns the author's entire termination interest unless there are any surviving children or grandchildren of the author, in which case the widow or widower owns one-half of the author's interest;

(B) the author's surviving children, and the surviving children of any dead child of the author, own the author's entire termination interest unless there is a widow or widower, in which case the ownership of one-half of the author's interest is divided among them;

(C) the rights of the author's children and grandchildren are in all cases divided among them and exercised on a per stirpes basis according to the number of such author's children represented; the share of the children of a dead child in a termination interest can be exercised only by the action of a majority of them.

(3) Termination of the grant may be effected at any time during a period of five years beginning at the end of thirty-five years from the date of execution of the grant; or, if the grant covers the right of publication of the work, the period begins at the end of thirty-five years from the date of publication of the work under the grant or at the end of forty years from the date of execution of the grant, whichever term ends earlier.

(4) The termination shall be effected by serving an advance notice in writing, signed by the number and proportion of owners of termination interests required under clauses (1) and (2) of this subsection, or by their duly authorized agents, upon the grantee or the grantee's successor in title.

(A) The notice shall state the effective date of the termination, which shall fall within the five-year period specified by clause (3) of this subsection, and the notice shall be served not less than two or more than ten years before that date. A copy of the notice shall be recorded in the Copyright Office before the effective date of termination, as a condition to its taking effect.

(B) The notice shall comply, in form, content, and manner of service, with requirements that the Register of Copyrights shall prescribe by regulation.

(5) Termination of the grant may be effected notwithstanding any agreement to the contrary, including an agreement to make a will or to make any future grant.

(b) EFFECT OF TERMINATION.—Upon the effective date of termination, all rights under this title that were covered by the terminated grants revert to the author, authors, and other persons owning termination interests under clauses (1) and (2) of subsection (a), including those owners who did not join in signing the notice of termination under clause (4) of subsection (a), but with the following limitations:

(1) A derivative work prepared under authority of the grant before its termination may continue to be utilized under the terms of the grant after its termination, but this privilege does not extend to the preparation after the termination of other derivative works based upon the copyrighted work covered by the terminated grant.

(2) The future rights that will revert upon termination of the grant become vested on the date the notice of termination has been served as provided by clause (4) of subsection (a). The rights vest in the author, authors, and other persons named in, and in the proportionate shares provided by, clauses (1) and (2) of subsection (a).

(3) Subject to the provisions of clause (4) of this subsection, a further grant, or agreement to make a further grant, of any right covered by a terminated grant is valid only if it is signed by the same number and proportion of the owners, in whom the right has vested under clause (2) of this subsection, as are required to terminate the grant under clauses (1) and (2) of subsection (a). Such further grant or agreement is effective with respect to all of the persons in whom the right it covers has vested under clause (2) of this subsection, including those who did not join in signing it. If any person dies after rights under a terminated grant have vested in him or her, that person's legal representatives, legatees, or heirs at law represent him or her for purposes of this clause.

(4) A further grant, or agreement to make a further grant, of any right covered by a terminated grant is valid only if it is made after the effective date of the termination. As an exception, however, an agreement for such a further grant may be made between the persons provided by clause (3) of this subsection and the original grantee or such grantee's successor in title, after the notice of termination has been served as provided by clause (4) of subsection (a).

(5) Termination of a grant under this section affects only those rights covered by the grants that arise under this title, and in no way affects rights arising under any other Federal, State, or foreign laws.

(6) Unless and until termination is effected under this section, the grant, if it does not provide otherwise, continues in effect for the term of copyright provided by this title.

## § 204. Execution of transfers of copyright ownership

(a) A transfer of copyright ownership, other than by operation of law, is not valid unless an instrument of conveyance, or a note or memorandum of the transfer, is in writing and signed by the owner of the rights conveyed or such owner's duly authorized agent.

(b) A certificate of acknowledgement is not required for the validity of a transfer, but is prima facie evidence of the execution of the transfer if—

(1) in the case of a transfer executed in the United States, the certificate is issued by a person authorized to administer oaths within the United States; or

(2) in the case of a transfer executed in a foreign country, the certificate is issued by a diplomatic or consular officer of the United States, or by a person authorized to administer oaths whose authority is proved by a certificate of such an officer.

## § 205. Recordation of transfers and other documents

(a) CONDITIONS FOR RECORDATION.—Any transfer of copyright ownership or other document pertaining to a copyright may be recorded in the Copyright Office if the document filed for recordation bears the actual signature of the person who executed it, or if it is accompanied by a sworn or official certification that it is a true copy of the original, signed document.

(b) CERTIFICATE OF RECORDATION.—The Register of Copyrights shall, upon receipt of a document as provided by subsection (a) and of the fee provided by section 708, record the document and return it with a certificate of recordation.

(c) RECORDATION AS CONSTRUCTIVE NOTICE.—Recordation of a document in the Copyright Office gives all persons constructive notice of the facts stated in the recorded document, but only if—

(1) the document, or material attached to it, specifically identifies the work to which it pertains so that, after the document is indexed by the Register of Copyrights, it would be revealed by a reasonable search under the title or registration number of the work; and

(2) registration has been made for the work.

(d) RECORDATION AS PREREQUISITE TO INFRINGEMENT SUIT.—No person claiming by virtue of a transfer to be the owner of copyright or of any exclusive right under a copyright is entitled to institute an infringement action under this title until the instrument of transfer under which such person claims has been recorded in the Copyright Office, but suit may be instituted after such recordation on a cause of action that arose before recordation.

(e) PRIORITY BETWEEN CONFLICTING TRANSFERS.—As between two conflicting transfers, the one executed first prevails if it is recorded, in the manner required to give constructive notice under subsection (c), within one month after its execution in the United States or within two months after its execution outside the United States, or at any time before recordation in such manner of the later transfer. Otherwise the later transfer prevails if recorded first in such manner, and if taken in good faith, for valuable consideration or on the basis of a binding promise to pay royalties, and without notice of the earlier transfer.

(f) PRIORITY BETWEEN CONFLICTING TRANSFER OF OWNERSHIP AND NONEXCLUSIVE LICENSE.—A nonexclusive license, whether recorded or not, prevails over a conflicting transfer of copyright ownership if the license is evidenced by a written instrument signed by the owner of the rights licensed or such owner's duly authorized agent, and if—

(1) the license was taken before execution of the transfer; or

(2) the license was taken in good faith before recordation of the transfer and without notice of it.

# Chapter 3.—DURATION OF COPYRIGHT

## § 301. Preemption with respect to other laws

(a) On and after January 1, 1978, all legal or equitable rights that are equivalent to any of the exclusive rights within the general scope of copyright as specified by section 106 in works of authorship that are fixed in a tangible medium of expression and come within the subject matter of copyright as specified by sections 102 and 103, whether created before or after that date and whether published or unpublished, are governed exclusively by this title. Thereafter, no person is entitled to any such right or equivalent right in any such work under the common law or statutes of any State.

(b) Nothing in this title annuls or limits any rights or remedies under the common law or statutes of any State with respect to—

(1) subject matter that does not come within the subject matter of copyright as specified by sections 102 and 103, including works of authorship not fixed in any tangible medium of expression; or

(2) any cause of action arising from undertakings commenced before January 1, 1978; or

(3) activities violating legal or equitable rights that are not equivalent to any of the exclusive rights within the general scope of copyright as specified by section 106.

(c) With respect to sound recordings fixed before February 15, 1972, any rights or remedies under the common law or statutes of any State shall not be annulled or limited by this title until February 15, 2047. The preemptive provisions of subsection (a) shall apply to any such rights and remedies pertaining to any cause of action arising from undertakings commenced on and after February 15, 2047. Notwithstanding the provisions of section 303, no sound recording fixed before February 15, 1972, shall be subject to copyright under this title before, on, or after February 15, 2047.

(d) Nothing in this title annuls or limits any rights or remedies under any other Federal statute.

## § 302. Duration of copyright: Works created on or after January 1, 1978

(a) IN GENERAL.—Copyright in a work created on or after January 1, 1978, subsists from its creation and, except as provided by the following subsections, endures for a term consisting of the life of the author and fifty years after the author's death.

(b) JOINT WORKS.—In the case of a joint work prepared by two or more authors who did not work for hire, the copyright endures for a term consisting of the life of the last surviving author and fifty years after such last surviving author's death.

(c) ANONYMOUS WORKS, PSEUDONYMOUS WORKS, AND WORKS MADE FOR HIRE.—In the case of an anonymous work, a pseudonymous work, or a work made for hire, the copyright endures for a term of seventy-five years from the year of its first publication, or a term of one hundred years from the year of its creation, whichever expires first. If, before the end of such term, the identity of one or more of the authors of an anonymous or pseudonymous work is revealed in the records of a registration made for that work under subsections (a) or (d) of section 408, or in the records provided by this subsection, the copyright in the work endures for the term specified by subsection (a) or (b), based on the life of the author or authors whose identity has been revealed. Any person having an interest in the copyright in an anonymous or pseudonymous work may at any time record, in records to be maintained by the Copyright Office for that purpose, a statement identifying one or more authors of the work; the statement shall also identify the person filing it, the nature of that person's interest, the source of the information recorded, and the particular work affected, and shall comply in form and content with requirements that the Register of Copyrights shall prescribe by regulation.

(d) RECORDS RELATING TO DEATH OF AUTHORS.—Any person having an interest in a copyright may at any time record in the Copyright Office a statement of the date of death of the author of the copyrighted work, or a statement that the author is still living on a particular date. The statement shall identify the person filing it, the nature of that person's interest, and the source of the information recorded, and shall comply in form and content with requirements that the Register of Copyrights shall prescribe by regulation. The Register shall maintain current records of information relating to the death of authors of copyrighted works, based on such recorded statements and, to the extent the Register considers practicable, on data contained in any of the records of the Copyright Office or in other reference sources.

(e) PRESUMPTION AS TO AUTHOR'S DEATH.—After a period of seventy five years from the year of first publication of a work, or a period of one hundred years from the year of its creation, whichever expires first, any person who obtains from the Copyright Office a certified report that the records provided by subsection (d) disclose nothing to indicate that the author of the work is living, or died less than fifty years before, is entitled to the benefit of a presumption that the author has been dead for at least fifty years. Reliance in good faith upon this presumption shall be a complete defense to any action for infringement under this title.

## § 303. Duration of copyright: Works created but not published or copyrighted before January 1, 1978

Copyright in a work created before January 1, 1978, but not theretofore in the public domain or copyrighted, subsists from January 1, 1978, and endures for the term provided by section 302. In no case, however, shall the term of copyright in such a work expire before December 31, 2002; and, if the work is published on or before December 31, 2002, the term of copyright shall not expire before December 31, 2027.

## § 304. Duration of copyright: Subsisting copyrights

(a) COPYRIGHTS IN THEIR FIRST TERM ON JANUARY 1, 1978.—Any copyright, the first term of which is subsisting on January 1, 1978, shall endure for twenty-eight years from the date it was originally secured: *Provided,* That in the case of any posthumous work or of any periodical, cyclopedic, or other composite work upon which the copyright was originally secured by the proprietor thereof, or of any work copyrighted by a corporate body (otherwise than as assignee or licensee of the individual author) or by an employer for whom such work is made for hire, the proprietor of such copyright shall be entitled to a renewal and extension of the copyright in such work for the further term of forty-seven years when application for such renewal and extension shall have been made to the Copyright Office and duly registered therein within one year prior to the expiration of the original term of copyright: *And provided further,* That in the case of any other copyrighted work, including a contribution by an individual author to a periodical or to a cyclopedic or other composite work, the author of such work, if still living, or the widow, widower, or children of the author, if the author be not living, or if such author, widow, widower, or children be not living, then the author's executors, or in the absence of a will, his or her next of kin shall be entitled to a renewal and extension of the copyright in such work for a further term of forty-seven years when application for such renewal and extension shall have been made to the Copyright Office and duly registered therein within one year prior to the expiration of the original term of copyright : *And provided further*, That in default of the registration of such application for renewal and extension, the copyright in any work shall terminate at the expiration of twenty-eight years from the date copyright was originally secured.

(b) COPYRIGHTS IN THEIR RENEWAL TERM OR REGISTERED FOR RENEWAL BEFORE JANUARY 1, 1978.—The duration of any copyright, the renewal term of which is subsisting at any time between December 31, 1976, and December 31, 1977, inclusive, or for which renewal registration is made between December 31, 1976, and December 31, 1977, inclusive, is extended to endure for a term of seventy-five years from the date copyright was originally secured.

(c) TERMINATION OF TRANSFERS AND LICENSES COVERING EXTENDED RENEWAL TERM.—In the case of any copyright subsisting in either its first or renewal term on January 1, 1978, other than a copyright in a work made for hire, the exclusive or nonexclusive grant of a transfer or license of the renewal copyright or any right under it, executed before January 1, 1978, by any of the persons designated by the second proviso of subsection (a) of this section, otherwise than by will, is subject to termination under the following conditions :

(1) In the case of a grant executed by a person or persons other than the author, termination of the grant may be effected by the surviving person or persons who executed it. In the case of a grant executed by one or more of the authors of the work, termination of the grant may be effected, to the extent of a particular author's share in the ownership of the renewal copyright, by the author who executed it or, if such author is dead, by the person or persons who, under clause (2) of this subsection, own and are entitled to exercise a total of more than one-half of that author's termination interest.

(2) Where an author is dead, his or her termination interest is owned, and may be exercised, by his widow or her widower and his or her children or grandchildren as follows :

(A) the widow or widower owns the author's entire termination interest unless there are any surviving children or grandchildren of the author, in which case the widow or widower owns one-half of the author's interest ;

(B) the author's surviving children, and the surviving children of any dead child of the author, own the author's entire termination interest unless there is a widow or widower, in which case the ownership of one-half of the author's interest is divided among them ;

(C) the rights of the author's children and grandchildren are in all cases divided among them and exercised on a per stirpes basis according to the number of such author's children represented ; the share of the children of a dead child in a termination interest can be exercised only by the action of a majority of them.

(3) Termination of the grant may be effected at any time during a period of five years beginning at the end of fifty-six years from the date copyright was originally secured, or beginning on January 1, 1978, whichever is later.

(4) The termination shall be effected by serving an advance notice in writing upon the grantee or the grantee's successor in title. In the case of a grant executed by a person or persons other than the author, the notice shall be signed by all of those entitled to terminate the grant under clause (1) of this subsection, or by their duly authorized agents. In the case of a grant executed by one or more of the authors of the work, the notice as to any one author's share shall be signed by that author or his or her duly authorized agent or, if that author is dead, by the number and proportion of the owners of his or her termination interest required under clauses (1) and (2) of this subsection, or by their duly authorized agents.

(A) The notice shall state the effective date of the termination, which shall fall within the five-year period specified by clause (3) of this subsection, and the notice shall be served not less than two or more than ten years before that date. A copy of the notice shall be recorded in the Copyright Office before the effective date of termination, as a condition to its taking effect.

(B) The notice shall comply, in form, content, and manner of service, with requirements that the Register of Copyrights shall prescribe by regulation.

(5) Termination of the grant may be effected notwithstanding any agreement to the contrary, including an agreement to make a will or to make any future grant.

(6) In the case of a grant executed by a person or persons other than the author, all rights under this title that were covered by the terminated grant revert, upon the effective date of termination, to all of those entitled to terminate the grant under clause (1) of this subsection. In the case of a grant executed by one or more of the authors of the work, all of a particular author's rights under this title that were covered by the terminated grant revert, upon the effective date of termination, to that author or, if that author is dead, to the persons owning his or her termination interest under clause (2) of this subsection, including those owners who did not join in signing the notice of termination under clause (4) of this subsection. In all cases the reversion of rights is subject to the following limitations:

(A) A derivative work prepared under authority of the grant before its termination may continue to be utilized under the terms of the grant after its termination, but this privilege does not extend to the preparation after the termination of other derivative works based upon the copyrighted work covered by the terminated grant.

(B) The future rights that will revert upon termination of the grant become vested on the date the notice of termination has been served as provided by clause (4) of this subsection.

(C) Where the author's rights revert to two or more persons under clause (2) of this subsection, they shall vest in those persons in the proportionate shares provided by that clause. In such a case, and subject to the provisions of subclause (D) of this clause, a further grant, or agreement to make a further grant, of a particular author's share with respect to any right covered by a terminated grant is valid only if it is signed by the same number and proportion of the owners, in whom the right has vested under this clause, as are required to terminate the grant under clause (2) of this subsection. Such further grant or agreement is effective with respect to all of the persons in whom the right it covers has vested under this subclause, including those who did not join in signing it. If any person dies after rights under a terminated grant have vested in him or her, that person's legal representatives, legatees, or heirs at law represent him or her for purposes of this subclause.

(D) A further grant, or agreement to make a further grant, of any right covered by a terminated grant is valid only if it is made after the effective date of the termination. As an exception, however, an agreement for such a further grant may be made between the author or any of the persons provided by the first sentence of clause (6) of this subsection, or between the persons provided by subclause (C) of this clause, and the original grantee or such grantee's successor in title, after the notice of termination has been served as provided by clause (4) of this subsection.

(E) Termination of a grant under this subsection affects only those rights covered by the grant that arise under this title, and in no way affects rights arising under any other Federal, State, or foreign laws.

(F) Unless and until termination is effected under this subsection, the grant, if it does not provide otherwise, continues in effect for the remainder of the extended renewal term.

### § 305. Duration of copyright: Terminal date

All terms of copyright provided by sections 302 through 304 run to the end of the calendar year in which they would otherwise expire.

### Chapter 4.—COPYRIGHT NOTICE, DEPOSIT, AND REGISTRATION

Sec.

### § 401. Notice of copyright: Visually perceptible copies

(a) GENERAL REQUIREMENT.—Whenever a work protected under this title is published in the United States or elsewhere by authority of the copyright owner, a notice of copyright as provided by this section shall be placed on all publicly distributed copies from which the work can be visually perceived, either directly or with the aid of a machine or device.

(b) FORM OF NOTICE.—The notice appearing on the copies. shall consist of the following three elements:

(1) the symbol © (the letter C in a circle), or the word "Copyright", or the abbreviation "Copr."; and

(2) the year of first publication of the work; in the case of compilations or derivative works incorporating previously published material, the year date of first publication of the compilation or derivative work is sufficient. The year date may be omitted where a pictorial, graphic, or sculptural work, with accompanying text matter, if any, is reproduced in or on greeting cards, postcards, stationery, jewelry, dolls, toys, or any useful articles; and

(3) the name of the owner of copyright in the work, or an abbreviation by which the name can be recognized, or a generally known alternative designation of the owner.

(c) Position of Notice.—The notice shall be affixed to the copies in such manner and location as to give reasonable notice of the claim of copyright. The Register of Copyrights shall prescribe by regulation, as examples, specific methods of affixation and positions of the notice on various types of works that will satisfy this requirement, but these specifications shall not be considered exhaustive.

## § 402. Notice of copyright: Phonorecords of sound recordings

(a) General Requirement.—Whenever a sound recording protected under this title is published in the United States or elsewhere by authority of the copyright owner, a notice of copyright as provided by this section shall be placed on all publicly distributed phonorecords of the sound recording.

(b) Form of Notice.—The notice appearing on the phonorecords shall consist of the following three elements:

(1) the symbol ℗ (the letter P in a circle); and

(2) the year of first publication of the sound recording; and

(3) the name of the owner of copyright in the sound recording, or an abbreviation by which the name can be recognized, or a generally known alternative designation of the owner; if the producer of the sound recording is named on the phonorecord labels or containers, and if no other name appears in conjunction with the notice, the producer's name shall be considered a part of the notice.

(c) Position of Notice.—The notice shall be placed on the surface of the phonorecord, or on the phonorecord label or container, in such manner and location as to give reasonable notice of the claim of copyright.

## § 403. Notice of copyright: Publications incorporating United States Government works

Whenever a work is published in copies or phonorecords consisting preponderantly of one or more works of the United States Government, the notice of copyright provided by sections 401 or 402 shall also include a statement identifying, either affirmatively or negatively, those portions of the copies or phonorecords embodying any work or works protected under this title.

## § 404. Notice of copyright: Contributions to collective works

(a) A separate contribution to a collective work may bear its own notice of copyright, as provided by sections 401 through 403. However, a single notice applicable to the collective work as a whole is sufficient to satisfy the requirements of sections 401 through 403 with respect to the separate contributions it contains (not including advertisements inserted on behalf of persons other than the owner of copyright in the collective work), regardless of the ownership of copyright in the contributions and whether or not they have been previously published.

(b) Where the person named in a single notice applicable to a collective work as a whole is not the owner of copyright in a separate contribution that does not bear its own notice, the case is governed by the provisions of section 406(a).

## § 405. Notice of copyright: Omission of notice

(a) EFFECT OF OMISSION ON COPYRIGHT.—The omission of the copyright notice prescribed by sections 401 through 403 from copies or phonorecords publicly distributed by authority of the copyright owner does not invalidate the copyright in a work if—

(1) the notice has been omitted from no more than a relatively small number of copies or phonorecords distributed to the public; or

(2) registration for the work has been made before or is made within five years after the publication without notice, and a reasonable effort is made to add notice to all copies or phonorecords that are distributed to the public in the United States after the omission has been discovered; or

(3) the notice has been omitted in violation of an express requirement in writing that, as a condition of the copyright owner's authorization of the public distribution of copies or phonorecords, they bear the prescribed notice.

(b) EFFECT OF OMISSION ON INNOCENT INFRINGERS.—Any person who innocently infringes a copyright, in reliance upon an authorized copy or phonorecord from which the copyright notice has been omitted, incurs no liability for actual or statutory damages under section 504 for any infringing acts committed before receiving actual notice that registration for the work has been made under section 408, if such person proves that he or she was misled by the omission of notice. In a suit for infringement in such a case the court may allow or disallow recovery of any of the infringer's profits attributable to the infringement, and may enjoin the continuation of the infringing undertaking or may require, as a condition or permitting the continuation of the infringing undertaking, that the infringer pay the copyright owner a reasonable license fee in an amount and on terms fixed by the court.

(c) REMOVAL OF NOTICE.—Protection under this title is not affected by the removal, destruction, or obliteration of the notice, without the authorization of the copyright owner, from any publicly distributed copies or phonorecords.

## § 406. Notice of copyright: Error in name or date

(a) ERROR IN NAME.—Where the person named in the copyright notice on copies or phonorecords publicly distributed by authority of the copyright owner is not the owner of copyright, the validity and ownership of the copyright are not affected. In such a case, however, any person who innocently begins an undertaking that infringes the copyright has a complete defense to any action for such infringement if such person proves that he or she was misled by the notice and began the undertaking in good faith under a purported transfer or license from the person named therein, unless before the undertaking was begun—

(1) registration for the work had been made in the name of the owner of copyright; or

(2) a document executed by the person named in the notice and showing the ownership of the copyright had been recorded.
The person named in the notice is liable to account to the copyright owner for all receipts from transfers or licenses purportedly made under the copyright by the person named in the notice.

(b) ERROR IN DATE.—When the year date in the notice on copies or phonorecords distributed by authority of the copyright owner is earlier than the year in which publication first occurred, any period computed from the year of first publication under section 302 is to be computed from the year in the notice. Where the year date is more than one year later than the year in which publication first occurred, the work is considered to have been published without any notice and is governed by the provisions of section 405.

(c) OMISSION OF NAME OR DATE.—Where copies or phonorecords publicly distributed by authority of the copyright owner contain no name or no date that could reasonably be considered a part of the notice, the work is considered to have been published without any notice and is governed by the provisions of section 405.

## § 407. Deposit of copies or phonorecords for Library of Congress

(a) Except as provided by subsection (c), and subject to the provisions of subsection (e), the owner of copyright or of the exclusive right of publication in a work published with notice of copyright in the United States shall deposit, within three months after the date of such publication—

(1) two complete copies of the best edition; or

(2) if the work is a sound recording, two complete phonorecords of the best edition, together with any printed or other visually perceptible material published with such phonorecords.

Neither the deposit requirements of this subsection nor the acquisition provisions of subsection (e) are conditions of copyright protection.

(b) The required copies or phonorecords shall be deposited in the Copyright Office for the use or disposition of the Library of Congress. The Register of Copyrights shall, when requested by the depositor and upon payment of the fee prescribed by section 708, issue a receipt for the deposit.

(c) The Register of Copyrights may by regulation exempt any categories of material from the deposit requirements of this section, or require deposit of only one copy or phonorecord with respect to any categories. Such regulations shall provide either for complete exemption from the deposit requirements of this section, or for alternative forms of deposit aimed at providing a satisfactory archival record of a work without imposing practical or financial hardships on the depositor, where the individual author is the owner of copyright in a pictorial, graphic, or sculptural work and (i) less than five copies of the work have been published, or (ii) the work has been published in a limited edition consisting of numbered copies, the monetary value of which would make the mandatory deposit of two copies of the best edition of the work burdensome, unfair, or unreasonable.

(d) At any time after publication of a work as provided by subsection (a), the Register of Copyrights may make written demand for the required deposit on any of the persons obligated to make the deposit under subsection (a). Unless deposit is made within three months after the demand is received, the person or persons on whom the demand was made are liable—

(1) to a fine of not more than $250 for each work; and

(2) to pay into a specially designated fund in the Library of Congress the total retail price of the copies or phonorecords demanded, or, if no retail price has been fixed, the reasonable cost of the Library of Congress of acquiring them; and

(3) to pay a fine of $2,500, in addition to any fine or liability imposed under clauses (1) and (2), if such person willfully or repeatedly fails or refuses to comply with such a demand.

(e) With respect to transmission programs that have been fixed and transmitted to the public in the United States but have not been published, the Register of Copyrights shall, after consulting with the Librarian of Congress and other interested organizations and officials, establish regulations governing the acquisition, through deposit or otherwise, of copies or phonorecords of such programs for the collections of the Library of Congress.

(1) The Librarian of Congress shall be permitted, under the standards and conditions set forth in such regulations, to make a fixation of a transmission program directly from a transmission to the public, and to reproduce one copy or phonorecord from such fixation for archival purposes.

(2) Such regulations shall also provide standards and procedures by which the Register of Copyrights may make written demand, upon the owner of the right of transmission in the United States, for the deposit of a copy or phonorecord of a specific transmission program. Such deposit may, at the option of the owner of the right of transmission in the United States, be accomplished by gift, by loan for purposes of reproduction, or by sale at a price not to exceed the cost of reproducing and supplying the copy or phonorecord. The regulations established under this clause shall provide reasonable periods of not less than three months for compliance with a demand, and shall allow for extensions of such periods and adjustments in the scope of the demand or the methods for fulfilling it, as reasonably warranted by the circumstances. Willful failure or refusal to comply with the conditions prescribed by such regulations shall subject the owner of the right of transmission in the United States to liability for an amount, not to exceed the cost of reproducing and supplying the copy or phonorecord in question, to be paid into a specially designated fund in the Library of Congress.

(3) Nothing in this subsection shall be construed to require the making or retention, for purposes of deposit, of any copy or phonorecord of an unpublished transmission program, the transmission of which occurs before the receipt of a specific written demand as provided by clause (2).

(4) No activity undertaken in compliance with regulations prescribed under clauses (1) or (2) of this subsection shall result in liability if intended solely to assist in the acquisition of copies or phonorecords under this subsection.

## § 408. Copyright registration in general

(a) REGISTRATION PERMISSIVE.—At any time during the subsistence of copyright in any published or unpublished work, the owner of copyright or of any exclusive right in the work may obtain registration of the copyright claim by delivering to the Copyright Office the deposit specified by this section, together with the application and fee specified by sections 409 and 708. Subject to the provisions of section 405(a), such registration is not a condition of copyright protection.

(b) DEPOSIT FOR COPYRIGHT REGISTRATION.—Except as provided by subsection (c), the material deposited for registration shall include—

(1) in the case of an unpublished work, one complete copy or phonorecord;

(2) in the case of a published work, two complete copies or phonorecords of the best edition;

(3) in the case of a work first published outside the United States, one complete copy or phonorecord as so published;

(4) in the case of a contribution to a collective work, one complete copy or phonorecord of the best edition of the collective work.

Copies or phonorecords deposited for the Library of Congress under section 407 may be used to satisfy the deposit provisions of this section, if they are accompanied by the prescribed application and fee, and by any additional identifying material that the Register may, by regulation, require. The Register shall also prescribe regulations establishing requirements under which copies or phonorecords acquired for the Library of Congress under subsection (e) of section 407, otherwise than by deposit, may be used to satisfy the deposit provisions of this section.

(c) ADMINISTRATIVE CLASSIFICATION AND OPTIONAL DEPOSIT.—

(1) The Register of Copyrights is authorized to specify by regulation the administrative classes into which works are to be placed for purposes of deposit and registration, and the nature of the copies or phonorecords to be deposited in the various classes specified. The regulations may require or permit, for particular classes, the deposit of identifying material instead of copies or phonorecords, the deposit of only one copy or phonorecord where two would normally be required, or a single registration for a group of related works. This administrative classification of works has no significance with respect to the subject matter of copyright or the exclusive rights provided by this title.

(2) Without prejudice to the general authority provided under clause (1), the Register of Copyrights shall establish regulations specifically permitting a single registration for a group of works by the same individual author, all first published as contributions to periodicals, including newspapers, within a twelve-month period, on the basis of a single deposit, application, and registration fee, under all of the following conditions—

(A) if each of the works as first published bore a separate copyright notice, and the name of the owner of copyright in the work, or an abbreviation by which the name can be recognized, or a generally known alternative designation of the owner was the same in each notice; and

(B) if the deposit consists of one copy of the entire issue of the periodical, or of the entire section in the case of a newspaper, in which each contribution was first published; and

(C) if the application identifies each work separately, including the periodical containing it and its date of first publication.

(3) As an alternative to separate renewal registrations under subsection (a) of section 304, a single renewal registration may be made for a group of works by the same individual author, all first published as contributions to periodicals, including newspapers, upon the filing of a single application and fee, under all of the following conditions:

(A) the renewal claimant or claimants, and the basis of claim or claims under section 304(a), is the same for each of the works; and

(B) the works were all copyrighted upon their first publication, either through separate copyright notice and registration or by virtue of a general copyright notice in the periodical issue as a whole; and

(C) the renewal application and fee are received not more than twenty-eight or less than twenty-seven years after the thirty-first day of December of the calendar year in which all of the works were first published; and

(D) the renewal application identifies each work separately, including the periodical containing it and its date of first publication.

(d) Corrections and Amplifications.—The Register may also establish, by regulation, formal procedures for the filing of an application for supplementary registration, to correct an error in a copyright registration or to amplify the information given in a registration. Such application shall be accompanied by the fee provided by section 708, and shall clearly identify the registration to be corrected or amplified. The information contained in a supplementary registration augments but does not supersede that contained in the earlier registration.

(e) Published Edition of Previously Registered Work.—Registration for the first published edition of a work previously registered in unpublished form may be made even though the work as published is substantially the same as the unpublished version.

## § 409. Application for copyright registration

The application for copyright registration shall be made on a form prescribed by the Register of Copyrights and shall include—

(1) the name and address of the copyright claimant;

(2) in the case of a work other than an anonymous or pseudonymous work, the name and nationality or domicile of the author or authors, and, if one or more of the authors is dead, the dates of their deaths;

(3) if the work is anonymous or pseudonymous, the nationality or domicile of the author or authors;

(4) in the case of a work made for hire, a statement to this effect;

(5) if the copyright claimant is not the author, a brief statement of how the claimant obtained ownership of the copyright;

(6) the title of the work, together with any previous or alternative titles under which the work can be identified;

(7) the year in which creation of the work was completed;

(8) if the work has been published, the date and nation of its first publication;

(9) in the case of a compilation or derivative work, an identification of any preexisting work or works that it is based on or incorporates, and a brief, general statement of the additional material covered by the copyright claim being registered;

(10) in the case of a published work containing material of which copies are required by section 601 to be manufactured in the United States, the names of the persons or organizations who performed the processes specified by subsection (c) of section 601 with respect to that material, and the places where those processes were performed; and

(11) any other information regarded by the Register of Copyrights as bearing upon the preparation or identification of the work or the existence, ownership, or duration of the copyright.

## § 410. Registration of claim and issuance of certificate

(a) When, after examination, the Register of Copyrights determines that, in accordance with the provisions of this title, the material deposited constitutes copyrightable subject matter and that the other legal and formal requirements of this title have been met, the Register shall register the claim and issue to the applicant a certificate of registration under the seal of the Copyright Office. The certificate shall contain the information given in the application, together with the number and effective date of the registration.

(b) In any case in which the Register of Copyrights determines that, in accordance with the provisions of this title, the material deposited does not constitute copyrightable subject matter or that the claim is invalid for any other reason, the Register shall refuse registration and shall notify the applicant in writing of the reasons for such refusal.

(c) In any judicial proceedings the certificate of a registration made before or within five years after first publication of the work shall constitute prima facie evidence of the validity of the copyright and of the facts stated in the certificate. The evidentiary weight to be accorded the certificate of a registration made thereafter shall be within the discretion of the court.

(d) The effective date of a copyright registration is the day on which an application, deposit, and fee, which are later determined by the Register of Copyrights or by a court of competent jurisdiction to be acceptable for registration, have all been received in the Copyright Office.

### § 411. Registration as prerequisite to infringement suit

(a) Subject to the provisions of subsection (b), no action for infringement of the copyright in any work shall be instituted until registration of the copyright claim has been made in accordance with this title. In any case, however, where the deposit, application, and fee required for registration have been delivered to the Copyright Office in proper form and registration has been refused, the applicant is entitled to institute an action for infringement if notice thereof, with a copy of the complaint, is served on the Register of Copyrights. The Register may, at his or her option, become a party to the action with respect to the issue of registrability of the copyright claim by entering an appearance within sixty days after such service, but the Register's failure to become a party shall not deprive the court of jurisdiction to determine that issue.

(b) In the case of a work consisting of sounds, images, or both, the first fixation of which is made simultaneously with its transmission, the copyright owner may, either before or after such fixation takes place, institute an action for infringement under section 501, fully subject to the remedies provided by sections 502 through 506 and sections 509 and 510, if, in accordance with requirements that the Register of Copyrights shall prescribe by regulation, the copyright owner—

(1) serves notice upon the infringer, not less than ten or more than thirty days before such fixation, identifying the work and the specific time and source of its first transmission, and declaring an intention to secure copyright in the work; and

(2) makes registration for the work within three months after its first transmission.

### § 412. Registration as prerequisite to certain remedies for infringement

In any action under this title, other than an action instituted under section 411(b), no award of statutory damages or of attorney's fees, as provided by sections 504 and 505, shall be made for—

(1) any infringement of copyright in an unpublished work commenced before the effective date of its registration; or

(2) any infringement of copyright commenced after first publication of the work and before the effective date of its registration, unless such registration is made within three months after the first publication of the work.

## Chapter 5.—COPYRIGHT INFRINGEMENT AND REMEDIES

### § 501. Infringement of copyright

(a) Anyone who violates any of the exclusive rights of the copyright owner as provided by sections 106 through 118, or who imports copies or phonorecords into the United States in violation of section 602, is an infringer of the copyright.

(b) The legal or beneficial owner of an exclusive right under a copyright is entitled, subject to the requirements of sections 205(d) and 411, to institute an action for any infringement of that particular right committed while he or she is the owner of it. The court may require such owner to serve written notice of the action with a copy of the complaint upon any person shown, by the records of the Copyright Office or otherwise, to have or claim an interest in the copyright, and shall require that such notice be served upon any person whose interest is likely to be affected by a decision in the case. The court may require the joinder, and shall permit the intervention, of any person having or claiming an interest in the copyright.

(c) For any secondary transmission by a cable system that embodies a performance or a display of a work which is actionable as an act of infringement under subsection (c) of section 111, a television broadcast station holding a copyright or other license to transmit or perform the same version of that work shall, for purposes of subsection (b) of this section, be treated as a legal or beneficial owner if such secondary transmission occurs within the local service area of that television station.

(d) For any secondary transmission by a cable system that is actionable as an act of infringement pursuant to section 111(c)(3), the following shall also have standing to sue: (i) the primary transmitter whose transmission has been altered by the cable system; and (ii) any broadcast station within whose local service area the secondary transmission occurs.

### § 502. Remedies for infringement: Injunctions

(a) Any court having jurisdiction of a civil action arising under this title may, subject to the provisions of section 1498 of title 28, grant temporary and final injunctions on such terms as it may deem reasonable to prevent or restrain infringement of a copyright.

(b) Any such injunction may be served anywhere in the United States on the person enjoined; it shall be operative throughout the United States and shall be enforceable, by proceedings in contempt or otherwise, by any United States court having jurisdiction of that person. The clerk of the court granting the injunction shall, when requested by any other court in which enforcement of the injunction is sought, transmit promptly to the other court a certified copy of all the papers in the case on file in such clerk's office.

## § 503. Remedies for infringement: Impounding and disposition of infringing articles

(a) At any time while an action under this title is pending, the court may order the impounding, on such terms as it may deem reasonable, of all copies or phonorecords claimed to have been made or used in violation of the copyright owner's exclusive rights, and of all plates, molds, matrices, masters, tapes, film negatives, or other articles by means of which such copies or phonorecords may be reproduced.

(b) As part of a final judgment or decree, the court may order the destruction or other reasonable disposition of all copies or phonorecords found to have been made or used in violation of the copyright owner's exclusive rights, and of all plates, molds, matrices, masters, tapes, film negatives, or other articles by means of which such copies or phonorecords may be reproduced.

## § 504. Remedies for infringement: Damages and profits

(a) In General.—Except as otherwise provided by this title, an infringer of copyright is liable for either—

(1) the copyright owner's actual damages and any additional profits of the infringer, as provided by subsection (b); or

(2) statutory damages, as provided by subsection (c).

(b) Actual Damages and Profits.—The copyright owner is entitled to recover the actual damages suffered by him or her as a result of the infringement, and any profits of the infringer that are attributable to the infringement and are not taken into account in computing the actual damages. In establishing the infringer's profits, the copyright owner is required to present proof only of the infringer's gross revenue, and the infringer is required to prove his or her deductible expenses and the elements of profit attributable to factors other than the copyrighted work.

(c) Statutory Damages.—

(1) Except as provided by clause (2) of this subsection, the copyright owner may elect, at any time before final judgment is rendered, to recover, instead of actual damages and profits, an award of statutory damages for all infringements involved in the action, with respect to any one work, for which any one infringer is liable individually, or for which any two or more infringers are liable jointly and severally, in a sum of not less than $250 or more than $10,000 as the court considers just. For the purposes of this subsection, all the parts of a compilation or derivative work constitute one work.

(2) In a case where the copyright owner sustains the burden of proving, and the court finds, that infringement was committed willfully, the court in its discretion may increase the award of statutory damages to a sum of not more than $50,000. In a case where the infringer sustains the burden of proving, and the court finds, that such infringer was not aware and had no reason to believe that his or her acts constituted an infringement of copyright, the court in its discretion may reduce the award of statutory damages to a sum of not less than $100. The court shall remit statutory damages in any case where an infringer believed and had reasonable grounds for believing that his or her use of the copyrighted work was a fair use under section 107, if the infringer was: (i) an employee or agent of a nonprofit educational institution, library, or archives acting within the scope of his or her employment who, or such institution, library, or archives itself, which infringed by reproducing the work in copies or phonorecords; or (ii) a public broadcasting entity which or a person who, as a regular part of the nonprofit activities of a public

broadcasting entity (as defined in subsection (g) of section 118) infringed by performing a published nondramatic literary work or by reproducing a transmission program embodying a performance of such a work.

## § 505. Remedies for infringement: Costs and attorney's fees

In any civil action under this title, the court in its discretion may allow the recovery of full costs by or against any party other than the United States or an officer thereof. Except as otherwise provided by this title, the court may also award a reasonable attorney's fee to the prevailing party as part of the costs.

## § 506. Criminal offenses

(a) CRIMINAL INFRINGEMENT.—Any person who infringes a copyright willfully and for purposes of commercial advantage or private financial gain shall be fined not more than $10,000 or imprisoned for not more than one year, or both: *Provided, however,* That any person who infringes willfully and for purposes of commercial advantage or private financial gain the copyright in a sound recording afforded by subsections (1), (2), or (3) of section 106 or the copyright in a motion picture afforded by subsections (1), (3), or (4) of section 106 shall be fined not more than $25,000 or imprisoned for not more than one year, or both, for the first such offense and shall be fined not more than $50,000 or imprisoned for not more than two years, or both, for any subsequent offense.

(b) FORFEITURE AND DESTRUCTION.—When any person is convicted of any violation of subsection (a), the court in its judgment of conviction shall, in addition to the penalty therein prescribed, order the forfeiture and destruction or other disposition of all infringing copies or phonorecords and all implements, devices, or equipment used in the manufacture of such infringing copies or phonorecords.

(c) FRAUDULENT COPYRIGHT NOTICE.—Any person who, with fraudulent intent, places on any article a notice of copyright or words of the same purport that such person knows to be false, or who, with fraudulent intent, publicly distributes or imports for public distribution any article bearing such notice or words that such person knows to be false, shall be fined not more than $2,500.

(d) FRAUDULENT REMOVAL OF COPYRIGHT NOTICE.—Any person who, with fraudulent intent, removes or alters any notice of copyright appearing on a copy of a copyrighted work shall be fined not more than $2,500.

(e) FALSE REPRESENTATION.—Any person who knowingly makes a false representation of a material fact in the application for copyright registration provided for by section 409, or in any written statement filed in connection with the application, shall be fined not more than $2,500.

## § 507. Limitations on actions

(a) CRIMINAL PROCEEDINGS.—No criminal proceeding shall be maintained under the provisions of this title unless it is commenced within three years after the cause of action arose.

(b) CIVIL ACTIONS.—No civil action shall be maintained under the provisions of this title unless it is commenced within three years after the claim accrued.

## § 508. Notification of filing and determination of actions

(a) Within one month after the filing of any action under this title, the clerks of the courts of the United States shall send written notification to the Register of Copyrights setting forth, as far as is shown by the papers filed in the court, the names and addresses of the parties and the title, author, and registration number of each work involved in the action. If any other copyrighted work is later included in the action by amendment, answer, or other pleading, the clerk shall also send a notification concerning it to the Register within one month after the pleading is filed.

(b) Within one month after any final order or judgment is issued in the case, the clerk of the court shall notify the Register of it, sending with the notification a copy of the order or judgment together with the written opinion, if any, of the court.

(c) Upon receiving the notifications specified in this section, the Register shall make them a part of the public records of the Copyright Office.

## § 509. Seizure and forfeiture

(a) All copies or phonorecords manufactured, reproduced, distributed, sold, or otherwise used, intended for use, or possessed with intent to use in violation of section 506(a), and all plates, molds, matrices, masters, tapes, film negatives, or other articles by means of which such copies or phonorecords may be reproduced, and all electronic, mechanical, or other devices for manufacturing, reproducing, or assembling such copies or phonorecords may be seized and forfeited to the United States.

(b) The applicable procedures relating to (i) the seizure, summary and judicial forfeiture, and condemnation of vessels, vehicles, merchandise, and baggage for violations of the customs laws contained in title 19, (ii) the disposition of such vessels, vehicles, merchandise, and baggage or the proceeds from the sale thereof, (iii) the remission or mitigation of such forfeiture, (iv) the compromise of claims, and (v) the award of compensation to informers in respect of such forfeitures, shall apply to seizures and forfeitures incurred, or alleged to have been incurred, under the provisions of this section, insofar as applicable and not inconsistent with the provisions of this section; except that such duties as are imposed upon any officer or employee of the Treasury Department or any other person with respect to the seizure and forfeiture of vessels, vehicles, merchandise; and baggage under the provisions of the customs laws contained in title 19 shall be performed with respect to seizure and forfeiture of all articles described in subsection (a) by such officers, agents, or other persons as may be authorized or designated for that purpose by the Attorney General.

## § 510. Remedies for alteration of programing by cable systems

(a) In any action filed pursuant to section 111(c)(3), the following remedies shall be available:

(1) Where an action is brought by a party identified in subsections (b) or (c) of section 501, the remedies provided by sections 502 through 505, and the remedy provided by subsection (b) of this section; and

(2) When an action is brought by a party identified in subsection (d) of section 501, the remedies provided by sections 502 and 505, together with any actual damages suffered by such party as a result of the infringement, and the remedy provided by subsection (b) of this section.

(b) In any action filed pursuant to section 111(c)(3), the court may decree that, for a period not to exceed thirty days, the cable system shall be deprived of the benefit of a compulsory license for one or more distant signals carried by such cable system.

## Chapter 6.—MANUFACTURING REQUIREMENTS AND IMPORTATION

Sec.
601. Manufacture, importation, and public distribution of certain copies.
602. Infringing importation of copies or phonorecords.
603. Importation prohibitions: Enforcement and disposition of excluded articles.

### § 601. Manufacture, importation, and public distribution of certain copies

(a) Prior to July 1, 1982, and except as provided by subsection (b), the importation into or public distribution in the United States of copies of a work consisting preponderantly of nondramtic literary material that is in the English language and is protected under this title is prohibited unless the portions consisting of such material have been manufactured in the United States or Canada.

(b) The provisions of subsection (a) do not apply—

(1) where, on the date when importation is sought or public distribution in the United States is made, the author of any substantial part of such material is neither a national nor a domiciliary of the United States or, if such author is a national of the United States, he or she has been domiciled outside the United States for a continuous period of at least one year immediately preceding that date; in the case of a work made for hire, the exemption provided by this clause does not apply unless a subsustantial part of the work was prepared for an employer or other person who is not a national or domiciliary of the United States or a domestic corporation or enterprise;

(2) where the United States Customs Service is presented with an import statement issued under the seal of the Copyright Office, in which case a total of no more than two thousand copies of any one such work shall be allowed entry; the import statement shall be issued upon request to the copyright owner or to a person designated by such owner at the time of registration for the work under section 408 or at any time thereafter;

(3) where importation is sought under the authority or for the use, other than in schools, of the Government of the United States or of any State or political subdivision of a State;

(4) where importation, for use and not for sale, is sought—

(A) by any person with respect to no more than one copy of any work at any one time;

(B) by any person arriving from outside the United States, with respect to copies forming part of such person's personal baggage; or

(C) by an organization operated for scholarly, educational, or religious purposes and not for private gain, with respect to copies intended to form a part of its library;

(5) where the copies are reproduced in raised characters for the use of the blind; or

(6) where, in addition to copies imported under clauses (3) and (4) of this subsection, no more than two thousand copies of any one such work, which have not been manufactured in the United States or Canada, are publicly distributed in the United States; or

(7) where, on the date when importation is sought or public distribution in the United States is made—

(A) the author of any substantial part of such material is an individual and receives compensation for the transfer or license of the right to distribute the work in the United States; and

(B) the first publication of the work has previously taken place outside the United States under a transfer or license granted by such author to a transferee or licensee who was not a national or domiciliary of the United States or a domestic corporation or enterprise; and

(C) there has been no publication of an authorized edition of the work of which the copies were manufactured in the United States; and

(D) the copies were reproduced under a transfer or license granted by such author or by the transferee or licensee of the right of first publication as mentioned in subclause (B), and the transferee or the licensee of the right of reproduction was not a national or domiciliary of the United States or a domestic corporation or enterprise.

(c) The requirement of this section that copies be manufactured in the United States or Canada is satisfied if—

(1) in the case where the copies are printed directly from type that has been set, or directly from plates made from such type, the setting of the type and the making of the plates have been performed in the United States or Canada; or

(2) in the case where the making of plates by a lithographic or photoengraving process is a final or intermediate step preceding the printing of the copies, the making of the plates has been performed in the United States or Canada; and

(3) in any case, the printing or other final process of producing multiple copies and any binding of the copies have been performed in the United States or Canada.

(d) Importation or public distribution of copies in violation of this section does not invalidate protection for a work under this title. However, in any civil action or criminal proceeding for infringement of the exclusive rights to reproduce and distribute copies of the work, the infringer has a complete defense with respect to all of the non-dramatic literary material comprised in the work and any other parts of the work in which the exclusive rights to reproduce and distribute copies are owned by the same person who owns such exclusive rights in the nondramatic literary material, if the infringer proves—

(1) that copies of the work have been imported into or publicly distributed in the United States in violation of this section by or with the authority of the owner of such exclusive rights; and

(2) that the infringing copies were manufactured in the United States or Canada in accordance with the provisions of subsection (c); and

(3) that the infringement was commenced before the effective date of registration for an authorized edition of the work, the copies of which have been manufactured in the United States or Canada in accordance with the provisions of subsection (c).

(e) In any action for infringement of the exclusive rights to reproduce and distribute copies of a work containing material required by this section to be manufactured in the United States or Canada, the copyright owner shall set forth in the complaint the names of the persons or organizations who performed the processes specified by subsection (c) with respect to that material, and the places where those processes were performed.

## § 602. Infringing importation of copies or phonorecords

(a) Importation into the United States, without the authority of the owner of copyright under this title, of copies or phonorecords of a work that have been acquired outside the United States is an infringement of the exclusive right to distribute copies or phonorecords under section 106, actionable under section 501. This subsection does not apply to—

(1) importation of copies or phonorecords under the authority or for the use of the Government of the United States or of any State or political subdivision of a State, but not including copies or phonorecords for use in schools, or copies of any audiovisual work imported for purposes other than archival use;

(2) importation, for the private use of the importer and not for distribution, by any person with respect to no more than one copy or phonorecord of any one work at any one time, or by any person arriving from outside the United States with respect to copies or phonorecords forming part of such person's personal baggage; or

(3) importation by or for an organization operated for scholarly, educational, or religious purposes and not for private gain, with respect to no more than one copy of an audiovisual work solely for its archival purposes, and no more than five copies or phonorecords of any other work for its library lending or archival purposes, unless the importation of such copies or phonorecords is part of an activity consisting of systematic reproduction or distribution, engaged in by such organization in violation of the provisions of section 108(g)(2).

(b) In a case where the making of the copies or phonorecords would have constituted an infringement of copyright if this title had been applicable, their importation is prohibited. In a case where the copies or phonorecords were lawfully made, the United States Customs Service has no authority to prevent their importation unless the provisions of section 601 are applicable. In either case, the Secretary of the Treasury is authorized to prescribe, by regulation, a procedure under which any person claiming an interest in the copyright in a particular work may, upon payment of a specified fee, be entitled to notification by the Customs Service of the importation of articles that appear to be copies or phonorecords of the work.

### § 603. Importation prohibitions: Enforcement and disposition of excluded articles

(a) The Secretary of the Treasury and the United States Postal Service shall separately or jointly make regulations for the enforcement of the provisions of this title prohibiting importation.

(b) These regulations may require, as a condition for the exclusion of articles under section 602—

(1) that the person seeking exclusion obtain a court order enjoining importation of the articles; or

(2) that the person seeking exclusion furnish proof, of a specified nature and in accordance with prescribed procedures, that the copyright in which such person claims an interest is valid and that the importation would violate the prohibition in section 602; the person seeking exclusion may also be required to post a surety bond for any injury that may result if the detention or exclusion of the articles proves to be unjustified.

(c) Articles imported in violation of the importation prohibitions of this title are subject to seizure and forfeiture in the same manner as property imported in violation of the customs revenue laws. Forfeited articles shall be destroyed as directed by the Secretary of the Treasury or the court, as the case may be; however, the articles may be returned to the country of export whenever it is shown to the satisfaction of the Secretary of the Treasury that the importer had no reasonable grounds for believing that his or her acts constituted a violation of law.

## Chapter 7.—COPYRIGHT OFFICE

### § 701. The Copyright Office: General responsibilities and organization

(a) All administrative functions and duties under this title, except as otherwise specified, are the responsibility of the Register of Copyrights as director of the Copyright Office of the Library of Congress. The Register of Copyrights, together with the subordinate officers and employees of the Copyright Office, shall be appointed by the Librarian of Congress, and shall act under the Librarian's general direction and supervision.

(b) The Register of Copyrights shall adopt a seal to be used on and after January 1, 1978, to authenticate all certified documents issued by the Copyright Office.

(c) The Register of Copyrights shall make an annual report to the Librarian of Congress of the work and accomplishments of the Copyright Office during the previous fiscal year. The annual report of the Register of Copyrights shall be published separately and as a part of the annual report of the Librarian of Congress.

(d) Except as provided by section 706(b) and the regulations issued thereunder, all actions taken by the Register of Copyrights under this title are subject to the provisions of the Administrative Procedure Act of June 11, 1946, as amended (c. 324, 60 Stat. 237, title 5, United States Code, Chapter 5, Subchapter II and Chapter 7).

### § 702. Copyright Office regulations

The Register of Copyrights is authorized to establish regulations not inconsistent with law for the administration of the functions and duties made the responsibility of the Register under this title. All regulations established by the Register under this title are subject to the approval of the Librarian of Congress.

### § 703. Effective date of actions in Copyright Office

In any case in which time limits are prescribed under this title for the performance of an action in the Copyright Office, and in which the last day of the prescribed period falls on a Saturday, Sunday, holiday, or other nonbusiness day within the District of Columbia or the Federal Government, the action may be taken on the next succeeding business day, and is effective as of the date when the period expired.

### § 704. Retention and disposition of articles deposited in Copyright Office

(a) Upon their deposit in the Copyright Office under sections 407 and 408, all copies, phonorecords, and identifying material, including those deposited in connection with claims that have been refused registration, are the property of the United States Government.

(b) In the case of published works, all copies, phonorecords, and identifying material deposited are available to the Library of Congress for its collections, or for exchange or transfer to any other library. In the case of unpublished works, the Library is entitled, under regulations that the Register of Copyrights shall prescribe, to select any deposits for its collections or for transfer to the National Archives of the United States or to a Federal records center, as defined in section 2901 of title 44.

(c) The Register of Copyrights is authorized, for specific or general categories of works, to make a facsimile reproduction of all or any part of the material deposited under section 408, and to make such reproduction a part of the Copyright Office records of the registration, before transferring such material to the Library of Congress as provided by subsection (b), or before destroying or otherwise disposing of such material as provided by subsection (d).

(d) Deposits not selected by the Library under subsection (b), or identifying portions or reproductions of them, shall be retained under the control of the Copyright Office, including retention in Government storage facilities, for the longest period considered practicable and desirable by the Register of Copyrights and the Librarian of Congress. After that period it is within the joint discretion of the Register and the Librarian to order their destruction or other disposition; but, in the case of unpublished works, no deposit shall be knowingly or intentionally destroyed or otherwise disposed of during its term of copyright unless a facsimile reproduction of the entire deposit has been made a part of the Copyright Office records as provided by subsection (c).

(e) The depositor of copies, phonorecords, or identifying material under section 408, or the copyright owner of record, may request retention, under the control of the Copyright Office, of one or more of such articles for the full term of copyright in the work. The Register of Copyrights shall prescribe, by regulation, the conditions under which such requests are to be made and granted, and shall fix the fee to be charged under section 708(a)(11) if the request is granted.

## § 705. Copyright Office records: Preparation, maintenance, public inspection, and searching

(a) The Register of Copyrights shall provide and keep in the Copyright Office records of all deposits, registrations, recordations, and other actions taken under this title, and shall prepare indexes of all such records.

(b) Such records and indexes, as well as the articles deposited in connection with completed copyright registrations and retained under the control of the Copyright Office, shall be open to public inspection.

(c) Upon request and payment of the fee specified by section 708, the Copyright Office shall make a search of its public records, indexes, and deposits, and shall furnish a report of the information they disclose with respect to any particular deposits, registrations, or recorded documents.

## § 706. Copies of Copyright Office records

(a) Copies may be made of any public records or indexes of the Copyright Office; additional certificates of copyright registration and copies of any public records or indexes may be furnished upon request and payment of the fees specified by section 708.

(b) Copies or reproductions of deposited articles retained under the control of the Copyright Office shall be authorized or furnished only under the conditions specified by the Copyright Office regulations.

## § 707. Copyright Office forms and publications

(a) CATALOG OF COPYRIGHT ENTRIES.—The Register of Copyrights shall compile and publish at periodic intervals catalogs of all copyright registrations. These catalogs shall be divided into parts in accordance with the various classes of works, and the Register has discretion to determine, on the basis of practicability and usefulness, the form and frequency of publication of each particular part.

(b) OTHER PUBLICATIONS.—The Register shall furnish, free of charge upon request, application forms for copyright registration and general informational material in connection with the functions of the Copyright Office. The Register also has the authority to publish compilations of information, bibliographies, and other material he or she considers to be of value to the public.

(c) DISTRIBUTION OF PUBLICATIONS.—All publications of the Copyright Office shall be furnished to depository libraries as specified under section 1905 of title 44, and, aside from those furnished free of charge, shall be offered for sale to the public at prices based on the cost of reproduction and distribution.

## § 708. Copyright Office fees

(a) The following fees shall be paid to the Register of Copyrights:

(1) for the registration of a copyright claim or a supplementary registration under section 408, including the issuance of a certificate of registration, $10;

(2) for the registration of a claim to renewal of a subsisting copyright in its first term under section 304(a), including the issuance of a certificate of registration, $6;

(3) for the issuance of a receipt for a deposit under section 407, $2;

(4) for the recordation, as provided by section 205, of a transfer of copyright ownership or other document of six pages or less, covering no more than one title, $10; for each page over six and each title over one, 50 cents additional;

(5) for the filing, under section 115(b), of a notice of intention to make phonorecords, $6;

(6) for the recordation, under section 302(c), of a statement revealing the identity of an author of an anonymous or pseudonymous work, or for the recordation, under section 302(d), of a statement relating to the death of an author, $10 for a document of six pages or less, covering no more than one title; for each page over six and for each title over one, $1 additional;

(7) for the issuance, under section 601, of an import statement, $3;

(8) for the issuance, under section 706, of an additional certificate of registration, $4;

(9) for the issuance of any other certification, $4; the Register of Copyrights has discretion, on the basis of their cost, to fix the fees for preparing copies of Copyright Office records, whether they are to be certified or not;

(10) for the making and reporting of a search as provided by section 705, and for any related services, $10 for each hour or fraction of an hour consumed;

(11) for any other special services requiring a substantial amount of time or expense, such fees as the Register of Copyrights may fix on the basis of the cost of providing the service.

(b) The fees prescribed by or under this section are applicable to the United States Government and any of its agencies, employees, or officers, but the Register of Copyrights has discretion to waive the requirement of this subsection in occasional or isolated cases involving relatively small amounts.

(c) All fees received under this section shall be deposited by the Register of Copyrights in the Treasury of the United States and shall be credited to the appropriation for necessary expenses of the Copyright Office.* The Register may, in accordance with regulations that he or she shall prescribe, refund any sum paid by mistake or in excess of the fee required by this section; however, before making a refund in any case involving a refusal to register a claim under section 410(b), the Register may deduct all or any part of the prescribed registration fee to cover the reasonable administrative costs of processing the claim.

## § 709. Delay in delivery caused by disruption of postal or other services

In any case in which the Register of Copyrights determines, on the basis of such evidence as the Register may by regulation require, that a deposit, application, fee, or any other material to be delivered to the Copyright Office by a particular date, would have been received in the Copyright Office in due time except for a general disruption or suspension of postal or other transportation or communications services, the actual receipt of such material in the Copyright Office within one month after the date on which the Register determines that the disruption or suspension of such services has terminated, shall be considered timely.

## § 710. Reproduction for use of the blind and physically handicapped: Voluntary licensing forms and procedures

The Register of Copyrights shall, after consultation with the Chief of the Division for the Blind and Physically Handicapped and other appropriate officials of the Library of Congress, establish by regulation standardized forms and procedures by which, at the time applications covering certain specified categories of nondramatic literary works are submitted for registration under section 408 of this title, the copyright owner may voluntarily grant to the Library of Congress a license to reproduce the copyrighted work by means of Braille or similar tactile symbols, or by fixation of a reading of the work in a phonorecord, or both, and to distribute the resulting copies or phonorecords solely for the use of the blind and physically handicapped and under limited conditions to be specified in the standardized forms.

## Chapter 8.—COPYRIGHT ROYALTY TRIBUNAL

Sec. 801. Copyright Royalty Tribunal: Establishment and purpose.
802. Membership of the Tribunal.
803. Procedures of the Tribunal.
804. Institution and conclusion of proceedings.
805. Staff of the Tribunal.
806. Administrative support of the Tribunal.
807. Deduction of costs of proceedings.
808. Reports.
809. Effective date of final determinations.
810. Judicial review.

## § 801. Copyright Royalty Tribunal: Establishment and purpose

(a) There is hereby created an independent Copyright Royalty Tribunal in the legislative branch.

(b) Subject to the provisions of this chapter, the purposes of the Tribunal shall be—

(1) to make determinations concerning the adjustment of reasonable copyright royalty rates as provided in sections 115 and 116, and to make determinations as to reasonable terms and rates of royalty payments as provided in section 118. The rates applicable under sections 115 and 116 shall be calculated to achieve the following objectives:

(A) To maximize the availability of creative works to the public;

*Sentence substituted by Pub. L. 95-94 (1977).

(B) To afford the copyright owner a fair return for his creative work and the copyright user a fair income under existing economic conditions;

(C) To reflect the relative roles of the copyright owner and the copyright user in the product made available to the public with respect to relative creative contribution, technological contribution, capital investment, cost, risk, and contribution to the opening of new markets for creative expression and media for their communication;

(D) To minimize any disruptive impact on the structure of the industries involved and on generally prevailing industry practices.

(2) to make determinations concerning the adjustment of the copyright royalty rates in section 111 solely in accordance with the following provisions:

(A) The rates established by section 111(d)(2)(B) may be adjusted to reflect (i) national monetary inflation or deflation or (ii) changes in the average rates charged cable subscribers for the basic service of providing secondary transmissions to maintain the real constant dollar level of the royalty fee per subscriber which existed as of the date of enactment of this Act: *Provided*, That if the average rates charged cable system subscribers for the basic service of providing secondary transmissions are changed so that the average rates exceed national monetary inflation, no change in the rates established by section 111(d)(2)(B) shall be permitted: *And provided further*, That no increase in the royalty fee shall be permitted based on any reduction in the average number of distant signal equivalents per subscriber. The Commission may consider all factors relating to the maintenance of such level of payments including, as an extenuating factor, whether the cable industry has been restrained by subscriber rate regulating authorities from increasing the rates for the basic service of providing secondary transmissions.

(B) In the event that the rules and regulations of the Federal Communications Commission are amended at any time after April 15, 1976, to permit the carriage by cable systems of additional television broadcast signals beyond the local service area of the primary transmitters of such signals, the royalty rates established by section 111(d)(2)(B) may be adjusted to insure that the rates for the additional distant signal equivalents resulting from such carriage are reasonable in the light of the changes effected by the amendment to such rules and regulations. In determining the reasonableness of rates proposed following an amendment of Federal Communications Commission rules and regulations, the Copyright Royalty Tribunal shall consider, among other factors, the economic impact on copyright owners and users: *Provided*, That no adjustment in royalty rates shall be made under this subclause with respect to any distant signal equivalent or fraction thereof represented by (i) carriage of any signal permitted under the rules and regulations of the Federal Communications Commission in effect on April 15, 1976, or the carriage of a signal of the same type (that is, independent, network, or noncommercial educational) substituted for such permitted signal, or (ii) a television broadcast signal first carried after April 15, 1976, pursuant to an individual waiver of the rules and regulations of the Federal Communications Commission, as such rules and regulations were in effect on April 15, 1976.

(C) In the event of any change in the rules and regulations of the Federal Communications Commission with respect to syndicated and sports program exclusivity after April 15, 1976, the rates established by section 111(d)(2)(B) may be adjusted to assure that such rates are reasonable in light of the changes to such rules and regulations, but any such adjustment shall apply only to the affected television broadcast signals carried on those systems affected by the change.

(D) The gross receipts limitations established by section 111(d)(2)(C) and (D) shall be adjusted to reflect national monetary inflation or deflation or changes in the average rates charged cable system subscribers for the basic service of providing secondary transmissions to maintain the real constant dollar value of the exemption provided by such section; and the royalty rate specified therein shall not be subject to adjustment; and

(3) to distribute royalty fees deposited with the Register of Copyrights under sections 111 and 116, and to determine, in cases where controversy exists, the distribution of such fees.

(c) As soon as possible after the date of enactment of this Act, and no later than six months following such date, the President shall publish a notice announcing the initial appointments provided in section 802, and shall designate an order of seniority among the initially-appointed commissioners for purposes of section 802(b).

## § 802. Membership of the Tribunal

(a) The Tribunal shall be composed of five commissioners appointed by the President with the advice and consent of the Senate for a term of seven years each; of the first five members appointed, three shall be designated to serve for seven years from the date of the notice specified in section 801(c), and two shall be designated to serve for five years from such date, respectively. Commissioners shall be compensated at the highest rate now or hereafter prescribe for grade 18 of the General Schedule pay rates (5 U.S.C. 5332).

(b) Upon convening the commissioners shall elect a chairman from among the commissioners appointed for a full seven-year term. Such chairman shall serve for a term of one year. Thereafter, the most senior commissioner who has not previously served as chairman shall serve as chairman for a period of one year, except that, if all commissioners have served a full term as chairman, the most senior commissioner who has served the least number of terms as chairman shall be designated as chairman.

(c) Any vacancy in the Tribunal shall not affect its powers and shall be filled, for the unexpired term of the appointment, in the same manner as the original appointment was made.

## § 803. Procedures of the Tribunal

(a) The Tribunal shall adopt regulations, not inconsistent with law, governing its procedure and methods of operation. Except as otherwise provided in this chapter, the Tribunal shall be subject to the provisions of the Administrative Procedure Act of June 11, 1946, as amended (c. 324, 60 Stat. 237, title 5, United States Code, chapter 5, subchapter II and chapter 7).

(b) Every final determination of the Tribunal shall be published in the Federal Register. It shall state in detail the criteria that the Tribunal determined to be applicable to the particular proceeding, the various facts that it found relevant to its determination in that proceeding, and the specific reasons for its determination.

## § 804. Institution and conclusion of proceedings

(a) With respect to proceedings under section 801(b)(1) concerning the adjustment of royalty rates as provided in sections 115 and 116, and with respect to proceedings under section 801(b)(2)(A) and (D)—

(1) on January 1, 1980, the Chairman of the Tribunal shall cause to be published in the Federal Register notice of commencement of proceedings under this chapter; and

(2) during the calendar years specified in the following schedule, any owner or user of a copyrighted work whose royalty rates are specified by this title, or by a rate established by the Tribunal, may file a petition with the Tribunal declaring that the petitioner requests an adjustment of the rate. The Tribunal shall make a determination as to whether the applicant has a significant interest in the royalty rate in which an adjustment is requested. If the Tribunal determines that the petitioner has a significant interest, the Chairman shall cause notice of this determination, with the reasons therefor, to be published in the Federal Register, together with notice of commencement of proceedings under this chapter.

(A) In proceedings under section 801(b)(2)(A) and (D), such petition may be filed during 1985 and in each subsequent fifth calendar year.

(B) In proceedings under section 801(b)(1) concerning the adjustment of royalty rates as provided in section 115, such petition may be filed in 1987 and in each subsequent tenth calendar year.

(C) In proceedings under section 801(b)(1) concerning the adjustment of royalty rates under section 116, such petition may be filed in 1990 and in each subsequent tenth calendar year.

(b) With respect to proceedings under subclause (B) or (C) of section 801(b)(2), following an event described in either of those subsections, any owner or user of a copyrighted work whose royalty rates are specified by section 111, or by a rate established by the Tribunal, may, within twelve months, file a petition with the Tribunal declaring that the petitioner requests an adjustment of the rate. In this event the Tribunal shall proceed as in subsection (a)(2), above. Any change in royalty rates made by the Tribunal pursuant to this subsection may be reconsidered in 1980, 1985, and each fifth calendar year thereafter, in accordance with the provisions in section 801(b)(2)(B) or (C), as the case may be.

(c) With respect to proceedings under section 801(b)(1), concerning the determination of reasonable terms and rates of royalty payments as provided in section 118, the Tribunal shall proceed when and as provided by that section.

(d) With respect to proceedings under section 801(b)(3), concerning the distribution of royalty fees in certain circumstances under sections 111 or 116, the Chairman of the Tribunal shall, upon determination by the Tribunal that a controversy exists concerning such distribution, cause to be published in the Federal Register notice of commencement of proceedings under this chapter.

(e) All proceedings under this chapter shall be initiated without delay following publication of the notice specified in this section, and the Tribunal shall render its final decision in any such proceeding within one year from the date of such publication.

## § 805. Staff of the Tribunal

(a) The Tribunal is authorized to appoint and fix the compensation of such employees as may be necessary to carry out the provisions of this chapter, and to prescribe their functions and duties.

(b) The Tribunal may procure temporary and intermittent services to the same extent as is authorized by section 3109 of title 5.

## § 806. Administrative support of the Tribunal

(a) The Library of Congress shall provide the Tribunal with necessary administrative services, including those related to budgeting, accounting, financial reporting, travel, personnel, and procurement. The Tribunal shall pay the Library for such services, either in advance or by reimbursement from the funds of the Tribunal, at amounts to be agreed upon between the Librarian and the Tribunal.

(b) The Library of Congress is authorized to disburse funds for the Tribunal, under regulations prescribed jointly by the Librarian of Congress and the Tribunal and approved by the Comptroller General. Such regulations shall establish requirements and procedures under which every voucher certified for payment by the Library of Congress under this chapter shall be supported with a certification by a duly authorized officer or employee of the Tribunal, and shall prescribe the responsibilities and accountability of said officers and employees of the Tribunal with respect to such certifications.

## § 807. Deduction of costs of proceedings

Before any funds are distributed pursuant to a final decision in a proceeding involving distribution of royalty fees, the Tribunal shall assess the reasonable costs of such proceeding.

## § 808. Reports

In addition to its publication of the reports of all final determinations as provided in section 803(b), the Tribunal shall make an annual report to the President and the Congress concerning the Tribunal's work during the preceding fiscal year, including a detailed fiscal statement of account.

## § 809. Effective date of final determinations

Any final determination by the Tribunal under this chapter shall become effective thirty days following its publication in the Federal Register as provided in section 803(b), unless prior to that time an appeal has been filed pursuant to section 810, to vacate, modify, or correct such determination, and notice of such appeal has been served on all parties who appeared before the Tribunal in the proceeding in question. Where the proceeding involves the distribution of royalty fees under sections 111 or 116, the Tribunal shall, upon the expiration of such thirty-day period, distribute any royalty fees not subject to an appeal filed pursuant to section 810.

## § 810. Judicial review

Any final decision of the Tribunal in a proceeding under section 801(b) may be appealed to the United States Court of Appeals, within thirty days after its publication in the Federal Register by an aggrieved party. The judicial review of the decision shall be had, in accordance with chapter 7 of title 5, on the basis of the record before the Tribunal. No court shall have jurisdiction to review a final decision of the Tribunal except as provided in this section.

TRANSITIONAL AND SUPPLEMENTARY PROVISIONS

SEC. 102. This Act becomes effective on January 1, 1978, except as otherwise expressly provided by this Act, including provisions of the first section of this Act. The provisions of sections 118, 304(b), and chapter 8 of title 17, as amended by the first section of this Act, take effect upon enactment of this Act.

SEC. 103. This Act does not provide copyright protection for any work that goes into the public domain before January 1, 1978. The exclusive rights, as provided by section 106 of title 17 as amended by the first section of this Act, to reproduce a work in phonorecords and to distribute phonorecords of the work, do not extend to any nondramatic musical work copyrighted before July 1, 1909.

SEC. 104. All proclamations issued by the President under section 1(e) or 9(b) of title 17 as it existed on December 31, 1977, or under previous copyright statutes of the United States, shall continue in force until terminated, suspended, or revised by the President.

SEC. 105. (a) (1) Section 505 of title 44 is amended to read as follows:

## "§ 505. Sale of duplicate plates

"The Public Printer shall sell, under regulations of the Joint Committee on Printing to persons who may apply, additional or duplicate stereotype or electrotype plates from which a Government publication is printed, at a price not to exceed the cost of composition, the metal, and making to the Government, plus 10 per centum, and the full amount of the price shall be paid when the order is filed.".

(2) The item relating to section 505 in the sectional analysis at the beginning of chapter 5 of title 44, is amended to read as follows:

"505. Sale of duplicate plates.".

(b) Section 2113 of title 44 is amended to read as follows:

## "§ 2113. Limitation on liability

"When letters and other intellectual productions (exclusive of patented material, published works under copyright protection, and unpublished works for which copyright registration has been made) come into the custody or possession of the Administrator of General Services, the United States or its agents are not liable for infringement of copyright or analogous rights arising out of use of the materials for display, inspection, research, reproduction, or other purposes.".

(c) In section 1498(b) of title 28, the phrase "section 101(b) of title 17" is amended to read "section 504(c) of title 17".

(d) Section 543(a)(4) of the Internal Revenue Code of 1954, as amended, is amended by striking out "(other than by reason of section 2 or 6 thereof)".

(e) Section 3202(a) of title 39 is amended by striking out clause (5). Section 3206 of title 39 is amended by deleting the words "subsections (b) and (c)" and inserting "subsection (b)" in subsection (a), and by deleting subsection (c). Section 3206(d) is renumbered (c).

(f) Subsection (a) of section 290(e) of title 15 is amended by deleting the phrase "section 8" and inserting in lieu thereof the phrase "section 105".

(g) Section 131 of title 2 is amended by deleting the phrase "deposit to secure copyright," and inserting in lieu thereof the phrase "acquisition of material under the copyright law,".

SEC. 106. In any case where, before January 1, 1978, a person has lawfully made parts of instruments serving to reproduce mechanically a copyrighted work under the compulsory license provisions of section 1(e) of title 17 as it existed on December 31, 1977, such person may continue to make and distribute such parts embodying the same mechanical reproduction without obtaining a new compulsory license under the terms of section 115 of title 17 as amended by the first section of this Act. However, such parts made on or after January 1, 1978, constitute phonorecords and are otherwise subject to the provisions of said section 115.

SEC. 107. In the case of any work in which an ad interim copyright is subsisting or is capable of being secured on December 31, 1977, under section 22 of title 17 as it existed on that date, copyright protection is hereby extended to endure for the term or terms provided by section 304 of title 17 as amended by the first section of this Act.

SEC. 108. The notice provisions of sections 401 through 403 of title 17 as amended by the first section of this Act apply to all copies or phonorecords publicly distributed on or after January 1, 1978. However, in the case of a work published before January 1, 1978, compliance with the notice provisions of title 17 either as it existed on December 31, 1977, or as amended by the first section of this Act, is adequate with respect to copies publicly distributed after December 31, 1977.

SEC. 109. The registration of claims to copyright for which the required deposit, application, and fee were received in the Copyright Office before January 1, 1978, and the recordation of assignments of copyright or other instruments received in the Copyright Office before January 1, 1978, shall be made in accordance with title 17 as it existed on December 31, 1977.

SEC. 110. The demand and penalty provisions of section 14 of title 17 as it existed on December 31, 1977, apply to any work in which copyright has been secured by publication with notice of copyright on or before that date, but any deposit and registration made after that date in response to a demand under that section shall be made in accordance with the provisions of title 17 as amended by the first section of this Act.

SEC. 111. Section 2318 of title 18 of the United States Code is amended to read as follows:

## "§ 2318. Transportation, sale or receipt of phonograph records bearing forged or counterfeit labels

"(a) Whoever knowingly and with fraudulent intent transports, causes to be transported, receives, sells, or offers for sale in interstate or foreign commerce any phonograph record, disk, wire, tape, film, or other article on which sounds are recorded, to which or upon which is stamped, pasted, or affixed any forged or counterfeited label, knowing the label to have been falsely made, forged, or counterfeited shall be fined not more than $10,000 or imprisoned for not more than one year, or both, for the first such offense and shall be fined not more than $25,000 or imprisoned for not more than two years, or both, for any subsequent offense.

"(b) When any person is convicted of any violation of subsection (a), the court in its judgment of conviction shall, in addition to the penalty therein prescribed, order the forfeiture and destruction or other disposition of all counterfeit labels and all articles to which counterfeit labels have been affixed or which were intended to have had such labels affixed.".

"(c) Except to the extent they are inconsistent with the provisions of this title, all provisions of section 509, title 17, United States Code, are applicable to violations of subsection (a).".

SEC. 112. All causes of action that arose under title 17 before January 1, 1978, shall be governed by title 17 as it existed when the cause of action arose.

SEC. 113. (a) The Librarian of Congress (hereinafter referred to as the "Librarian") shall establish and maintain in the Library of Congress a library to be known as the American Television and Radio Archives (hereinafter referred to as the "Archives"). The purpose of the Archives shall be to preserve a permanent record of the television and radio programs which are the heritage of the people of the United States and to provide access to such programs to historians and scholars without encouraging or causing copyright infringement.

(1) The Librarian, after consultation with interested organizations and individuals, shall determine and place in the Archives such copies and phonorecords of television and radio programs transmitted to the public in the United States and in other countries which are of present or potential public or cultural interest, historical significance, cognitive value, or otherwise worthy of preservation, including copies and phonorecords of published and unpublished transmission programs—

(A) acquired in accordance with sections 407 and 408 of title 17 as amended by the first section of this Act; and

(B) transferred from the existing collections of the Library of Congress; and

(C) given to or exchanged with the Archives by other libraries, archives, organizations, and individuals; and

(D) purchased from the owner thereof.

(2) The Librarian shall maintain and publish appropriate catalogs and indexes of the collections of the Archives, and shall make such collections available for study and research under the conditions prescribed under this section.

(b) Notwithstanding the provisions of section 106 of title 17 as amended by the first section of this Act, the Librarian is authorized with respect to a transmission program which consists of a regularly scheduled newscast or on-the-spot coverage of news events and, under standards and conditions that the Librarian shall prescribe by regulation—

(1) to reproduce a fixation of such a program, in the same or another tangible form, for the purposes of preservation or security or for distribution under the conditions of clause (3) of this subsection; and

(2) to compile, without abridgment or any other editing, portions of such fixations according to subject matter, and to reproduce such compilations for the purpose of clause (1) of this subsection; and

(3) to distribute a reproduction made under clause (1) or (2) of this subsection—

(A) by loan to a person engaged in research; and

(B) for deposit in a library or archives which meets the requirements of section 108(a) of title 17 as amended by the first section of this Act,

in either case for use only in research and not for further reproduction or performance.

(c) The Librarian or any employee of the Library who is acting under the authority of this section shall not be liable in any action for copyright infringement committed by any other person unless the Librarian or such employee knowingly participated in the act of infringement committed by such person. Nothing in this section shall be construed to excuse or limit liability under title 17 as amended by the first section of this Act for any act not authorized by that title or this section, or for any act performed by a person not authorized to act under that title or this section.

(d) This section may be cited as the "American Television and Radio Archives Act".

SEC. 114. There are hereby authorized to be appropriated such funds as may be necessary to carry out the purposes of this Act.

SEC. 115. If any provision of title 17, as amended by the first section of this Act, is declared unconstitutional, the validity of the remainder of this title is not affected.

Approved October 19, 1976.

# NOTES

1. The "computer program" definition was added by Pub. L. 96-517, §10(a), December 12, 1980, 94 Stat. 3028.

2. Section 117, as currently in effect, is included in the text of the statute. The legislation that added it, Pub. L. 96-517, §10(b), December 12, 1980, 94 Stat. 3028, also deleted the old section 117, which was part of the 1976 Copyright Law as initially enacted. It was captioned "Scope of exclusive rights: Use in conjunction with computer and similar information systems." The text was as follows: "Notwithstanding the provisions of sections 106 through 116 and 118, this title does not afford to the owner of copyright in a work of greater or lesser rights with respect to the use of the work in conjunction with automatic systems capable of storing, processing, retrieving, or transferring information, or in conjunction with any similar device, machine, or process, than those afforded to works under the law, whether title 17 or the common law or statutes of a State, in effect on December 31, 1977, as held applicable and construed by a court in an action brought under this title."

# Appendix 2
## SELECTED COPYRIGHT OFFICE REGULATIONS

## List of Copyright Office Regulations, Copyright Royalty Tribunal Regulations

Below is a list of the regulations of the Copyright Office and of the Copyright Royalty Tribunal. The regulations are published in Title 37 of the Code of Federal Regulations approximately each October, as of the preceding July 1. In between, regulations and proposed regulations are published in the *Federal Register*. (Proposed regulations as of January 1, 1982 are included below with the *Federal Register* citation.)

### LIST OF COPYRIGHT OFFICE REGULATIONS

| Section | Regulation |
|---------|-----------|
| 201.1 | Communications with the Copyright Office |
| 201.2 | Information given by the Copyright Office |
| 201.4 | Recordations of transfers and other documents |
| 201.5 | Corrections and amplifications of copyright registrations; applications for supplementary registrations |
| 201.6 | Payment and refund of Copyright Office fees |
| 201.8 | Import statements |
| 201.9 | Recordation of agreements between copyright owners and public broadcast entities |
| 201.10 | Notice of termination of transfers and licenses covering extended renewal term |
| 201.11 | Notices of identity and signal carriage complement of cable systems<br>Notices recorded prior to Feb. 10, 1978<br>Notices recorded between Feb. 10 and July 30, 1978<br>Notices recorded July 31, 1978 and following |
| 201.12 | Recordation of certain contracts by cable systems located outside the forty-eight contiguous states |
| 201.13 | Notices of objection to certain noncommercial performances of nondramatic literary or musical works |
| 201.14 | Warnings of copyright for use by certain libraries and archives |
| 201.15 | Voluntary license to permit reproduction of nondramatic literary works solely for use of the blind and physically handicapped |
| 201.16 | Recordation and certification of coin-operated phonorecord players |
| 201.17 | Statement of account covering compulsory licenses for secondary transmissions by cable systems |

## LIST OF COPYRIGHT ROYALTY TRIBUNAL REGULATIONS

| Section | Regulation |
|---------|------------|
| | remove section 307.4 and amend sections 307.2 and 307.3. 46 *Federal Register* 55276, 11/9/81.] |

*Part 308—Adjustment of Royalty Fee for Compulsory License*
*for Secondary Transmission by Cable Systems*

| | |
|---------|------------|
| 308.1 | General |
| 308.2 | Royalty fee for compulsory license for secondary transmission by cable systems |

## COPYRIGHT NOTICE PLACEMENTS AND LOCATIONS ON COPIES

### §201.20 Methods of affixation and positions of the copyright notice on various types of works.

#### (a) General

(1) This section specifies examples of methods of affixation and positions of the copyright notice on various types of works that will satisfy the notice requirement of section 401(c) of title 17 of the United States Code, as amended by Pub. L. 94-553. A notice considered "acceptable" under this regulation shall be considered to satisfy the requirement of that section that it be "affixed to the copies in such manner and location as to give reasonable notice of the claim of copyright." As provided by that section, the examples specified in this regulation shall not be considered exhaustive of methods of affixation and positions giving reasonable notice of the claim of copyright.

(2) The provisions of this section are applicable to copies publicly distributed on or after December 1, 1981. This section does not establish any rules concerning the form of the notice or the legal sufficiency of particular notices, except with respect to methods of affixation and positions of notice. The adequacy or legal sufficiency of a copyright notice is determined by the law in effect at the time of first publication of the work.

#### (b) Definitions. For the purposes of this section:

(1) The terms "audiovisual works," "collective works," "copies," "device," "fixed," "machine," "motion picture," "pictorial, graphic, and sculptural works," and their variant forms, have the meanings given to them in section 101 of title 17.

(2) "Title 17" means title 17 of the United States Code, as amended by Pub. L. 94-553.

(3) In the case of a work consisting preponderantly of leaves on which the work is printed or otherwise reproduced on both sides, a "page" is one side of a leaf; where the preponderance of the leaves are printed on one side only, the terms "page" and "leaf" mean the same.

(4) A work is published in "book form" if the copies embodying it consist of multiple leaves bound, fastened, or assembled in a predetermined order, as, for example, a volume, booklet, pamphlet, or multipage folder. For the purpose of this section, a work need not consist of textual matter in order to be considered published in "book form."

(5) A "title page" is a page, or two consecutive pages facing each other, appearing at or near the front of the copies of a work published in book form, on which the complete title of the work is prominently stated and on which the names of the author or authors, the name of the publisher, the place of publication, or some combination of them, are given.

(6) The meaning of the terms "front," "back," "first," "last," and "following," when used in connection with works published in book form, with vary in relation to the physical form of the copies depending upon the particular language in which the work is written.

(7) In the case of a work published in book form with a hard or soft cover, the "front page" and "back page" of the copies are the outsides of the front and back covers; where there is no cover, the "front page" and "back page" are the pages visible at the front and back of the copies before they are opened.

(8) A "masthead" is a body of information appearing in approximately the same location in most issues of a newspaper, magazine, journal, review, or other periodical or serial, typically containing the title of the periodical or serial, information about the staff, periodicity of issues, operation, and subscription and editorial policies, of the publication.

(9) A "single-leaf work" is a work published in copies consisting of a single leaf, including copies on which the work is printed or otherwise reproduced on either one side or on both sides of the leaf, and also folders which, without cutting or tearing the copies, can be opened out to form a single leaf. For the purpose of this section, a work need not consist of textual matter in order to be considered a "single-leaf work."

**(c) Manner or affixation and position generally.**

(1) In all cases dealt with in this section, the acceptability of a notice depends upon its being permanently legible to an ordinary user of the work under normal conditions of use, and affixed to the copies in such manner and position that, when affixed, it is not concealed from view upon reasonable examination.

(2) Where, in a particular case, a notice does not appear in one of the precise locations prescribed in this section but a person looking in one of those locations would be reasonably certain to find a notice in another somewhat different location, that notice will be acceptable under this section.

**(d) Works published in book form.** In the case of works published in book form, a notice reproduced on the copies in any of the following positions is acceptable:

(1) The title page, if any;

(2) The page immediately following the title page, if any;

(3) Either side of the front cover, if any; or, if there is no front cover, either side of the front leaf of the copies;

(4) Either side of the back cover, if any; or, if there is no back cover, either side of the back leaf of the copies;

(5) The first page of the main body of the work;

(6) The last page of the main body of the work;

(7) Any page between the front page and the first page of the main body of the work, if: (i) There are no more than ten pages between the front page and the first page of the main body of the work; and (ii) the notice is reproduced prominently and is set apart from other matter on the page where it appears;

(8) Any page between the last page of the main body of the work and back page, if: (i) There are no more than ten pages between the last page of the main body of the work and the back page; and (ii) the notice is reproduced prominently and is set apart from the other matter on the page where it appears;

(9) In the case of a work published as an issue of a periodical or serial, in addition to any of the locations listed in paragraphs (d)(1) through (8) of this section, a notice

is acceptable if it is located: (i) As a part of, or adjacent to, the masthead; (ii) on the page containing the masthead if the notice is reproduced prominently and is set apart from the other matter appearing on the page; or (iii) adjacent to a prominent heading, appearing at or near the front of the issue, containing the title of the periodical or serial and any combination of the volume and issue number and date of the issue;

(10) In the case of a musical work, in addition to any of the locations listed in paragraphs (d)(1) through (9) of this section, a notice is acceptable if it is located on the first page of music.

**(e) Single-leaf works.** In the case of single-leaf works, a notice reproduced on the copies anywhere on the front or back of the leaf is acceptable.

**(f) Contributions to collective works.** For a separate contribution to a collective work to be considered to "bear its own notice of copyright," as provided by 17 U.S.C. 404, a notice reproduced on the copies in any of the following positions is acceptable:

(1) Where the separate contribution is reproduced on a single page, a notice is acceptable if it appears: (i) Under the title of the contribution on that page; (ii) adjacent to the contribution; or (iii) on the same page if, through format, wording, or both, the application of the notice to the particular contribution is made clear;

(2) Where the separate contribution is reproduced on more than one page of the collective work, a notice is acceptable if it appears: (i) Under a title appearing at or near the beginning of the contribution; (ii) on the first page of the main body of the contribution; (iii) immediately following the end of the contribution; or (iv) on any of the pages where the contribution appears, if: (A) The contribution is repro- duced on no more than twenty pages of the collective work; (B) the notice is reproduced prominently and is set apart from other matter on the page where it appears; and (C) through format, wording, or both, the application of the notice to the particular contribution is made clear;

(3) Where the separate contribution is a musical work, in addition to any of the locations listed in paragraphs (f)(1) and (2) of this section, a notice is acceptable if it is located on the first page of music of the contribution;

(4) As an alternative to placing the notice on one of the pages where a separate contribution itself appears, the contribution is considered to "bear its own notice" if the notice appears clearly in juxtaposition with a separate listing of the contribution by title, or if the contribution is untitled, by a description reasonably identifying the contribution: (i) On the page bearing the copyright notice for the collective work as a whole, if any; or (ii) in a clearly identified and readily accessible table of contents or listing of acknowledgments appearing near the front or back of the collective work as a whole.

**(g) Works reproduced in machine-readable copies.** For works reproduced in machine-readable copies (such as magnetic tapes or disks, punched cards, or the like, from which the work cannot ordinarily be visually perceived except with the aid of a machine or device,* each of the following constitute examples of acceptable methods of affixation and position of notice:

(1) A notice embodied in the copies in machine-readable form in such a manner

* A footnote to the regulations states: "Works published in a form requiring the use of a machine or device for purposes of optical enlargement (such as film, filmstrips, slide films, and works published in any variety of microform) and works published in visually perceptible form but used in connection with optical scanning devices, are not within this category."

that on visually perceptible printouts it appears either with or near the title, or at the end of the work;

(2) A notice that is displayed at the user's terminal at sign on;

(3) A notice that is continuously on terminal display; or

(4) A legible notice reproduced durably, so as to withstand normal use, on a gummed or other label securely affixed to the copies or to a box, reel, cartridge, cassette, or other container used as a permanent receptacle for the copies.

**(h) Motion pictures and other audiovisual works.**

(1) The following constitute examples of acceptable methods of affixation and positions of the copyright notice on motion pictures and other audiovisual works: A notice that is embodied in the copies by a photomechanical or electronic process, in such a position that it ordinarily would appear whenever the work is performed in its entirety, and that is located: (i) with or near the title; (ii) with the cast, credits, and similar information; (iii) at or immediately following the beginning of the work; or (iv) at or immediately preceding the end of the work.

(2) In the case of an untitled motion picture or other audiovisual work whose duration is sixty seconds or less, in addition to any of the locations listed in paragraph (h)(1) of this section, a notice that is embodied in the copies by a photomechanical or electronic process, in such a position that it ordinarily would appear to the projectionist or broadcaster when preparing the work for performance, is acceptable if it is located on the leader of the film or tape immediately preceding the beginning of the work.

(3) In the case of a motion picture or other audiovisual work that is distributed to the public for private use, the notice may be affixed, in addition to the locations specified in paragraph (h)(1) of this section, on the housing or container, if it is a permanent receptacle for the work.

**(i) Pictorial, graphic, and sculptural works.** The following constitute examples of acceptable methods of affixation and positions of the copyright notice on various forms of pictorial, graphic, and sculptural works:

(1) Where a work is reproduced in two-dimensional copies, a notice affixed directly or by means of a label cemented, sewn, or otherwise attached durably, so as to withstand normal use, on the front or back of the copies, or to any backing, mounting, matting, framing, or other material to which the copies are durably attached, so as to withstand normal use, or in which they are permanently housed, is acceptable.

(2) Where a work is reproduced in three-dimensional copies, a notice affixed directly or by means of a label cemented, sewn, or otherwise attached durably, so as to withstand normal use, to any visible portion of the work, or to any base, mounting, framing, or other material on which the copies are durably attached, so as to withstand normal use, or in which they are permanently housed, is acceptable.

(3) Where, because of the size or physical characteristics of the material in which the work is reproduced in copies, it is impossible or extremely impracticable to affix a notice to the copies directly or by means of a durable label, a notice is acceptable if it appears on a tag that is of durable material, so as to withstand normal use, and that is attached to the copy with sufficient durability that it will remain with the copy while it is passing through its normal channels of commerce.

(4) Where a work is reproduced in copies consisting of sheetlike or strip materials bearing multiple or continuous reproductions of the work, the notice may be applied: (i) To the reproduction itself; (ii) to the margin, selvage, or reverse side of the material

at frequent and regular intervals; or (iii) if the material contains neither a selvage nor a reverse side, to tags or labels, attached to the copies and to any spools, reels, or containers housing them in such a way that a notice is visible while the copies are passing through their normal channels of commerce.

(5) If the work is permanently housed in a container, such as a game or puzzle box, a notice reproduced on the permanent container is acceptable.

## DEPOSITS UNDER SECTION 407

### §202.19 Deposit of published copies or phonorecords for the Library of Congress.

(a) **General.** This section prescribes rules pertaining to the deposit of copies and phonorecords of published works for the Library of Congress under section 407 of title 17 of the United States Code, as amended by Pub. L. 94-553. The provisions of this section are not applicable to the deposit of copies and phonorecords for purposes of copyright registration under section 408 of title 17, except as expressly adopted in §202.20 of these regulations.

(b) **Definitions.** For the purposes of this section:

(1) (i) The "best edition" of a work is the edition, published in the United States at any time before the date of deposit, that the Library of Congress determines to be most suitable for its purposes.

(ii) Criteria for selection of the "best edition" from among two or more published editions of the same version of the same work are set forth in the statement entitled "Best Edition of Published Copyrighted Works for the Collections of the Library of Congress" (hereafter referred to as the "Best Edition Statement") in effect at the time of deposit. Copies of the Best Edition Statement are available upon request made to the Acquisitions and Processing Division of the Copyright Office. [The "Best Edition statement" is set forth later on in this appendix.]

(iii) Where no specific criteria for the selection of the "best edition" are established in the Best Edition Statement, that edition which, in the judgment of the Library of Congress, represents the highest quality for its purposes shall be considered the "best edition." In such cases:

(A) When the Copyright Office is aware that two or more editions of a work have been published it will consult with other appropriate officials of the Library of Congress to obtain instructions as to the "best edition" and (except in cases for which special relief is granted) will require deposit of that edition; and

(B) when a potential depositor is uncertain which of two or more published editions comprises the "best edition," inquiry should be made to the Acquisitions and Processing Division of the Copyright Office.

(iv) Where differences between two or more "editions" of a work represent variations in copyrightable content, each edition is considered a separate version, and hence a different work, for the purpose of this section, and criteria of "best edition" based on such differences do not apply.

(2) A "complete" copy includes all elements comprising the unit of publication of the best edition of the work, including elements that, if considered separately, would not be copyrightable subject matter or would otherwise be exempt from mandatory deposit requirements under paragraph (c) of this section. In the case of sound recordings, a "complete" phonorecord includes the phonorecord, together with any printed or other visually perceptible material published with such phono-

record (such as textual or pictorial matter appearing on record sleeves or album covers, or embodied in leaflets or booklets included in a sleeve, album, or other container). In the case of a musical composition published in copies only, or in both copies and phonorecords:

(i) if the only publication of copies in the United States took place by the rental, lease, or lending of a full score and parts, a full score is a "complete" copy; and

(ii) if the only publication of copies in the United States took place by the rental, lease, or lending of a conductor's score and parts, a conductor's score is a "complete" copy. In the case of a motion picture, a copy is "complete" if the reproduction of all of the visual and aural elements comprising the copyrightable subject matter in the work is clean, undamaged, undeteriorated, and free of splices, and if the copy itself and its physical housing are free of any defects that would interfere with the performance of the work or that would cause mechanical, visual, or audible defects or distortions.

(3) The terms "copies," "collective work," "device," "fixed," "literary work," "machine," "motion picture," "phonorecord," "publication," "sound recording," and "useful article," and their variant forms, have the meanings given to them in section 101 of title 17.

(4) "Title 17" means title 17 of the United States Code, as amended by Pub. L. 94-553.

**(c) Exemptions from deposit requirements.** The following categories of material are exempt from the deposit requirements of section 407(a) of title 17:

(1) Diagrams and models, illustrating scientific or technical works or formulating scientific or technical information in linear or three-dimensional form, such as an architectural or engineering blueprint, plan, or design, a mechanical drawing, or an anatomical model.

(2) Greeting cards, picture postcards, and stationery.

(3) Lectures, sermons, speeches, and addresses when published individually and not as a collection of the works of one or more authors.

(4) Literary, dramatic, and musical works published only as embodied in phonorecords. This category does not exempt the owner of copyright, or of the exclusive right of publication, in a sound recording resulting from the fixation of such works in a phonorecord from the applicable deposit requirements for the sound recording.

(5) Literary works, including computer programs and automated data bases, published in the United States only in the form of machine-readable copies (such as magnetic tape or disks, punched cards, or the like) from which the work cannot ordinarily be visually perceived except with the aid of a machine or device. Works published in a form requiring the use of a machine or device for purposes of optical enlargement (such as film, filmstrips, slide films, and works published in any variety of microform), and works published in visually perceivable form but used in connection with optical scanning devices, are not within this category and are subject to the applicable deposit requirements.

(6) Three-dimensional sculptural works, and any works published only as reproduced in or on jewelry, dolls, toys, games, plaques, floor coverings, wallpaper and similar commercial wall coverings, textile and other fabrics, packaging material, or any useful article. Globes, relief models, and similar cartographic representations of area are not within this category and are subject to the applicable deposit requirements.

(7) Prints, labels, and other advertising matter published in connection with the

rental, lease, lending, licensing, or sale of articles of merchandise, works of authorship, or services.

(8) Tests, and answer material for tests, when published separately from other literary works.

(9) Works first published as individual contributions to collective works. This category does not exempt the owner of copyright, or of the exclusive right of publication, in the collective work as a whole from the applicable deposit requirements for the collective work.

(10) Works first published outside the United States and later published in the United States without change in copyrightable content, if:

(i) Registration for the work was made under 17 U.S.C. 403 before the work was published in the United States; or

(ii) registration for the work was made under 17 U.S.C. 406 after the work was published in the United States but before a demand for deposit is made under 17 U.S.C. 407(d).

(11) Works published only as embodied in a soundtrack that is an integral part of a motion picture. This category does not exempt the owner of copyright, or of the exclusive right of publication, in the motion picture from the applicable deposit requirements for the motion picture.

(12) Motion pictures that consist of television transmission programs and that have been published, if at all, only by reason of a license or other grant to a nonprofit institution of the right to make a fixation of such programs directly from a transmission to the public, with or without the right to make further uses of such fixations.

**(d) Nature of required deposit.**

(1) Subject to the provisions of paragraph (d)(2) of this section, the deposit required to satisfy the provisions of section 407(a) of title 17 shall consist of

(i) in the case of published works other than sound recordings, two complete copies of the best edition; and

(ii) in the case of published sound recordings, two complete phonorecords of the best edition.

(2) In the case of certain published works not exempt from deposit requirements under paragraph (c) of this section, the following special provisions shall apply:

(i) In the case of published three-dimensional cartographic representations of area, such as globes and relief models, the deposit of one complete copy of the best edition of the work will suffice in lieu of the two copies required by paragraph (d)(1) of this section.

(ii) In the case of published motion pictures, the deposit of one complete copy of the best edition of the work will suffice in lieu of the two copies required by paragraph (d)(1) of this section. Any deposit for a published motion picture must be accompanied by a separate description of its contents, such as a continuity, pressbook, or synopsis. The Library of Congress may, at its sole discretion, enter into an agreement permitting the return of copies of published motion pictures to the depositor under certain conditions and establishing certain rights and obligations with respect to such copies. In the event of termination of such an agreement by the Library it shall not be subject to reinstatement, nor shall the depositor or any successor in interest of the depositor be entitled to any similar or subsequent agreement with the Library, unless at the sole discretion of the Library it would be in the best interests of the Library to reinstate the agreement or enter into a new agreement.

(iii) In the case of any published work deposited in the form of a hologram, the deposit shall be accompanied by:

(A) Two sets of precise instructions for displaying the image fixed in the hologram; and

(B) two sets of identifying material in compliance with §202.21 of these regulations and clearly showing the displayed image.

(iv) In any case where an individual author is the owner of copyright in a published pictorial or graphic work and (A) less than five copies of the work have been published, or (B) the work has been published and sold or offered for sale in a limited edition consisting of no more than three hundred numbered copies, the deposit of one complete copy of the best edition of the work or, alternatively, the deposit of photographs or other identifying material in compliance with §202.21 of these regulations, will suffice in lieu of the two copies required by paragraph (d)(1) of this section.

(v) In the case of a musical composition published in copies only, or in both copies and phonorecords, if the only publication of copies in the United States took place by rental, lease, or lending, the deposit of one complete copy of the best edition will suffice in lieu of the two copies required by paragraph (d)(1) of this section.

(vi) In the case of published multimedia kits that are prepared for use in systematic instructional activities and that include literary works, audiovisual works, sound recordings, or any combination of such works, the deposit of one complete copy of the best edition will suffice in lieu of the two copies required by paragraph (d)(1) of this section.

### (e) Special relief.

(1) In the case of any published work not exempt from deposit under paragraph (c) of this section the Register of Copyrights may, after consultation with other appropriate officials of the Library of Congress and upon such conditions as the Register may determine after such consultation:

(i) Grant an exemption from the deposit requirements of section 407(a) of title 17 on an individual basis for single works or series or groups of works; or

(ii) permit the deposit of one copy or phonorecord, or alternative identifying material in lieu of the two copies or phonorecords required by paragraph (d)(1) of this section; or

(iii) permit the deposit of incomplete copies or phonorecords, or copies or phonorecords other than those normally comprising the best edition.

(2) Any decisions as to whether to grant such special relief, and the conditions under which special relief is to be granted, shall be made by the Register of Copyrights after consultation with other appropriate officials of the Library of Congress, and shall be based upon the acquisition policies of the Library of Congress then in force.

(3) Requests for special relief under this paragraph shall be made in writing to the Chief, Acquisitions and Processing Division of the Copyright Office, shall be signed by or on behalf of the owner of copyright or of the exclusive right of publication in the work, and shall set forth specific reasons why the request should be granted.

(4) The Register of Copyrights may, after consultation with other appropriate officials of the Library of Congress, terminate any ongoing or continuous grant of special relief. Notice of termination shall be given in writing and shall be sent to

the individual person or organization to whom the grant of special relief had been given, at the last address shown in the records of the Copyright Office. A notice of termination may be given at any time, but it shall state a specific date of termination that is at least 30 days later than the date the notice is mailed. Termination shall not affect the validity of any deposit earlier made under the grant of special relief.

**(f) Submission and receipt of copies and phonorecords.**

(1) All copies and phonorecords deposited in the Copyright Office will be considered to be deposited only in compliance with section 407 of title 17 unless they are accompanied by:

(i) An application for registration of claim to copyright, or

(ii) a clear written request that they be held for connection with a separately forwarded application.

Copies or phonorecords deposited without such an accompanying application written request will not be connected with or held for receipt of separate applications, and will not satisfy the deposit provisions of section 408 of title 17 or §202.20 of these regulations. Any written request that copies or phonorecords be held for connection with a separately forwarded application must appear in a letter or similar document accompanying the deposit; a request or instruction appearing on the packaging, wrapping, or container for the deposit will not be effective for this purpose.

(2) All copies and phonorecords deposited in the Copyright Office under section 407 of title 17, unless accompanied by written instructions to the contrary, will be considered to be deposited by the person or persons named in the copyright notice on the work.

(3) Upon request by the depositor made at the time of the deposit, the Copyright Office will issue a certificate of receipt for the deposit of copies or phonorecords of a work under this section.

Certificates of receipt will be issued in response to requests made after the date of deposit only if the requesting party is identified in the records of the Copyright Office as having made the deposit. In either case, requests for a certificate of receipt must be in writing and accompanied by a fee of $2. A certificate of receipt will include identification of the depositor, the work deposited, and the nature and format of the copy or phonorecord deposited, together with the date of the receipt.

"BEST EDITION" OF PUBLISHED COPYRIGHTED WORKS FOR THE COLLECTIONS OF THE LIBRARY OF CONGRESS

The Copyright Law (Title 17, United States Code) requires that copies or phonorecords deposited in the Copyright Office be of the "best edition" of the work. The law states that "The 'best edition' of work is the edition, published in the United States at any time before the date of deposit, that the Library of Congress determines to be most suitable for its purposes."

When two or more editions of the same version of a work have been published, the one of the highest quality is generally considered to be the best edition. In judging quality, the Library of Congress will adhere to the criteria set forth below in all but exceptional circumstances.

Where differences between editions represent variations in copyrightable content, each edition is a separate version and "best edition" standards based on such differences do not apply. Each such version is a separate work for the purposes of the Copyright Law.

Appearing below are lists of criteria to be applied in determining the best edition of each of several types of material. The criteria are listed in descending order of importance. In deciding between two editions, a criterion-by-criterion comparison should be made. The edition which first fails to satisfy a criterion is to be considered of inferior quality and will not be an acceptable deposit. For example, if a comparison is made between two hardbound editions of a book, one a trade edition printed on acid-free paper and the other a specially bound edition printed on average paper, the former will be the best edition because the type of paper is a more important criterion than the binding.

Under regulations of the Copyright Office, potential depositors may request authorization to deposit copies or phonorecords of other than the best edition of a specific work (e.g., a microform rather than a printed edition of a serial).

### I. PRINTED TEXTUAL MATTER

A. *Paper, Binding, and Packaging:*
1. Archival-quality rather than less-permanent paper.
2. Hard cover rather than soft cover.
3. Library binding rather than commercial binding.
4. Trade edition rather than book club edition.
5. Sewn rather than glue-only binding.
6. Sewn or glued rather than stapled or spiral-bound.
7. Stapled rather than spiral-bound or plastic-bound.
8. Bound rather than looseleaf, except when future looseleaf insertions are to be issued.
9. Slipcased rather than nonslipcased.
10. With protective folders rather than without (for broadsides).
11. Rolled rather than folded (for broadsides).
12. With protective coatings rather than without (except broadsides, which should not be coated).

B. *Rarity:*
1. Special limited edition having the greatest number of special features.
2. Other limited edition rather than trade edition.
3. Special binding rather than trade binding.

C. *Illustrations:*
1. Illustrated rather than unillustrated.
2. Illustrations in color rather than black and white.

D. *Special Features:*
1. With thumb notches or index tabs rather than without.
2. With aids to use such as overlays and magnifiers rather than without.

E. *Size:*
1. Larger rather than smaller sizes. (Except that large-type editions for the partially-sighted are not required in place of editions employing type of more conventional size.)

### II. PHOTOGRAPHS

A. Size and finish, in descending order of preference:
1. The most widely distributed edition.
2. 8 × 10-inch glossy print.
3. Other size or finish.

B. Unmounted rather than mounted.
C. Archival-quality rather than less permanent paper stock or printing process.

### III. MOTION PICTURES

A. Film rather than another medium. Film editions are listed below in descending order of preference.
  1. Preprint material, by special arrangement.
  2. Film gauge in which most widely distributed.
  3. 35 mm rather than 16 mm.
  4. 16 mm rather than 8 mm.
  5. Special formats (e.g., 65 mm) only in exceptional cases.
  6. Open reel rather than cartridge or cassette.
B. Videotape rather than videodisc. Videotape editions are listed below in descending order of preference.
  1. Tape gauge in which most widely distributed.
  2. Two-inch tape.
  3. One-inch tape.
  4. Three-quarter-inch tape cassette.
  5. One-half-inch tape cassette.

### IV. OTHER GRAPHIC MATTER

A. *Paper and Printing:*
  1. Archival quality rather than less-permanent paper.
  2. Color rather than black and white.
B. *Size and Content:*
  1. Larger rather than smaller size.
  2. In the case of cartographic works, editions with the greatest amount of information rather than those with less detail.
C. *Rarity:*
  1. The most widely distributed edition rather than one of limited distribution.
  2. In the case of a work published only in a limited, numbered edition, one copy outside the numbered series but otherwise identical.
  3. A photographic reproduction of the original, by special arrangement only.
D. *Text and Other Materials:* 1. Works with annotations, accompanying tabular or textual matter, or other interpretive aids rather than those without them.
E. *Binding and Packaging:*
  1. Bound rather than unbound.
  2. If editions have different binding, apply the criteria in I.A.2–1.A.7, above.
  3. Rolled rather than folded.
  4. With protective coatings rather than without.

### V. PHONORECORDS

A. Disc rather than tape.
B. With special enclosures rather than without.
C. Open-reel rather than cartridge.
D. Cartridge rather than cassette.
E. Quadraphonic rather than stereophonic.
F. True stereophonic rather than monaural.
G. Monaural rather than electronically rechanneled stereo.

## VI. MUSICAL COMPOSITIONS

A. *Fullness of Score:* 1. *Vocal music:* a. With orchestral accompaniment—
  i. Full score and parts, if any, rather than conductor's score and parts, if any. (In cases of compositions published only by rental, lease, or lending, this requirement is reduced to full score only.)
  ii. Conductor's score and parts, if any, rather than condensed score and parts, if any. (In cases of compositions published only by rental, lease, or lending, this requirement is reduced to conductor's score only.)
  b. Unaccompanied: Open score (each part on separate staff) rather than closed score (all parts condensed to two staves).
  2. *Instrumental music:*
  a. Full score and parts, if any, rather than conductor's score and parts, if any. (In cases of compositions published only by rental, lease, or lending, this requirement is reduced to full score only.)
  b. Conductor's score and parts, if any, rather than condensed score and parts, if any. (In cases of compositions published only by rental, lease, or lending, this requirement is reduced to conductor's score only.)
B. *Printing and Paper:* 1. Archival-quality rather than less-permanent paper.
C. *Binding and Packaging:*
  1. Special limited editions rather than trade editions.
  2. Bound rather than unbound.
  3. If editions have different binding, apply the criteria in I.A.2–I.A.12, above.
  4. With protective folders rather than without.

## VII. MICROFORMS

A. *Related Materials.* 1. With indexes, study guides, or other printed matter rather than without.
B. *Permanence and Appearance:*
  1. Silver halide rather than any other emulsion.
  2. Positive rather than negative.
  3. Color rather than black and white.
C. *Format (newspapers and newspaper-formatted serials):* 1. Reel microfilm rather than any other microform.
D. *Format (all other materials):*
  1. Microfiche rather than reel microfilm.
  2. Reel microfilm rather than microform cassettes.
  3. Microfilm cassettes rather than micro-opaque prints.
E. *Sizes:* 1. 35 mm rather than 16 mm.

## VIII. WORKS EXISTING IN MORE THAN ONE MEDIUM

Editions are listed below in descending order of preference.

A. Newspapers, dissertations and theses, newspaper-formatted serials:
  1. Microform.
  2. Printed matter.
B. All other materials:
  1. Printed matter.
  2. Microform.
  3. Phonorecord.

(Effective: January 1, 1978.)

## §202.21 Deposit of identifying material instead of copies.

(a) **General.** Subject to the specific provisions of paragraphs (f) and (g) of this section, in any case where the deposit of identifying material is permitted or requested under §202.19 or §202.20 of these regulations, the material shall consist of photographic prints, transparencies, photostats, drawings, or similar two-dimensional reproductions or rendering of the work, in a form visually perceivable without the aid of a machine or device. In the case of pictorial or graphic works, such material shall reproduce the actual colors employed in the work. In all other cases, such material may be in black and white or may consist of a reproduction of the actual colors.

(b) **Completeness; number of sets.** As many pieces of identifying material as are necessary to show clearly the entire copyrightable content of the work for which deposit is being made, or for which registration is being sought, shall be submitted. Except in cases falling under the provisions of §202.19(d)(2)(iii) or §202.20(c)(2)(iii) with respect to holograms, only one set of such complete identifying material is required.

(c) **Size.** All pieces of identifying material must be of uniform size. Photographic transparencies must be 35 mm. in size, and must be fixed in cardboard, plastic, or similar mounts to facilitate identification, handling, and storage. All other types of identifying material must be not less than 5 × 7 inches and not more than 9 × 12 inches, but preferably 8 × 10 inches. Except in the case of transparencies, the image of the work must be either lifesize or larger, or if less than lifesize must be at least four inches in its greatest dimension.

(d) **Title and dimensions.** At least one piece of identifying material must, on its front, back, or mount, indicate the title of the work and an exact measurement of one or more dimensions of the work.

(e) **Copyright notice.** In the case of works published with notice of copyright, the notice and its position on the work must be clearly shown on at least one piece of identifying material. Where necessary because of the size or position of the notice, a separate drawing or the like showing the exact appearance and content of the notice, its position on the work must be clearly shown on at least one piece of identifying material. Where necessary because of the size or position of the notice, a separate drawing or the like showing the exact appearance and content of the notice, its dimensions, and its specific position on the work shall be submitted.

(f) For separate registration of an unpublished work that is fixed, or a published work that is published, only as embodied in a soundtrack that is an integral part of a motion picture, identifying material deposited in lieu of an actual copy or copies of the motion picture shall consist of:

(1) a transcription of the entire work, or a reproduction of the entire work on a phonorecord; and

(2) photographs or other reproductions from the motion picture showing the title of the motion picture, the soundtrack credits, and the copyright notice for the soundtrack, if any. The provisions of paragraphs (b), (c), (d) and (e) of this §202.21 do not apply to identifying material deposited under this paragraph (f).

(g) In the case of unpublished motion pictures (including transmission programs that have been fixed and transmitted to the public, but have not been published), identifying material deposited in lieu of an actual copy shall consist of either:

(1) an audio cassette or other phonorecord reproducing the entire soundtrack or other sound portion of the motion picture, and a description of the motion picture; or

(2) a set consisting of one frame enlargement or similar visual reproduction from each ten minute segment of the motion picture, and a description of the motion picture. In either case the "description" may be a continuity, a pressbook, or a synopsis, but in all cases it must include:

(i) the title or continuing title of the work, and the episode title, if any;

(ii) the nature and general content of the program;

(iii) the date when the work was first fixed and whether or not fixation was simultaneous with first transmission;

(iv) the date of first transmission, if any;

(v) the running time; and

(vi) the credit appearing on the work, if any. The provisions of paragraphs (b), (c), (d) and (e) of this §202.21 do not apply to identifying material submitted under this paragraph (g).

## §202.20 Deposit of copies and phonorecords for copyright registration.

**(a) General.** This section prescribes rules pertaining to the deposit of copies and phonorecords of published and unpublished works for the purpose of copyright registration under section 408 of title 17 of the United States Code, as amended by Pub. L. 94-553. The provisions of this section are not applicable to the deposit of copies and phonorecords for the Library of Congress under section 407 of title 17, except as expressly adopted in §202.19 of these regulations.

**(b) Definitions.** For the purposes of this section:

(1) The "best edition" of a work has the meaning set forth in §202.19(b)(1) of these regulations.

(2) A "complete" copy or phonorecord means the following:

(i) *Unpublished works.* Subject to the requirements of paragraph (vi) of this §202.20(b)(2), a "complete" copy or phonorecord of an unpublished work is a copy or phonorecord representing the entire copyrightable content of the work for which registration is sought;

(ii) *Published works.* Subject to the requirements of paragraphs (iii) through (vi) of this §202.20(b)(2), a "complete" copy or phonorecord of a published work includes all elements comprising the applicable unit of publication of the work, including elements that, if considered separately, would not be copyrightable subject matter. However, even where certain physically separable elements included in the applicable unit of publication are missing from the deposit, a copy or phonorecord will be considered "complete" for purposes of registration where:

(A) The copy or phonorecord deposited contains all parts of the work for which registration is sought; and

(B) the removal of the missing elements did not physically damage the copy or phonorecord or garble its contents; and

(C) the work is exempt from the mandatory deposit requirements under section 407 of title 17 of the United States Code and §202.19(c) of these regulations, or the copy deposited consists entirely of a container, wrapper, or holder, such as an envelope, sleeve, jacket, slipcase, box, bag, folder, binder, or other receptacle acceptable for deposit under paragraph (c)(2) of this section;

(iii) *Contributions to collective works.* In the case of a published contribution to a collective work, a "complete" copy or phonorecord is the entire collective work including the contribution or, in the case of a newspaper, the entire section including the contribution;

(iv) *Sound recordings.* In the case of published sound recordings, a "complete" phonorecord has the meaning set forth in §202.19(b)(2) of these regulations;

(v) *Musical scores.* In the case of a musical composition published in copies only, or in both copies and phonorecords:

(a) If the only publication of copies took place by the rental, lease, or lending of a full score and parts, a full score is a "complete" copy; and

(b) if the only publication of copies took place by the rental, lease, or lending of a conductor's score and parts, a conductor's score is a "complete" copy;

(vi) *Motion pictures.* In the case of a published or unpublished motion picture, a copy is "complete" if the reproduction of all of the visual and aural elements comprising the copyrightable subject matter in the work is clean, undamaged, undeteriorated, and free of splices, and if the copy itself and its physical housing are free of any defects that would interfere with the performance of the work or that would cause mechanical, visual, or audible defects or distortions.

(3) The terms "copy," "collective work," "device," "fixed," "literary work," "machine," "motion picture," "phonorecord," "publication," "sound recording," "transmission program," and "useful article," and their variant forms, have the meanings given to them in section 101 of title 17.

(4) A "secure test" is a non-marketed test administered under supervision at specified centers on specific dates, all copies of which are accounted for and either destroyed or returned to restricted locked storage following each administration. For these purposes a test is not marketed if copies are not sold but it is distributed and used in such a manner that ownership and control of copies remain with the test sponsor or publisher.

(5) "Title 17" means title 17 of the United States Code, as amended by Pub. L. 94-553.

(6) For the purposes of determining the applicable deposit requirements under this §202.20 only, the following shall be considered as unpublished motion pictures: motion pictures that consist of television transmission programs and that have been published, if at all, only by reason of a license or other grant to a nonprofit institution of the right to make a fixation of such programs directly from a transmission to the public, with or without the right to make further uses of such fixations.

**(c) Nature of required deposit.**

(1) Subject to the provisions of paragraph (c)(2) of this section, the deposit required to accompany an application for registration of claim to copyright under section 408 of title 17 shall consist of:

(i) In the case of unpublished works, one complete copy or phonorecord.

(ii) In the case of works first published in the United States before January 1, 1978, two complete copies or phonorecords of the work as first published.

(iii) In the case of works first published in the United States on or after January 1, 1978, two complete copies or phonorecords of the best edition.

(iv) In the case of works first published outside of the United States, whenever published, one complete copy or phonorecord of the work as first published. For the purposes of this section, any works simultaneously first published within and outside of the United States shall be considered to be first published in the United States.

(2) In the case of certain works, the special provisions set forth in this clause shall apply. In any case where this clause specifies that one copy or phonorecord may be submitted, that copy or phonorecord shall represent the best edition, or the work as first published, as set forth in paragraph (c)(1) of this section.

(i) *General.* In the following cases the deposit of one complete copy or phonorecord will suffice in lieu of two copies or phonorecords:

(A) Published three-dimensional cartographic representations of area, such as globes and relief models;

(B) published diagrams illustrating scientific or technical works or formulating scientific or technical information in linear or other two-dimensional form such as an architectural or engineering blueprint, or a mechanical drawing;

(C) published greeting cards, picture postcards, and stationery;

(D) lectures, sermons, speeches, and addresses published individually and not as a collection of the works of one or more authors;

(E) published contributions to a collective work;

(F) musical compositions published in copies only, or in both copies and phonorecords, if the only publication of copies took place by rental, lease, or lending;

(G) published multimedia kits that are prepared for use in systematic instructional activities and that include literary works, audiovisual works, sound recordings, or any combination of such works; and

(H) works exempted from the requirement of depositing identifying material under §202.20(c)(2)(ix)(B)(5) of these regulations.

(ii) *Motion pictures.* In the case of published motion pictures, the deposit of one complete copy will suffice in lieu of two copies. The deposit of a copy or copies for any published or unpublished motion picture must be accompanied by a separate description of its contents, such as a continuity, pressbook, or synopsis. The Library of Congress may, at its sole discretion, enter into an agreement permitting the return of copies of published motion pictures to the depositor under certain conditions and establishing certain rights and obligations of the Library of Congress with respect to such copies. In the event of termination of such an agreement by the Library, it shall not be subject to reinstatement, nor shall the depositor or any successor in interest of the depositor be entitled to any similar or subsequent agreement with the Library, unless at the sole discretion of the Library it would be in the best interests of the Library to reinstate the agreement or enter into a new agreement. In the case of unpublished motion pictures (including television transmission programs that have been fixed and transmitted to the public, but have not been published), the deposit of identifying material in compliance with §202.21 of these regulations may be made and will suffice in lieu of an actual copy.

(iii) *Holograms.* In the case of any work deposited in the form of a hologram, the copy or copies shall be accompanied by:

(A) Precise instructions for displaying the image fixed in the hologram; and

(B) photographs or other identifying material complying with §202.21 of these regulations and clearly showing the displayed image. The number of sets of instructions and identifying material shall be the same as the number of copies required.

(iv) *Certain pictorial and graphic works.* In any case of any unpublished pictorial or graphic work, deposit of identifying material in compliance with §202.21 of these regulations may be made and will suffice in lieu of deposit of an actual copy. In the case of a published pictorial or graphic work, deposit of one complete copy, or of identifying material in compliance with §202.21 of these regulations, may be made and will suffice in lieu of deposit of two actual copies where an individual author is the owner of copyright and either:

(A) Less than five copies of the work have been published, or

(B) the work has been published and sold or offered for sale in a limited edition consisting of no more than three hundred numbered copies.

(v) *Commercial prints and labels.* In the case of prints, labels, and other advertising matter published in connection with the rental, lease, lending, licensing, or sale of articles of merchandise, works of authorship, or services, the deposit of one complete copy will suffice in lieu of two copies. Where the print or label is published in a larger work, such as a newspaper or other periodical, one copy of the entire page or pages upon which it appears may be submitted in lieu of the entire larger work. In the case of prints or labels physically inseparable from a three-dimensional object, identifying material complying with §202.21 of these regulations must be submitted rather than an actual copy or copies except under the conditions of paragraph (c)(2)(ix)(B)(6) of this section.

(vi) *Tests.* In the case of tests, and answer material for tests, published separately from other literary works, the deposit of one complete copy will suffice in lieu of two copies. In the case of any secure test the Copyright Office will return the deposit to the applicant promptly after examination: *Provided,* that sufficient portions, description, or the like are retained so as to constitute a sufficient archival record of the deposit.

(vii) *Machine-readable works.* In cases where an unpublished literary work is fixed, or a published literary work is published in the United States, only in the form of machine-readable copies (such as magnetic tape or disks, punched cards, or the like) from which the work cannot ordinarily be perceived except with the aid of a machine or device,* the deposit shall consist of:

(A) For published or unpublished computer programs, one copy of identifying portions of the program, reproduced in a form visually perceptible without the aid of a machine or device, either on paper or in microform. For these purposes, "identifying portions" shall mean either the first and last twenty-five pages or equivalent units of the program if reproduced on paper, or at least the first and last twenty-five pages or equivalent units of the program if reproduced in microform, together with the page or equivalent unit containing the copyright notice, if any.

(B) For published and unpublished automated data bases, compilations, statistical compendia, and other literary works so fixed or published, one copy or identifying portions of the work, reproduced in a form visually perceptible without the aid of a machine or device, either on paper or in microform. For these purposes:

(1) "identifying portions" shall mean either the first and last twenty-five pages or equivalent units of the work if reproduced on paper, or at least the first and last twenty-five pages or equivalent units of work if reproduced on microform, or, in the case of automated data bases comprising separate and distinct data files, representative portions of each separate data file consisting of either 50 complete data records from each file or the entire file, whichever is less; and

(2) "data file" and "file" mean a group of data records pertaining to a common subject matter, regardless of the physical size of the records or the number of data items included in them. (In the case of revised versions of such data bases, the portions deposited must contain representative data records which have been added or modified.)

* A footnote in the regulations provides: "Works published in a form requiring the use of a machine or device for purposes of optical enlargement (such as film, filmstrips, slide films, and works published in any variety of microform), and works published in visually perceptible form but used in connection with optical scanning devices, are not within this category."

In any case where the deposit comprises representative portions of each separate file of an automated data base as indicated above, it shall be accompanied by a typed or printed descriptive statement containing: The title of the data base; the name and address of the copyright claimant; the name and content of each separate file within the data base, including the subject matter involved, the origin(s) of the data, and the approximate number of individual records within the file; and a description of the exact contents of any machine-readable copyright notice employed in or with the work and the manner and frequency with which it is displayed (e.g., at user's terminal only at sign-on, or continuously on terminal display, or on printouts, etc.). If a visually perceptible copyright notice is placed on any copies of the work (such as magnetic tape reels) or their container, a sample of such notice must also accompany the statement.

(viii) *Works reproduced in or on sheetlike materials.* In the case of any unpublished work that is fixed, or any published work that is published, only in the form of a two-dimensional reproduction on sheetlike materials such as textile and other fabrics, wallpaper and similar commercial wall coverings, carpeting, floor tile, and similar commercial floor coverings, and wrapping paper and similar packaging material, the deposit shall consist of one copy in the form of an actual swatch or piece of such material sufficient to show all elements of the work in which copyright is claimed and the copyright notice appearing on the work, if any. If the work consists of a repeated pictorial or graphic design, the complete design and at least part of one repetition must be shown. If the sheetlike material in or on which a published work has been reproduced has been embodied in or attached to a three-dimensional object, such as wearing apparel, furniture, or any other three-dimensional manufactured article, and the work has been published only in that form, the deposit must consist of identifying material complying with §202.21 of these regulations instead of a copy.

(ix) *Works reproduced in or on three-dimensional objects.*

(A) In the following cases the deposit must consist of identifying material complying with §202.21 of these regulations instead of a copy or copies:

(1) Any three-dimensional sculptural work, including any illustration or formulation of artistic expression or information in three-dimensional form. Examples of such works include statues, carvings, ceramics, moldings, constructions, models, and maquettes; and

(2) any two-dimensional or three-dimensional work that, if unpublished, has been fixed, or, if published, has been published only in or on jewelry, dolls, toys, games, or any three-dimensional useful article.

(B) In the following cases, the requirements of paragraph (A) of this §202.20(c)(2)(ix) for the deposit of identifying material shall not apply:

(1) Works that are reproduced by intaglio or relief printing methods on two-dimensional materials such as paper or fabrics;

(2) three-dimensional cartographic representations of area, such as globes and relief models;

(3) works that have been fixed or published in or on a useful article that comprises one of the elements of the unit of publication of an educational or instructional kit which also includes a literary or audiovisual work, a sound recording, or any combination of such works;

(4) published works exempt from the deposit of copies under section 407 of title

17 and §202.19(c) of these regulations, where the "complete" copy of the work within the meaning of paragraph (b)(2) of this section consists of a reproduction of the work on two-dimensional materials such as paper or fabrics;

(5) published works consisting of multiple parts that are packaged and published in a box or similar container with flat sides and with dimensions of no more than 12 × 24 × 6 inches, and that include among the copyrightable elements of the work, in addition to any copyrightable element on the box or other container, three or more three-dimensional, physically separable parts; and

(6) works reproduced on three-dimensional containers or holders such as boxes, cases, and cartons, where the container or holder can be readily opened out, unfolded, slit at the corners, or in some other way made adaptable for flat storage, and the copy, when flattened, does not exceed 96 inches in any dimension.

(x) Soundtracks. For separate registration of an unpublished work that is fixed, or a published work that is published, only as embodied in a soundtrack that is an integral part of a motion picture, the deposit of identifying material in compliance with §202.21 of these regulations will suffice in lieu of an actual copy or copies of the motion picture.

(xi) Oversize deposits. In any case where the deposit otherwise required by this section exceeds 96 inches in any dimension, identifying material complying with §202.21 of these regulations must be submitted instead of an actual copy or copies.

**(d) Special relief.**

(1) In any case the Register of Copyrights may, after consultation with other appropriate officials of the Library of Congress and upon such conditions as the Register may determine after such consultation:

(i) Permit the deposit of one copy or phonorecord, or alternative identifying material, in lieu of the one or two copies or phonorecords otherwise required by paragraph (c)(1) of this section;

(ii) permit the deposit of incomplete copies or phonorecords, or copies or phono-records other than those normally comprising the best edition; or

(iii) permit the deposit of an actual copy or copies, in lieu of the identifying material otherwise required by this section.

(2) Any decision as to whether to grant such relief, and the condition under which special relief is to be granted, shall be made by the Register of Copyrights after consultation with other appropriate officials of the Library of Congress, and shall be based upon the acquisition policies of the Library of Congress then in force and the archival and examining requirements of the Copyright Office.

(3) Requests for special relief under this paragraph may be combined with requests for special relief under §202.19(e) of the regulations. Whether so combined or made solely under this paragraph, such requests shall be made in writing to the Chief, Examining Division of the Copyright Office, shall be signed by or on behalf of the person signing the application for registration, and shall set forth specific reasons why the request should be granted.

(4) The Register of Copyrights may, after consultation with other appropriate officials of the Library of Congress, terminate any ongoing or continuous grant of special relief. Notice of termination shall be given in writing and shall be sent to the individual person or organization to whom the grant of special relief had been given, at the last address shown in the records of the Copyright Office. A notice of termination may be given at any time, but it shall state a specific date of termination

that is at least 30 days later than the date the notice is to be mailed. Termination shall not affect the validity of any deposit or registration earlier made under the grant of special relief.

(e) *Use of copies and phonorecords deposited for the Library of Congress.* Copies and phonorecords deposited for the Library of Congress under section 407 of title 17 and §202.19 of these regulations may be used to satisfy the deposit provisions of this section if they are accompanied by an application for registration of claim to copyright in the work represented by the deposit, or connected with such an application under the conditions set forth in §202.19(f)(1) of these regulations.

# Appendix 3
## APPLICATION FORMS FOR REGISTRATION
## OF COPYRIGHTS

# Filling Out Application Form TX

*Detach and read these instructions before completing this form. Make sure all applicable spaces have been filled in before you return this form.*

## BASIC INFORMATION

**When to Use This Form:** Use Form TX for registration of published or unpublished non-dramatic literary works, excluding periodicals or serial issues. This class includes a wide variety of works: fiction, non-fiction, poetry, textbooks, reference works, directories, catalogs, advertising copy, compilations of information, and computer programs. For periodicals and serials, use Form SE.

**Deposit to Accompany Application:** An application for copyright registration must be accompanied by a deposit consisting of copies or phonorecords representing the entire work for which registration is to be made. The following are the general deposit requirements as set forth in the statute:

**Unpublished Work:** Deposit one complete copy (or phonorecord).

**Published Work:** Deposit two complete copies (or phonorecords) of the best edition.

**Work First Published Outside the United States:** Deposit one complete copy (or phonorecord) of the first foreign edition.

**Contribution to a Collective Work:** Deposit one complete copy (or phonorecord) of the best edition of the collective work.

**The Copyright Notice:** For published works the law provides that a copyright notice in a specified form "shall be placed on all publicly distributed copies from which the work can be visually perceived." Use of the copyright notice is the responsibility of the copyright owner and does not require advance permission from the Copyright Office. The required form of the notice for copies generally consists of three elements: (1) the symbol "©", or the word "Copyright," or the abbreviation "Copr."; (2) the year of first publication; and (3) the name of the owner of copyright. For example: "© 1981 Constance Porter." The notice is to be affixed to the copies "in such manner and location as to give reasonable notice of the claim of copyright."

For further information about copyright registration, notice, or special questions relating to copyright problems, write:

Information and Publications Section, LM-455
Copyright Office
Library of Congress
Washington, D.C. 20559

## LINE-BY-LINE INSTRUCTIONS

### 1 SPACE 1: Title

**Title of This Work:** Every work submitted for copyright registration must be given a title to identify that particular work. If the copies or phonorecords of the work bear a title (or an identifying phrase that could serve as a title), transcribe that wording *completely* and *exactly* on the application. Indexing of the registration and future identification of the work will depend on the information you give here.

**Previous or Alternative Titles:** Complete this space if there are any additional titles for the work under which someone searching for the registration might be likely to look, or under which a document pertaining to the work might be recorded.

**Publication as a Contribution:** If the work being registered is a contribution to a periodical, serial, or collection, give the title of the contribution in the "Title of this Work" space. Then, in the line headed "Publication as a Contribution," give information about the collective work in which the contribution appeared.

### 2 SPACE 2: Author(s)

**General Instructions:** After reading these instructions, decide who are the "authors" of this work for copyright purposes. Then, unless the work is a "collective work," give the requested information about every "author" who contributed any appreciable amount of copyrightable matter to this version of the work. If you need further space, request additional Continuation sheets. In the case of a collective work, such as an anthology, collection of essays, or encyclopedia, give information about the author of the collective work as a whole.

**Name of Author:** The fullest form of the author's name should be given. Unless the work was "made for hire," the individual who actually created the work is its "author." In the case of a work made for hire, the statute provides that "the employer or other person for whom the work was prepared is considered the author."

**What is a "Work Made for Hire"?** A "work made for hire" is defined as: (1) "a work prepared by an employee within the scope of his or her employment"; or (2) "a work specially ordered or commissioned for use as a contribution to a collective work, as a part of a motion picture or other audiovisual work, as a translation, as a supplementary work, as a compilation, as an instructional text, as a test, as answer material for a test, or as an atlas, if the parties expressly agree in a written instrument signed by them that the work shall be considered a work made for hire." If you have checked "Yes" to indicate that the work was "made for hire," you must give the full legal name of the employer (or other person for whom the work was prepared). You may also include the name of the employee along with the name of the employer (for example: "Elster Publishing Co., employer for hire of John Ferguson").

**"Anonymous" or "Pseudonymous" Work:** An author's contribution to a work is "anonymous" if that author is not identified on the copies or phonorecords of the work. An author's contribution to a work is "pseudonymous" if that author is identified on the copies or phonorecords under a fictitious name. If the work is "anonymous" you may: (1) leave the line blank; or (2) state "anonymous" on the line; or (3) reveal the author's identity. If the work is "pseudonymous" you may: (1) leave the line blank; or (2) give the pseudonym and identify it as such (for example: "Huntley Haverstock, pseudonym"); or (3) reveal the author's name, making clear which is the real name and which is the pseudonym (for example: "Judith Barton, whose pseudonym is Madeline Elster"). However, the citizenship or domicile of the author **must** be given in all cases.

**Dates of Birth and Death:** If the author is dead, the statute requires that the year of death be included in the application unless the work is anonymous or pseudonymous. The author's birth date is optional, but is useful as a form of identification. Leave this space blank if the author's contribution was a "work made for hire."

**Author's Nationality or Domicile:** Give the country of which the author is a citizen, or the country in which the author is domiciled. Nationality or domicile **must** be given in all cases.

**Nature of Authorship:** After the words "Nature of Authorship" give a brief general statement of the nature of this particular author's contribution to the work. Examples: "Entire text"; "Coauthor of entire text"; "Chapters 11-14"; "Editorial revisions"; "Compilation and English translation"; "New text."

## 3 SPACE 3: Creation and Publication

**General Instructions:** Do not confuse "creation" with "publication." Every application for copyright registration must state "the year in which creation of the work was completed." Give the date and nation of first publication only if the work has been published.

**Creation:** Under the statute, a work is "created" when it is fixed in a copy or phonorecord for the first time. Where a work has been prepared over a period of time, the part of the work existing in fixed form on a particular date constitutes the created work on that date. The date you give here should be the year in which the author completed the particular version for which registration is now being sought, even if other versions exist or if further changes or additions are planned.

**Publication:** The statute defines "publication" as "the distribution of copies or phonorecords of a work to the public by sale or other transfer of ownership, or by rental, lease, or lending"; a work is also "published" if there has been an "offering to distribute copies or phonorecords to a group of persons for purposes of further distribution, public performance, or public display." Give the full date (month, day, year) when, and the country where, publication first occurred. If first publication took place simultaneously in the United States and other countries, it is sufficient to state "U.S.A."

## 4 SPACE 4: Claimant(s)

**Name(s) and Address(es) of Copyright Claimant(s):** Give the name(s) and address(es) of the copyright claimant(s) in this work even if the claimant is the same as the author. Copyright in a work belongs initially to the author of the work (including, in the case of a work made for hire, the employer or other person for whom the work was prepared). The copyright claimant is either the author of the work or a person or organization to whom the copyright initially belonging to the author has been transferred.

**Transfer:** The statute provides that, if the copyright claimant is not the author, the application for registration must contain "a brief statement of how the claimant obtained ownership of the copyright." If any copyright claimant named in space 4 is not an author named in space 2, give a brief, general statement summarizing the means by which that claimant obtained ownership of the copyright. Examples: "By written contract"; "Transfer of all rights by author"; "Assignment"; "By will." Do not attach transfer documents or other attachments or riders.

## 5 SPACE 5: Previous Registration

**General Instructions:** The questions in space 5 are intended to find out whether an earlier registration has been made for this work and, if so, whether there is any basis for a new registration. As a general rule, only one basic copyright registration can be made for the same version of a particular work.

**Same Version:** If this version is substantially the same as the work covered by a previous registration, a second registration is not generally possible unless: (1) the work has been registered in unpublished form and a second registration is now being sought to cover this first published edition; or (2) someone other than the author is identified as copyright claimant in the earlier registration, and the author is now seeking registration in his or her own name. If either of these two exceptions apply, check the appropriate box and give the earlier registration number and date. Otherwise, do not submit Form TX; instead, write the Copyright Office for information about supplementary registration or recordation of transfers of copyright ownership.

**Changed Version:** If the work has been changed, and you are now seeking registration to cover the additions or revisions, check the last box in space 5, give the earlier registration number and date, and complete both parts of space 6 in accordance with the instructions below.

**Previous Registration Number and Date:** If more than one previous registration has been made for the work, give the number and date of the latest registration.

## 6 SPACE 6: Derivative Work or Compilation

**General Instructions:** Complete space 6 if this work is a "changed version," "compilation," or "derivative work," and if it incorporates one or more earlier works that have already been published or registered for copyright, or that have fallen into the public domain. A "compilation" is defined as "a work formed by the collection and assembling of preexisting materials or of data that are selected, coordinated, or arranged in such a way that the resulting work as a whole constitutes an original work of authorship." A "derivative work" is "a work based on one or more preexisting works." Examples of derivative works include translations, fictionalizations, abridgments, condensations, or "any other form in which a work may be recast, transformed, or adapted." Derivative works also include works "consisting of editorial revisions, annotations, or other modifications" if these changes, as a whole, represent an original work of authorship.

**Preexisting Material (space 6a):** For derivative works, complete this space and space 6b. In space 6a identify the preexisting work that has been recast, transformed, or adapted. An example of preexisting material might be: "Russian version of Goncharov's 'Oblomov'." Do not complete space 6a for compilations.

**Material Added to This Work (space 6b):** Give a brief, general statement of the new material covered by the copyright claim for which registration is sought. **Derivative work** examples include: "Foreword, editing, critical annotations"; "Translation"; "Chapters 11-17." If the work is a **compilation**, describe both the compilation itself and the material that has been compiled. Example: "Compilation of certain 1917 Speeches by Woodrow Wilson." A work may be both a derivative work and compilation, in which case a sample statement might be: "Compilation and additional new material."

## 7 SPACE 7: Manufacturing Provisions

**General Instructions:** The copyright statute currently provides, as a general rule, that the copies of a published work "consisting preponderantly of nondramatic literary material in the English language" be manufactured in the United States or Canada in order to be lawfully imported and publicly distributed in the United States. If the work being registered is unpublished or not in English, leave this space blank. Complete this space if registration is sought for a published work "consisting preponderantly of nondramatic literary material that is in the English language." Identify those who manufactured the copies and where those manufacturing processes were performed. As an exception to the manufacturing provisions, the statute prescribes that, where manufacture has taken place outside the United States or Canada, a maximum of 2000 copies of the foreign edition may be imported into the United States without affecting the copyright owners' rights. For this purpose, the Copyright Office will issue an Import Statement upon request and payment of a fee of $3 at the time of registration or at any later time. For further information about import statements, write for Form IS.

## 8 SPACE 8: Reproduction for Use of Blind or Physically Handicapped Individuals

**General Instructions:** One of the major programs of the Library of Congress is to provide Braille editions and special recordings of works for the exclusive use of the blind and physically handicapped. In an effort to simplify and speed up the copyright licensing procedures that are a necessary part of this program, section 710 of the copyright statute provides for the establishment of a voluntary licensing system to be tied in with copyright registration. Copyright Office regulations provide that you may grant a license for such reproduction and distribution solely for the use of persons who are certified by competent authority as unable to read normal printed material as a result of physical limitations. The license is entirely voluntary, nonexclusive, and may be terminated upon 90 days notice.

**How to Grant the License:** If you wish to grant it, check one of the three boxes in space 8. Your check in one of these boxes, together with your signature in space 10, will mean that the Library of Congress can proceed to reproduce and distribute under the license without further paperwork. For further information, write for Circular R63.

## 9,10,11 SPACE 9, 10, 11: Fee, Correspondence, Certification, Return Address

**Deposit Account:** If you maintain a Deposit Account in the Copyright Office, identify it in space 9. Otherwise leave the space blank and send the fee of $10 with your application and deposit.

**Correspondence** (space 9): This space should contain the name, address, area code, and telephone number of the person to be consulted if correspondence about this application becomes necessary.

**Certification** (space 10): The application can not be accepted unless it bears the date and the **handwritten signature** of the author or other copyright claimant, or of the owner of exclusive right(s), or of the duly authorized agent of author, claimant, or owner of exclusive right(s).

**Address for Return of Certificate** (space 11): The address box must be completed legibly since the certificate will be returned in a window envelope.

# FORM TX

UNITED STATES COPYRIGHT OFFICE

REGISTRATION NUMBER

TX        TXU

EFFECTIVE DATE OF REGISTRATION

Month     Day     Year

---

**DO NOT WRITE ABOVE THIS LINE. IF YOU NEED MORE SPACE, USE A SEPARATE CONTINUATION SHEET.**

**1**

**TITLE OF THIS WORK ▼**

**PREVIOUS OR ALTERNATIVE TITLES ▼**

**PUBLICATION AS A CONTRIBUTION** If this work was published as a contribution to a periodical, serial, or collection, give information about the collective work in which the contribution appeared. **Title of Collective Work ▼**

If published in a periodical or serial give: **Volume ▼**     **Number ▼**     **Issue Date ▼**     **On Pages ▼**

**2**

**a**

**NAME OF AUTHOR ▼**

**DATES OF BIRTH AND DEATH**
Year Born ▼     Year Died ▼

Was this contribution to the work a "work made for hire"?
☐ Yes
☐ No

**AUTHOR'S NATIONALITY OR DOMICILE**
Name of Country
OR { Citizen of ▶
Domiciled in ▶

**WAS THIS AUTHOR'S CONTRIBUTION TO THE WORK**
Anonymous? ☐ Yes ☐ No
Pseudonymous? ☐ Yes ☐ No
If the answer to either of these questions is "Yes," see detailed instructions.

**NATURE OF AUTHORSHIP** Briefly describe nature of the material created by this author in which copyright is claimed. ▼

**NOTE**

Under the law, the "author" of a "work made for hire" is generally the employer, not the employee (see instructions). For any part of this work that was "made for hire" check "Yes" in the space provided, give the employer (or other person for whom the work was prepared) as "Author" of that part, and leave the space for dates of birth and death blank.

**b**

**NAME OF AUTHOR ▼**

**DATES OF BIRTH AND DEATH**
Year Born ▼     Year Died ▼

Was this contribution to the work a "work made for hire"?
☐ Yes
☐ No

**AUTHOR'S NATIONALITY OR DOMICILE**
Name of Country
OR { Citizen of ▶
Domiciled in ▶

**WAS THIS AUTHOR'S CONTRIBUTION TO THE WORK**
Anonymous? ☐ Yes ☐ No
Pseudonymous? ☐ Yes ☐ No
If the answer to either of these questions is "Yes," see detailed instructions.

**NATURE OF AUTHORSHIP** Briefly describe nature of the material created by this author in which copyright is claimed. ▼

**c**

**NAME OF AUTHOR ▼**

**DATES OF BIRTH AND DEATH**
Year Born ▼     Year Died ▼

Was this contribution to the work a "work made for hire"?
☐ Yes
☐ No

**AUTHOR'S NATIONALITY OR DOMICILE**
Name of Country
OR { Citizen of ▶
Domiciled in ▶

**WAS THIS AUTHOR'S CONTRIBUTION TO THE WORK**
Anonymous? ☐ Yes ☐ No
Pseudonymous? ☐ Yes ☐ No
If the answer to either of these questions is "Yes," see detailed instructions.

**NATURE OF AUTHORSHIP** Briefly describe nature of the material created by this author in which copyright is claimed. ▼

**3**

**YEAR IN WHICH CREATION OF THIS WORK WAS COMPLETED** This information must be given in all cases. ◀ Year

**DATE AND NATION OF FIRST PUBLICATION OF THIS PARTICULAR WORK**
Complete this information ONLY if this work has been published. Month ▶ _____ Day ▶ _____ Year ▶ _____ ◀ Nation

**4**

**COPYRIGHT CLAIMANT(S)** Name and address must be given even if the claimant is the same as the author given in space 2.▼

**TRANSFER** If the claimant(s) named here in space 4 are different from the author(s) named in space 2, give a brief statement of how the claimant(s) obtained ownership of the copyright.▼

APPLICATION RECEIVED

ONE DEPOSIT RECEIVED

TWO DEPOSITS RECEIVED

REMITTANCE NUMBER AND DATE

DO NOT WRITE HERE OFFICE USE ONLY

---

**MORE ON BACK ▶**
• Complete all applicable spaces (numbers 5-11) on the reverse side of this page.
• See detailed instructions.
• Sign the form at line 10.

DO NOT WRITE HERE

Page 1 of_____pages

See instructions before completing this space.

**DO NOT WRITE ABOVE THIS LINE. IF YOU NEED MORE SPACE, USE A SEPARATE CONTINUATION SHEET.**

**PREVIOUS REGISTRATION** Has registration for this work, or for an earlier version of this work, already been made in the Copyright Office?

☐ Yes ☐ No If your answer is "Yes," why is another registration being sought? (Check appropriate box) ▼

☐ This is the first published edition of a work previously registered in unpublished form.

☐ This is the first application submitted by this author as copyright claimant.

☐ This is a changed version of the work, as shown by space 6 on this application.

If your answer is "Yes," give: **Previous Registration Number** ▼          **Year of Registration** ▼

**5**

**DERIVATIVE WORK OR COMPILATION** Complete both space 6a & 6b for a derivative work; complete only 6b for a compilation.

**a. Preexisting Material** Identify any preexisting work or works that this work is based on or incorporates. ▼

**b. Material Added to This Work** Give a brief, general statement of the material that has been added to this work and in which copyright is claimed. ▼

**6**

See instructions before completing this space.

**MANUFACTURERS AND LOCATIONS** If this is a published work consisting preponderantly of nondramatic literary material in English, the law may require that the copies be manufactured in the United States or Canada for full protection. If so, the names of the manufacturers who performed certain processes, and the places where these processes were performed **must** be given. See instructions for details.

**Names of Manufacturers** ▼          **Places of Manufacture** ▼

**7**

**REPRODUCTION FOR USE OF BLIND OR PHYSICALLY HANDICAPPED INDIVIDUALS** A signature on this form at space 10, and a check in one of the boxes here in space 8, constitutes a non-exclusive grant of permission to the Library of Congress to reproduce and distribute solely for the blind and physically handicapped and under the conditions and limitations prescribed by the regulations of the Copyright Office: (1) copies of the work identified in space 1 of this application in Braille (or similar tactile symbols); or (2) phonorecords embodying a fixation of a reading of that work; or (3) both.

a ☐ Copies and Phonorecords          b ☐ Copies Only          c ☐ Phonorecords Only

**8**

See instructions.

**DEPOSIT ACCOUNT** If the registration fee is to be charged to a Deposit Account established in the Copyright Office, give name and number of Account.

**Name** ▼          **Account Number** ▼

**CORRESPONDENCE** Give name and address to which correspondence about this application should be sent. Name/Address/Apt/City/State/Zip ▼

**9**

Be sure to give your daytime phone ◀ number.

Area Code & Telephone Number ▶

**CERTIFICATION\*** I, the undersigned, hereby certify that I am the

Check one ▶

☐ author
☐ other copyright claimant
☐ owner of exclusive right(s)
☐ authorized agent of _____

of the work identified in this application and that the statements made by me in this application are correct to the best of my knowledge.

Name of author or other copyright claimant, or owner of exclusive right(s) ▲

**Typed or printed name and date** ▼ If this is a published work, this date must be the same as or later than the date of publication given in space 3.

_____ date ▶ _____

☞ Handwritten signature (X) ▼

**10**

**MAIL CERTIFI-CATE TO**

Name ▼

Number/Street/Apartment Number ▼

**Certificate will be mailed in window envelope**

City/State/ZIP ▼

**Have you:**
• Completed all necessary spaces?
• Signed your application in space 10?
• Enclosed check or money order for $10 payable to *Register of Copyrights*?
• Enclosed your deposit material with the application and fee?

**MAIL TO:** Register of Copyrights, Library of Congress, Washington, D.C. 20559

**11**

☆ U.S. GOVERNMENT PRINTING OFFICE: 1981: 355-304                    Nov. 1981-400,000

# Filling Out Application Form SE

*Detach and read these instructions before completing this form. Make sure all applicable spaces have been filled in before you return this form.*

## BASIC INFORMATION

**When To Use This Form:** Use a separate Form SE for registration of each individual issue of a serial, Class SE. A serial is defined as a work issued or intended to be issued in successive parts bearing numerical or chronological designations and intended to be continued indefinitely. This class includes a variety of works: periodicals; newspapers; annuals; the journals, proceedings, transactions, etc., of societies. Do not use Form SE to register an individual contribution to a serial. Request Form TX for such contributions.

**Deposit to Accompany Application:** An application for copyright registration must be accompanied by a deposit consisting of copies or phonorecords representing the entire work for which registration is to be made. The following are the general deposit requirements as set forth in the statute:

**Unpublished Work:** Deposit one complete copy (or phonorecord).

**Published Work:** Deposit two complete copies (or phonorecords) of the best edition.

**Work First Published Outside the United States:** Deposit one complete copy (or phonorecord) of the first foreign edition.

**Mailing Requirements:** It is important that you send the application, the deposit copy or copies, and the $10 fee together in the same envelope or package. The Copyright Office cannot process them unless they are received together. Send to: *Register of Copyrights, Library of Congress, Washington, D.C. 20559.*

**The Copyright Notice:** For published works, the law provides that a copyright notice in a specified form "shall be placed on all publicly distributed copies from which the work can be visually perceived." Use of the copyright notice is the responsibility of the copyright owner and does not require advance permission from the Copyright Office. The required form of the notice for copies generally consists of three elements: (1) the symbol "©"; or the word "Copyright"; or the abbreviation "Copr."; (2) the year of first publication; and (3) the name of the owner of copyright. For example: "© 1981 National News Publishers, Inc." The notice is to be affixed to the copies "in such manner and location as to give reasonable notice of the claim of copyright." For further information about copyright registration, notice, or special questions relating to copyright problems, write:

> Information and Publications Section, LM-455
> Copyright Office, Library of Congress, Washington, D.C. 20559

## LINE-BY-LINE INSTRUCTIONS

### 1 SPACE 1: Title

**Title of This Serial:** Every work submitted for copyright registration must be given a title to identify that particular work. If the copies or phonorecords of the work bear a title (or an identifying phrase that could serve as a title), copy that wording *completely* and *exactly* on the application. Give the volume and number of the periodical issue for which you are seeking registration. The "Date on copies" in space 1 should be the date appearing on the actual copies (for example: "June 1981," "Winter 1981"). Indexing of the registration and future identification of the work will depend on the information you give here.

**Previous or Alternative Titles:** Complete this space only if there are any additional titles for the serial under which someone searching for the registration might be likely to look, or under which a document pertaining to the work might be recorded.

### 2 SPACE 2: Author(s)

**General Instructions:** After reading these instructions, decide who are the "authors" of this work for copyright purposes. In the case of a serial issue, the organization which directs the creation of the serial issue as a whole is generally considered the author of the "collective work" (see "Nature of Authorship") whether it employs a staff or uses the efforts of volunteers. Where, however, an individual is independently responsible for the serial issue, name that person as author of the "collective work."

**Name of Author:** The fullest form of the author's name should be given. In the case of a "work made for hire," the statute provides that "the employer or other person for whom the work was prepared is considered the author." If this issue is a "work made for hire," the author's name will be the full legal name of the hiring organization, corporation, or individual. The title of the periodical should not ordinarily be listed as "author" because the title itself does not usually correspond to a legal entity capable of authorship. When an individual creates an issue of a serial independently and not as an "employee" of an organization or corporation, that individual should be listed as the "author."

**Author's Nationality or Domicile:** Give the country of which the author is a citizen, or the country in which the author is domiciled. Nationality or domicile **must** be given in all cases. The citizenship of an organization formed under United States Federal or state law should be stated as "U.S.A."

**What is a "Work Made for Hire"?** A "work made for hire" is defined as: (1) "a work prepared by an employee within the scope of his or her employment"; or (2) "a work specially ordered or commissioned for use as a contribution to a collective work, as a part of a motion picture or other audiovisual work, as a translation, as a supplementary work, as a compilation, as an instructional text, as a test, as answer material for a test, or as an atlas, if the parties expressly agree in a written instrument signed by them that the work shall be considered a work made for hire." An organization that uses the efforts of volunteers in the creation of a "collective work" (see "Nature of Authorship") may also be considered the author of a "work made for hire" even though those volunteers were not specifically paid by the organization. In the case of a "work made for hire," give the full legal name of the employer and check "Yes" to indicate that the work was made for hire. You may also include the name of the employee along with the name of the employer (for example: "Elster Publishing Co., employer for hire of John Ferguson").

**"Anonymous" or "Pseudonymous" Work:** Leave this space **blank** if the serial is a "work made for hire." An author's contribution to a work is "anonymous" if that author is not identified on the copies or phonorecords of the work. An author's contribution to a work is "pseudonymous" if that author is identified on the copies or phonorecords under a fictitious name. If the work is "anonymous" you may: (1) leave the line blank; or (2) state "anonymous" on the line; or (3) reveal the author's identity. If the work is "pseudonymous" you may: (1) leave the line blank; or (2) give the pseudonym and identify it as such (for example: "Huntley Haverstock, pseudonym"); or (3) reveal the author's name, making clear which is the real name and which is the pseudonym (for example: "Judith Barton, whose pseudonym is Madeline Elster"). However, the citizenship or domicile of the author **must** be given in all cases.

**Dates of Birth and Death:** Leave this space blank if the author's contribution was a "work made for hire." If the author is dead, the statute requires that the year of death be included in the application unless the work is anonymous or pseudonymous. The author's birth date is optional, but is useful as a form of identification.

**Nature of Authorship:** Give a brief statement of the nature of the particular author's contribution to the work. If an organization directed, controlled, and supervised the creation of the serial issue as a whole, check the box "collective work." The term "collective work" means that the author is responsible for compilation and editorial revision, and may also be responsible for certain individual contributions to the serial issue. Further examples of "Authorship" which may apply both to organizational and to individual authors are "Entire text"; "Entire text and/or illustrations"; "Editorial revision, compilation, plus additional new material."

# 3 SPACE 3: Creation and Publication

**General Instructions:** Do not confuse "creation" with "publication." Every application for copyright registration must state "the year in which creation of the work was completed." Give the date and nation of first publication only if the work has been published.

**Creation:** Under the statute, a work is "created" when it is fixed in a copy or phonorecord for the first time. Where a work has been prepared over a period of time, the part of the work existing in fixed form on a particular date constitutes the created work on that date. The date you give here should be the year in which this particular issue first was completed.

**Publication:** The statute defines "publication" as "the distribution of copies or phonorecords of a work to the public by sale or other transfer of ownership, or by rental, lease, or lending"; a work is also "published" if there has been an "offering to distribute copies or phonorecords to a group of persons for purposes of further distribution, public performance, or public display." Give the full date (month, day, year) when, and the country where, publication of this particular issue first occurred. If first publication took place simultaneously in the United States and other countries, it is sufficient to state "U.S.A."

# 4 SPACE 4: Claimant(s)

**Name(s) and Address(es) of Copyright Claimant(s):** This space must be completed. Give the name(s) and address(es) of the copyright claimant(s) of this work even if the claimant is the same as the author named in space 2. Copyright in a work belongs initially to the author of the work (including, in the case of a work made for hire, the employer or other person for whom the work was prepared). The copyright claimant is either the author of the work or a person or organization to whom the copyright initially belonging to the author has been transferred.

**Transfer:** The statute provides that, if the copyright claimant is not the author, the application for registration must contain "a brief statement of how the claimant obtained ownership of the copyright." A transfer of copyright ownership (other than one brought about by operation of law) must be in writing. If any copyright claimant named in space 4 is not an author named in space 2, give a brief, general statement describing the means by which that claimant obtained ownership of the copyright from the original author. Examples: "By written contract"; "Written transfer of all rights by author"; "Assignment"; "Inherited by will." Do not attach the actual document of transfer or other attachments or riders.

# 5 SPACE 5: Previous Registration

**General Instructions:** This space applies only rarely to serials. Complete space 5 if this particular issue has been registered earlier or if it contains a substantial amount of material that has been previously registered. Do not complete this space if the previous registrations are simply those made for earlier issues.

**Previous Registration:**
**a. Check this box** if this issue has been registered in unpublished form and a second registration is now sought to cover the first published edition.

**b. Check this box** if someone other than the author is identified as copyright claimant in the earlier registration and the author is now seeking registration in his or her own name. If the work in question is a contribution to a collective work, as opposed to the issue as a whole, file Form TX, not Form SE.

**c. Check this box** (and complete space 6) if this particular issue, or a substantial portion of the material in it, has been previously registered and you are now seeking registration for the additions and revisions which appear in this issue for the first time.

**Previous Registration Number and Date:** Complete this line if you checked one of the boxes above. If more than one previous registration has been made for the issue or for material in it, give only the number and year date for the latest registration.

# 6 SPACE 6: Derivative Work or Compilation

**General Instructions:** Complete space 6 if this issue is a "changed version," "compilation," or "derivative work," which incorporates one or more earlier works that have already been published or registered for copyright, or that have fallen into the public domain. Do not complete space 6 for an issue consisting of entirely new material appearing for the first time, such as a new issue of a continuing serial. A "compilation" is defined as "a work formed by the collection and assembling of preexisting materials or of data that are se-

lected, coordinated, or arranged in such a way that the resulting work as a whole constitutes an original work of authorship." A "derivative work" is "a work based on one or more preexisting works." Examples of derivative works include translations, fictionalizations, abridgments, condensations, or "any other form in which a work may be recast, transformed, or adapted." Derivative works also include works "consisting of editorial revisions, annotations, or other modifications" if these changes, as a whole, represent an original work of authorship.

**Preexisting Material (space 6a):** For derivative works, complete this space and space 6b. In space 6a identify the preexisting work that has been recast, transformed, adapted, or updated. Example: "1978 Morgan Co. Sales Catalog." Do not complete space 6a for compilations.

**Material Added to This Work (space 6b):** Give a brief, general statement of the new material covered by the copyright claim for which registration is sought. **Derivative work** examples include: "Editorial revisions and additions to the Catalog"; "Translation"; "Additional material." If a periodical issue is a **compilation**, describe both the compilation itself and the material that has been compiled. Examples: "Compilation of previously published journal articles"; "Compilation of previously published data." An issue may be both a derivative work and a compilation, in which case a sample statement might be: "Compilation of [describe] and additional new material."

# 7 SPACE 7: Manufacturing Provisions

**General Instructions:** The copyright statute currently provides, as a general rule, that the copies of a published work "consisting preponderantly of nondramatic literary material in the English language" be manufactured in the United States or Canada in order to be lawfully imported and publicly distributed in the United States. If the work being registered is unpublished or not in English, leave this space blank. Complete this space if registration is sought for a published work "consisting preponderantly of nondramatic literary material that is in the English language." Identify those who manufactured the copies and where those manufacturing processes were performed. As an exception to the manufacturing provisions, the statute prescribes that, where manufacture has taken place outside the United States or Canada, a maximum of 2000 copies of the foreign edition may be imported into the United States without affecting the copyright owners' rights. For this purpose, the Copyright Office will issue an Import Statement upon request and payment of a fee of $3 at the time of registration or at any later time. For further information about import statements, write for Form IS.

# 8 SPACE 8: Reproduction for Use of Blind or Physically Handicapped Individuals

**General Instructions:** One of the major programs of the Library of Congress is to provide Braille editions and special recordings of works for the exclusive use of the blind and physically handicapped. In an effort to simplify and speed up the copyright licensing procedures that are a necessary part of this program, section 710 of the copyright statute provides for the establishment of a voluntary licensing system to be tied in with copyright registration. Copyright Office regulations provide that you may grant a license for such reproduction and distribution solely for the use of persons who are certified by competent authority as unable to read normal printed material as a result of physical limitations. The license is entirely voluntary, nonexclusive, and may be terminated upon 90 days notice.

**How to Grant the License:** If you wish to grant it, check one of the three boxes in space 8. Your check in one of these boxes, together with your signature in space 10, will mean that the Library of Congress can proceed to reproduce and distribute under the license without further paperwork. For further information, write for Circular R63.

# 9,10,11 SPACE 9, 10, 11: Fee, Correspondence, Certification, Return Address

**Deposit Account:** If you maintain a Deposit Account in the Copyright Office, identify it in space 9. Otherwise leave the space blank and send the fee of $10 with your application and deposit.

**Correspondence (space 9):** This space should contain the name, address, area code, and telephone number of the person to be consulted if correspondence about this application becomes necessary.

**Certification (space 10):** The application cannot be accepted unless it bears the date and the **handwritten signature** of the author or other copyright claimant, or of the owner of exclusive right(s), or of the duly authorized agent of the author, claimant, or owner of exclusive right(s).

**Address for Return of Certificate (space 11):** The address box must be completed legibly since the certificate will be returned in a window envelope.

# FORM SE
UNITED STATES COPYRIGHT OFFICE

REGISTRATION NUMBER

_____

_____ U

EFFECTIVE DATE OF REGISTRATION

_____

Month          Day          Year

**DO NOT WRITE ABOVE THIS LINE. IF YOU NEED MORE SPACE, USE A SEPARATE CONTINUATION SHEET.**

## 1

**TITLE OF THIS SERIAL ▼**

Volume ▼          Number ▼          Date on Copies ▼          Frequency of Publication ▼

**PREVIOUS OR ALTERNATIVE TITLES ▼**

## 2

**a**

**NAME OF AUTHOR ▼**

**DATES OF BIRTH AND DEATH**
Year Born ▼          Year Died ▼

Was this contribution to the work a "work made for hire"?
☐ Yes
☐ No

**AUTHOR'S NATIONALITY OR DOMICILE**
Name of Country
OR { Citizen of ▶ _____
Domiciled in ▶ _____

**WAS THIS AUTHOR'S CONTRIBUTION TO THE WORK**
Anonymous?   ☐ Yes ☐ No
Pseudonymous?   ☐ Yes ☐ No

If the answer to either of these questions is "Yes," see detailed instructions.

**NATURE OF AUTHORSHIP**   Briefly describe nature of the material created by this author in which copyright is claimed. ▼
☐ Collective Work     Other: _____

### NOTE
Under the law, the "author" of a "work made for hire" is generally the employer, not the employee (see instructions). For any part of this work that was "made for hire" check "Yes" in the space provided, give the employer (or other person for whom the work was prepared) as "Author" of that part, and leave the space for dates of birth and death blank.

**b**

**NAME OF AUTHOR ▼**

**DATES OF BIRTH AND DEATH**
Year Born ▼          Year Died ▼

Was this contribution to the work a "work made for hire"?
☐ Yes
☐ No

**AUTHOR'S NATIONALITY OR DOMICILE**
Name of country
OR { Citizen of ▶ _____
Domiciled in ▶ _____

**WAS THIS AUTHOR'S CONTRIBUTION TO THE WORK**
Anonymous?   ☐ Yes ☐ No
Pseudonymous?   ☐ Yes ☐ No

If the answer to either of these questions is "Yes," see detailed instructions.

**NATURE OF AUTHORSHIP**   Briefly describe nature of the material created by this author in which copyright is claimed. ▼
☐ Collective Work     Other: _____

**c**

**NAME OF AUTHOR ▼**

**DATES OF BIRTH AND DEATH**
Year Born ▼          Year Died ▼

Was this contribution to the work a "work made for hire"?
☐ Yes
☐ No

**AUTHOR'S NATIONALITY OR DOMICILE**
Name of Country
OR { Citizen of ▶ _____
Domiciled in ▶ _____

**WAS THIS AUTHOR'S CONTRIBUTION TO THE WORK**
Anonymous?   ☐ Yes ☐ No
Pseudonymous?   ☐ Yes ☐ No

If the answer to either of these questions is "Yes," see detailed instructions.

**NATURE OF AUTHORSHIP**   Briefly describe nature of the material created by this author in which copyright is claimed. ▼
☐ Collective Work     Other: _____

## 3

**YEAR IN WHICH CREATION OF THIS ISSUE WAS COMPLETED**   This information must be given in all cases.
◀ Year

**DATE AND NATION OF FIRST PUBLICATION OF THIS PARTICULAR ISSUE**
Complete this information Month ▶ _____ Day ▶ _____ Year ▶ _____
ONLY if this work has been published.
◀ Nation

## 4

**COPYRIGHT CLAIMANT(S)** Name and address must be given even if the claimant is the same as the author given in space 2.▼

See instructions before completing this space.

**TRANSFER** If the claimant(s) named here in space 4 are different from the author(s) named in space 2, give a brief statement of how the claimant(s) obtained ownership of the copyright.▼

**DO NOT WRITE HERE OFFICE USE ONLY**

APPLICATION RECEIVED
_____
ONE DEPOSIT RECEIVED
_____
TWO DEPOSITS RECEIVED
_____
REMITTANCE NUMBER AND DATE

**MORE ON BACK ▶**   • Complete all applicable spaces (numbers 5-11) on the reverse side of this page
• See detailed instructions.          • Sign the form at line 10.

**DO NOT WRITE HERE**
Page 1 of _____ pages

| EXAMINED BY | FORM SE |
|---|---|
| CHECKED BY | |
| ☐ CORRESPONDENCE Yes | FOR COPYRIGHT OFFICE USE ONLY |
| ☐ DEPOSIT ACCOUNT FUNDS USED | |

**DO NOT WRITE ABOVE THIS LINE. IF YOU NEED MORE SPACE, USE A SEPARATE CONTINUATION SHEET.**

**PREVIOUS REGISTRATION**   Has registration for this issue, or for an earlier version of this particular issue, already been made in the Copyright Office?

☐ Yes ☐ No  If your answer is "Yes," why is another registration being sought? (Check appropriate box) ▼

a. ☐ This is the first published version of an issue previously registered in unpublished form.

b. ☐ This is the first application submitted by this author as copyright claimant.

c. ☐ This is a changed version of this issue, as shown by space 6 on this application.

If your answer is "Yes," give: **Previous Registration Number** ▼          **Year of Registration** ▼

**5**

**DERIVATIVE WORK OR COMPILATION**   Complete both space 6a & 6b for a derivative work; complete only 6b for a compilation.

a.   **Preexisting Material**   Identify any preexisting work or works that this work is based on or incorporates. ▼

b.   **Material Added to This Work**   Give a brief, general statement of the material that has been added to this work and in which copyright is claimed. ▼

**6**

See instructions before completing this space.

**MANUFACTURERS AND LOCATIONS**   If this is a published work consisting preponderantly of nondramatic literary material in English, the law may require that the copies be manufactured in the United States or Canada for full protection. If so, the names of the manufacturers who performed certain processes, and the places where these processes were performed **must** be given. See instructions for details.

**Names of Manufacturers** ▼          **Places of Manufacture** ▼

**7**

**REPRODUCTION FOR USE OF BLIND OR PHYSICALLY HANDICAPPED INDIVIDUALS**      A signature on this form at space 10, and a check in one of the boxes here in space 8, constitutes a non-exclusive grant of permission to the Library of Congress to reproduce and distribute solely for the blind and physically handicapped and under the conditions and limitations prescribed by the regulations of the Copyright Office: (1) copies of the work identified in space 1 of this application in Braille (or similar tactile symbols); or (2) phonorecords embodying a fixation of a reading of that work; or (3) both.

a ☐ Copies and Phonorecords          b ☐ Copies Only          c ☐ Phonorecords Only

**8**

See instructions.

**DEPOSIT ACCOUNT**   If the registration fee is to be charged to a Deposit Account established in the Copyright Office, give name and number of Account.

**Name** ▼          **Account Number** ▼

**CORRESPONDENCE**   Give name and address to which correspondence about this application should be sent.   Name/Address/Apt/City/State/Zip ▼

Area Code & Telephone Number ▶

**9**

Be sure to give your daytime phone ◀ number.

**CERTIFICATION\***   I, the undersigned, hereby certify that I am the

Check one ▶

☐ author
☐ other copyright claimant
☐ owner of exclusive right(s)
☐ authorized agent of

of the work identified in this application and that the statements made by me in this application are correct to the best of my knowledge.          Name of author or other copyright claimant, or owner of exclusive right(s) ▲

**10**

**Typed or printed name and date ▼** If this is a published work, this date must be the same as or later than the date of publication given in space 3.

_____ date ▶ _____

Handwritten signature (X) ▼

| MAIL CERTIFI- CATE TO | Name ▼ |
|---|---|
| **Certificate will be mailed in window envelope** | Number/Street/Apartment Number ▼ |
| | City/State/ZIP ▼ |

**Have you:**
• Completed all necessary spaces?
• Signed your application in space 10?
• Enclosed check or money order for $10 payable to *Register of Copyrights?*
• Enclosed your deposit material with the application and fee?

**MAIL TO:** Register of Copyrights, Library of Congress, Washington, D.C. 20559.

**11**

\* 17 U.S.C. § 506(e): Any person who knowingly makes a false representation of a material fact in the application for copyright registration provided for by section 409, or in any written statement filed in connection with the application, shall be fined not more than $2,500.

☆ U.S. GOVERNMENT PRINTING OFFICE: 1981: 355–308          Nov. 1981-200,000

# Filling Out Application Form VA

*Detach and read these instructions before completing this form. Make sure all applicable spaces have been filled in before you return this form.*

## BASIC INFORMATION

**When to Use This Form:** Use Form VA for copyright registration of published or unpublished works of the visual arts. This category consists of "pictorial, graphic, or sculptural works," including two-dimensional and three-dimensional works of fine, graphic, and applied art, photographs, prints and art reproductions, maps, globes, charts, technical drawings, diagrams, and models.

**What Does Copyright Protect?** Copyright in a work of the visual arts protects those pictorial, graphic, or sculptural elements that, either alone or in combination, represent an "original work of authorship." The statute declares: "In no case does copyright protection for an original work of authorship extend to any idea, procedure, process, system, method of operation, concept, principle, or discovery, regardless of the form in which it is described, explained, illustrated, or embodied in such work."

**Works of Artistic Craftsmanship and Designs:** "Works of artistic craftsmanship" are registrable on Form VA, but the statute makes clear that protection extends to "their form" and not to "their mechanical or utilitarian aspects." The "design of a useful article" is considered copyrightable "only if, and only to the extent that, such design incorporates pictorial, graphic, or sculptural features that can be identified separately from, and are capable of existing independently of, the utilitarian aspects of the article."

**Labels and Advertisements:** Works prepared for use in connection with the sale or advertisement of goods and services are registrable if they contain "original work of authorship." Use Form VA if the copyrightable material in the work you are registering is mainly pictorial or graphic; use Form TX if it consists mainly of text. NOTE. Words and short phrases such as names, titles, and slogans cannot be protected by copyright, and the same is true of standard symbols, emblems, and other commonly used graphic designs that are in the public domain. When used commercially, material of that sort can sometimes be protected under state laws of unfair competition or under the Federal trademark laws. For information about trademark registration, write to the Commissioner of Patents and Trademarks, Washington, D.C. 20231.

**Deposit to Accompany Application:** An application for copyright registration must be accompanied by a deposit consisting of copies representing the entire work for which registration is to be made

> **Unpublished Work:** Deposit one complete copy.
>
> **Published Work.** Deposit two complete copies of the best edition.
>
> **Work First Published Outside the United States:** Deposit one complete copy of the first foreign edition.
>
> **Contribution to a Collective Work:** Deposit one complete copy of the best edition of the collective work.

**The Copyright Notice:** For published works, the law provides that a copyright notice in a specified form "shall be placed on all publicly distributed copies from which the work can be visually perceived." Use of the copyright notice is the responsibility of the copyright owner and does not require advance permission from the Copyright Office. The required form of the notice for copies generally consists of three elements: (1) the symbol "©", or the word "Copyright," or the abbreviation "Copr."; (2) the year of first publication; and (3) the name of the owner of copyright. For example: "© 1981 Constance Porter." The notice is to be affixed to the copies "in such manner and location as to give reasonable notice of the claim of copyright."

For further information about copyright registration, notice, or special questions relating to copyright problems, write:

Information and Publications Section, LM-455
Copyright Office, Library of Congress, Washington, D.C. 20559

> **PRIVACY ACT ADVISORY STATEMENT Required by the Privacy Act of 1974 (PL. 93-579)**
> The authority for requesting this information is title 17 U.S.C. secs. 409 and 410. Furnishing the requested information is voluntary. But if the information is not furnished, it may be necessary to delay or refuse registration and you may not be entitled to certain relief, remedies, and benefits provided in chapters 4 and 5 of title 17, U.S.C.
> The principal uses of the requested information are the establishment and maintenance of a public record and the examination of the application for compliance with legal requirements.
> Other routine uses include public inspection and copying, preparation of public indexes, preparation of public catalogs of copyright registrations, and preparation of search reports upon request.
> NOTE No other advisory statement will be given in connection with this application. Please keep this statement and refer to it if we communicate with you regarding this application

## LINE-BY-LINE INSTRUCTIONS

### 1 SPACE 1: Title

**Title of This Work:** Every work submitted for copyright registration must be given a title to identify that particular work. If the copies of the work bear a title (or an identifying phrase that could serve as a title), transcribe that wording *completely* and *exactly* on the application. Indexing of the registration and future identification of the work will depend on the information you give here.

**Previous or Alternative Titles:** Complete this space if there are any additional titles for the work under which someone searching for the registration might be likely to look, or under which a document pertaining to the work might be recorded.

**Publication as a Contribution:** If the work being registered is a contribution to a periodical, serial, or collection, give the title of the contribution in the "Title of This Work" space. Then, in the line headed "Publication as a Contribution," give information about the collective work in which the contribution appeared.

**Nature of This Work:** Briefly describe the general nature or character of the pictorial, graphic, or sculptural work being registered for copyright. Examples: "Oil Painting"; "Charcoal Drawing"; "Etching"; "Sculpture"; "Map"; "Photograph"; "Scale Model"; "Lithographic Print"; "Jewelry Design"; "Fabric Design."

### 2 SPACE 2: Author(s)

**General Instructions:** After reading these instructions, decide who are the "authors" of this work for copyright purposes. Then, unless the work is a "collective work," give the requested information about every "author" who contributed any appreciable amount of copyrightable matter to this version of the work. If you need further space, request additional Continuation Sheets. In the case of a collective work, such as a catalog of paintings or collection of cartoons by various authors, give information about the author of the collective work as a whole.

**Name of Author:** The fullest form of the author's name should be given. Unless the work was "made for hire," the individual who actually created the work is its "author." In the case of a work made for hire, the statute provides that "the employer or other person for whom the work was prepared is considered the author."

**What is a "Work Made for Hire"?** A "work made for hire" is defined as: (1) "a work prepared by an employee within the scope of his or her employment"; or (2) "a work specially ordered or commissioned for use as a contribution to a collective work, as a part of a motion picture or other audiovisual work, as a translation, as a supplementary work, as a compilation, as an instructional text, as a test, as answer material for a test, or as an atlas, if the parties expressly agree in a written instrument signed by them that the work shall be considered a work made for hire." If you have checked "Yes" to indicate that the work was "made for hire," you must give the full legal name of the employer (or other person for whom the work was prepared). You may also include the name of the employee along with the name of the employer (for example: "Elster Publishing Co., employer for hire of John Ferguson").

**"Anonymous" or "Pseudonymous" Work:** An author's contribution to a work is "anonymous" if that author is not identified on the copies or phonorecords of the work. An author's contribution to a work is "pseudonymous" if that author is identified on the copies or phonorecords under a fictitious name. If the work is "anonymous" you may: (1) leave the line blank; or (2) state "anonymous" on the line; or (3) reveal the author's identity. If the work is "pseudonymous" you may: (1) leave the line blank; or (2) give the pseudonym and identify it as such (for example: "Huntley Haverstock, pseudonym"); or (3) reveal the author's name, making clear which is the real name and which is the pseudonym (for example: "Henry Leek, whose pseudonym is Priam Farrel"). However, the citizenship or domicile of the author **must** be given in all cases.

**Dates of Birth and Death:** If the author is dead, the statute requires that the year of death be included in the application unless the work is anonymous or pseudonymous. The author's birth date is optional, but is useful as a form of identification. Leave this space blank if the author's contribution was a "work made for hire."

**Author's Nationality or Domicile:** Give the country of which the author is a citizen, or the country in which the author is domiciled. Nationality or domicile **must** be given in all cases.

**Nature of Authorship:** Give a brief general statement of the nature of this particular author's contribution to the work. Examples: "Painting"; "Photograph"; "Silk Screen Reproduction"; "Co-author of Cartographic Material"; "Technical Drawing"; "Text and Artwork."

## 3 SPACE 3: Creation and Publication

**General Instructions:** Do not confuse "creation" with "publication." Every application for copyright registration must state "the year in which creation of the work was completed." Give the date and nation of first publication only if the work has been published.

**Creation:** Under the statute, a work is "created" when it is fixed in a copy or phonorecord for the first time. Where a work has been prepared over a period of time, the part of the work existing in fixed form on a particular date constitutes the created work on that date. The date you give here should be the year in which the author completed the particular version for which registration is now being sought, even if other versions exist or if further changes or additions are planned.

**Publication:** The statute defines "publication" as "the distribution of copies or phonorecords of a work to the public by sale or other transfer of ownership, or by rental, lease, or lending"; a work is also "published" if there has been an "offering to distribute copies or phonorecords to a group of persons for purposes of further distribution, public performance, or public display." Give the full date (month, day, year) when, and the country where, publication first occurred. If first publication took place simultaneously in the United States and other countries, it is sufficient to state "U.S.A."

## 4 SPACE 4: Claimant(s)

**Name(s) and Address(es) of Copyright Claimant(s):** Give the name(s) and address(es) of the copyright claimant(s) in this work even if the claimant is the same as the author. Copyright in a work belongs initially to the author of the work (including, in the case of a work made for hire, the employer or other person for whom the work was prepared.) The copyright claimant is either the author of the work or a person or organization to whom the copyright initially belonging to the author has been transferred.

**Transfer:** The statute provides that, if the copyright claimant is not the author, the application for registration must contain "a brief statement of how the claimant obtained ownership of the copyright." If any copyright claimant named in space 4 is not an author named in space 2, give a brief, general statement summarizing the means by which that claimant obtained ownership of the copyright. Examples: "By written contract"; "Transfer of all rights by author"; "Assignment"; "By will." Do not attach transfer documents or other attachments or riders.

## 5 SPACE 5: Previous Registration

**General Instructions:** The questions in space 5 are intended to find out whether an earlier registration has been made for this work and, if so, whether there is any basis for a new registration. As a rule, only one basic copyright registration can be made for the same version of a particular work.

**Same Version:** If this version is substantially the same as the work covered by a previous registration, a second registration is not generally possible unless: (1) the work has been registered in unpublished form and a second registration is now being sought to cover this first published edition; or (2) some-

one other than the author is identified as copyright claimant in the earlier registration, and the author is now seeking registration in his or her own name. If either of these two exceptions apply, check the appropriate box and give the earlier registration number and date. Otherwise, do not submit Form VA; instead, write the Copyright Office for information about supplementary registration or recordation of transfers of copyright ownership.

**Changed Version:** If the work has been changed, and you are now seeking registration to cover the additions or revisions, check the last box in space 5, give the earlier registration number and date, and complete both parts of space 6 in accordance with the instructions below.

**Previous Registration Number and Date:** If more than one previous registration has been made for the work, give the number and date of the latest registration.

## 6 SPACE 6: Derivative Work or Compilation

**General Instructions:** Complete space 6 if this work is a "changed version," "compilation," or "derivative work," and if it incorporates one or more earlier works that have already been published or registered for copyright, or that have fallen into the public domain. A "compilation" is defined as "a work formed by the collection and assembling of preexisting materials or of data that are selected, coordinated, or arranged in such a way that the resulting work as a whole constitutes an original work of authorship." A "derivative work" is "a work based on one or more preexisting works." Examples of derivative works include reproductions of works of art, sculptures based on drawings, lithographs based on paintings, maps based on previously published sources, or "any other form in which a work may be recast, transformed, or adapted." Derivative works also include works "consisting of editorial revisions, annotations, or other modifications" if these changes, as a whole, represent an original work of authorship.

**Preexisting Material (space 6a):** Complete this space **and** space 6b for derivative works. In this space identify the preexisting work that has been recast, transformed, or adapted. Examples of preexisting material might be "Grunewald Altarpiece"; or "19th century quilt design." Do not complete this space for compilations.

**Material Added to This Work (space 6b):** Give a brief, general statement of the **additional** new material covered by the copyright claim for which registration is sought. In the case of a derivative work, identify this new material. Examples: "Adaptation of design and additional artistic work"; "Reproduction of painting by photolithography"; "Additional cartographic material"; "Compilation of photographs." If the work is a compilation, give a brief, general statement describing both the material that has been compiled **and** the compilation itself. Example: "Compilation of 19th Century Political Cartoons."

## 7,8,9 SPACE 7, 8, 9: Fee, Correspondence, Certification, Return Address

**Deposit Account:** If you maintain a Deposit Account in the Copyright Office, identify it in space 7. Otherwise leave the space blank and send the fee of $10 with your application and deposit.

**Correspondence** (space 7): This space should contain the name, address, area code, and telephone number of the person to be consulted if correspondence about this application becomes necessary.

**Certification** (space 8): The application cannot be accepted unless it bears the date and the **handwritten signature** of the author or other copyright claimant, or of the owner of exclusive right(s), or of the duly authorized agent of the author, claimant, or owner of exclusive right(s).

**Address for Return of Certificate** (space 9): The address box must be completed legibly since the certificate will be returned in a window envelope.

# MORE INFORMATION

## Form of Deposit for Works of the Visual Arts

**Exceptions to General Deposit Requirements:** As explained on the reverse side of this page, the statutory deposit requirements (generally one copy for unpublished works and two copies for published works) will vary for particular kinds of works of the visual arts. The copyright law authorizes the Register of Copyrights to issue regulations specifying "the administrative classes into which works are to be placed for purposes of deposit and registration, and the nature of the copies or phonorecords to be deposited in the various classes specified." For particular classes, the regulations may require or permit "the deposit of identifying material instead of copies or phonorecords," or "the deposit of only one copy or phonorecord where two would normally be required."

**What Should You Deposit?** The detailed requirements with respect to the kind of deposit to accompany an application on Form VA are contained in the Copyright

Office Regulations. The following does not cover all of the deposit requirements, but is intended to give you some general guidance.

**For an Unpublished Work,** the material deposited should represent the entire copyrightable content of the work for which registration is being sought.

**For a Published Work,** the material deposited should generally consist of two complete copies of the best edition. Exceptions: (1) For certain types of works, one complete copy may be deposited instead of two. These include greeting cards, postcards, stationery, labels, advertisements, scientific drawings, and globes; (2) For most three-dimensional sculptural works, and for certain two-dimensional works, the Copyright Office Regulations require deposit of identifying material (photographs or drawings in a specified form) rather than copies; and (3) Under certain circumstances, for works published in five copies or less or in limited, numbered editions, the deposit may consist of one copy or of identifying reproductions.

# FORM VA

UNITED STATES COPYRIGHT OFFICE

REGISTRATION NUMBER

VA          VAU

EFFECTIVE DATE OF REGISTRATION

_____
Month          Day          Year

**DO NOT WRITE ABOVE THIS LINE. IF YOU NEED MORE SPACE, USE A SEPARATE CONTINUATION SHEET.**

## 1

TITLE OF THIS WORK ▼                     NATURE OF THIS WORK ▼ See instructions

PREVIOUS OR ALTERNATIVE TITLES ▼

PUBLICATION AS A CONTRIBUTION   If this work was published as a contribution to a periodical, serial, or collection, give information about the collective work in which the contribution appeared.   **Title of Collective Work ▼**

If published in a periodical or serial give: Volume ▼      Number ▼          Issue Date ▼          On Pages ▼

## 2

**a**

NAME OF AUTHOR ▼                         DATES OF BIRTH AND DEATH
                                         Year Born ▼          Year Died ▼

Was this contribution to the work a     AUTHOR'S NATIONALITY OR DOMICILE     WAS THIS AUTHOR'S CONTRIBUTION TO
"work made for hire"?                   Name of Country                      THE WORK                        If the answer to either
☐ Yes                          OR { Citizen of ▶_____        Anonymous?    ☐ Yes ☐ No       of these questions is
☐ No                                { Domiciled in ▶_____       Pseudonymous? ☐ Yes ☐ No       "Yes," see detailed
                                                                                                            instructions.

NATURE OF AUTHORSHIP   Briefly describe nature of the material created by this author in which copyright is claimed. ▼

### NOTE

Under the law,
the "author" of a
"work made for
hire" is generally
the employer,
not the em-
ployee (see in-
structions). For
any part of this
work that was
"made for hire"
check "Yes" in
the space pro-
vided, give the
employer (or
other person for
whom the work
was prepared)
as "Author" of
that part, and
leave the space
for dates of birth
and death blank.

**b**

NAME OF AUTHOR ▼                         DATES OF BIRTH AND DEATH
                                         Year Born ▼          Year Died ▼

Was this contribution to the work a     AUTHOR'S NATIONALITY OR DOMICILE     WAS THIS AUTHOR'S CONTRIBUTION TO
"work made for hire"?                   Name of Country                      THE WORK                        If the answer to either
☐ Yes                          OR { Citizen of ▶_____        Anonymous?    ☐ Yes ☐ No       of these questions is
☐ No                                { Domiciled in ▶_____       Pseudonymous? ☐ Yes ☐ No       "Yes," see detailed
                                                                                                            instructions.

NATURE OF AUTHORSHIP   Briefly describe nature of the material created by this author in which copyright is claimed. ▼

**c**

NAME OF AUTHOR ▼                         DATES OF BIRTH AND DEATH
                                         Year Born ▼          Year Died ▼

Was this contribution to the work a     AUTHOR'S NATIONALITY OR DOMICILE     WAS THIS AUTHOR'S CONTRIBUTION TO
"work made for hire"?                   Name of Country                      THE WORK                        If the answer to either
☐ Yes                          OR { Citizen of ▶_____        Anonymous?    ☐ Yes ☐ No       of these questions is
☐ No                                { Domiciled in ▶_____       Pseudonymous? ☐ Yes ☐ No       "Yes," see detailed
                                                                                                            instructions.

NATURE OF AUTHORSHIP   Briefly describe nature of the material created by this author in which copyright is claimed. ▼

## 3

YEAR IN WHICH CREATION OF THIS         DATE AND NATION OF FIRST PUBLICATION OF THIS PARTICULAR WORK
WORK WAS COMPLETED This information     Complete this information Month ▶_____ Day ▶_____ Year ▶_____
                   must be given       ONLY if this work
          ◀ Year  in all cases.        has been published.                                         ◀ Nation

## 4

COPYRIGHT CLAIMANT(S) Name and address must be given even if the claimant is the     APPLICATION RECEIVED
same as the author given in space 2.▼
                                                                                      ONE DEPOSIT RECEIVED

                                                                                      TWO DEPOSITS RECEIVED

See instructions
before completing
this space.                                                                           REMITTANCE NUMBER AND DATE

TRANSFER If the claimant(s) named here in space 4 are different from the author(s) named
in space 2, give a brief statement of how the claimant(s) obtained ownership of the copyright.▼

DO NOT WRITE HERE
OFFICE USE ONLY

**MORE ON BACK ▶** • Complete all applicable spaces (numbers 5-9) on the reverse side of this page     **DO NOT WRITE HERE**
                  • See detailed instructions.          • Sign the form at line 8.
                                                                                      Page 1 of_____pages

| EXAMINED BY | | FORM VA |
|---|---|---|
| CHECKED BY | | |
| ☐ CORRESPONDENCE Yes | | FOR COPYRIGHT OFFICE USE ONLY |
| ☐ DEPOSIT ACCOUNT FUNDS USED | | |

**DO NOT WRITE ABOVE THIS LINE. IF YOU NEED MORE SPACE, USE A SEPARATE CONTINUATION SHEET.**

**PREVIOUS REGISTRATION** Has registration for this work, or for an earlier version of this work, already been made in the Copyright Office?
☐ Yes ☐ No If your answer is "Yes," why is another registration being sought? (Check appropriate box) ▼

☐ This is the first published edition of a work previously registered in unpublished form.

☐ This is the first application submitted by this author as copyright claimant.

☐ This is a changed version of the work, as shown by space 6 on this application.

If your answer is "Yes," give: **Previous Registration Number ▼**     **Year of Registration ▼**

**5**

**DERIVATIVE WORK OR COMPILATION** Complete both space 6a & 6b for a derivative work; complete only 6b for a compilation.
a. **Preexisting Material** Identify any preexisting work or works that this work is based on or incorporates. ▼

b. **Material Added to This Work** Give a brief, general statement of the material that has been added to this work and in which copyright is claimed.▼

**6**

See instructions before completing this space.

**DEPOSIT ACCOUNT** If the registration fee is to be charged to a Deposit Account established in the Copyright Office, give name and number of Account.
**Name ▼**     **Account Number ▼**

**7**

**CORRESPONDENCE** Give name and address to which correspondence about this application should be sent.   Name/Address/Apt/City/State/Zip ▼

Area Code & Telephone Number ▶

Be sure to give your daytime phone ◀ number.

**CERTIFICATION\*** I, the undersigned, hereby certify that I am the
Check only one ▼

☐ author

☐ other copyright claimant

☐ owner of exclusive right(s)

☐ authorized agent of_____
Name of author or other copyright claimant, or owner of exclusive right(s) ▲

**8**

of the work identified in this application and that the statements made
by me in this application are correct to the best of my knowledge.

**Typed or printed name and date ▼** If this is a published work, this date must be the same as or later than the date of publication given in space 3.

_____ date ▶ _____

Handwritten signature (X) ▼

| MAIL CERTIFI- CATE TO | Name ▼ | Have you: |
|---|---|---|
| | Number/Street/Apartment Number ▼ | • Completed all necessary spaces? • Signed your application in space 8? • Enclosed check or money order for $10 payable to *Register of Copyrights*? • Enclosed your deposit material with the application and fee? |
| Certificate will be mailed in window envelope | City/State/ZIP ▼ | **MAIL TO:** Register of Copyrights, Library of Congress, Washington, D.C. 20559 |

**9**

\* 17 U.S.C. § 506(e): Any person who knowingly makes a false representation of a material fact in the application for copyright registration provided for by section 409, or in any written statement filed in connection with the application. shall be fined not more than $2.500.

☆ U.S. GOVERNMENT PRINTING OFFICE: 1981: 355–312

Nov. 1981-600,000

# Filling Out Application Form PA

*Detach and read these instructions before completing this form. Make sure all applicable spaces have been filled in before you return this form.*

## BASIC INFORMATION

**When to Use This Form:** Use Form PA for registration of published or unpublished works of the performing arts. This class includes works prepared for the purpose of being "performed" directly before an audience or indirectly "by means of any device or process." Works of the performing arts include: (1) musical works, including any accompanying words; (2) dramatic works, including any accompanying music; (3) pantomimes and choreographic works; and (4) motion pictures and other audiovisual works.

**Deposit to Accompany Application:** An application for copyright registration must be accompanied by a deposit consisting of copies or phonorecords representing the entire work for which registration is to be made. The following are the general deposit requirements as set forth in the statute:

**Unpublished Work:** Deposit one complete copy (or phonorecord).

**Published Work:** Deposit two complete copies (or phonorecords) of the best edition.

**Work First Published Outside the United States:** Deposit one complete copy (or phonorecord) of the first foreign edition.

**Contribution to a Collective Work:** Deposit one complete copy (or phonorecord) of the best edition of the collective work.

**Motion Pictures:** Deposit both of the following: (1) a separate written description of the contents of the motion picture; and (2) for a published work, one complete copy of the best edition of the motion picture; or, for an unpublished work, one complete copy of the motion picture or identifying material. Identifying material may be either an audiorecording of the entire soundtrack or one frame enlargement or similar visual print from each 10-minute segment.

**The Copyright Notice:** For published works, the law provides that a copyright notice in a specified form "shall be placed on all publicly distributed copies from which the work can be visually perceived." Use of the copyright notice is the responsibility of the copyright owner and does not require advance permission from the Copyright Office. The required form of the notice for copies generally consists of three elements: (1) the symbol "©", or the word "Copyright," or the abbreviation "Copr."; (2) the year of first publication; and (3) the name of the owner of copyright. For example: "© 1981 Constance Porter." The notice is to be affixed to the copies "in such manner and location as to give reasonable notice of the claim of copyright."

For further information about copyright registration, notice, or special questions relating to copyright problems, write:

Information and Publications Section, LM-455
Copyright Office
Library of Congress
Washington, D.C. 20559

## LINE-BY-LINE INSTRUCTIONS

### 1 SPACE 1: Title

**Title of This Work:** Every work submitted for copyright registration must be given a title that particular work. If the copies or phonorecords of the work bear a title (or an identifying phrase that could serve as a title), transcribe that wording *completely* and *exactly* on the application. Indexing of the registration and future identification of the work will depend on the information you give here. If the work you are registering is an entire "collective work" (such as a collection of plays or songs), give the overall title of the collection. If you are registering one or more individual contributions to a collective work, give the title of each contribution, followed by the title of the collection. Example: "'A Song for Elinda' in *Old and New Ballads for Old and New People*."

**Previous or Alternative Titles:** Complete this space if there are any additional titles for the work under which someone searching for the registration might be likely to look, or under which a document pertaining to the work might be recorded.

**Nature of This Work:** Briefly describe the general nature or character of the work being registered for copyright. Examples: "Music"; "Song Lyrics"; "Words and Music"; "Drama"; "Musical Play"; "Choreography"; "Pantomime"; "Motion Picture"; "Audiovisual Work."

### 2 SPACE 2: Author(s)

**General Instructions:** After reading these instructions, decide who are the "authors" of this work for copyright purposes. Then, unless the work is a "collective work," give the requested information about every "author" who contributed any appreciable amount of copyrightable matter to this version of the work. If you need further space, request additional Continuation Sheets. In the case of a collective work, such as a songbook or a collection of plays, give information about the author of the collective work as a whole.

**Name of Author:** The fullest form of the author's name should be given. Unless the work was "made for hire," the individual who actually created the work is its "author." In the case of a work made for hire, the statute provides that "the employer or other person for whom the work was prepared is considered the author."

**What is a "Work Made for Hire"?** A "work made for hire" is defined as: (1) "a work prepared by an employee within the scope of his or her employment"; or (2) "a work specially ordered or commissioned for use as a contribution to a collective work, as a part of a motion picture or other audiovisual work, as a translation, as a supplementary work, as a compilation, as an instructional text, as a test, as answer material for a test, or as an atlas, if the parties expressly agree in a written instrument signed by them that the work shall be considered a work made for hire." If you have checked "Yes" to indicate that the work was "made for hire," you must give the full legal name of the employer (or other person for whom the work was prepared). You may also include the name of the employee along with the name of the employer (for example: "Elster Music Co., employer for hire of John Ferguson").

**"Anonymous" or "Pseudonymous" Work:** An author's contribution to a work is "anonymous" if that author is not identified on the copies or phonorecords of the work. An author's contribution to a work is "pseudonymous" if that author is identified on the copies or phonorecords under a fictitious name. If the work is "anonymous" you may: (1) leave the line blank; or (2) state "anonymous" on the line; or (3) reveal the author's identity. If the work is "pseudonymous" you may: (1) leave the line blank; or (2) give the pseudonym and identify it as such (for example: "Huntley Haverstock, pseudonym"); or (3) reveal the author's name, making clear which is the real name and which is the pseudonym (for example: "Judith Barton, whose pseudonym is Madeline Elster"). However, the citizenship or domicile of the author must be given in all cases.

**Dates of Birth and Death:** If the author is dead, the statute requires that the year of death be included in the application unless the work is anonymous or pseudonymous. The author's birth date is optional, but is useful as a form of identification. Leave this space blank if the author's contribution was a "work made for hire."

**Author's Nationality or Domicile:** Give the country of which the author is a citizen, or the country in which the author is domiciled. Nationality or domicile must be given in all cases.

**Nature of Authorship:** Give a brief general statement of the nature of this particular author's contribution to the work. Examples: "Words"; "Co-Author of Music"; "Words and Music"; "Arrangement"; "Co-Author of Book and Lyrics"; "Dramatization"; "Screen Play"; "Compilation and English Translation"; "Editorial Revisions."

## 3 SPACE 3: Creation and Publication

**General Instructions:** Do not confuse "creation" with "publication." Every application for copyright registration must state "the year in which creation of the work was completed." Give the date and nation of first publication only if the work has been published.

**Creation:** Under the statute, a work is "created" when it is fixed in a copy or phonorecord for the first time. Where a work has been prepared over a period of time, the part of the work existing in fixed form on a particular date constitutes the created work on that date. The date you give here should be the year in which the author completed the particular version for which registration is now being sought, even if other versions exist or if further changes or additions are planned.

**Publication:** The statute defines "publication" as "the distribution of copies or phonorecords of a work to the public by sale or other transfer of ownership, or by rental, lease, or lending"; a work is also "published" if there has been an "offering to distribute copies or phonorecords to a group of persons for purposes of further distribution, public performance, or public display." Give the full date (month, day, year) when, and the country where, publication first occurred. If first publication took place simultaneously in the United States and other countries, it is sufficient to state "U.S.A."

## 4 SPACE 4: Claimant(s)

**Name(s) and Address(es) of Copyright Claimant(s):** Give the name(s) and address(es) of the copyright claimant(s) in this work even if the claimant is the same as the author. Copyright in a work belongs initially to the author of the work (including, in the case of a work made for hire, the employer or other person for whom the work was prepared). The copyright claimant is either the author of the work or a person or organization to whom the copyright initially belonging to the author has been transferred.

**Transfer:** The statute provides that, if the copyright claimant is not the author, the application for registration must contain "a brief statement of how the claimant obtained ownership of the copyright." If any copyright claimant named in space 4 is not an author named in space 2, give a brief, general statement summarizing the means by which that claimant obtained ownership of the copyright. Examples: "By written contract"; "Transfer of all rights to author"; "Assignment"; "By will." Do not attach transfer documents or other attachments or riders.

## 5 SPACE 5: Previous Registration

**General Instructions:** The questions in space 5 are intended to find out whether an earlier registration has been made for this work and, if so, whether there is any basis for a new registration. As a general rule, only one basic copyright registration can be made for the same version of a particular work.

**Same Version:** If this version is substantially the same as the work covered by a previous registration, a second registration is not generally possible unless: (1) the work has been registered in unpublished form and a second registration is now being sought to cover this first published edition; or (2) someone other than the author is identified as copyright claimant in the earlier registration, and the author is now seeking registration in his or her own name. If either of these two exceptions apply, check the appropriate box and give the earlier registration number and date. Otherwise, do not submit Form PA; instead, write the Copyright Office for information about supplementary registration or recordation of transfers of copyright ownership.

**Changed Version:** If the work has been changed, and you are now seeking registration to cover the additions or revisions, check the last box in space 5, give the earlier registration number and date, and complete both parts of space 6 in accordance with the instructions below.

**Previous Registration Number and Date:** If more than one previous registration has been made for the work, give the number and date of the latest registration.

## 6 SPACE 6: Derivative Work or Compilation

**General Instructions:** Complete space 6 if this work is a "changed version," "compilation," or "derivative work," and if it incorporates one or more earlier works that have already been published or registered for copyright, or that have fallen into the public domain. A "compilation" is defined as "a work formed by the collection and assembling of preexisting materials or of data that are selected, coordinated, or arranged in such a way that the resulting work as a whole constitutes an original work of authorship." A "derivative work" is "a work based on one or more preexisting works." Examples of derivative works include musical arrangements, dramatizations, translations, abridgments, condensations, motion picture versions, or "any other form in which a work may be recast, transformed, or adapted." Derivative works also include works "consisting of editorial revisions, annotations, or other modifications" if these changes, as a whole, represent an original work of authorship.

**Preexisting Material (space 6a):** Complete this space and space 6b for derivative works. In this space identify the preexisting work that has been recast, transformed, or adapted. For example, the preexisting material might be: "French version of Hugo's 'Le Roi s'amuse'." Do not complete this space for compilations.

**Material Added to This Work (space 6b):** Give a brief, general statement of the additional new material covered by the copyright claim for which registration is sought. In the case of a derivative work, identify this new material. Examples: "Arrangement for piano and orchestra"; "Dramatization for television"; "New film version"; "Revisions throughout; Act III completely new." If the work is a compilation, give a brief, general statement describing both the material that has been compiled and the compilation itself. Example: "Compilation of 19th Century Military Songs."

## 7,8,9 SPACE 7, 8, 9: Fee, Correspondence, Certification, Return Address

**Deposit Account:** If you maintain a Deposit Account in the Copyright Office, identify it in space 7. Otherwise leave the space blank and send the fee of $10 with your application and deposit.

**Correspondence (space 7):** This space should contain the name, address, area code, and telephone number of the person to be consulted if correspondence about this application becomes necessary.

**Certification (space 8):** The application cannot be accepted unless it bears the date and the **handwritten signature** of the author or other copyright claimant, or of the owner of exclusive right(s), or of the duly authorized agent of the author, claimant, or owner of exclusive right(s).

**Address for Return of Certificate (space 9):** The address box must be completed legibly since the certificate will be returned in a window envelope.

# MORE INFORMATION

**How To Register a Recorded Work:** If the musical or dramatic work that you are registering has been recorded (as a tape, disk, or cassette), you may choose either copyright application Form PA or Form SR, Performing Arts or Sound Recordings, depending on the purpose of the registration.

Form PA should be used to register the underlying musical composition or dramatic work. Form SR has been developed specifically to register a "sound recording" as defined by the Copyright Act—a work resulting from the "fixation of a series of sounds," separate and distinct from the underlying musical or dramatic work. Form SR should be used when the copyright claim is limited to the sound recording itself. (In one instance, Form SR may also be used to file for a copyright registration for both kinds of works—see (4) below.) Therefore:

(1) **File Form PA** if you are seeking to register the musical or dramatic work, not the "sound recording," even though what you deposit for copyright purposes may be in the form of a phonorecord.

(2) **File Form PA** if you are seeking to register the audio portion of an audiovisual work, such as a motion picture soundtrack; these are considered integral parts of the audiovisual work.

(3) **File Form SR** if you are seeking to register the "sound recording" itself, that is, the work that results from the fixation of a series of musical, spoken, or other sounds, but not the underlying musical or dramatic work.

(4) **File Form SR** if you are the copyright claimant for both the underlying musical or dramatic work and the sound recording, *and* you prefer to register both on the same form.

(5) **File both forms PA and SR** if the copyright claimant for the underlying work and sound recording differ, or you prefer to have separate registration for them.

**"Copies" and "Phonorecords":** To register for copyright, you are required to deposit "copies" or "phonorecords." These are defined as follows:

Musical compositions may be embodied (fixed) in "copies," objects from which a work can be read or visually perceived, directly or with the aid of a machine or device, such as manuscripts, books, sheet music, film, and videotape. They may also be fixed in "phonorecords," objects embodying fixations of sounds, such as tapes and phonograph disks, commonly known as phonograph records. For example, a song (the work to be registered) can be reproduced in sheet music ("copies") or phonograph records ("phonorecords"), or both.

# FORM PA
UNITED STATES COPYRIGHT OFFICE

REGISTRATION NUMBER

| PA | PAU |

EFFECTIVE DATE OF REGISTRATION

| Month | Day | Year |

**DO NOT WRITE ABOVE THIS LINE. IF YOU NEED MORE SPACE, USE A SEPARATE CONTINUATION SHEET.**

## 1

TITLE OF THIS WORK ▼

PREVIOUS OR ALTERNATIVE TITLES ▼

NATURE OF THIS WORK ▼ See instructions

## 2

**a** NAME OF AUTHOR ▼

DATES OF BIRTH AND DEATH
Year Born ▼     Year Died ▼

Was this contribution to the work a "work made for hire"?
☐ Yes
☐ No

AUTHOR'S NATIONALITY OR DOMICILE
Name of Country
OR { Citizen of ▶
{ Domiciled in ▶

WAS THIS AUTHOR'S CONTRIBUTION TO THE WORK
Anonymous?   ☐ Yes ☐ No
Pseudonymous?   ☐ Yes ☐ No
If the answer to either of these questions is "Yes," see detailed instructions.

NATURE OF AUTHORSHIP   Briefly describe nature of the material created by this author in which copyright is claimed. ▼

**NOTE**

Under the law, the "author" of a "work made for hire" is generally the employer, not the employee (see instructions). For any part of this work that was "made for hire" check "Yes" in the space provided, give the employer (or other person for whom the work was prepared) as "Author" of that part, and leave the space for dates of birth and death blank.

**b** NAME OF AUTHOR ▼

DATES OF BIRTH AND DEATH
Year Born ▼     Year Died ▼

Was this contribution to the work a "work made for hire"?
☐ Yes
☐ No

AUTHOR'S NATIONALITY OR DOMICILE
Name of Country
OR { Citizen of ▶
{ Domiciled in ▶

WAS THIS AUTHOR'S CONTRIBUTION TO THE WORK
Anonymous?   ☐ Yes ☐ No
Pseudonymous?   ☐ Yes ☐ No
If the answer to either of these questions is "Yes," see detailed instructions.

NATURE OF AUTHORSHIP   Briefly describe nature of the material created by this author in which copyright is claimed. ▼

**c** NAME OF AUTHOR ▼

DATES OF BIRTH AND DEATH
Year Born ▼     Year Died ▼

Was this contribution to the work a "work made for hire"?
☐ Yes
☐ No

AUTHOR'S NATIONALITY OR DOMICILE
Name of Country
OR { Citizen of ▶
{ Domiciled in ▶

WAS THIS AUTHOR'S CONTRIBUTION TO THE WORK
Anonymous?   ☐ Yes ☐ No
Pseudonymous?   ☐ Yes ☐ No
If the answer to either of these questions is "Yes," see detailed instructions.

NATURE OF AUTHORSHIP   Briefly describe nature of the material created by this author in which copyright is claimed. ▼

## 3

YEAR IN WHICH CREATION OF THIS WORK WAS COMPLETED   This information must be given in all cases.   ◀ Year

DATE AND NATION OF FIRST PUBLICATION OF THIS PARTICULAR WORK
Complete this information Month ▶         Day ▶         Year ▶
ONLY if this work has been published.         ◀ Nation

## 4

COPYRIGHT CLAIMANT(S) Name and address must be given even if the claimant is the same as the author given in space 2.▼

See instructions before completing this space.

TRANSFER If the claimant(s) named here in space 4 are different from the author(s) named in space 2, give a brief statement of how the claimant(s) obtained ownership of the copyright.▼

APPLICATION RECEIVED

ONE DEPOSIT RECEIVED

TWO DEPOSITS RECEIVED

REMITTANCE NUMBER AND DATE

DO NOT WRITE HERE OFFICE USE ONLY

**MORE ON BACK ▶**
• Complete all applicable spaces (numbers 5-9) on the reverse side of this page.
• See detailed instructions.
• Sign the form at line 8.

DO NOT WRITE HERE
Page 1 of _____ pages

| EXAMINED BY | FORM PA |
|---|---|
| CHECKED BY | |
| ☐ CORRESPONDENCE Yes | FOR COPYRIGHT OFFICE USE ONLY |
| ☐ DEPOSIT ACCOUNT FUNDS USED | |

**DO NOT WRITE ABOVE THIS LINE. IF YOU NEED MORE SPACE, USE A SEPARATE CONTINUATION SHEET.**

**PREVIOUS REGISTRATION** Has registration for this work, or for an earlier version of this work, already been made in the Copyright Office?
☐ Yes ☐ No If your answer is "Yes," why is another registration being sought? (Check appropriate box) ▼
☐ This is the first published edition of a work previously registered in unpublished form.
☐ This is the first application submitted by this author as copyright claimant.
☐ This is a changed version of the work, as shown by space 6 on this application.
If your answer is "Yes," give: **Previous Registration Number** ▼          **Year of Registration** ▼

**5**

**DERIVATIVE WORK OR COMPILATION** Complete both space 6a & 6b for a derivative work; complete only 6b for a compilation.
a. **Preexisting Material** Identify any preexisting work or works that this work is based on or incorporates. ▼

b. **Material Added to This Work** Give a brief, general statement of the material that has been added to this work and in which copyright is claimed. ▼

**6**

See instructions before completing this space.

**DEPOSIT ACCOUNT** If the registration fee is to be charged to a Deposit Account established in the Copyright Office, give name and number of Account.
**Name** ▼                              **Account Number** ▼

**7**

**CORRESPONDENCE** Give name and address to which correspondence about this application should be sent.   Name/Address/Apt/City/State/Zip ▼

Area Code & Telephone Number ▶

Be sure to give your daytime phone ◀ number.

**CERTIFICATION\*** I, the undersigned, hereby certify that I am the
Check only one ▼
☐ author
☐ other copyright claimant
☐ owner of exclusive right(s)
☐ authorized agent of_____
          Name of author or other copyright claimant, or owner of exclusive right(s) ▲

**8**

of the work identified in this application and that the statements made
by me in this application are correct to the best of my knowledge.

**Typed or printed name and date** ▼ If this is a published work, this date must be the same as or later than the date of publication given in space 3.

_____ date ▶ _____

☛ **Handwritten signature (X)** ▼

**MAIL CERTIFI- CATE TO**

Certificate will be mailed in window envelope

Name ▼

Number/Street/Apartment Number ▼

City/State/ZIP ▼

**Have you:**
• Completed all necessary spaces?
• Signed your application in space 8?
• Enclosed check or money order for $10 payable to *Register of Copyrights?*
• Enclosed your deposit material with the application and fee?
**MAIL TO:** Register of Copyrights, Library of Congress, Washington, D.C. 20559.

**9**

\* 17 U.S.C. § 506(e): Any person who knowingly makes a false representation of a material fact in the application for copyright registration provided for by section 409, or in any written statement filed in connection with the application. shall be fined not more than $2,500.

☆ U.S. GOVERNMENT PRINTING OFFICE: 1981: 355–306

●          Nov. 1981-700,000

# Filling Out Application Form SR

*Detach and read these instructions before completing this form. Make sure all applicable spaces have been filled in before you return this form.*

## BASIC INFORMATION

**When to Use This Form:** Use Form SR for copyright registration of published or unpublished sound recordings. It should be used where the copyright claim is limited to the sound recording itself, and it may also be used where the same copyright claimant is seeking simultaneous registration of the underlying musical, dramatic, or literary work embodied in the phonorecord.

With one exception, "sound recordings" are works that result from the fixation of a series of musical, spoken, or other sounds. The exception is for the audio portions of audiovisual works, such as a motion picture soundtrack or an audio cassette accompanying a filmstrip; these are considered a part of the audiovisual work as a whole.

**Deposit to Accompany Application:** An application for copyright registration of a sound recording must be accompanied by a deposit consisting of phonorecords representing the entire work for which registration is to be made.

**Unpublished Work:** Deposit one complete phonorecord.

**Published Work:** Deposit two complete phonorecords of the best edition, together with "any printed or other visually perceptible material" published with the phonorecords.

**Work First Published Outside the United States:** Deposit one complete phonorecord of the first foreign edition.

**Contribution to a Collective Work:** Deposit one complete phonorecord of the best edition of the collective work.

**The Copyright Notice:** For published sound recordings, the law provides that a copyright notice in a specified form "shall be placed on all publicly distributed phonorecords of the sound recording." Use of the copyright notice is the responsibility of the copyright owner and does not require advance permission from the Copyright Office. The required form of the notice for phonorecords of sound recordings consists of three elements: (1) the symbol "℗" (the letter "P" in a circle); (2) the year of first publication of the sound recording; and (3) the name of the owner of copyright. For example: "℗ 1981 Rittenhouse Record Co." The notice is to be "placed on the surface of the phonorecord, or on the label or container, in such manner and location as to give reasonable notice of the claim of copyright." For further information about copyright, write:

Information and Publications Section, LM-455
Copyright Office, Library of Congress, Washington, D.C. 20559

## LINE-BY-LINE INSTRUCTIONS

### 1 SPACE 1: Title

**Title of This Work:** Every work submitted for copyright registration must be given a title to identify that particular work. If the phonorecords or any accompanying printed material bear a title (or an identifying phrase that could serve as a title), transcribe that wording completely and exactly on the application. Indexing of the registration and future identification of the work may depend on the information you give here.

**Nature of Material Recorded:** Indicate the general type or character of the works or other material embodied in the recording. The box marked "Literary" should be checked for nondramatic spoken material of all sorts, including narration, interviews, panel discussions, and training material. If the material recorded is not musical, dramatic, or literary in nature, check "Other" and briefly describe the type of sounds fixed in the recording. For example: "Sound Effects"; "Bird Calls"; "Crowd Noises."

**Previous or Alternative Titles:** Complete this space if there are any additional titles for the work under which someone searching for the registration might be likely to look, or under which a document pertaining to the work might be recorded.

### 2 SPACE 2: Author(s)

**General Instructions:** After reading these instructions, decide who are the "authors" of this work for copyright purposes. Then, unless the work is a "collective work," give the requested information about every "author" who contributed any appreciable amount of copyrightable matter to this version of the work. If you need further space, request additional Continuation Sheets. In the case of a collective work, such as a collection of previously published or registered sound recordings, give information about the author of the collective work as a whole. If you are submitting this Form SR to cover the recorded musical, dramatic, or literary work as well as the sound recording itself, it is important for space 2 to include full information about the various authors of all of the material covered by the copyright claim, making clear the nature of each author's contribution.

**Name of Author:** The fullest form of the author's name should be given. Unless the work was "made for hire," the individual who actually created the work is its "author." In the case of a work made for hire, the statute provides that "the employer or other person for whom the work was prepared is considered the author."

**What is a "Work Made for Hire"?** A "work made for hire" is defined as: (1) "a work prepared by an employee within the scope of his or her employment"; or (2) "a work specially ordered or commissioned for use as a contribution to a collective work, as a part of a motion picture or other audiovisual work, as a translation, as a supplementary work, as a compilation, as an instructional text, as a test, as answer material for a test, or as an atlas, if the parties expressly agree in a written instrument signed by them that the work shall be considered a work made for hire." If you have checked "Yes" to indicate that the work was "made for hire," you must give the full legal name of the employer (or other person for whom the work was prepared). You may also include the name of the employee along with the name of the employer (for example: "Elster Record Co., employer for hire of John Ferguson").

**"Anonymous" or "Pseudonymous" Work:** An author's contribution to a work is "anonymous" if that author is not identified on the copies or phonorecords of the work. An author's contribution to a work is "pseudonymous" if that author is identified on the copies or phonorecords under a fictitious name. If the work is "anonymous" you may: (1) leave the line blank; or (2) state "anonymous" on the line; or (3) reveal the author's identity. If the work is "pseudonymous" you may: (1) leave the line blank; or (2) give the pseudonym and identify it as such (for example: "Huntley Haverstock, pseudonym"); or (3) reveal the author's name, making clear which is the real name and which is the pseudonym (for example: "Judith Barton, whose pseudonym is Madeline Elster"). However, the citizenship or domicile of the author **must** be given in all cases.

**Dates of Birth and Death:** If the author is dead, the statute requires that the year of death be included in the application unless the work is anonymous or pseudonymous. The author's birth date is optional, but is useful as a form of identification. Leave this space blank if the author's contribution was a "work made for hire."

**Author's Nationality or Domicile:** Give the country of which the author is a citizen, or the country in which the author is domiciled. Nationality or domicile **must** be given in all cases.

**Nature of Authorship:** Give a brief general statement of the nature of this particular author's contribution to the work. If you are submitting this Form SR to cover both the sound recording and the underlying musical, dramatic, or literary work, make sure that the precise nature of each author's contribution is reflected here. Examples where the authorship pertains to the recording: "Sound Recording"; "Performance and Recording"; "Compilation and Remixing of Sounds." Examples where the authorship pertains to both the recording and the underlying work: "Words, Music, Performance, Recording"; "Arrangement of Music and Recording"; "Compilation of Poems and Reading."

## 3 SPACE 3: Creation and Publication

**General Instructions:** Do not confuse "creation" with "publication." Every application for copyright registration must state "the year in which creation of the work was completed." Give the date and nation of first publication only if the work has been published.

**Creation:** Under the statute, a work is "created" when it is fixed in a copy or phonorecord for the first time. Where a work has been prepared over a period of time, the part of the work existing in fixed form on a particular date constitutes the created work on that date. The date you give here should be the year in which the author completed the particular version for which registration is now being sought, even if other versions exist or if further changes or additions are planned.

**Publication:** The statute defines "publication" as "the distribution of copies or phonorecords of a work to the public by sale or other transfer of ownership, or by rental, lease, or lending"; a work is also "published" if there has been an "offering to distribute copies or phonorecords to a group of persons for purposes of further distribution, public performance, or public display." Give the full date (month, day, year) when, and the country where, publication first occurred. If first publication took place simultaneously in the United States and other countries, it is sufficient to state "U.S.A."

## 4 SPACE 4: Claimant(s)

**Name(s) and Address(es) of Copyright Claimant(s):** Give the name(s) and address(es) of the copyright claimant(s) in this work even if the claimant is the same as the author. Copyright in a work belongs initially to the author of the work (including, in the case of a work made for hire, the employer or other person for whom the work was prepared). The copyright claimant is either the author of the work or a person or organization to whom the copyright initially belonging to the author has been transferred.

**Transfer:** The statute provides that, if the copyright claimant is not the author, the application for registration must contain "a brief statement of how the claimant obtained ownership of the copyright." If any copyright claimant named in space 4 is not an author named in space 2, give a brief, general statement summarizing the means by which that claimant obtained ownership of the copyright. Examples: "By written contract"; "Transfer of all rights by author"; "Assignment"; "By will." Do not attach transfer documents or other attachments or riders.

## 5 SPACE 5: Previous Registration

**General Instructions:** The questions in space 5 are intended to find out whether an earlier registration has been made for this work and, if so, whether there is any basis for a new registration. As a rule, only one basic copyright registration can be made for the same version of a particular work.

**Same Version:** If this version is substantially the same as the work covered by a previous registration, a second registration is not generally possible unless: (1) the work has been registered in unpublished form and a second registration is now being sought to cover this first published edition; or (2) someone other than the author is identified as copyright claimant in the earlier registration, and the author is now seeking registration in his or her own name. If either of these two exceptions apply, check the appropriate box and give the earlier registration number and date. Otherwise, do not submit Form SR; instead, write the Copyright Office for information about supplementary registration or recordation of transfers of copyright ownership.

**Changed Version:** If the work has been changed, and you are now seeking registration to cover the additions or revisions, check the last box in space 5, give the earlier registration number and date, and complete both parts of space 6 in accordance with the instructions below.

**Previous Registration Number and Date:** If more than one previous registration has been made for the work, give the number and date of the latest registration.

## 6 SPACE 6: Derivative Work or Compilation

**General Instructions:** Complete space 6 if this work is a "changed version," "compilation," or "derivative work," and if it incorporates one or more earlier works that have already been published or registered for copyright, or that have fallen into the public domain, or sound recordings that were fixed before February 15, 1972. A "compilation" is defined as "a work formed by the collection and assembling of preexisting materials or of data that are selected, coordinated, or arranged in such a way that the resulting work as a whole constitutes an original work of authorship." A "derivative work" is "a work based on one or more preexisting works." Examples of derivative works include recordings reissued with substantial editorial revisions or abridgments of the recorded sounds, and recordings republished with new recorded material, or "any other form in which a work may be recast, transformed, or adapted." Derivative works also include works "consisting of editorial revisions, annotations, or other modifications" if these changes, as a whole, represent an original work of authorship.

**Preexisting Material (space 6a):** Complete this space **and** space 6b for derivative works. In this space identify the preexisting work that has been recast, transformed, or adapted. For example, the preexisting material might be: "1970 recording by Sperryville Symphony of Bach Double Concerto." Do not complete this space for compilations.

**Material Added to This Work (space 6b):** Give a brief, general statement of the additional new material covered by the copyright claim for which registration is sought. In the case of a derivative work, identify this new material. Examples: "Recorded performances on bands 1 and 3"; "Remixed sounds from original multitrack sound sources"; "New words, arrangement, and additional sounds." If the work is a compilation, give a brief, general statement describing both the material that has been compiled and the compilation itself. Example: "Compilation of 1938 Recordings by various swing bands."

## 7,8,9 SPACE 7, 8, 9: Fee, Correspondence, Certification, Return Address

**Deposit Account:** If you maintain a Deposit Account in the Copyright Office, identify it in space 7. Otherwise leave the space blank and send the fee of $10 with your application and deposit.

**Correspondence** (space 7): This space should contain the name, address, area code, and telephone number of the person to be consulted if correspondence about this application becomes necessary.

**Certification** (space 8): The application cannot be accepted unless it bears the date and the **handwritten signature** of the author or other copyright claimant, or of the owner of exclusive right(s), or of the duly authorized agent of the author, claimant, or owner of exclusive right(s).

**Address for Return of Certificate** (space 9): The address box must be completed legibly since the certificate will be returned in a window envelope.

# MORE INFORMATION

**"Works":** "Works" are the basic subject matter of copyright; they are what authors create and copyright protects. The statute draws a sharp distinction between the "work" and "any material object in which the work is embodied."

**"Copies" and "Phonorecords":** These are the two types of material objects in which "works" are embodied. In general, **"copies"** are objects from which a work can be read or visually perceived, directly or with the aid of a machine or device, such as manuscripts, books, sheet music, film, and videotape. **"Phonorecords"** are objects embodying fixations of sounds, such as audio tapes and phonograph disks. For example, a song (the "work") can be reproduced in sheet music ("copies") or phonograph disks ("phonorecords"), or both.

**"Sound Recordings":** These are "works," not "copies" or "phonorecords." "Sound recordings" are "works that result from the fixation of a series of musical, spoken, or other sounds, but not including the sounds accompanying a motion picture or other audiovisual work." Example:When a record company issues a new release, the release will typically involve two distinct "works": the "musical work" that has been recorded, and the "sound recording" as a separate work in itself. The material objects that the record company sends out are "phonorecords": physical reproductions of both the "musical work" and the "sound recording."

## Should You File More Than One Application? If your work consists of a recorded musical, dramatic, or literary work, and both that "work," and the sound recording as a separate "work," are eligible for registration, the application form you should file depends on the following:

**File Only Form SR if:** The copyright claimant is the same for both the musical, dramatic, or literary work and for the sound recording, and you are seeking a single registration to cover both of these "works."

**File Only Form PA (or Form TX) if:** You are seeking to register only the musical, dramatic, or literary work, not the sound recording. Form PA is appropriate for works of the performing arts; Form TX is for nondramatic literary works.

**Separate Applications Should Be Filed on Form PA (or Form TX) and on Form SR if:** (1) The copyright claimant for the musical, dramatic, or literary work is different from the copyright claimant for the sound recording; or (2) You prefer to have separate registrations for the musical, dramatic, or literary work and for the sound recording.

# FORM SR
UNITED STATES COPYRIGHT OFFICE

REGISTRATION NUMBER

SR       SRU

EFFECTIVE DATE OF REGISTRATION

Month      Day      Year

**DO NOT WRITE ABOVE THIS LINE. IF YOU NEED MORE SPACE, USE A SEPARATE CONTINUATION SHEET.**

## 1

**TITLE OF THIS WORK ▼**

**PREVIOUS OR ALTERNATIVE TITLES ▼**

**NATURE OF MATERIAL RECORDED ▼** See instructions.
- ☐ Musical    ☐ Musical-Dramatic
- ☐ Dramatic    ☐ Literary
- ☐ Other _____

## 2

### a

**NAME OF AUTHOR ▼**

**DATES OF BIRTH AND DEATH**
Year Born ▼      Year Died ▼

Was this contribution to the work a "work made for hire"?
- ☐ Yes
- ☐ No

**AUTHOR'S NATIONALITY OR DOMICILE**
Name of Country
OR { Citizen of ▶ _____
{ Domiciled in ▶ _____

**WAS THIS AUTHOR'S CONTRIBUTION TO THE WORK**
Anonymous? ☐ Yes ☐ No
Pseudonymous? ☐ Yes ☐ No
If the answer to either of these questions is "Yes," see detailed instructions.

**NATURE OF AUTHORSHIP** Briefly describe nature of the material created by this author in which copyright is claimed. ▼

**NOTE**

Under the law, the "author" of a "work made for hire" is generally the employer, not the employee (see instructions). For any part of this work that was "made for hire" check "Yes" in the space provided, give the employer (or other person for whom the work was prepared) as "Author" of that part, and leave the space for dates of birth and death blank.

### b

**NAME OF AUTHOR ▼**

**DATES OF BIRTH AND DEATH**
Year Born ▼      Year Died ▼

Was this contribution to the work a "work made for hire"?
- ☐ Yes
- ☐ No

**AUTHOR'S NATIONALITY OR DOMICILE**
Name of Country
OR { Citizen of ▶ _____
{ Domiciled in ▶ _____

**WAS THIS AUTHOR'S CONTRIBUTION TO THE WORK**
Anonymous? ☐ Yes ☐ No
Pseudonymous? ☐ Yes ☐ No
If the answer to either of these questions is "Yes," see detailed instructions.

**NATURE OF AUTHORSHIP** Briefly describe nature of the material created by this author in which copyright is claimed. ▼

### c

**NAME OF AUTHOR ▼**

**DATES OF BIRTH AND DEATH**
Year Born ▼      Year Died ▼

Was this contribution to the work a "work made for hire"?
- ☐ Yes
- ☐ No

**AUTHOR'S NATIONALITY OR DOMICILE**
Name of Country
OR { Citizen of ▶ _____
{ Domiciled in ▶ _____

**WAS THIS AUTHOR'S CONTRIBUTION TO THE WORK**
Anonymous? ☐ Yes ☐ No
Pseudonymous? ☐ Yes ☐ No
If the answer to either of these questions is "Yes," see detailed instructions.

**NATURE OF AUTHORSHIP** Briefly describe nature of the material created by this author in which copyright is claimed. ▼

## 3

**YEAR IN WHICH CREATION OF THIS WORK WAS COMPLETED** This information must be given ◀ Year in all cases.

**DATE AND NATION OF FIRST PUBLICATION OF THIS PARTICULAR WORK**
Complete this information Month ▶ _____ Day ▶ _____ Year ▶ _____
ONLY if this work has been published. ◀ Nation

## 4

**COPYRIGHT CLAIMANT(S)** Name and address must be given even if the claimant is the same as the author given in space 2.▼

See instructions before completing this space.

**TRANSFER** If the claimant(s) named here in space 4 are different from the author(s) named in space 2, give a brief statement of how the claimant(s) obtained ownership of the copyright.▼

APPLICATION RECEIVED

ONE DEPOSIT RECEIVED

TWO DEPOSITS RECEIVED

REMITTANCE NUMBER AND DATE

DO NOT WRITE HERE OFFICE USE ONLY

**MORE ON BACK ▶**
- Complete all applicable spaces (numbers 5-9) on the reverse side of this page.
- See detailed instructions.
- Sign the form at line 8.

DO NOT WRITE HERE
Page 1 of _____ pages

**DO NOT WRITE ABOVE THIS LINE. IF YOU NEED MORE SPACE, USE A SEPARATE CONTINUATION SHEET.**

**PREVIOUS REGISTRATION** Has registration for this work, or for an earlier version of this work, already been made in the Copyright Office?
☐ Yes ☐ No  If your answer is "Yes," why is another registration being sought? (Check appropriate box) ▼
☐ This is the first published edition of a work previously registered in unpublished form.
☐ This is the first application submitted by this author as copyright claimant.
☐ This is a changed version of the work, as shown by space 6 on this application.
If your answer is "Yes," give: **Previous Registration Number** ▼        **Year of Registration** ▼

**5**

**DERIVATIVE WORK OR COMPILATION** Complete both space 6a & 6b for a derivative work; complete only 6b for a compilation.
a.  **Preexisting Material** Identify any preexisting work or works that this work is based on or incorporates. ▼

b.  **Material Added to This Work** Give a brief, general statement of the material that has been added to this work and in which copyright is claimed. ▼

**6**

See instructions
before completing
this space

**DEPOSIT ACCOUNT** If the registration fee is to be charged to a Deposit Account established in the Copyright Office, give name and number of Account.
**Name** ▼                                                          **Account Number** ▼

**7**

**CORRESPONDENCE** Give name and address to which correspondence about this application should be sent.  Name/Address/Apt/City/State/Zip ▼

Area Code & Telephone Number ▶

Be sure to
give your
daytime phone
◀ number

**CERTIFICATION\*** I, the undersigned, hereby certify that I am the
Check one ▼
☐ author
☐ other copyright claimant
☐ owner of exclusive right(s)
☐ authorized agent of_____
                                    Name of author or other copyright claimant, or owner of exclusive right(s) ▲

of the work identified in this application and that the statements made
by me in this application are correct to the best of my knowledge.

**Typed or printed name and date** ▼ If this is a published work, this date must be the same as or later than the date of publication given in space 3.

_____                                  date ▶ _____

☞        **Handwritten signature (X)** ▼

**8**

**MAIL
CERTIFI-
CATE TO**

Certificate
will be
mailed in
window
envelope

Name ▼

Number/Street/Apartment Number ▼

City/State/ZIP ▼

**Have you:**
● Completed all necessary
  spaces?
● Signed your application in space
  8?
● Enclosed check or money order
  for $10 payable to *Register of
  Copyrights*?
● Enclosed your deposit material
  with the application and fee?
**MAIL TO:** Register of Copyrights,
Library of Congress, Washington,
D.C. 20559

**9**

## FORM RE

UNITED STATES COPYRIGHT OFFICE
LIBRARY OF CONGRESS
WASHINGTON, D.C. 20559

# APPLICATION FOR
## *Renewal Registration*

---

### HOW TO REGISTER A RENEWAL CLAIM:

- **First:** Study the information on this page and make sure you know the answers to two questions:

  (1) What are the renewal time limits in your case?

  (2) Who can claim the renewal?

- **Second:** Turn this page over and read through the specific instructions for filling out Form RE. Make sure, before starting to complete the form, that the copyright is now eligible for renewal, that you are authorized to file a renewal claim, and that you have all of the information about the copyright you will need.

- **Third:** Complete all applicable spaces on Form RE, following the line-by-line instructions on the back of this page. Use typewriter, or print the information in dark ink.

- **Fourth:** Detach this sheet and send your completed Form RE to: Register of Copyrights, Library of Congress, Washington, D.C. 20559. Unless you have a Deposit Account in the Copyright Office, your application must be accompanied by a check or money order for $6, payable to: *Register of Copyrights*. Do not send copies, phonorecords, or supporting documents with your renewal application.

---

**WHAT IS RENEWAL OF COPYRIGHT?** For works originally copyrighted between January 1, 1950 and December 31, 1977, the statute now in effect provides for a first term of copyright protection lasting for 28 years, with the possibility of renewal for a second term of 47 years. If a valid renewal registration is made for a work, its total copyright term is 75 years (a first term of 28 years, plus a renewal term of 47 years). Example: For a work copyrighted in 1960, the first term will expire in 1988, but if renewed at the proper time the copyright will last through the end of 2035.

**SOME BASIC POINTS ABOUT RENEWAL:**

(1) There are strict time limits and deadlines for renewing a copyright.

(2) Only certain persons who fall into specific categories named in the law can claim renewal.

(3) The new copyright law does away with renewal requirements for works first copyrighted after 1977. However, copyrights that were already in their first copyright term on January 1, 1978 (that is, works originally copyrighted between January 1, 1950 and December 31, 1977) **still have to be renewed** in order to be protected for a second term.

**TIME LIMITS FOR RENEWAL REGISTRATION:** The new copyright statute provides that, in order to renew a copyright, the renewal application and fee must be received in the Copyright Office "within one year prior to the expiration of the copyright." It also provides that all terms of copyright will run through the end of the year in which they would otherwise expire. Since all copyright terms will expire on December 31st of their last year, all periods for renewal registration will run from December 31th of the 27th year of the copyright and will end on December 31st of the following year.

To determine the time limits for renewal in your case:

(1) First, find out the date of original copyright for the work. (In the case of works originally registered in unpublished form, the date of copyright is the date of registration; for published works, copyright begins on the date of first publication.)

(2) Then add 28 years to the year the work was originally copyrighted.

Your answer will be the calendar year during which the copyright will be eligible for renewal, and December 31st of that year will be the renewal deadline. Example: A work originally copyrighted on April 19, 1957, will be eligible for renewal between December 31, 1984, and December 31, 1985.

**WHO MAY CLAIM RENEWAL:** Renewal copyright may be claimed only by those persons specified in the law. Except in the case of four specific types of works, the law gives the right to claim renewal to the individual author of the work, regardless of who owned the copyright during the original term. If the author is dead, the statute gives the right to claim renewal to certain of the author's beneficiaries (widow and children, executors, or next of kin, depending on the circumstances). The present owner (proprietor) of the copyright is entitled to claim renewal only in four specified cases, as explained in more detail on the reverse of this page.

**CAUTION:** Renewal registration is possible only if an acceptable application and fee are **received** in the Copyright Office during the renewal period and before the renewal deadline. If an acceptable application and fee are not received before the renewal deadline, the work falls into the public domain and the copyright cannot be renewed. The Copyright Office has no discretion to extend the renewal time limits.

---

# INSTRUCTIONS FOR COMPLETING FORM RE

## SPACE 1: RENEWAL CLAIM(S)

• **General Instructions:** In order for this application to result in a valid renewal, space 1 must identify one or more of the persons who are entitled to renew the copyright under the statute. Give the full name and address of each claimant, with a statement of the basis of each claim, using the wording given in these instructions.

• **Persons Entitled to Renew:**

A. The following persons may claim renewal in all types of works except those enumerated in Paragraph B, below:

1. The author, if living. State the claim as: *the author.*

2. The widow, widower, and/or children of the author, if the author is not living. State the claim as: *the widow (widower) of the author* ............ (Name of author)

and/or *the child (children) of the deceased author* ............ (Name of author)

3. The author's executor(s), if the author left a will and if there is no surviving widow, widower, or child. State the claim as: *the executor(s) of the author* ............

(Name of author)

4. The next of kin of the author, if the author left no will and if there is no surviving widow, widower, or child. State the claim as: *the next of kin of the deceased author* ............ *there being no will.* (Name of author)

B. In the case of the following four types of works, the proprietor (owner of the copyright at the time of renewal registration) may claim renewal:

1. Posthumous work (a work as to which no copyright assignment or other contract for exploitation has occurred during the author's lifetime). State the claim as: *proprietor of copyright in a posthumous work.*

2. Periodical, cyclopedic, or other composite work. State the claim as: *proprietor of copyright in a composite work.*

3. "Work copyrighted by a corporate body otherwise than as assignee or licensee of the individual author." State the claim as: *proprietor of copyright in a work copyrighted by a corporate body otherwise than as assignee or licensee of the individual author.* (This type of claim is considered appropriate in relatively few cases.)

4. Work copyrighted by an employer for whom such work was made for hire. State the claim as: *proprietor of copyright in a work made for hire.*

## SPACE 2: WORK RENEWED

• **General Instructions:** This space is to identify the particular work being renewed. The information given here should agree with that appearing in the certificate of original registration.

• **Title:** Give the full title of the work, together with any subtitles or descriptive wording included with the title in the original registration. In the case of a musical composition, give the specific instrumentation of the work.

• **Renewable Matter:** Copyright in a new version of a previous work (such as an arrangement, translation, dramatization, compilation, or work republished with new matter) covers only the additions, changes, or other new material appearing for the first time in that version. If this work was a new version, state in general the new matter upon which copyright was claimed.

• **Contribution to Periodical, Serial, or other Composite Work:** Separate renewal registration is possible for a work published as a contribution to a periodical, serial, or other composite work, whether the contribution was copyrighted independently or as part of the larger work in which it appeared. Each contribution published in a separate issue ordinarily requires a separate renewal registration. However, the new law provides an alternative, permitting groups of periodical contributions by the same individual author to be combined under a single renewal application and fee in certain cases.

If this renewal application covers a single contribution, give all of the requested information in space 2. If you are seeking to renew a group of contributions, include a reference such as "See space 5" in space 2 and give the requested information about all of the contributions in space 5.

## SPACE 3: AUTHOR(S)

• **General Instructions:** The copyright secured in a new version of a work is independent of any copyright protection in material published earlier. The only "authors" of a new version are those who contributed copyrightable matter to it. Thus, for renewal purposes, the person who wrote the original version on which the new work is based cannot be regarded as an "author" of the new version, unless that person also contributed to the new matter.

• **Authors of Renewable Matter:** Give the full names of all authors who contributed copyrightable matter to this particular version of the work.

## SPACE 4: FACTS OF ORIGINAL REGISTRATION

• **General Instructions:** Each item in space 4 should agree with the information appearing in the original registration for the work. If the work being renewed is a single contribution to a periodical or composite work that was not separately registered, give information about the particular issue in which the contribution appeared. You may leave this space blank if you are completing space 5.

• **Original Registration Number:** Give the full registration number, which is a series of numerical digits, preceded by one or more letters. The registration number appears in the upper right hand corner of the certificate of registration.

• **Original Copyright Claimant:** Give the name in which ownership of the copyright was claimed in the original registration.

• **Date of Publication or Registration:** Give only one date. If the original registration gave a publication date, it should be transcribed here; otherwise the registration was for an unpublished work, and the date of registration should be given.

## SPACE 5: GROUP RENEWALS

• **General Instructions:** A single renewal registration can be made for a group of works if all of the following statutory conditions are met: (1) all of the works were written by the same author, who is named in space 3 and who is or was an individual (not an employer for hire); (2) all of the works were first published as contributions to periodicals (including newspapers) and were copyrighted on their first publication; (3) the renewal claimant or claimants, and the basis of claim or claims, as stated in space 1, is the same for all of the works; (4) the renewal application and fee are "received not more than 28 or less than 27 years after the 31st day of December of the calendar year in which all of the works were first published"; and (5) the renewal application identifies each work separately, including the periodical containing it and the date of first publication.

**Time Limits for Group Renewals:** To be renewed as a group, all of the contributions must have been first published during the same calendar year. For example, suppose six contributions by the same author were published on April 1, 1960, July 1, 1960, November 1, 1960, February 1, 1961, July 1, 1961, and March 1, 1962. The three 1960 copyrights can be combined and renewed at any time during 1988, and the two 1961 copyrights can be renewed as a group during 1989, but the 1962 copyright must be renewed by itself, in 1990.

**Identification of Each Work:** Give all of the requested information for each contribution. The registration number should be that for the contribution itself if it was separately registered, and the registration number for the periodical issue if it was not.

## SPACES 6, 7 AND 8: FEE, MAILING INSTRUCTIONS, AND CERTIFICATION

• **Deposit Account and Mailing Instructions (Space 6):** If you maintain a Deposit Account in the Copyright Office, identify it in Space 6. Otherwise, you will need to send the renewal registration fee of $6 with your form. The space headed "Correspondence" should contain the name and address of the person to be consulted if correspondence about the form becomes necessary.

• **Certification (Space 7):** The renewal application is not acceptable unless it bears the handwritten signature of the renewal claimant or the duly authorized agent of the renewal claimant.

• **Address for Return of Certificate (Space 8):** The address box must be completed legibly, since the certificate will be returned in a window envelope.

# FORM RE

UNITED STATES COPYRIGHT OFFICE

REGISTRATION NUMBER

EFFECTIVE DATE OF RENEWAL REGISTRATION

...... ...... ......
(Month)          (Day)          (Year)

DO NOT WRITE ABOVE THIS LINE.   FOR COPYRIGHT OFFICE USE ONLY

**①** Renewal Claimant(s)

**RENEWAL CLAIMANT(S), ADDRESS(ES), AND STATEMENT OF CLAIM: (See Instructions)**

1
Name ........................
Address ..........................
Claiming as ..........................
(Use appropriate statement from instructions)

2
Name ........................
Address ..........................
Claiming as ..........................
(Use appropriate statement from instructions)

3
Name ........................
Address ..........................
Claiming as ..........................
(Use appropriate statement from instructions)

**②** Work Renewed

**TITLE OF WORK IN WHICH RENEWAL IS CLAIMED:**

**RENEWABLE MATTER:**

**CONTRIBUTION TO PERIODICAL OR COMPOSITE WORK:**
Title of periodical or composite work: ..........................
If a periodical or other serial, give:  Vol. ............... No. ............... Issue Date ...............

**③** Author(s)

**AUTHOR(S) OF RENEWABLE MATTER:**

**④** Facts of Original Registration

**ORIGINAL REGISTRATION NUMBER:**

**ORIGINAL COPYRIGHT CLAIMANT:**

**ORIGINAL DATE OF COPYRIGHT:**
• If the original registration for this work was made in published form, give:
DATE OF PUBLICATION: ...............
(Month)   (Day)   (Year)

} OR {

• If the original registration for this work was made in unpublished form, give:
DATE OF REGISTRATION: ...............
(Month)   (Day)   (Year)

| | | EXAMINED BY: .......... | RENEWAL APPLICATION RECEIVED: | FOR COPYRIGHT OFFICE USE ONLY |
| | | CHECKED BY: .......... | | |
| | | DEPOSIT ACCOUNT FUNDS USED: ☐ | REMITTANCE NUMBER AND DATE: | |

**DO NOT WRITE ABOVE THIS LINE**

**RENEWAL FOR GROUP OF WORKS BY SAME AUTHOR:** To make a single registration for a group of works by the same individual author published as contributions to periodicals (see instructions), give full information about each contribution. If more space is needed, request continuation sheet (Form RE/CON).

**⑤**
**Renewal for Group of Works**

**1**
Title of Contribution: ................................................................
Title of Periodical: ................................. Vol. ...... No. ...... Issue Date ...............
Date of Publication: ............................... Registration Number ...................
(Month)      (Day)      (Year)

**2**
Title of Contribution: ................................................................
Title of Periodical: ................................. Vol. ...... No. ...... Issue Date ...............
Date of Publication: ............................... Registration Number ...................
(Month)      (Day)      (Year)

**3**
Title of Contribution: ................................................................
Title of Periodical: ................................. Vol. ...... No. ...... Issue Date ...............
Date of Publication: ............................... Registration Number ...................
(Month)      (Day)      (Year)

**4**
Title of Contribution: ................................................................
Title of Periodical: ................................. Vol. ...... No. ...... Issue Date ...............
Date of Publication: ............................... Registration Number ...................
(Month)      (Day)      (Year)

**5**
Title of Contribution: ................................................................
Title of Periodical: ................................. Vol. ...... No. ...... Issue Date ...............
Date of Publication: ............................... Registration Number ...................
(Month)      (Day)      (Year)

**6**
Title of Contribution: ................................................................
Title of Periodical: ................................. Vol. ...... No. ...... Issue Date ...............
Date of Publication: ............................... Registration Number ...................
(Month)      (Day)      (Year)

**7**
Title of Contribution: ................................................................
Title of Periodical: ................................. Vol. ...... No. ...... Issue Date ...............
Date of Publication: ............................... Registration Number ...................
(Month)      (Day)      (Year)

**DEPOSIT ACCOUNT:** (If the registration fee is to be charged to a Deposit Account established in the Copyright Office, give name and number of Account.)

Name: ...................................................
Account Number: ........................................

**CORRESPONDENCE:** (Give name and address to which correspondence about this application should be sent.)

Name: ...................................................
Address: .................................................
                                    (Apt.)
.................................................
(City)          (State)          (ZIP)

**⑥**
**Fee and Correspondence**

**CERTIFICATION:** I, the undersigned, hereby certify that I am the: (Check one)
☐ renewal claimant        ☐ duly authorized agent of: ...............................
                                                    (Name of renewal claimant)
of the work identified in this application, and that the statements made by me in this application are correct to the best of my knowledge.

☞ Handwritten signature: (X) ........................................
Typed or printed name: ..............................................
                                    Date .............................

**⑦**
**Certification (Application must be signed)**

MAIL CERTIFICATE TO

.................................................
(Name)
.................................................
(Number, Street and Apartment Number)
.................................................
(City)          (State)          (ZIP code)

(Certificate will be mailed in window envelope)

**⑧**
**Address for Return of Certificate**

☆ U.S. GOVERNMENT PRINTING OFFICE : 1977 O—248-639

Nov. 1977—100,000

**FORM CA**

UNITED STATES COPYRIGHT OFFICE
LIBRARY OF CONGRESS
WASHINGTON, D.C. 20559

**USE THIS FORM WHEN:**

- An earlier registration has been made in the Copyright Office; and
- Some of the facts given in that registration are incorrect or incomplete; and
- You want to place the correct or complete facts on record.

# Application for
# Supplementary Copyright Registration

### To Correct or Amplify Information Given in the
### Copyright Office Record of an Earlier Registration

**What is "Supplementary Copyright Registration"?** Supplementary registration is a special type of copyright registration provided for in section 408(d) of the copyright law.

**Purpose of Supplementary Registration.** As a rule, only one basic copyright registration can be made for the same work. To take care of cases where information in the basic registration turns out to be incorrect or incomplete, the law provides for "the filing of an application for supplementary registration, to correct an error in a copyright registration or to amplify the information given in a registration."

**Earlier Registration Necessary.** Supplementary registration can be made only if a basic copyright registration for the same work has already been completed.

**Who May File.** Once basic registration has been made for a work, any author or other copyright claimant, or owner of any exclusive right in the work, who wishes to correct or amplify the information given in the basic registration, may submit Form CA.

**Please Note:**

- Do not use Form CA to correct errors in statements on the copies or phonorecords of the work in question, or to reflect changes in the content of the work. If the work has been changed substantially, you should consider making an entirely new registration for the revised version to cover the additions or revisions.

- Do not use Form CA as a substitute for renewal registration. For works originally copyrighted between January 1, 1950 and December 31, 1977, registration of a renewal claim within strict time limits is necessary to extend the first 28-year copyright term to the full term of 75 years. This cannot be done by filing Form CA.

- Do not use Form CA as a substitute for recording a transfer of copyright or other document pertaining to rights under a copyright. Recording a document under section 205 of the statute gives all persons constructive notice of the facts stated in the document and may have other important consequences in cases of infringement or conflicting transfers. Supplementary registration does not have that legal effect.

**How to Apply for Supplementary Registration:**

**First:** Study the information on this page to make sure that filing an application on Form CA is the best procedure to follow in your case.

**Second:** Turn this page over and read through the specific instructions for filling out Form CA. Make sure, before starting to complete the form, that you have all of the detailed information about the basic registration you will need.

**Third:** Complete all applicable spaces on this form, following the line-by-line instructions on the back of this page. Use typewriter, or print the information in dark ink.

**Fourth:** Detach this sheet and send your completed Form CA to: Register of Copyrights, Library of Congress, Washington, D.C. 20559. Unless you have a Deposit Account in the Copyright Office, your application must be accompanied by a check or money order for $10 payable to Register of Copyrights. Do not send copies, phonorecords, or supporting documents with your application, since they cannot be made part of the record of a supplementary registration.

**What Happens When a Supplementary Registration is Made?** When a supplementary registration is completed, the Copyright Office will assign it a new registration number in the appropriate registration category, and issue a certificate of supplementary registration under that number. The basic registration will not be expunged or cancelled, and the two registrations will both stand in the Copyright Office records. The supplementary registration will have the effect of calling the public's attention to a possible error or omission in the basic registration, and of placing the correct facts or the additional information on official record. Moreover, if the person on whose behalf Form CA is submitted is the same as the person identified as copyright claimant in the basic registration, the Copyright Office will place a note referring to the supplementary registration in its records of the basic registration.

PLEASE READ DETAILED INSTRUCTIONS ON REVERSE

Please read the following line-by-line instructions carefully and refer to them while completing Form CA.

# INSTRUCTIONS

## For Completing FORM CA (Supplementary Registration)

### PART A: BASIC INSTRUCTIONS

• **General Instructions:** The information in this part identifies the basic registration to be corrected or amplified. Each item must agree exactly with the information as it already appears in the basic registration (even if the purpose of filing Form CA is to change one of these items).

• **Title of Work:** Give the title as it appears in the basic registration, including previous or alternative titles if they appear.

• **Registration Number:** This is a series of numerical digits, pre-ceded by one or more letters. The registration number appears in the upper right hand corner of the certificate of registration.

• **Registration Date:** Give the year when the basic registration was completed.

• **Name(s) of Author(s) and Name(s) of Copyright Claimant(s):** Give all of the names as they appear in the basic registration.

### PART B: CORRECTION

• **General Instructions:** Complete this part **only** if information in the basic registration was incorrect at the time that basic registration was made. Leave this part blank and complete Part C, instead, if your purpose is to add, update, or clarify information rather than to rectify an actual error.

• **Location and Nature of Incorrect Information:** Give the line number and the heading or description of the the space in the basic registration where the error occurs (for example: "Line number 3 . . . Citizenship of author").

• **Incorrect Information as it Appears in Basic Registration:** Transcribe the erroneous statement exactly as it appears in the basic registration.

• **Corrected Information:** Give the statement as it should have appeared.

• **Explanation of Correction (Optional):** If you wish, you may add an explanation of the error or its correction.

### PART C: AMPLIFICATION

• **General Instructions:** Complete this part if you want to provide any of the following: (1) additional information that could have been given but was omitted at the time of basic registration; (2) changes in facts, such as changes of title or address of claimant, that have occurred since the basic registration; or (3) explanations clarifying information in the basic registration.

• **Location and Nature of Information to be Amplified:** Give the line number and the heading or description of the space in the basic registration where the information to be amplified appears.

• **Amplified Information:** Give a statement of the added, updated, or explanatory information as clearly and succinctly as possible.

• **Explanation of Amplification (Optional):** If you wish, you may add an explanation of the amplification.

### PARTS D, E, F, G: CONTINUATION, FEE, MAILING INSTRUCTIONS AND CERTIFICATION

• **Continuation (Part D):** Use this space if you do not have enough room in Parts B or C

• **Deposit Account and Mailing Instructions (Part E):** If you maintain a Deposit Account in the Copyright Office, identify it in Part E. Otherwise, you will need to send the registration fee of $10 with your form. The space headed "Correspondence" should contain the name and address of the person to be consulted if correspondence about the form becomes necessary.

• **Certification (Part F):** The application is not acceptable unless it bears the handwritten signature of the author, or other copyright claimant, or of the owner of exclusive right(s), or of the duly authorized agent of such author, claimant, or owner.

• **Address for Return of Certificate (Part G):** The address box must be completed legibly, since the certificate will be returned in a window envelope.

**FORM CA**
UNITED STATES COPYRIGHT OFFICE

REGISTRATION NUMBER

| TX | TXU | PA | PAU | VA | VAU | SR | SRU | RE |

Effective Date of Supplementary Registration

. . . . . . . . . . . . . . . . . .    . . . . . . .    . . . . . . . . . . .
MONTH                                    DAY                 YEAR

**DO NOT WRITE ABOVE THIS LINE—FOR COPYRIGHT OFFICE USE**

**Ⓐ**
**Basic
Instructions**

TITLE OF WORK:

REGISTRATION NUMBER OF BASIC REGISTRATION:

YEAR OF BASIC REGISTRATION:

NAME(S) OF AUTHOR(S):

NAME(S) OF COPYRIGHT CLAIMANT(S):

**Ⓑ**
**Correction**

LOCATION AND NATURE OF INCORRECT INFORMATION IN BASIC REGISTRATION:
Line Number . . . . . . . . . . . Line Heading or Description . . . . . . . . . . . . . . . . . . . . . . . . . . . . . . . . . . . . . . . . . . . . . . . . . . . . . . . . . .

INCORRECT INFORMATION AS IT APPEARS IN BASIC REGISTRATION:

CORRECTED INFORMATION:

EXPLANATION OF CORRECTION: (Optional)

**Ⓒ**
**Amplification**

LOCATION AND NATURE OF INFORMATION IN BASIC REGISTRATION TO BE AMPLIFIED:
Line Number . . . . . . . . . . . Line Heading or Description . . . . . . . . . . . . . . . . . . . . . . . . . . . . . . . . . . . . . . . . . . . . . . . . . . . . . .

AMPLIFIED INFORMATION:

EXPLANATION OF AMPLIFIED INFORMATION: (Optional)

| | | FORM CA RECEIVED | FOR COPYRIGHT OFFICE USE ONLY |
|---|---|---|---|
| | EXAMINED BY: . . . . . . . . . . . | | |
| | CHECKED BY: . . . . . . . . . . . | | |
| | CORRESPONDENCE ☐ YES | REMITTANCE NUMBER AND DATE | |
| | REFERENCE TO THIS REGISTRATION ADDED TO BASIC REGISTRATION ☐ YES ☐ NO | DEPOSIT ACCOUNT FUNDS USED ☐ | |

**DO NOT WRITE ABOVE THIS LINE: FOR COPYRIGHT OFFICE USE ONLY**

**CONTINUATION OF:** (Check which): ☐ PART B OR ☐ PART C

**D** Continuation

---

**DEPOSIT ACCOUNT:** If the registration fee is to be charged to a Deposit Account established in the Copyright Office, give name and number of Account:

Name . . . . . . . . . . . . . . . . . . . . . . . . . . . . . . . . . . . . . . . . . . . . . . . . . . . Account Number . . . . . . . . . . . . . . . . . .

**CORRESPONDENCE:** Give name and address to which correspondence should be sent:

Name . . . . . . . . . . . . . . . . . . . . . . . . . . . . . . . . . . . . . . . . . . . . . . . . . . . . . . . . . . . . Apt. No. . . . . . . . . . . . . . . . .

Address . . . . . . . . . . . . . . . . . . . . . . . . . . . . . . . . . . . . . . . . . . . . . . . . . . . . . . . . . . . . . . . . . . . . . . . . . . . . . . . . . . . . .
(Number and Street)　　　　　　　　　　　(City)　　　　　(State)　　　　(ZIP Code)

**E** Deposit Account and Mailing Instructions

---

**CERTIFICATION** ✱ I, the undersigned, hereby certify that I am the: (Check one)

☐ author ☐ other copyright claimant ☐ owner of exclusive right(s) ☐ authorized agent of: . . . . . . . . . . . . . . . . . . . . . . . . . . . . . . . . .
(Name of author or other copyright claimant, or owner of exclusive right(s))

of the work identified in this application and that the statements made by me in this application are correct to the best of my knowledge.

Handwritten signature: (X) . . . . . . . . . . . . . . . . . . . . . . . . . . . . . . . . . . . . . . . . .

Typed or printed name. . . . . . . . . . . . . . . . . . . . . . . . . . . . . . . . . . . . . . . . . . .

Date: . . . . . . . . . . . . . . . . . . . . . . . . . . . . . . . . . . . . . . . .

✱ 17 USC §506(e): FALSE REPRESENTATION — Any person who knowingly makes a false representation of a material fact in the application for copyright registration provided for by section 409, or in any written statement filed in connection with the application, shall be fined not more than $2,500.

**F** Certification (Application must be signed)

---

| . . . . . . . . . . . . . . . . . . . . . . . . . . . . . . . . . . . . . . . . . . . . . . . . . . . . . . | **MAIL CERTIFICATE TO** | **G** Address for Return of Certificate |
|---|---|---|
| (Name) | | |
| . . . . . . . . . . . . . . . . . . . . . . . . . . . . . . . . . . . . . . . . . . | | |
| (Number, Street and Apartment Number) | | |
| . . . . . . . . . . . . . . . . . . . . . . . . . . . . . . . . . . . . . . . . . . | (Certificate will be mailed in window envelope) | |
| (City)　　　(State)　　　(ZIP code) | | |

**FORM GR/CP**

UNITED STATES COPYRIGHT OFFICE
LIBRARY OF CONGRESS
WASHINGTON, D.C. 20559

---

**THIS FORM:**

- Can be used solely as an adjunct to a basic application for copyright registration.
- Is not acceptable unless submitted together with Form TX, Form PA, or Form VA.
- Is acceptable only if the group of works listed on it all qualify for a single copyright registration under 17 U.S.C. § 408 (c)(2).

---

# ADJUNCT APPLICATION
## for Copyright Registration for a
## Group of Contributions to Periodicals

**WHEN TO USE FORM GR/CP:** Form GR/CP is the appropriate adjunct application form to use when you are submitting a basic application on Form TX, Form PA, or Form VA, for a group of works that qualify for a single registration under section 408(c)(2) of the copyright statute.

**WHEN DOES A GROUP OF WORKS QUALIFY FOR A SINGLE REGISTRATION UNDER 17 U.S.C. §408 (c)(2)?**
The statute provides that a single copyright registration for a group of works can be made if **all** of the following conditions are met:

(1) All of the works are by the same author, who is an individual (not an employer for hire); and

(2) All of the works were first published as contributions to periodicals (including newspapers) within a twelve-month period; and

(3) Each of the contributions as first published bore a separate copyright notice, and the name of the owner of copyright in the work (or an abbreviation or alternative designation of the owner) was the same in each notice; and

(4) One copy of the entire periodical issue or newspaper section in which each contribution was first published must be deposited with the application; and

(5) The application must identify each contribution separately, including the periodical containing it and the date of its first publication.

**How to Apply for Group Registration:**

*First:* Study the information on this page to make sure that all of the works you want to register together as a group qualify for a single registration.

*Second:* Turn this page over and read through the detailed instructions for group registration. Decide which form you should use for the basic registration (Form TX for nondramatic literary works; or Form PA for musical, dramatic, and other works of the performing arts; or Form VA for pictorial and graphic works). Be sure that you have all of the information you need before you start filling out both the basic and the adjunct application forms.

*Third:* Complete the basic application form, following the detailed instructions accompanying it **and the special instructions on the reverse of this page**.

*Fourth:* Complete the adjunct application on Form GR/CP and mail it, together with the basic application form and the required copy of each contribution, to: Register of Copyrights, Library of Congress, Washington, D.C. 20559. Unless you have a Deposit Account in the Copyright Office, your application and copies must be accompanied by a check or money order for $10, payable to: *Register of Copyrights.*

# PROCEDURE FOR GROUP REGISTRATION

## TWO APPLICATION FORMS MUST BE FILED

When you apply for a single registration to cover a group of contributions to periodicals, you must submit two application forms:

(1) A basic application on either Form TX, or Form PA, or Form VA. It must contain all of the information required for copyright registration except the titles and information concerning publication of the contributions.

(2) An adjunct application on Form GR/CP. The purpose of this form is to provide separate identification for each of the contributions and to give information about their first publication, as required by the statute.

## WHICH BASIC APPLICATION FORM TO USE

The basic application form you choose to submit should be determined by the nature of the contributions you are registering. As long as they meet the statutory qualifications for group registration (outlined on the reverse of this page), the contributions can be registered together even if they are entirely different in nature, type, or content. However, you must choose which of three forms is generally the most appropriate on which to submit your basic application:

**Form TX:** for nondramatic literary works consisting primarily of text. Examples are fiction, verse, articles, news stories, features, essays, reviews, editorials, columns, quizzes, puzzles, and advertising copy.

**Form PA:** for works of the performing arts. Examples are music, drama, choreography, and pantomimes.

**Form VA:** for works of the visual arts. Examples are photographs, drawings, paintings, prints, art reproductions, cartoons, comic strips, charts, diagrams, maps, pictorial ornamentation, and pictorial or graphic material published as advertising.

If your contributions differ in nature, choose the form most suitable for the majority of them. However, if any of the contributions consists preponderantly of nondramatic text matter in English, you should file Form TX for the entire group. This is because Form TX is the only form containing spaces for information about the manufacture of copies, which the statute requires to be given for certain works.

## REGISTRATION FEE FOR GROUP REGISTRATION

The fee for registration of a group of contributions to periodicals is $10, no matter how many contributions are listed on Form GR/CP. Unless you maintain a Deposit Account in the Copyright Office, the registration fee must accompany your application forms and copies. Make your remittance payable to: *Register of Copyrights.*

## WHAT COPIES SHOULD BE DEPOSITED FOR GROUP REGISTRATION?

The application forms you file for group registration must be accompanied by one complete copy of each contribution listed in Form GR/CP, exactly as the contribution was first published in a periodical. The deposit must consist of the entire issue of the periodical containing the contribution; or, if the contribution was first published in a newspaper, the deposit should consist of the entire section in which the contribution appeared. Tear sheets or proof copies are not acceptable for deposit.

## COPYRIGHT NOTICE REQUIREMENTS

For published works, the law provides that a copyright notice in a specified form "shall be placed on all publicly distributed copies from which the work can be visually perceived." The required form of the notice generally consists of three elements: (1) the symbol "©", or the word "Copyright", or the abbreviation "Copr."; (2) the year of first publication of the work; and (3) the name of the owner of copyright in the work, or an abbreviation or alternative form of the name. For example: "© 1978 Samuel Craig"

Among the conditions for group registration of contributions to periodicals, the statute establishes two requirements involving the copyright notice:

(1) Each of the contributions as first published must have borne a separate copyright notice; and

(2) "The name of the owner of copyright in the work, or an abbreviation by which the name can be recognized, or a generally known alternative designation of the owner" must have been the same in each notice.

## HOW TO FILL OUT THE BASIC APPLICATION FORM WHEN APPLYING FOR GROUP REGISTRATION

In general, the instructions for filling out the basic application (Form TX, Form PA, or Form VA) apply to group registrations. In addition, please observe the following specific instructions:

**Space 1 (Title):** Do not give information concerning any of the contributions in space 1 of the basic application. Instead, in the block headed "Title of this Work", state: "See Form GR/CP, attached". Leave the other blocks in space 1 blank.

**Space 2 (Author):** Give the name and other information concerning the author of all of the contributions listed in Form GR/CP. To qualify for group registration, all of the contributions must have been written by the same individual author.

**Space 3 (Creation and Publication):** In the block calling for the year of creation, give the year of creation of the last of the contributions to be completed. Leave the block calling for the date and nation of first publication blank.

**Space 4 (Claimant):** Give all of the requested information, which must be the same for all of the contributions listed on Form GR/CP.

**Other spaces:** Complete all of the applicable spaces, and be sure that the form is signed in the certification space.

## HOW TO FILL OUT FORM GR/CP

### PART A: IDENTIFICATION OF APPLICATION

• **Identification of Basic Application:** Indicate, by checking one of the boxes, which of the basic application forms (Form TX, or Form PA, or Form VA) you are filing for registration.

• **Identification of Author and Claimant:** Give the name of the individual author exactly as it appears in line 2 of the basic application, and give the name of the copyright claimant exactly as it appears in line 4 of the basic application. These must be the same for all of the contributions listed in Part B of Form GR/CP.

### PART B: REGISTRATION FOR GROUP OF CONTRIBUTIONS

• **General Instructions:** Under the statute, a group of contributions to periodicals will qualify for a single registration only if the application "identifies each work separately, including the periodical containing it and its date of first publication." Part B of the Form GR/CP provides lines enough to list 19 separate contributions; if you need more space, use additional Forms GR/CP. If possible, list the contributions in the order of their publication, giving the earliest first. Number each line consecutively.

• **Important:** All of the contributions listed on Form GR/CP must have been published within a single twelve-month period. This does not mean that all of the contributions must have been published during the same calendar year, but it does mean that, to be grouped in a single application, the earliest and latest contributions must not have been published more than twelve months apart. Example: Contributions published on April 1, 1978, July 1, 1978, and March 1, 1979, could be grouped together, but a contribution published on April 15, 1979, could not be registered with them as part of the group.

• **Title of Contribution:** Each contribution must be given a title that is capable of identifying that particular work and of distinguishing it from others. If the contribution as published in the periodical bears a title (or an identifying phrase that could serve as a title), transcribe its wording completely and exactly.

• **Identification of Periodical:** Give the over-all title of the periodical in which the contribution was first published, together with the volume and issue number (if any) and the issue date.

• **Pages:** Give the number of the page of the periodical issue on which the contribution appeared. If the contribution covered more than one page, give the inclusive pages, if possible.

• **First Publication:** The statute defines "publication" as "the distribution of copies or phonorecords of a work to the public by sale or other transfer of ownership, or by rental, lease, or lending"; a work is also "published" if there has been an "offering to distribute copies or phonorecords to a group of persons for purposes of further distribution, public performance, or public display." Give the full date (month, day, and year) when, and the country where, publication of the periodical issue containing the contribution first occurred. If first publication took place simultaneously in the United States and other countries, it is sufficient to state "U.S.A."

---

**NOTE:** The advantage of group registration is that it allows any number of works published within a twelve-month period to be registered "on the basis of a single deposit, application, and registration fee." On the other hand, group registration may also have disadvantages under certain circumstances. If infringement of a published work begins before the work has been registered, the copyright owner can still obtain the ordinary remedies for copyright infringement (including injunctions, actual damages and profits, and impounding and disposition of infringing articles). However, in that situation—where the copyright in a published work is infringed before registration is made—the owner cannot obtain special remedies (statutory damages and attorney's fees) unless registration was made within three months after first publication of the work.

# ADJUNCT APPLICATION
## *for*
## *Copyright Registration for a*
## *Group of Contributions to Periodicals*

- Use this adjunct form only if your are making a single registration for a group of contributions to periodicals, and you are also filing a basic application on Form TX, Form PA, or Form VA. Follow the instructions, attached.
- Number each line in Part B consecutively. Use additional Forms GR/CP if you need more space.
- Submit this adjunct form with the basic application form. Clip (do not tape or staple) and fold all sheets together before submitting them.

## FORM GR/CP

UNITED STATES COPYRIGHT OFFICE

| REGISTRATION NUMBER |
|---|
| TX       PA       VA |

| EFFECTIVE DATE OF REGISTRATION |
|---|
| (Month)         (Day)         (Year) |

| FORM GR/CP RECEIVED |
|---|
| Page _____ of _____ pages |

---

**DO NOT WRITE ABOVE THIS LINE. FOR COPYRIGHT OFFICE USE ONLY**

**(A)**

**Identification of Application**

**IDENTIFICATION OF BASIC APPLICATION:**
- This application for copyright registration for a group of contributions to periodicals is submitted as an adjunct to an application filed on: (Check which)

☐ Form TX          ☐ Form PA          ☐ Form VA

**IDENTIFICATION OF AUTHOR AND CLAIMANT:** (Give the name of the author and the name of the copyright claimant in all of the contributions listed in Part B of this form. The names should be the same as the names given in spaces 2 and 4 of the basic application.)

Name of Author: ....................................................................................

Name of Copyright Claimant: ....................................................................

**(B)**

**Registration For Group of Contributions**

**COPYRIGHT REGISTRATION FOR A GROUP OF CONTRIBUTIONS TO PERIODICALS:** (To make a single registration for a group of works by the same individual author, all first published as contributions to periodicals within a 12-month period (see instructions), give full information about each contribution. If more space is needed, use additional Forms GR/CP.)

☐ Title of Contribution: .......................................................
Title of Periodical: ................................. Vol...... No...... Issue Date....... Pages........
Date of First Publication: .................................. Nation of First Publication ..............
(Month) (Day) (Year) (Country)

☐ Title of Contribution: .......................................................
Title of Periodical: ................................. Vol...... No...... Issue Date....... Pages........
Date of First Publication: .................................. Nation of First Publication ..............
(Month) (Day) (Year) (Country)

☐ Title of Contribution: .......................................................
Title of Periodical: ................................. Vol...... No...... Issue Date....... Pages........
Date of First Publication: .................................. Nation of First Publication ..............
(Month) (Day) (Year) (Country)

☐ Title of Contribution: .......................................................
Title of Periodical: ................................. Vol...... No...... Issue Date....... Pages........
Date of First Publication: .................................. Nation of First Publication ..............
(Month) (Day) (Year) (Country)

☐ Title of Contribution: .......................................................
Title of Periodical: ................................. Vol...... No...... Issue Date....... Pages........
Date of First Publication: .................................. Nation of First Publication
(Month) (Day) (Year) (Country)

☐ Title of Contribution: .......................................................
Title of Periodical: ................................. Vol...... No...... Issue Date....... Pages........
Date of First Publication: .................................. Nation of First Publication ..............
(Month) (Day) (Year) (Country)

☐ Title of Contribution: .......................................................
Title of Periodical: ................................. Vol...... No...... Issue Date....... Pages........
Date of First Publication: .................................. Nation of First Publication ..............
(Month) (Day) (Year) (Country)

FOR
COPYRIGHT
OFFICE
USE
ONLY

**DO NOT WRITE ABOVE THIS LINE. FOR COPYRIGHT OFFICE USE ONLY**

☐ Title of Contribution: . . . . . . . . . . . . . . . . . . . . . . . . . . . . . . . . . . . . . . . . . . . . . . . . . . . . . . . . . . . . . . . . . . . .
Title of Periodical: . . . . . . . . . . . . . . . . . . . . . . . . . . . . . . . . . . . . . . Vol. . . . . . No. . . . . . Issue Date . . . . . . . . . Pages. . . . . . . . . .
Date of First Publication: . . . . . . . . . . . . . . . . . . . . . . . . . . . . . Nation of First Publication . . . . . . . . . . . . . . . . . . . . . . . . . . .
(Month)        (Day)        (Year)                        (Country)

Ⓑ
**Continued**

☐ Title of Contribution: . . . . . . . . . . . . . . . . . . . . . . . . . . . . . . . . . . . . . . . . . . . . . . . . . . . . . . . . . . . . . . . . . . . .
Title of Periodical: . . . . . . . . . . . . . . . . . . . . . . . . . . . . . . . . . . . . . . Vol. . . . . . No. . . . . . Issue Date . . . . . . . . . Pages. . . . . . . . . .
Date of First Publication: . . . . . . . . . . . . . . . . . . . . . . . . . . . Nation of First Publication . . . . . . . . . . . . . . . . . . . . . . . . . . .
(Month)        (Day)        (Year)                        (Country)

☐ Title of Contribution: . . . . . . . . . . . . . . . . . . . . . . . . . . . . . . . . . . . . . . . . . . . . . . . . . . . . . . . . . . . . . . . . . . . .
Title of Periodical: . . . . . . . . . . . . . . . . . . . . . . . . . . . . . . . . . . . . . . Vol. . . . . . No. . . . . . Issue Date . . . . . . . . . Pages. . . . . . . . . .
Date of First Publication: . . . . . . . . . . . . . . . . . . . . . . . . . . . Nation of First Publication . . . . . . . . . . . . . . . . . . . . . . . . . . .
(Month)        (Day)        (Year)                        (Country)

☐ Title of Contribution: . . . . . . . . . . . . . . . . . . . . . . . . . . . . . . . . . . . . . . . . . . . . . . . . . . . . . . . . . . . . . . . . . . . .
Title of Periodical: . . . . . . . . . . . . . . . . . . . . . . . . . . . . . . . . . . . . . . Vol. . . . . . No. . . . . . Issue Date . . . . . . . . . Pages. . . . . . . . . .
Date of First Publication: . . . . . . . . . . . . . . . . . . . . . . . . . . . Nation of First Publication . . . . . . . . . . . . . . . . . . . . . . . . . . .
(Month)        (Day)        (Year)                        (Country)

☐ Title of Contribution: . . . . . . . . . . . . . . . . . . . . . . . . . . . . . . . . . . . . . . . . . . . . . . . . . . . . . . . . . . . . . . . . . . . .
Title of Periodical: . . . . . . . . . . . . . . . . . . . . . . . . . . . . . . . . . . . . . . Vol. . . . . . No. . . . . . Issue Date . . . . . . . . . Pages. . . . . . . . . .
Date of First Publication: . . . . . . . . . . . . . . . . . . . . . . . . . . . Nation of First Publication . . . . . . . . . . . . . . . . . . . . . . . . . . .
(Month)        (Day)        (Year)                        (Country)

☐ Title of Contribution: . . . . . . . . . . . . . . . . . . . . . . . . . . . . . . . . . . . . . . . . . . . . . . . . . . . . . . . . . . . . . . . . . . . .
Title of Periodical: . . . . . . . . . . . . . . . . . . . . . . . . . . . . . . . . . . . . . . Vol. . . . . . No. . . . . . Issue Date . . . . . . . . . Pages. . . . . . . . . .
Date of First Publication: . . . . . . . . . . . . . . . . . . . . . . . . . . . Nation of First Publication . . . . . . . . . . . . . . . . . . . . . . . . . . .
(Month)        (Day)        (Year)                        (Country)

☐ Title of Contribution: . . . . . . . . . . . . . . . . . . . . . . . . . . . . . . . . . . . . . . . . . . . . . . . . . . . . . . . . . . . . . . . . . . . .
Title of Periodical: . . . . . . . . . . . . . . . . . . . . . . . . . . . . . . . . . . . . . . Vol. . . . . . No. . . . . . Issue Date . . . . . . . . . Pages. . . . . . . . . .
Date of First Publication: . . . . . . . . . . . . . . . . . . . . . . . . . . . Nation of First Publication . . . . . . . . . . . . . . . . . . . . . . . . . . .
(Month)        (Day)        (Year)                        (Country)

☐ Title of Contribution: . . . . . . . . . . . . . . . . . . . . . . . . . . . . . . . . . . . . . . . . . . . . . . . . . . . . . . . . . . . . . . . . . . . .
Title of Periodical: . . . . . . . . . . . . . . . . . . . . . . . . . . . . . . . . . . . . . . Vol. . . . . . No. . . . . . Issue Date . . . . . . . . . Pages. . . . . . . . . .
Date of First Publication: . . . . . . . . . . . . . . . . . . . . . . . . . . . Nation of First Publication . . . . . . . . . . . . . . . . . . . . . . . . . . .
(Month)        (Day)        (Year)                        (Country)

☐ Title of Contribution: . . . . . . . . . . . . . . . . . . . . . . . . . . . . . . . . . . . . . . . . . . . . . . . . . . . . . . . . . . . . . . . . . . . .
Title of Periodical: . . . . . . . . . . . . . . . . . . . . . . . . . . . . . . . . . . . . . . Vol. . . . . . No. . . . . . Issue Date . . . . . . . . . Pages. . . . . . . . . .
Date of First Publication: . . . . . . . . . . . . . . . . . . . . . . . . . . . Nation of First Publication . . . . . . . . . . . . . . . . . . . . . . . . . . .
(Month)        (Day)        (Year)                        (Country)

☐ Title of Contribution: . . . . . . . . . . . . . . . . . . . . . . . . . . . . . . . . . . . . . . . . . . . . . . . . . . . . . . . . . . . . . . . . . . . .
Title of Periodical: . . . . . . . . . . . . . . . . . . . . . . . . . . . . . . . . . . . . . . Vol. . . . . . No. . . . . . Issue Date . . . . . . . . . Pages. . . . . . . . . .
Date of First Publication: . . . . . . . . . . . . . . . . . . . . . . . . . . . Nation of First Publication . . . . . . . . . . . . . . . . . . . . . . . . . . .
(Month)        (Day)        (Year)                        (Country)

☐ Title of Contribution: . . . . . . . . . . . . . . . . . . . . . . . . . . . . . . . . . . . . . . . . . . . . . . . . . . . . . . . . . . . . . . . . . . . .
Title of Periodical: . . . . . . . . . . . . . . . . . . . . . . . . . . . . . . . . . . . . . . Vol. . . . . . No. . . . . . Issue Date . . . . . . . . . Pages. . . . . . . . . .
Date of First Publication: . . . . . . . . . . . . . . . . . . . . . . . . . . . Nation of First Publication . . . . . . . . . . . . . . . . . . . . . . . . . . .
(Month)        (Day)        (Year)                        (Country)

☐ Title of Contribution: . . . . . . . . . . . . . . . . . . . . . . . . . . . . . . . . . . . . . . . . . . . . . . . . . . . . . . . . . . . . . . . . . . . .
Title of Periodical: . . . . . . . . . . . . . . . . . . . . . . . . . . . . . . . . . . . . . . Vol. . . . . . No. . . . . . Issue Date . . . . . . . . . Pages. . . . . . . . . .
Date of First Publication: . . . . . . . . . . . . . . . . . . . . . . . . . . . Nation of First Publication . . . . . . . . . . . . . . . . . . . . . . . . . . .
(Month)        (Day)        (Year)                        (Country)

Nov. 1977—25,000

GPO : 1977—O-248-623

# Appendix 4
## TEXTS OF VARIOUS GUIDELINES DEVELOPED UNDER OFFICIAL AUSPICES

Notwithstanding the general exclusive rights that a copyright owner has, they are not infringed upon by the fair use of a copyrighted work [107]. This is not a new concept. "Fair use," as a judicial doctrine, was part of our copyright law even before the Copyright Act of 1909. Nonetheless, the scope of its application to educational uses of copyrighted materials has not been significantly developed in court cases. In 1975, members of the House Judiciary Committee encouraged representatives of educators and publishers to meet together to develop some standards as to permissible educational uses of copyrighted materials. Meetings were held and resulted in the two sets of guidelines included in this appendix. The guidelines do not have the binding effect of a law. However, they are part of the new law's legislative history, and the Senate-House Conference report on the bill states that the conferees accept them "as part of their understanding of fair use."

## Legislative History's Fair Use Guidelines for Educators

### BOOKS AND PERIODICALS

The purpose of the following guidelines is to state the minimum and not the maximum standards of educational fair use under Section 107 of H.R. 2223. The parties agree that the conditions determining the extent of permissible copying for educational purposes may change in the future; that certain types of copying permitted under these guidelines may not be permissible in the future; and conversely that in the future other types of copying not permitted under these guidelines may be permissible under revised guidelines.

Moreover, the following statement of guidelines is not intended to limit the types of copying permitted under the standards of fair use under judicial decision and which are stated in Section 107 of the Copyright Revision Bill. There may be instances in which copying which does not fall within the guidelines stated below may nonetheless be permitted under the criteria of fair use.

### I. SINGLE COPYING FOR TEACHERS

A single copy may be made of any of the following by or for a teacher at his or her individual request for his or her scholarly research or use in teaching or preparation to teach a class:

A. A chapter from a book;

B. An article from a periodical or newspaper;

C. A short story, short essay or short poem, whether or not from a collective work;

D. A chart, graph, diagram, drawing, cartoon, or picture from a book, periodical, or newspaper.

## II. MULTIPLE COPIES FOR CLASSROOM USE

Multiple copies (not to exceed, in any event, more than one copy per pupil in a course) may be made by or for the teacher giving the course for classroom use or discussion; *provided that:*

A. The copying meets the tests of brevity and spontaneity as defined below; *and,*

B. Meets the cumulative effect test as defined below; *and,*

C. Each copy includes a notice of copyright.

### Definitions

*Brevity*

i. Poetry: (a) A complete poem if less than 250 words and if printed on not more than two pages, or (b) from a longer poem, an excerpt of not more than 250 words.

ii. Prose: (a) Either a complete article, story or essay of less than 2,500 words, or (b) an excerpt from any prose work of not more than 1,000 words or 10% of the work, whichever is less, but in any event a minimum of 500 words.

[Each of the numerical limits stated in "i" and "ii" above may be expanded to permit the completion of an unfinished line of a poem or of an unfinished prose paragraph.]

iii. Illustration: One chart, graph, diagram, drawing, cartoon or picture per book or per periodical issue.

iv. "Special" works: Certain works in poetry, prose or in "poetic prose" which often combine language with illustrations and which are intended sometimes for children and at other times for a more general audience fall short of 2,500 words in their entirety. Paragraph "ii" above, notwithstanding such "special works," may not be reproduced in their entirety; however, an excerpt comprising not more than two of the published pages of such special work and containing not more than 10% of the words found in the text thereof, may be reproduced.

*Spontaneity*

i. The copying is at the instance and inspiration of the individual teacher, and

ii. The inspiration and decision to use the work and the moment of its use for maximum teaching effectiveness are so close in time that it would be unreasonable to expect a timely reply to a request for permission.

*Cumulative Effect*

i. The copying of the material is for only one course in the school in which the copies are made.

ii. Not more than one short poem, article, story, essay or two excerpts may be copied from the same author, nor more than three from the same collective work or periodical volume during one class term.

iii. There shall not be more than nine instances of such multiple copying for one course during one class term.

[The limitations stated in "ii" and "iii" above shall not apply to current news periodicals and newspapers and current news sections of other periodicals.]

## III. PROHIBITIONS AS TO I AND II ABOVE

Notwithstanding any of the above, the following shall be prohibited:

A. Copying shall not be used to create or to replace or substitute for anthologies, compilations or collective works. Such replacement or substitution may occur whether copies of various works or excerpts therefrom are accumulated or are reproduced and used separately.

B. There shall be no copying of or from works intended to be "consumable" in the course of study or of teaching. These include workbooks, exercises, standardized tests and test booklets and answer sheets and like consumable material.

C. Copying shall not:
   a. substitute for the purchase of books, publisher's reprints or periodicals;
   b. be directed by higher authority;
   c. be repeated with respect to the same item by the same teacher from term to term.

D. No charge shall be made to the student beyond the actual cost of the photocopying.

## MUSIC

The purpose of the following guidelines is to state the minimum and not the maximum standards of educational fair use under Section 107 of H.R. 2223. The parties agree that the conditions determining the extent of permissible copying for educational purposes may change in the future; that certain types of copying permitted under these guidelines may not be permissible in the future; and conversely that in the future other types of copying not permitted under these guidelines may be permissible under revised guidelines.

Moreover, the following statement of guidelines is not intended to limit the types of copying permitted under the standards of fair use under judicial decision and which are stated in Section 107 of the Copyright Revision Bill. There may be instances in which copying which does not fall within the guidelines stated below may nonetheless be permitted under the criteria of fair use.

## A. PERMISSIBLE USES

1. Emergency copying to replace purchased copies which for any reason are not available for an imminent performance, provided purchased replacement copies shall be substituted in due course.

2. For academic purposes other than performance, single or multiple copies of excerpts of works may be made, provided that the excerpts do not comprise a part of the whole which would constitute a performable unit such as a section, movement or aria, but in no case more than (10%) of the whole work. The number of copies shall not exceed one copy per pupil.

3. Printed copies which have been purchased may be edited or simplified, provided that the fundamental character of the work is not distorted or the lyrics, if any, altered, or lyrics added if none exist.

4. A single copy of recordings of performances by students may be made for evaluation or rehearsal purposes and may be retained by the educational institution or individual teacher.

5. A single copy of a sound recording (such as a tape, disc or cassette) of copy-

righted music may be made from sound recordings owned by an educational institution or an individual teacher for the purpose of constructing aural exercises or examinations and may be retained by the educational institution or individual teacher. (This pertains only to the copyright of the music itself and not to any copyright which may exist in the sound recording.)

## B. PROHIBITIONS

1. Copying to create or replace or substitute for anthologies, compilations or collective works.
2. Copying of or from works intended to be "consumable" in the course of study or of teaching, such as workbooks, exercises, standardized tests and answer sheets and like material.
3. Copying for the purpose of performance, except as in A(1) above.
4. Copying for the purpose of substituting for the purchase of music, except as in A(1) and A(2) above.
5. Copying without inclusion of the copyright notice which appears on the printed copy.

# 1981 Negotiated Guidelines Concerning Off-Air Videorecording and Fair Use in Education

This part of the appendix consists of remarks and materials inserted into the *Congressional Record* by Congressman Kastenmeier (*Congressional Record* E4751, daily edition, October 14, 1981).

I am pleased to announce today that a negotiating committee of interested parties, developed by the Judiciary Committee, has drafted guidelines for use by copyright owners and educators which will go a long way toward resolving the lingering problems associated with off-air videotaping of copyright works for educational purposes. I thank, and congratulate, the negotiating committee for their efforts, which will, I believe, greatly assist in clarifying the procedures which educators may follow in their use of broadcasted copyrighted materials. These guidelines will help solve an important problem, hopefully without further legislation and litigation. As chairman of the House Judiciary Subcommittee on Courts, Civil Liberties, and the Administration of Justice, which has jurisdiction over our copyright system, I share the view of the negotiating committee that these guidelines reach an appropriate balance between the proprietary rights of copyright owners and the instructional needs of educational institutions. I recognize that beyond these guidelines specific permissions from copyright proprietors may be required under the Copyright Law. I am pleased to insert the guidelines in the *Record* for printing in order to assist in their widest possible dissemination.

August 31, 1981

Hon. Robert W. Kastenmeier,
*Chairman, Subcommittee on Courts, Civil Liberties,*
*and Administration of Justice, Committee on the Judiciary,*
*U.S. House of Representatives, Washington, D.C.*

Dear Congressman Kastenmeier: We are forwarding herewith the "Guidelines for Off-Air Recording of Broadcast Programming for Educational Purposes," developed by the Negotiating Committee appointed by your subcommittee.

The Negotiating Committee has concurred that these guidelines reach an appropriate balance between the proprietary rights of copyright owners and the instructional needs of educational institutions. The Negotiating Committee recognized that beyond these guidelines, specific licenses or permissions from copyright proprietors may be required under the Copyright Law. The Committee believes that these guidelines should be reviewed periodically at reasonable intervals.

In accordance with what we believe was your intent, the Negotiating Committee has limited its discussion to nonprofit educational institutions and to television programs broadcast for reception by the general public without charge. Within the guidelines, the Negotiating Committee does not intend that off-air recordings by teachers under fair use be permitted to be intentionally substituted in the school curriculum for a standard practice of purchase or license of the same educational material by the institution concerned.

Sincerely,

Eileen D. Cooke, Co-Chairman
Leonard Wasser, Co-Chairman

MEMBERS OF THE NEGOTIATING TEAM*
Eugene Aleinikoff, Agency for Instructional Television
Joseph Bellon, CBS
Ivan Bender, Association of Media Producers
James Bouras, Motion Picture Association of America
Eileen D. Cooke, American Library Association
Bernard Freitag, National Education Association
Howard Hitchens, Association for Educational Communications and Technology
Irwin Karp, Authors League of America
John McGuire, Screen Actors Guild
Frank Norwood, Joint Council on Educational Communications
Ernest Ricca, Directors Guild of America
Carol Risher, Association of American Publishers
James Popham, National Association of Broadcasters
Judith Bressler, ABC
Eric H. Smith, Public Broadcasting Service
Sheldon Steinbach, American Council on Education
August W. Steinhilber, National School Boards Association
Leonard Wasser, Writers Guild of America, East
Sanford Wolff, American Federation of Television and Radio Artists

---

* *Author's note:* The *Congressional Record* text included superscript numbers next to the names of Messrs. Bender, Bouras, and Wolff. These, and the related footnotes, are omitted here. The note related to Mr. Wolff reports that "As a result of a summer hiatus, the guidelines have not yet been submitted to the AFTRA National Governing Board." The notes with respect to the other individuals refer to certain letters which are reported on in this appendix following the text of the guidelines.

# Guidelines for Off-Air Recording of Broadcast Programming for Educational Purposes*

In March 1978, Congressman Robert Kastenmeier, Chairman of the House Sub-committee on Courts, Civil Liberties, and Administration of Justice, appointed a Negotiating Committee consisting of representatives of educational organizations, copyright proprietors, and creative guilds and unions. The following guidelines reflect the Negotiating Committee's consensus as to the application of "fair use" to the recording, retention, and use of television broadcast programs for educational purposes. They specify periods of retention and use of such off-air recordings in classrooms and similar places devoted to instruction and for home-bound instruction. The purpose of establishing these guidelines is to provide standards for both owners and users of copyrighted television programs.

1. The guidelines were developed to apply only to off-air recording by non-profit educational institutions.

2. A broadcast program may be recorded off-air simultaneously with broadcast transmission (including simultaneous cable retransmission) and retained by a non-profit educational institution for a period not to exceed the first forty-five (45) consecutive calendar days after date of recording. Upon conclusion of such retention period, all off-air recordings must be erased or destroyed immediately. "Broadcast programs" are television programs transmitted by television stations for reception by the general public without charge.

3. Off-air recordings may be used once by individual teachers in the course of relevant teaching activities, and repeated once only when instructional reinforcement is necessary, in classrooms and similar places devoted to instruction within a single building, cluster or campus, as well as in the homes of students receiving formalized home instruction, during the first ten (10) consecutive school days in the forty-five (45) calendar day retention period. "School days" are school session days—not counting weekends, holidays, vacations, examination periods, or other scheduled interruptions—within the forty-five (45) calendar day retention period.

4. Off-air recordings may be made only at the request of and used by individual teachers and may not be regularly recorded in anticipation of requests. No broadcast

---

* Author's note: The Congressional Record text of the guidelines is followed by letters from the Motion Picture Association of America, Inc., the Association of Media Producers, and from Ivan Bender, the General Counsel of Films, Inc.

The Motion Picture Association noted that it "will take no position on the . . . guidelines" but also named several member companies which "assent to the guidelines," i.e., Avco Embassy Pictures Corp., Filmways Pictures, Inc., Metro-Goldwyn-Mayer Film Co., Paramount Pictures Corp., Twentieth Century-Fox Film Corp., and Universal Pictures, a division of Universal City Studios, Inc.

The Association of Media Producers letter reports that the association's board of directors voted not to endorse the guidelines. The letter states: "The guidelines are not in keeping with the principal objectives of our industry, and we are fearful that they may seriously jeopardize the future well-being of the small but vital educational media industry, its markets, and the availability of a broad variety of instructional materials essential to maintaining quality educational programs."

The letter from Mr. Bender, who was a member of the Negotiating Committee, notes that he had recommended adoption of the guidelines by the board of the Association of Media Producers; that his recommendation also reflected the "overwhelming opinion throughout my company [Films, Inc.] on this issue," that the question was narrowly defeated by the AMP board; and that he believes "that adoption of the guidelines would be a positive development in the educational audio-visual industry."

program may be recoreded (sic) off-air more than once at the request of the same teacher, regardless of the number of times the program may be broadcast.

5. A limited number of copies may be reproduced from each off-air recording to meet the legitimate needs of teachers under these guidelines. Each such additional copy shall be subject to all provisions governing the original recording.

6. After the first ten (10) consecutive school days, off-air recordings may be used up to the end of the forty-five (45) calendar day retention period only for teacher evaluation purposes, i.e., to determine whether or not to include the broadcast program in the teaching curriculum, and may not be used in the recording institution for student exhibition or any other non-evaluation purposes without authorization.

7. Off-air recordings need not be used in their entirety, but the recorded programs may not be altered from their original content. Off-air recordings may not be physically or electronically combined or merged to constitute teaching anthologies or compilations.

8. All copies of off-air recordings must include the copyright notice on the broadcast notice as recorded.

9. Educational institutions are expected to establish appropriate control procedures to maintain the integrity of these guidelines.

This part of the appendix is composed of excerpts from the September 29, 1976, Senate-House Conference report.

## Conference Substitute

The conference substitute adopts the provisions of section 108 as amended by the House bill. In doing so, the conferees have noted two letters dated September 22, 1976, sent respectively to John L. McClellan, Chairman of the Senate Judiciary Subcommittee on Patents, Trademarks, and Copyrights, and to Robert W. Kastenmeier, Chairman of the House Judiciary Subcommittee on Courts, Civil Liberties, and the Administration of Justice. The letters, from the Chairman of the National Commission on New Technological Uses of Copyrighted Works (CONTU), Stanley H. Fuld, transmitted a document consisting of "guidelines interpreting the provision in subsection 108(g)(2) of S. 22, as approved by the House Committee on the Judiciary." Chairman Fuld's letters explain that, following lengthy consultations with the parties concerned, the Commission adopted these guidelines as fair and workable and with the hope that the conferees on S. 22 may find that they merit inclusion in the conference report. The letters add that, although time did not permit securing signatures of the representatives of the principal library organizations or of the organizations representing publishers and authors on these guidelines, the Commission had received oral assurances from these representatives that the guidelines are acceptable to their organizations.

The conference committee understands that the guidelines are not intended as, and cannot be considered, explicit rules or directions governing any and all cases, now or in the future. It is recognized that their purpose is to provide guidance in the most commonly encountered interlibrary photocopying situations, that they are not intended to be limiting or determinative in themselves or with respect to other situations, and that they deal with an evolving situation that will undoubtedly require their continuous reevaluation and adjustment. With these qualifications, the conference committee agrees that the guidelines are a reasonable interpretation of the proviso of section 108(g)(2) in the most common situations to which they apply today.

The text of the library reproduction guidelines appears on the following two pages.

# Photocopying—Interlibrary Arrangements

## INTRODUCTION

Subsection 108(g)(2) of the bill deals, among other things, with limits on interlibrary arrangements for photocopying. It prohibits systematic photocopying of copyrighted materials but permits interlibrary arrangements "that do not have, as their purpose or effect, that the library or archives receiving such copies or phonorecords for distribution does so in such aggregate quantities as to substitute for a subscription to or purchase of such work."

The National Commission on New Technological Uses of Copyrighted Works offered its good offices to the House and Senate subcommittees in bringing the interested parties together to see if agreement could be reached on what a realistic definition would be of "such aggregate quantities." The Commission consulted with the parties and suggested the interpretation which follows, on which there has been substantial agreement by the principal library, publisher, and author organizations. The Commission considers the guidelines which follow to be a workable and fair interpretation of the intent of the proviso portion of subsection 108(g)(2).

These guidelines are intended to provide guidance in the application of section 108 to the most frequently encountered interlibrary case: a library's obtaining from another library, in lieu of interlibrary loan, copies of articles from relatively recent issues of periodicals—those published within five years prior to the date of the request. The guidelines do not specify what aggregate quantity of copies of an article or articles published in a periodical, the issue date of which is more than five years prior to the date when the request for the copy thereof is made, constitutes a substitute for a subscription to such periodical. The meaning of the proviso to subsection 108(g)(2) in such case is left to future interpretation.

The point has been made that the present practice on interlibrary loans and use of photocopies in lieu of loans may be supplemented or even largely replaced by a system in which one or more agencies or institutions, public or private, exist for the specific purpose of providing a central source for photocopies. Of course, these guidelines would not apply to such a situation.

## GUIDELINES FOR THE PROVISO OF SUBSECTION 108(g)(2)

1. As used in the proviso of subsection 108(g)(2), the words ". . . such aggregate quantities as to substitute for a subscription to or purchase of such work" shall mean:

(a) with respect to any given periodical (as opposed to any given issue of a periodical), filled requests of a library or archives (a "requesting entity") within any calendar year for a total of six or more copies of an article or articles published in such periodical within five years prior to the date of the request. These guidelines specifically shall not apply, directly or indirectly, to any request of a requesting entity for a copy or copies of an article or articles published in any issue of a periodical, the publication date of which is more than five years prior to the date when the request is made. These guidelines do not define the meaning, with respect to such a request, of ". . . such aggregate quantities as to substitute for a subscription to [such periodical]."

(b) with respect to any other material described in subsection 108(d) (including fiction and poetry), filled requests of a requesting entity within any calendar year for a total of six or more copies or phonorecords of or from any given work (including a collective work) during the entire period when such material shall be protected by copyright.

2. In the event that a requesting entity—

(a) shall have in force or shall have entered an order for a subscription to a periodical, or

(b) has within its collection, or shall have entered an order for, a copy or phonorecord of any other copyrighted work,

material from either category of which it desires to obtain by copy from another library or archives (the "supplying entity"), because the material to be copied is not reasonably available for use by the requesting entity itself, then the fulfillment of such request shall be treated as though the requesting entity made such copy from its own collection. A library or archives may request a copy or phonorecord from a supplying entity only under those circumstances where the requesting entity would have been able, under the other provisions of section 108, to supply such copy from materials in its own collection.

3. No request for a copy or phonorecord of any material to which these guidelines apply may be fulfilled by the supplying entity unless such request is accompanied by a representation by the requesting entity that the request was made in conformity with these guidelines.

4. The requesting entity shall maintain records of all requests made by it for copies or phonorecords of any materials to which these guidelines apply and shall maintain records of the fulfillment of such requests, which records shall be retained until the end of the third complete calendar year after the end of the calendar year in which the respective request shall have been made.

5. As part of the review provided for in subsection 108(i), these guidelines shall be reviewed not later than five years from the effective date of this bill.

# Appendix 5
## TEXT OF THE COPYRIGHT ACT OF 1909

Boldface numbers in the margin of the text (e.g., **N1, N2,** etc.) refer to notes at the end of this appendix. These notes represent amendments made to the Copyright Act of 1909 up to the time of the enactment of the 1976 Copyright Law. Ellipses have been inserted to indicate deletions of nonpertinent material from the original document's footnotes.

# Title 17—Copyrights

### (Revised to January 1, 1973)

## Chapter 1—Registration of Copyrights

§ 1. Exclusive rights as to copyrighted works.
§ 2. Rights of author or proprietor of unpublished work.
§ 3. Protection of component parts of work copyrighted; composite works or periodicals.
§ 4. All writings of author included.
§ 5. Classification of works for registration.
§ 6. Registration of prints and labels.
§ 7. Copyright on compilations of works in public domain or of copyrighted works; subsisting copyrights not affected.
§ 8. Copyright not to subsist in works in public domain, or published prior to July 1, 1909, and not already copyrighted, or Government publications; publication by Government of copyrighted material.
§ 9. Authors or proprietors, entitled; aliens.
§ 10. Publication of work with notice.
§ 11. Registration of claim and issuance of certificate.
§ 12. Works not reproduced for sale.
§ 13. Deposit of copies after publication; action or proceeding for infringement.
§ 14. Same; failure to deposit; demand; penalty.
§ 15. Same; postmaster's receipt; transmission by mail without cost.
§ 16. Mechanical work to be done in United States.
§ 17. Affidavit to accompany copies.
§ 18. Making false affidavit.
§ 19. Notice; form.

§ 1. Exclusive Rights as to Copyrighted Works.—Any person entitled thereto, upon complying with the provisions of this title, shall have the exclusive right:

(a) To print, reprint, publish, copy, and vend the copyrighted work;

(b) To translate the copyrighted work into other languages or dialects, or make any other version thereof, if it be a literary work; to dramatize it if it be a nondramatic work; to convert it into a novel or other nondramatic work if it be a drama; to arrange or adapt it if it be a musical work; to complete, execute, and finish it if it be a model or design for a work of art;

(c) To deliver, authorize the delivery of, read, or present the copyrighted work in public for profit if it be a lecture, sermon, address or similar production, or other nondramatic literary work; to make or procure the making of any transcription or record thereof by or from which, in whole or in part, it may in any manner or by any method be exhibited, delivered, presented, produced, or reproduced; and to play or perform it in public for profit, and to exhibit, represent, produce, or reproduce it in any manner or by any method whatsoever. The damages for the infringement by broadcast of any work referred to in this subsection shall not exceed the sum of $100 where the infringing broadcaster shows that he was not aware that he was infringing and that such infringement could not have been reasonably foreseen; and

(d) To perform or represent the copyrighted work publicly if it be a drama or, if it be a dramatic work and not reproduced in copies for sale, to vend any manuscript or any record whatsoever thereof; to make or to procure the making of any transcription or record thereof by or from which, in whole or in part, it may in any manner or by any method be exhibited, performed, represented, produced, or reproduced; and to exhibit, perform, represent, produce, or reproduce it in any manner or by any method whatsoever; and

(e) To perform the copyrighted work publicly for profit if it be a musical composition; and for the purpose of public performance for profit, and for the purposes set forth in subsection (a) hereof, to make any arrangement or setting of it or of the melody of it in any system of notation or any form of record in which the thought of an author may be recorded and from which it may be read or reproduced: *Provided*, That the provisions of this title, so far as they secure copyright controlling the parts of instruments serving to reproduce mechanically the musical work, shall include only compositions published and copyrighted after July 1, 1909, and shall not include the works of a foreign author or composer unless the foreign state or nation of which such author or composer is a citizen or subject grants, either by treaty, convention, agreement, or law, to citizens of the United States similar rights. And as a condition of extending the copyright control to such mechanical reproductions, that whenever the owner of a musical copyright has used or permitted or knowingly acquiesced in the use of the copyrighted work upon the parts of instruments serving to reproduce mechanically the musical work, any other person may make similar use of the copyrighted work upon the payment to the copyright proprietor of a royalty of 2 cents on each such part manufactured, to be paid by the manufacturer thereof; and the copyright proprietor may require, and if so the manufacturer shall furnish, a report under oath on the 20th day of each month on the number of parts of instruments manufactured during the previous month serving to reproduce mechanically said musical work, and royalties shall be due on the parts manufactured during any month upon the 20th of the next succeeding month. The payment of the royalty provided for by this section shall free the articles or devices for which such royalty has been paid from further contribution to the copyright except in case of public performance for profit. It shall be the duty of the copyright owner, if he uses the musical composition himself for the manufacture of parts of instruments serving to reproduce mechanically the musical work, or licenses others to do so, to file notice thereof, accompanied by a recording fee, in the copyright office, and any failure to file such notice shall be a complete defense to any suit, action, or proceeding for any infringement of such copyright.

In case of failure of such manufacturer to pay to the copyright proprietor within thirty days after demand in writing the full sum of royalties due at said rate at the date of such demand, the court may award taxable costs to the plaintiff and a reasonable counsel fee, and the court may, in its discretion, enter judgment therein for any sum in addition over the amount found to be due as royalty in accordance with the terms of this title, not exceeding three times such amount.

The reproduction or rendition of a musical composition by or upon coin-operated machines shall not be deemed a public performance for profit unless a fee is charged for admission to the place where such reproduction or rendition occurs.

(f) [1] To reproduce and distribute to the public by sale or other transfer of ownership, or by rental, lease, or lending, reproductions of the copyrighted work if it be a sound recording: *Provided*, That the exclusive right of the owner of a copyright in a sound recording to reproduce it is limited to the right to duplicate the sound recording in a tangible form that directly or indirectly recaptures the actual sounds fixed in the recording: *Provided further*, That this right does not extend to the making or duplication of another sound recording that is an independent fixation of other sounds, even though such sounds imitate or simulate those in the copyrighted sound recording; or to reproductions made by transmitting organizations exclusively for their own use.

§ 2. RIGHTS OF AUTHOR OR PROPRIETOR OF UNPUBLISHED WORK.—Nothing in this title shall be construed to annul or limit the right of the author or proprietor of an unpublished work, at common law or in equity, to prevent the copying, publication, or use of such unpublished work without his consent, and to obtain damages therefor.

§ 3. PROTECTION OF COMPONENT PARTS OF WORK COPYRIGHTED; COMPOSITE WORKS OR PERIODICALS.—The copyright provided by this title shall protect all the copyrightable component parts of the work copyrighted, and all matter therein in which copyright is already subsisting, but without extending the duration or scope of such copyright. The copyright upon composite works or periodicals shall give to the proprietor thereof all the rights in respect thereto which he would have if each part were individually copyrighted under this title.

§ 4. ALL WRITINGS OF AUTHOR INCLUDED.—The works for which copyright may be secured under this title shall include all the writings of an author.

§ 5. CLASSIFICATION OF WORKS FOR REGISTRATION.—The application for registration shall specify to which of the following classes the work in which copyright is claimed belongs:

---

[1] Section 1(f) was added by the Act of October 15, 1971, Pub. L. 92–140, 85 Stat. 391. This act also added section 5(n), added a sentence at the end of section 19, amended the first sentence of section 20, and added three sentences at the end of section 26. The Act specified that the provisions cited in this footnote shall take effect four months after its enactment, that these provisions "shall apply only to sound recordings fixed, published, and copyrighted on and after the effective date of this Act and before January 1, 1975," and that nothing in title 17, United States Code, as amended by these provisions "shall be applied retrospectively or be construed as affecting in any way rights with respect to sound recordings fixed before the effective date of this Act."

(a) Books, including composite and cyclopedic works, directories, gazetteers, and other compilations.

(b) Periodicals, including newspapers.

(c) Lectures, sermons, addresses (prepared for oral delivery).

(d) Dramatic or dramatico-musical compositions.

(e) Musical compositions.

(f) Maps.

(g) Works of art; models or designs for works of art.

(h) Reproductions of a work of art.

(i) Drawings or plastic works of a scientific or technical character.

(j) Photographs.

(k) Prints and pictorial illustrations including prints or labels used for articles of merchandise.

(l) Motion-picture photoplays.

(m) Motion pictures other than photoplays.

(n)[1] Sound recordings.

The above specifications shall not be held to limit the subject matter of copyright as defined in section 4 of this title, nor shall any error in classification invalidate or impair the copyright protection secured under this title.

§ 6. REGISTRATION OF PRINTS AND LABELS.—Commencing July 1, 1940, the Register of Copyrights is charged with the registration of claims to copyright properly presented, in all prints and labels published in connection with the sale or advertisement of articles of merchandise, including all claims to copyright in prints and labels pending in the Patent Office and uncleared at the close of business June 30, 1940. There shall be paid for registering a claim of copyright in any such print or label not a trade-mark $6, which sum shall cover the expense of furnishing a certificate of such registration, under the seal of the Copyright Office, to the claimant of copyright.

§ 7. COPYRIGHT ON COMPILATIONS OF WORKS IN PUBLIC DOMAIN OR OF COPYRIGHTED WORKS; SUBSISTING COPYRIGHTS NOT AFFECTED.— Compilations or abridgments, adaptations, arrangements, dramatizations, translations, or other versions of works in the public domain or of copyrighted works when produced with the consent of the proprietor of the copyright in such works, or works republished with new matter, shall be regarded as new works subject to copyright under the provisions of this title; but the publication of any such new works shall not affect the force or validity of any subsisting copyright upon

---

[1] Section 5(n) was added by the Act of October 15, 1971, Pub. L. 92–140, 85 Stat. 391. [. . .]

the matter employed or any part thereof, or be construed to imply an exclusive right to such use of the original works, or to secure or extend copyright in such original works.

§ 8. COPYRIGHT NOT TO SUBSIST IN WORKS IN PUBLIC DOMAIN, OR PUBLISHED PRIOR TO JULY 1, 1909, AND NOT ALREADY COPYRIGHTED, OR GOVERNMENT PUBLICATIONS; PUBLICATION BY GOVERNMENT OF COPYRIGHTED MATERIAL.—No copyright shall subsist in the original text of any work which is in the public domain, or in any work which was published in this country or any foreign country prior to July 1, 1909, and has not been already copyrighted in the United States, or in any publication of the United States Government, or any reprint, in whole or in part, thereof, except that the Postmaster General may secure copyright on behalf of the United States in the whole or any part of the publications authorized by section 2506 of title 39.[1]

The publication or republication by the Government, either separately or in a public document, of any material in which copyright is subsisting shall not be taken to cause any abridgment or annulment of the copyright or to authorize any use or appropriation of such copyright material without the consent of the copyright proprietor.

§ 9. AUTHORS OR PROPRIETORS, ENTITLED: ALIENS.—The author or proprietor of any work made the subject of copyright by this title, or his executors, administrators, or assigns, shall have copyright for such work under the conditions and for the terms specified in this title: *Provided, however*, That the copyright secured by this title shall extend to the work of an author or proprietor who is a citizen or subject of a foreign state or nation only under the conditions described in subsections (a), (b), or (c) below:

(a) When an alien author or proprietor shall be domiciled within the United States at the time of the first publication of his work; or

(b) When the foreign state or nation of which such author or proprietor is a citizen or subject grants, either by treaty, convention, agreement, or law, to citizens of the United States the benefit of copyright on substantially the same basis as to its own citizens, or copyright protection, substantially equal to the protection secured to such foreign author under this title or by treaty; or when such foreign state or nation is a party to an international agreement which provides for reciprocity in the granting of copyright, by the terms of which agreement the United States may, at its pleasure, become a party thereto.

---

[1] A further exception was provided by a statute enacted in 1968, Pub. L. 90–396, 82 Stat. 339, 340, amending Title 15 of the United States Code (15 U.S.C. 272), authorizing the Secretary of Commerce, at section 290(e), to secure copyright and renewal thereof on behalf of the United States as author or proprietor "in all or any part of any standard reference data which he prepares or makes available under this chapter."

The existence of the reciprocal conditions aforesaid shall be determined by the President of the United States, by proclamation made from time to time, as the purposes of this title may require: *Provided*, That whenever the President shall find that the authors, copyright owners, or proprietors of works first produced or published abroad and subject to copyright or to renewal of copyright under the laws of the United States, including works subject to ad interim copyright, are or may have been temporarily unable to comply with the conditions and formalities prescribed with respect to such works by the copyright laws of the United States, because of the disruption or suspension of facilities essential for such compliance, he may by proclamation grant such extension of time as he may deem appropriate for the fulfillment of such conditions or formalities by authors, copyright owners, or proprietors who are citizens of the United States or who are nationals of countries which accord substantially equal treatment in this respect to authors, copyright owners, or proprietors who are citizens of the United States: *Provided further*, That no liability shall attach under this title for lawful uses made or acts done prior to the effective date of such proclamation in connection with such works, or in respect to the continuance for one year subsequent to such date of any business undertaking or enterprise lawfully undertaken prior to such date involving expenditure or contractual obligation in connection with the exploitation, production, reproduction, circulation, or performance of any such work.

The President may at any time terminate any proclamation authorized herein or any part thereof or suspend or extend its operation for such period or periods of time as in his judgment the interests of the United States may require.

(c) When the Universal Copyright Convention, signed at Geneva on September 6, 1952, shall be in force [1] between the United States of America and the foreign state or nation of which such author is a citizen or subject, or in which the work was first published. Any work to which copyright is extended pursuant to this subsection shall be exempt from the following provisions of this title: (1) The requirement in section 1 (e) that a foreign state or nation must grant to United States citizens mechanical reproduction rights similar to those specified therein; (2) the obligatory deposit requirements of the first sentence of section 13; (3) the provisions of sections 14, 16, 17, and 18; (4) the import prohibitions of section 107, to the extent that they are related to the manufacturing requirements of section 16; and (5) the require-

---

[1] The Universal Copyright Convention came into force with respect to the United States of America on September 16, 1955. [. . .]

ments of sections 19 and 20: *Provided, however,* That such exemptions shall apply only if from the time of first publication all the copies of the work published with the authority of the author or other copyright proprietor shall bear the symbol © accompanied by the name of the copyright proprietor and the year of first publication placed in such manner and location as to give reasonable notice of claim of copyright.

Upon the coming into force of the Universal Copyright Convention in a foreign state or nation as hereinbefore provided, every book or periodical of a citizen or subject thereof in which ad interim copyright was subsisting on the effective date of said coming into force shall have copyright for twenty-eight years from the date of first publication abroad without the necessity of complying with the further formalities specified in section 23 of this title.

The provisions of this subsection shall not be extended to works of an author who is a citizen of, or domiciled in the United States of America regardless of place of first publication, or to works first published in the United States.

§ 10. PUBLICATION OF WORK WITH NOTICE.—Any person entitled thereto by this title may secure copyright for his work by publication thereof with the notice of copyright required by this title; and such notice shall be affixed to each copy thereof published or offered for sale in the United States by authority of the copyright proprietor, except in the case of books seeking ad interim protection under section 22 of this title.

§ 11. REGISTRATION OF CLAIM AND ISSUANCE OF CERTIFICATE.—Such person may obtain registration of his claim to copyright by complying with the provisions of this title, including the deposit of copies, and upon such compliance the Register of Copyrights shall issue to him the certificates provided for in section 209 of this title.

§ 12. WORKS NOT REPRODUCED FOR SALE.—Copyright may also be had of the works of an author, of which copies are not reproduced for sale, by the deposit, with claim of copyright, of one complete copy of such work if it be a lecture or similar production or a dramatic, musical, or dramatico-musical composition; of a title and description, with one print taken from each scene or act, if the work be a motion-picture photoplay; of a photographic print if the work be a photograph; of a title and description, with not less than two prints taken from different sections of a complete motion picture, if the work be a motion picture other than a photoplay; or of a photograph or other identifying reproduction thereof, if it be a work of art or a plastic work or drawing. But the privilege of registration of copyright secured hereunder shall not exempt the copyright proprietor from the deposit of copies, under sections 13 and 14 of this title, where the work is later reproduced in copies for sale.

§ 13. DEPOSIT OF COPIES AFTER PUBLICATION; ACTION OR PROCEEDING FOR INFRINGEMENT.—After copyright has been secured by publication of the work with the notice of copyright as provided in section 10 of this title, there shall be promptly deposited in the Copyright Office or in the mail addressed to the Register of Copyrights, Washington, District of Columbia, two complete copies of the best edition thereof then published, or if the work is by an author who is a citizen or subject of a foreign state or nation and has been published in a foreign country, one complete copy of the best edition then published in such foreign country, which copies or copy, if the work be a book or periodical, shall have been produced in accordance with the manufacturing provisions specified in section 16 of this title; or if such work be a contribution to a periodical, for which contribution special registration is requested, one copy of the issue or issues containing such contribution; or if the work belongs to a class specified in subsections (g), (h), (i) or (k) of section 5 of this title, and if the Register of Copyrights determines that it is impracticable to deposit copies because of their size, weight, fragility, or monetary value he may permit the deposit of photographs or other identifying reproductions in lieu of copies of the work as published under such rules and regulations as he may prescribe with the approval of the Librarian of Congress; or if the work is not reproduced in copies for sale there shall be deposited the copy, print, photograph, or other identifying reproduction provided by section 12 of this title, such copies or copy, print, photograph, or other reproduction to be accompanied in each case by a claim of copyright. No action or proceeding shall be maintained for infringement of copyright in any work until the provisions of this title with respect to the deposit of copies and registration of such work shall have been complied with.

§ 14. SAME; FAILURE TO DEPOSIT; DEMAND; PENALTY.—Should the copies called for by section 13 of this title not be promptly deposited as provided in this title, the Register of Copyrights may at any time after the publication of the work, upon actual notice, require the proprietor of the copyright to deposit them, and after the said demand shall have been made, in default of the deposit of copies of the work within three months from any part of the United States, except an outlying territorial possession of the United States, or within six months from any outlying territorial possession of the United States, or from any foreign country, the proprietor of the copyright shall be liable to a fine of $100 and to pay to the Library of Congress twice the amount of the retail price of the best edition of the work, and the copyright shall become void.

§ 15. SAME; POSTMASTER'S RECEIPT; TRANSMISSION BY MAIL WITHOUT COST.—The postmaster to whom are delivered the articles deposited as provided in sections 12 and 13 of this title shall, if requested, give a receipt therefor and shall mail them to their destination without cost to the copyright claimant.

§ 16. MECHANICAL WORK TO BE DONE IN UNITED STATES.—Of the printed book or periodical specified in section 5, subsections (a) and (b), of this title, except the original text of a book or periodical of foreign origin in a language or languages other than English, the text of all copies accorded protection under this title, except as below provided, shall be printed from type set within the limits of the United States, either by hand or by the aid of any kind of typesetting machine, or from plates made within the limits of the United States from type set therein, or, if the text be produced by lithographic process, or photoengraving process, then by a process wholly performed within the limits of the United States, and the printing of the text and binding of the said book shall be performed within the limits of the United States; which requirements shall extend also to the illustrations within a book consisting of printed text and illustrations produced by lithographic process, or photoengraving process, and also to separate lithographs or photoengravings, except where in either case the subjects represented are located in a foreign country and illustrate a scientific work or reproduce a work of art: *Provided, however,* That said requirements shall not apply to works in raised characters for the use of the blind, or to books or periodicals of foreign origin in a language or languages other than English, or to works printed or produced in the United States by any other process than those above specified in this section, or to copies of books or periodicals, first published abroad in the English language, imported into the United States within five years after first publication in a foreign state or nation up to the number of fifteen hundred copies of each such book or periodical if said copies shall contain notice of copyright in accordance with sections 10, 19, and 20 of this title and if ad interim copyright in said work shall have been obtained pursuant to section 22 of this title prior to the importation into the United States of any copy except those permitted by the provisions of section 107 of this title: *Provided further,* That the provisions of this section shall not affect the right of importation under the provisions of section 107 of this title.

§ 17. AFFIDAVIT TO ACCOMPANY COPIES.—In the case of the book the copies so deposited shall be accompanied by an affidavit under the official seal of any officer authorized to administer oaths within the United States, duly made by the person claiming copyright or by his duly authorized agent or representative residing in the United States, or by the printer who has printed the book, setting forth that the copies deposited have been printed from type set within the limits of the

United States or from plates made within the limits of the United States from type set therein; or, if the text be produced by lithographic process, or photoengraving process, that such process was wholly performed within the limits of the United States and that the printing of the text and binding of the said book have also been performed within the limits of the United States. Such affidavit shall state also the place where and the establishment or establishments in which such type was set or plates made or lithographic process, or photoengraving process or printing and binding were performed and the date of the completion of the printing of the book or the date of publication.

§ 18. Making False Affidavit.—Any person who, for the purpose of obtaining registration of a claim to copyright, shall knowingly make a false affidavit as to his having complied with the above conditions shall be deemed guilty of a misdemeanor, and upon conviction thereof shall be punished by a fine of not more than $1,000, and all of his rights and privileges under said copyright shall thereafter be forfeited.

§ 19. Notice; Form.[1]—The notice of copyright required by section 10 of this title shall consist either of the word "Copyright", the abbreviation "Copr.", or the symbol ©, accompanied by the name of the copyright proprietor, and if the work be a printed literary, musical, or dramatic work, the notice shall include also the year in which the copyright was secured by publication. In the case, however, of copies of works specified in subsections (f) to (k), inclusive, of section 5 of this title, the notice may consist of the letter C enclosed within a circle, thus ©, accompanied by the initials, monogram, mark, or symbol of the copyright proprietor: *Provided*, That on some accessible portion of such copies or of the margin, back, permanent base, or pedestal, or of the substance on which such copies shall be mounted, his name shall appear. But in the case of works in which copyright was subsisting on July 1, 1909, the notice of copyright may be either in one of the forms prescribed herein or may consist of the following words: "Entered according to Act of Congress, in the year     , by A. B., in the office of the Librarian of Congress, at Washington, D.C.," or, at his option, the word "Copyright", together with the year the copyright was entered and the name of the party by whom it was taken out; thus, "Copyright, 19—, by A. B." In the case of reproductions of works specified in subsection (n) of section 5 of this title, the notice shall consist of the symbol ℗ (the letter P in a circle), the year of first publication of the sound recording, and the name of the owner of copyright in the sound recording, or an abbreviation by which the name can be recognized, or a generally known alternative designation of the owner:

---

[1] The last sentence of section 19 was added by the Act of October 15, 1971, Pub. L. 92–140, 85 Stat. 391.[...]

*Provided,* That if the producer of the sound recording is named on the labels or containers of the reproduction, and if no other name appears in conjunction with the notice, his name shall be considered a part of the notice.

§ 20. SAME; PLACE OF APPLICATION OF; ONE NOTICE IN EACH VOLUME OR NUMBER OF NEWSPAPER OR PERIODICAL.[1]—The notice of copyright shall be applied, in the case of a book or other printed publication, upon its title page or the page immediately following, or if a periodical either upon the title page or upon the first page of text of each separate number or under the title heading, or if a musical work either upon its title page or the first page of music, or if a sound recording on the surface of reproductions thereof or on the label or container in such manner and location as to give reasonable notice of the claim of copyright. One notice of copyright in each volume or in each number of a newspaper or periodical published shall suffice.

§ 21. SAME; EFFECT OF ACCIDENTAL OMISSION FROM COPY OR COPIES.—Where the copyright proprietor has sought to comply with the provisions of this title with respect to notice, the omission by accident or mistake of the prescribed notice from a particular copy or copies shall not invalidate the copyright or prevent recovery for infringement against any person who, after actual notice of the copyright, begins an undertaking to infringe it, but shall prevent the recovery of damages against an innocent infringer who has been misled by the omission of the notice; and in a suit for infringement no permanent injunction shall be had unless the copyright proprietor shall reimburse to the innocent infringer his reasonable outlay innocently incurred if the court, in its discretion, shall so direct.

§ 22. AD INTERIM PROTECTION OF BOOK OF PERIODICAL PUBLISHED ABROAD.—In the case of a book or periodical first published abroad in the English language, the deposit in the Copyright Office, not later than six months after its publication abroad, of one complete copy of the foreign edition, with a request for the reservation of the copyright and a statement of the name and nationality of the author and of the copyright proprietor and of the date of publication of the said book or periodical, shall secure to the author or proprietor an ad interim copyright therein, which shall have all the force and effect given to copyright by this title, and shall endure until the expiration of five years after the date of first publication abroad.

§ 23. SAME; EXTENSION TO FULL TERM.—Whenever within the period of such ad interim protection an authorized edition of such

---

[1] The first sentence of section 20 was amended by the Act of October 15, 1971, Pub. L. 92–140, 85 Stat. 391. [...]

books or periodicals shall be published within the United States, in accordance with the manufacturing provisions specified in section 16 of this title, and whenever the provisions of this title as to deposit of copies, registration, filing of affidavits, and the printing of the copyright notice shall have been duly complied with, the copyright shall be extended to endure in such book or periodical for the term provided in this title.

§ 24. DURATION; RENEWAL AND EXTENSION.[1]—The copyright secured by this title shall endure for twenty-eight years from the date of first publication, whether the copyrighted work bears the author's true name or is published anonymously or under an assumed name: *Provided*, That in the case of any posthumous work or of any periodical, cyclopedic, or other composite work upon which the copyright was originally secured by the proprietor thereof, or of any work copyrighted by a corporate body (otherwise than as assignee or licensee of the individual author) or by an employer for whom such work is made for hire, the proprietor of such copyright shall be entitled to a renewal and extension of the copyright in such work for the further term of twenty-eight years when application for such renewal and extension shall have been made to the copyright office and duly registered therein within one year prior to the expiration of the original term of copyright: *And provided further*, That in the case of any other copyrighted work, including a contribution by an individual author to a periodical or to a cyclopedic or other composite work, the author of such work, if still living, or the widow, widower, or children of the author, if the author be not living, or if such author, widow, widower, or children be not living, then the author's executors, or in the absence of a will, his next of kin shall be entitled to a renewal and extension of the copyright in such work for a further term of twenty-eight years when application for such renewal and extension shall have been made to the copyright office and duly registered therein within one year prior to the expiration of the original term of copyright:[2] *And provided further*, That in default of the registration of such application for renewal and extension, the copyright in any work shall determine at the expiration of twenty-eight years from first publication.

---

[1] Private Law 92–60, enacted December 15, 1971, provides specially for a term of 75 years from that date, or from the later date of first publication, for the various editions of "Science and Health" by Mary Baker Eddy. [...]
further information is needed on this subject.

[2] A series of eight acts, the most recent being the Act of October 25, 1972, Pub. L. 92–566, 86 Stat. 1170, which cites the seven earlier acts, has extended until December 31, 1974, copyrights previously renewed in which the second term would otherwise have expired between September 19, 1962 and December 31, 1974. [...]

§ 25. RENEWAL OF COPYRIGHTS REGISTERED IN PATENT OFFICE UNDER REPEALED LAW.—Subsisting copyrights originally registered in the Patent Office prior to July 1, 1940, under section 3 of the act of June 18, 1874, shall be subject to renewal in behalf of the proprietor upon application made to the Register of Copyrights within one year prior to the expiration of the original term of twenty-eight years.

§ 26. TERMS DEFINED.[1]—In the interpretation and construction of this title "the date of publication" shall in the case of a work of which copies are reproduced for sale or distribution be held to be the earliest date when copies of the first authorized edition were placed on sale, sold, or publicly distributed by the proprietor of the copyright or under his authority, and the word "author" shall include an employer in the case of works made for hire. For the purposes of this section and sections 10, 11, 13, 14, 21, 101, 106, 109, 209, 215, but not for any other purpose, a reproduction of a work described in subsection 5(n) shall be considered to be a copy thereof. "Sound recordings" are works that result from the fixation of a series of musical, spoken, or other sounds, but not including the sounds accompanying a motion picture. "Reproductions of sound recordings" are material objects in which sounds other than those accompanying a motion picture are fixed by any method now known or later developed, and from which the sounds can be perceived, reproduced, or otherwise communicated, either directly or with the aid of a machine or device, and include the "parts of instruments serving to reproduce mechanically the musical work", "mechanical reproductions", and "interchangeable parts, such as discs or tapes for use in mechanical music-producing machines" referred to in sections 1(e) and 101(e) of this title.

§ 27. COPYRIGHT DISTINCT FROM PROPERTY IN OBJECT COPYRIGHTED; EFFECT OF SALE OF OBJECT, AND OF ASSIGNMENT OF COPYRIGHT.—The copyright is distinct from the property in the material object copyrighted, and the sale or conveyance, by gift or otherwise, of the material object shall not of itself constitute a transfer of the copyright, nor shall the assignment of the copyright constitute a transfer of the title to the material object; but nothing in this title shall be deemed to forbid, prevent, or restrict the transfer of any copy of a copyrighted work the possession of which has been lawfully obtained.

§ 28. ASSIGNMENTS AND BEQUESTS.—Copyright secured under this title or previous copyright laws of the United States may be assigned, granted, or mortgaged by an instrument in writing signed by the proprietor of the copyright, or may be bequeathed by will.

---

[1] The last three sentences of section 26 were added by the Act of October 15, 1971, Pub. L. 92–140, 85 Stat. 391. [...]

§ 29. SAME; EXECUTED IN FOREIGN COUNTRY; ACKNOWLEDGMENT AND CERTIFICATE.—Every assignment of copyright executed in a foreign country shall be acknowledged by the assignor before a consular officer or secretary of legation of the United States authorized by law to administer oaths or perform notarial acts. The certificate of such acknowledgment under the hand and official seal of such consular officer or secretary of legation shall be prima facie evidence of the execution of the instrument.

§ 30. SAME; RECORD.—Every assignment of copyright shall be recorded in the copyright office within three calendar months after its execution in the United States or within six calendar months after its execution without the limits of the United States, in default of which it shall be void as against any subsequent purchaser or mortgagee for a valuable consideration, without notice, whose assignment has been duly recorded.

§ 31. SAME; CERTIFICATE OF RECORD.—The Register of Copyrights shall, upon payment of the prescribed fee, record such assignment, and shall return it to the sender with a certificate of record attached under seal of the copyright office, and upon the payment of the fee prescribed by this title he shall furnish to any person requesting the same a certified copy thereof under the said seal.

§ 32. SAME; USE OF NAME OF ASSIGNEE IN NOTICE.—When an assignment of the copyright in a specified book or other work has been recorded the assignee may substitute his name for that of the assignor in the statutory notice of copyright prescribed by this title.

## Chapter 2—Infringement Proceedings [1]

§ 101. Infringement:
   (a) Injunction.
   (b) Damages and profits; amounts; other remedies.
   (c) Impounding during action.
   (d) Destruction of infringing copies and plates.
   (e) Interchangeable parts for use in mechanical music-producing machines.
§ 104. Willful infringement for profit.
§ 105. Fraudulent notice of copyright, or removal or alteration of notice.
§ 106. Importation of article bearing false notice or piratical copies of copyrighted work.
§ 107. Importation, during existence of copyright, of piratical copies, or of copies not produced in accordance with section 16 of this title.
§ 108. Forfeiture and destruction of articles prohibited importation.
§ 109. Importation of prohibited articles; regulations; proof of deposit of copies by complainants.

---

[1] Sections 101(f), 102, 103, 110, and 111 were repealed by the Act of June 25, 1948, ch. 646, § 39, 62 Stat. 869, at 931, 936, and 996, effective September 1, 1948. However, see sections 1338, 1400, 1498, and 2072, Title 28, United States Code.

§ 112. Injunctions ; service and enforcement.
§ 113. Transmission of certified copies of papers for enforcement of injunction by other court.
§ 114. Review of orders, judgments, or decrees.
§ 115. Limitations.
§ 116. Costs ; attorney's fees.

§ 101. INFRINGEMENT.—If any person shall infringe the copyright in any work protected under the copyright laws of the United States such person shall be liable :

(a) INJUNCTION.—To an injunction restraining such infringement ;

(b) DAMAGES AND PROFITS ; AMOUNT ; OTHER REMEDIES.—To pay to the copyright proprietor such damages as the copyright proprietor may have suffered due to the infringement, as well as all the profits which the infringer shall have made from such infringement, and in proving profits the plaintiff shall be required to prove sales only, and the defendant shall be required to prove every element of cost which he claims, or in lieu of actual damages and profits, such damages as to the court shall appear to be just, and in assessing such damages the court may, in its discretion, allow the amounts as hereinafter stated, but in case of a newspaper reproduction of a copyrighted photograph, such damages shall not exceed the sum of $200 nor be less than the sum of $50, and in the case of the infringement of an undramatized or non-dramatic work by means of motion pictures, where the infringer shall show that he was not aware that he was infringing, and that such infringement could not have been reasonably foreseen, such damages shall not exceed the sum of $100 ; and in the case of an infringement of a copyrighted dramatic or dramatico-musical work by a maker of motion pictures and his agencies for distribution thereof to exhibitors, where such infringer shows that he was not aware that he was infringing a copyrighted work, and that such infringements could not reasonably have been foreseen, the entire sum of such damages recoverable by the copyright proprietor from such infringing maker and his agencies for the distribution to exhibitors of such infringing motion picture shall not exceed the sum of $5,000 nor be less than $250, and such damages shall in no other case exceed the sum of $5,000 nor be less than the sum of $250, and shall not be regarded as a penalty. But the foregoing exceptions shall not deprive the copyright proprietor of any other remedy given him under this law, nor shall the limitation as to the amount of recovery apply to infringements occurring after the actual notice to a defendant, either by service of process in a suit or other written notice served upon him.

First. In the case of a painting, statue, or sculpture, $10 for every infringing copy made or sold by or found in the possession of the infringer or his agents or employees ;

Second. In the case of any work enumerated in section 5 of this title, except a painting, statue, or sculpture, $1 for every infringing copy made or sold by or found in the possession of the infringer or his agents or employees;

Third. In the case of a lecture, sermon, or address, $50 for every infringing delivery;

Fourth. In the case of a dramatic or dramatico-musical or a choral or orchestral composition, $100 for the first and $50 for every subsequent infringing performance; in the case of other musical compositions $10 for every infringing performance;

(c) IMPOUNDING DURING ACTION.—To deliver up on oath, to be impounded during the pendency of the action, upon such terms and conditions as the court may prescribe, all articles alleged to infringe a copyright;

(d) DESTRUCTION OF INFRINGING COPIES AND PLATES. To deliver up on oath for destruction all the infringing copies or devices, as well as all plates, molds, matrices, or other means for making such infringing copies as the court may order.

(e)[1] INTERCHANGEABLE PARTS FOR USE IN MECHANICAL MUSIC-PRODUCING MACHINES.—Interchangeable parts, such as discs or tapes for use in mechanical music-producing machines adapted to reproduce copyrighted musical works, shall be considered copies of the copyrighted musical works which they serve to reproduce mechanically for the purposes of this section 101 and sections 106 and 109 of this title, and the unauthorized manufacture, use, or sale of such interchangeable parts shall constitute an infringement of the copyrighted work rendering the infringer liable in accordance with all provisions of this title dealing with infringements of copyright and, in a case of willful infringement for profit, to criminal prosecution pursuant to section 101 of this title. Whenever any person, in the absence of a license agreement, intends to use a copyrighted musical composition upon the parts of instruments serving to reproduce mechanically the musical work, relying upon the compulsory license provision of this title, he shall serve notice of such intention, by registered mail, upon the copyright proprietor at his last address disclosed by the records of the copyright office, sending to the copyright office a duplicate of such notice.

[(f) See footnote 1, page 205, *supra*.]

[§ 102. See footnote 1, page 205, *supra*.]

[§ 103. See footnote 1, page 205, *supra*.]

---

[1] The former section 101(e) was deleted in its entirety and the present language was substituted by the Act of October 15, 1971, Pub. L. 92–140, 85 Stat. 391, effective immediately upon enactment.

§ 104. WILLFUL INFRINGEMENT FOR PROFIT.—Any person who will-
N3 fully and for profit shall infringe any copyright secured by this title, or who shall knowingly and willfully aid or abet such infringement, shall be deemed guilty of a misdemeanor, and upon conviction thereof shall be punished by imprisonment for not exceeding one year or by a fine of not less than $100 nor more than $1,000, or both, in the discretion of the court: *Provided, however*, That nothing in this title shall be so construed as to prevent the performance of religious or secular works such as oratorios, cantatas, masses, or octavo choruses by public schools, church choirs, or vocal societies, rented, borrowed, or obtained from some public library, public school, church choir, school choir, or vocal society, provided the performance is given for charitable or educational purposes and not for profit.

§ 105. FRAUDULENT NOTICE OF COPYRIGHT, OR REMOVAL OR ALTERATION OF NOTICE.—Any person who, with fraudulent intent, shall insert or impress any notice of copyright required by this title, or words of the same purport, in or upon any uncopyrighted article, or with fraudulent intent shall remove or alter the copyright notice upon any article duly copyrighted shall be guilty of a misdemeanor, punishable by a fine of not less than $100 and not more than $1,000. Any person who shall knowingly issue or sell any article bearing a notice of United States copyright which has not been copyrighted in this country, or who shall knowingly import any article bearing such notice or words of the same purport, which has not been copyrighted in this country, shall be liable to a fine of $100.

§ 106. IMPORTATION OF ARTICLE BEARING FALSE NOTICE OR PIRATICAL COPIES OF COPYRIGHTED WORK.—The importation into the United States of any article bearing a false notice of copyright when there is no existing copyright thereon in the United States, or of any piratical copies of any work copyrighted in the United States, is prohibited.

§ 107. IMPORTATION, DURING EXISTENCE OF COPYRIGHT, OF PIRATICAL COPIES, OR OF COPIES NOT PRODUCED IN ACCORDANCE WITH SECTION 16 OF THIS TITLE.—During the existence of the American copyright in any book the importation into the United States of any piratical copies thereof or of any copies thereof (although authorized by the author or proprietor) which have not been produced in accordance with the manufacturing provisions specified in section 16 of this title, or any plates of the same not made from type set within the limits of the United States, or any copies thereof produced by lithographic or photoengraving process not performed within the limits of the United States, in accordance with the provisions of section 16 of this title, is prohibited: *Provided, however*, That, except as regards piratical copies, such prohibition shall not apply:

(a) To works in raised characters for the use of the blind.

(b) To a foreign newspaper or magazine, although containing matter copyrighted in the United States printed or reprinted by authority of the copyright proprietor, unless such newspaper or magazine contains also copyright matter printed or reprinted without such authorization.

(c) To the authorized edition of a book in a foreign language or languages of which only a translation into English has been copyrighted in this country.

(d) To any book published abroad with the authorization of the author or copyright proprietor when imported under the circumstances stated in one of the four subdivisions following, that is to say:

First. When imported, not more than one copy at one time, for individual use and not for sale; but such privilege of importation shall not extend to a foreign reprint of a book by an American author copyrighted in the United States.

Second. When imported by the authority or for the use of the United States.

Third. When imported, for use and not for sale, not more than one copy of any such book in any one invoice, in good faith by or for any society or institution incorporated for educational, literary, philosophical, scientific or religious purposes, or for the encouragement of the fine arts, or for any college, academy, school, or seminary of learning, or for any State, school, college, university, or free public library in the United States.

Fourth. When such books form parts of libraries or collections purchased en bloc for the use of societies, institutions, or libraries designated in the foregoing paragraph, or form parts of the libraries or personal baggage belonging to persons or families arriving from foreign countries and are not intended for sale: *Provided*, That copies imported as above may not lawfully be used in any way to violate the rights of the proprietor of the American copyright or annul or limit the copyright protection secured by this title, and such unlawful use shall be deemed an infringement of copyright.

§ 108. FORFEITURE AND DESTRUCTION OF ARTICLES PROHIBITED IMPORTATION.—Any and all articles prohibited importation by this title which are brought into the United States from any foreign country (except in the mails) shall be seized and forfeited by like proceedings as those provided by law for the seizure and condemnation of property imported into the United States in violation of the customs revenue laws. Such articles when forfeited shall be destroyed in such manner as the Secretary of the Treasury or the court, as the case may be, shall direct: *Provided, however*, That all copies of authorized editions of copyright books imported in the mails or otherwise in violation of the provisions of this title may be exported and returned to the country of export whenever it is shown to the satisfaction of the Secretary of the Treasury, in a written application, that such importation does not involve willful negligence or fraud.

§ 109. IMPORTATION OF PROHIBITED ARTICLES; REGULATIONS; PROOF OF DEPOSIT OF COPIES BY COMPLAINANTS.—The Secretary of the Treasury and the Postmaster General are hereby empowered and required to make and enforce individually or jointly such rules and regulations as shall prevent the importation into the United States of articles prohibited importation by this title, and may require, as conditions precedent to exclusion of any work in which copyright is claimed, the copyright proprietor or any person claiming actual or potential injury by reason of actual or contemplated importations of copies of such work to file with the Post Office Department or the Treasury Department a certificate of the Register of Copyrights that the provisions of section 13 of this title have been fully complied with, and to give notice of such compliance to postmasters or to customs officers at the ports of entry in the United States in such form and accompanied by such exhibits as may be deemed necessary for the practical and efficient administration and enforcement of the provisions of sections 106 and 107 of this title.

[§ 110. See footnote 1, page 205, *supra*.]

[§ 111. See footnote 1, page 205, *supra*.]

§ 112. INJUNCTIONS; SERVICE AND ENFORCEMENT.—Any court mentioned in section 1338 of Title 28 or judge thereof shall have power, upon complaint filed by any party aggrieved, to grant injunctions to prevent and restrain the violation of any right secured by this title, according to the course and principles of courts of equity, on such terms as said court or judge may deem reasonable. Any injunction that may be granted restraining and enjoining the doing of anything forbidden by this title may be served on the parties against whom such injunction may be granted anywhere in the United States, and shall be operative throughout the United States and be enforceable by proceedings in contempt or otherwise by any other court or judge possessing jurisdiction of the defendants.

§ 113. TRANSMISSION OF CERTIFIED COPIES OF PAPERS FOR ENFORCEMENT OF INJUNCTION BY OTHER COURT.—The clerk of the court or judge granting the injunction, shall, when required so to do by the court hearing the application to enforce said injunction, transmit without delay to said court a certified copy of all the papers in said cause that are on file in his office.

§ 114. REVIEW OF ORDERS, JUDGMENTS, OR DECREES.—The orders, judgments, or decrees of any court mentioned in section 1338 of Title

28 arising under the copyright laws of the United States may be reviewed on appeal in the manner and to the extent now provided by law for the review of cases determined in said courts, respectively.

§ 115. LIMITATIONS.—(a) CRIMINAL PROCEEDINGS.—No criminal proceedings shall be maintained under the provisions of this title unless the same is commenced within three years after the cause of action arose.

(b) CIVIL ACTIONS.—No civil action shall be maintained under the provisions of this title unless the same is commenced within three years after the claim accrued.

§ 116. COSTS; ATTORNEY'S FEES.—In all actions, suits, or proceedings under this title, except when brought by or against the United States or any officer thereof, full costs shall be allowed, and the court may award to the prevailing party a reasonable attorney's fee as part of the costs.

## Chapter 3—Copyright Office

§ 201. COPYRIGHT OFFICE; PRESERVATION OF RECORDS.—All records and other things relating to copyrights required by law to be preserved shall be kept and preserved in the copyright office, Library of Congress, District of Columbia, and shall be under the control of the register of copyrights, who shall, under the direction and supervision of the Librarian of Congress, perform all the duties relating to the registration of copyrights.

§ 202. REGISTER, ASSISTANT REGISTER, AND SUBORDINATES.—There shall be appointed by the Librarian of Congress a Register of Copyrights, and one Assistant Register of Copyrights, who shall have authority during the absence of the Register of Copyrights to attach the copyright office seal to all papers issued from the said office and to sign such certificates and other papers as may be necessary. There shall also be appointed by the Librarian such subordinate assistants to the register as may from time to time be authorized by law.

§ 203. SAME; DEPOSIT OF MONEYS RECEIVED; REPORTS.—The Register of Copyrights shall make daily deposits in some bank in the District of Columbia, designated for this purpose by the Secretary of the Treasury as a national depository, of all moneys received to be applied as copyright fees, and shall make weekly deposits with the Secretary of the Treasury, in such manner as the latter shall direct, of all copyright fees actually applied under the provisions of this title, and annual deposits of sums received which it has not been possible to apply as copyright fees or to return to the remitters, and shall also make monthly reports to the Secretary of the Treasury and to the Librarian of Congress of the applied copyright fees for each calendar month, together with a statement of all remittances received, trust funds on hand, moneys refunded, and unapplied balances.

§ 204. SAME; BOND.—The Register of Copyrights shall give bond to the United States in the sum of $20,000, in form to be approved by the General Counsel for the Department of the Treasury and with sureties satisfactory to the Secretary of the Treasury, for the faithful discharge of his duties.

§ 205. SAME; ANNUAL REPORT.—The Register of Copyrights shall make an annual report to the Librarian of Congress, to be printed in the annual report on the Library of Congress, of all copyright business for the previous fiscal year, including the number and kind of works which have been deposited in the copyright office during the fiscal year, under the provisions of this title.

§ 206. SEAL OF COPYRIGHT OFFICE.—The seal used in the copyright office on July 1, 1909, shall be the seal of the copyright office, and by it all papers issued from the copyright office requiring authentication shall be authenticated.

§ 207. RULES FOR REGISTRATION OF CLAIMS.[1]—Subject to the approval of the Librarian of Congress, the Register of Copyrights shall be authorized to make rules and regulations for the registration of claims to copyright as provided by this title.

§ 208. RECORD BOOKS IN COPYRIGHT OFFICE.—The Register of Copyrights shall provide and keep such record books in the copyright office as are required to carry out the provisions of this title, and when-

---

[1] Published in the *Federal Register* and Title 37 of the *Code of Federal Regulations.*
[. . .]

ever deposit has been made in the copyright office of a copy of any work under the provisions of this title he shall make entry thereof.

§ 209. CERTIFICATE OF REGISTRATION; EFFECT AS EVIDENCE; RECEIPT FOR COPIES DEPOSITED.—In the case of each entry the person recorded as the claimant of the copyright shall be entitled to a certificate of registration under seal of the copyright office, to contain the name and address of said claimant, the name of the country of which the author of the work is a citizen or subject, and when an alien author domiciled in the United States at the time of said registration, then a statement of that fact, including his place of domicile, the name of the author (when the records of the copyright office shall show the same), the title of the work which is registered for which copyright is claimed, the date of the deposit of the copies of such work, the date of publication if the work has been reproduced in copies for sale, or publicly distributed, and such marks as to class designation and entry number as shall fully identify the entry. In the case of a book, the certificate shall also state the receipt of the affidavit, as provided by section 17 of this title, and the date of the completion of the printing, or the date of the publication of the book, as stated in the said affidavit. The Register of Copyrights shall prepare a printed form for the said certificate, to be filled out in each case as above provided for in the case of all registrations made after July 1, 1909, and in the case of all previous registrations so far as the copyright office record books shall show such facts, which certificate, sealed with the seal of the copyright office, shall, upon payment of the prescribed fee, be given to any person making application for the same. Said certificate shall be admitted in any court as prima facie evidence of the facts stated therein. In addition to such certificate the register of copyrights shall furnish, upon request, without additional fee, a receipt for the copies of the work deposited to complete the registration.

§ 210. CATALOG OF COPYRIGHT ENTRIES; EFFECT AS EVIDENCE.—The Register of Copyrights shall fully index all copyright registrations and assignments and shall print at periodic intervals a catalog of the titles of articles deposited and registered for copyright, together with suitable indexes, and at stated intervals shall print complete and indexed catalog for each class of copyright entries, and may thereupon, if expedient, destroy the original manuscript catalog cards containing the titles included in such printed volumes and representing the entries made during such intervals. The current catalog of copyright entries and the index volumes herein provided for shall be admitted in any court as prima facie evidence of the facts stated therein as regards any copyright registration.

§ 211. SAME; DISTRIBUTION AND SALE; DISPOSAL OF PROCEEDS.—The said printed current catalogs as they are issued shall be promptly distributed by the Superintendent of Documents to the collectors of customs of the United States and to the postmasters of all exchange offices of receipt of foreign mails, in accordance with revised list of such collectors of customs and postmasters prepared by the Secretary of the Treasury and the Postmaster General, and they shall also be furnished in whole or in part to all parties desiring them at a price to be determined by the Register of Copyrights for each part of the catalog not exceeding $75 for the complete yearly catalog of copyright entries. The consolidated catalogs and indexes shall also be supplied to all persons ordering them at such prices as may be fixed by the Register of Copyrights, and all subscriptions for the catalogs shall be received by the Superintendent of Documents, who shall forward the said publications; and the moneys thus received shall be paid into the Treasury of the United States and accounted for under such laws and Treasury regulations as shall be in force at the time.

§ 212. RECORDS AND WORKS DEPOSITED IN COPYRIGHT OFFICE OPEN TO PUBLIC INSPECTION; TAKING COPIES OF ENTRIES.—The record books of the copyright office, together with the indexes to such record books, and all works deposited and retained in the copyright office, shall be open to public inspection; and copies may be taken of the copyright entries actually made in such record books, subject to such safeguards and regulations as shall be prescribed by the Register of Copyrights and approved by the Librarian of Congress.

§ 213. DISPOSITION OF ARTICLES DEPOSITED IN OFFICE.—Of the articles deposited in the copyright office under the provisions of the copyright laws of the United States, the Librarian of Congress shall determine what books and other articles shall be transferred to the permanent collections of the Library of Congress, including the law library, and what other books or articles shall be placed in the reserve collections of the Library of Congress for sale or exchange, or be transferred to other governmental libraries in the District of Columbia for use therein.

§ 214. DESTRUCTION OF ARTICLES DEPOSITED IN OFFICE REMAINING UNDISPOSED OF; REMOVAL OF BY AUTHOR OR PROPRIETOR; MANUSCRIPTS OF UNPUBLISHED WORKS.—Of any articles undisposed of as above provided, together with all titles and correspondence relating thereto, the Librarian of Congress and the Register of Copyrights jointly shall, at suitable intervals, determine what of these received during any period of years it is desirable or useful to preserve in the permanent files of the copyright office, and, after due notice as hereinafter provided, may within their discretion cause the remaining articles and other things to be destroyed: *Provided*, That there shall be printed in the Catalog of Copyright Entries from February to November, inclusive, a statement of the years of receipt of such articles and a notice to permit any author, copyright proprietor, or other lawful claimant to claim and remove before the expiration of the month of December of that year anything found which relates to any of his productions deposited or registered for copyright within the period of years stated, not reserved or disposed of as provided for in this title. No manuscript of an unpublished work shall be destroyed during its term of copyright without specific notice to the copyright proprietor of record, permitting him to claim and remove it.

§ 215. Fees.—The Register of Copyrights shall receive, and the persons to whom the services designated are rendered shall pay, the following fees:

For the registration of a claim to copyright in any work, including a print or label used for articles of merchandise, $6; for the registration of a claim to renewal of copyright, $4; which fees shall include a certificate for each registration: *Provided*, That only one registration fee shall be required in the case of several volumes of the same book published and deposited at the same time: *And provided further*, That with respect to works of foreign origin, in lieu of payment of the copyright fee of $6 together with one copy of the work and application, the foreign author or proprietor may at any time within six months from the date of first publication abroad deposit in the Copyright Office an application for registration and two copies of the work which shall be accompanied by a catalog card in form and content satisfactory to the Register of Copyrights.

For every additional certificate of registration, $2.

For certifying a copy of an application for registration of copyright, and for all other certifications, $3.

For recording every assignment, agreement, power of attorney or other paper not exceeding six pages, $5; for each additional page or less, 50 cents; for each title over one in the paper recorded, 50 cents additional.

For recording a notice of use, or notice of intention to use, $3, for each notice of not more than five titles; and 50 cents for each additional title.

For any requested search of Copyright Office records, works deposited, or other available material, or services rendered in connection therewith, $5, for each hour of time consumed.

§ 216. When the Day for Taking Action Falls on Saturday, Sunday, or a Holiday.—When the last day for making any deposit or application, or for paying any fee, or for delivering any other material to the Copyright Office falls on Saturday, Sunday, or a holiday within the District of Columbia, such action may be taken on the next succeeding business day.

# NOTES

1. By the Act of December 31, 1974, Pub. L. 93-573, 88 Stat. 1873, the phrase "and before January 1, 1975" was stricken.

2. By the Act of December 31, 1974, Pub. L. 93-573, 88 Stat. 1873, the December 31, 1974 date was further extended until December 31, 1976.

3. By the Act of December 31, 1974, Pub. L. 93-573, 88 Stat. 1873, Section 104 was amended to read as follows:

### § 104. Willful infringement for profit

(a) Except as provided in subsection (b), any person who willfully and for profit shall infringe any copyright secured by this title, or who shall knowingly and willfully aid or abet such infringement, shall be deemed guilty of a misdemeanor, and upon conviction thereof shall be punished by imprisonment for not exceeding one year or by a fine of not less than $100 nor more than $1,000, or both, in the discretion of the court: Provided, however, That nothing in this title shall be so construed as to prevent the performance of religious or secular works such as oratorios, cantatas, masses, or octavo choruses by public schools, church choirs, or vocal societies, rented, borrowed, or obtained from some public library, public school, church choir, school choir, or vocal society, provided the performance is given for charitable or educational purposes and not for profit.

(b) Any person who willfully and for profit shall infringe any copyright provided by section 1 (f) of this title, or who should knowingly and willfully aid or abet such infringement, shall be fined not more than $25,000 or imprisoned not more than one year, or both, for the first offense and shall be fined not more than $50,000 or imprisoned not more than two years, or both, for any subsequent offense.

# INDEX